Baptism

and the

Plan of Salvation

Restoring the New Testament Gospel

By
Steven A. Carlson

GUARDIAN
PUBLISHING, LLC

This edition published in April 2009 in association with

Guardian Publishing, LLC
Holt, Michigan

Acknowledgements

This book is dedicated to my brothers and sisters in Christ who are not professional theologians, along with all others who look at life through a similar lens. When my first book, <u>Baptism and the Battle for Souls</u>, proved a bit challenging for the layman, I decided it would be a good idea to address the topic of baptism in simpler terms. Therefore, this is essentially the same book as the first, with the same chapters and headings, offered in a simple, easy-to-understand writing style.

As before, I would like to thank those who offered their assistance as I labored to provide a thorough study of the subject of baptism. These include my parents, Elton (a minister) and Edna Carlson, and my brother Phil, as well as Mr. W. Robert Palmer, a retired minister who unfortunately passed away prior to publishing. I would also like to thank Paul and Betty Stacy, a retired minister and his wife, who provided valuable insights into the subject matter of this book, and to my proofreading/editing team consisting of Annette Bobko and my three children, Michael, Adam, and Crystal Carlson. A friend and school teacher by the name of Debbie Schneider also aided immensely, offering helpful advice. I would also like to thank my remarkable wife, Denise, who was relatively patient as I spent hour upon hour in my office studying and writing.

I would like to acknowledge my friend and former minister, Greg Steere, who taught Greek and helped me immensely in assuring that the Greek presented in this book does not misrepresent the biblical authors' intended meaning. Most of all, however, I would like to recognize the invaluable contribution from my brother, Tim Carlson, who is also a minister and whose theological expertise far exceeds my own. His knowledge of biblical history has helped to make this book one that I am pleased to present. Thanks a lot, Tim.

Preface

In the book of Hebrews, we are told that baptism is an *'elementary principle of Christ'* along with certain other basics that include both repentance and faith (Hebrews 6: 1-2). Unfortunately, over the centuries baptism has become one of the most divisive issues in all of Scripture. While it was originally intended to unify the church (Acts 2: 41; 1 Corinthians 12: 13; Ephesians 4: 4-5), the attitudes that men have taken toward baptism seem to have caused more division than unity.

Addressing any topic that sparks heated debate (e.g., water baptism, gifts of the spirit, baptism with the Holy Spirit, etc.) is always challenging since men are very passionate in their beliefs. This leads many people to become very emotional when it comes to discussing baptism. Few are ever willing to consider a point of view that does not harmonize with their own. They believe what they believe; therefore, everyone else must be wrong.

Sadly, a large number of people do not even know why they believe as they do. It is simply what they have learned from their spiritual teachers. Since baptism is such an emotionally-charged subject, we should begin by considering some areas where we can find common ground. Therefore, the following paragraphs offer guidelines that will serve as a basis for the discussion that follows.

*   *   *   *   *

We must begin with the understanding that the Bible is the one true and complete Word of God. Without this initial premise very little can be accomplished. If a survey was done asking men their opinion of the Bible, we would discover many who accept by faith that it is God's Word. We would also find some who flatly deny the spiritual authority of Scripture. Then there would be those who question the *complete* authority of Scripture, while still claiming belief in both God and Jesus. They could be skeptical about the authenticity of an event recorded in Scripture, or they may wish to challenge the legitimacy of one or more of the commands handed down by Jesus or the apostles.

When someone rejects the teaching of a portion of Scripture, that person is essentially rejecting the entire work as God's revelation to mankind. After all, if it is God's Word, we must accept the Bible from cover to cover. For those who have decided they need only believe part of the Bible, the principles discussed in this book will have little meaning. On the other hand, those who recognize the Bible as God's spirit-breathed message to mankind will hopefully discover a genuine examination of baptism as it is revealed in God's Word.

*   *   *   *   *

Of course, recognizing that the Bible is the true Word of God means accepting that the purpose of Scripture, as it is written (especially in the original Hebrew and Greek text), is to communicate to us the *entire* will of God with respect to mankind (2 Timothy 3: 16-17). Therefore, if we accept the spiritual authority of Scripture, it is important that we not only draw our beliefs from the Bible, but that we draw our beliefs from the Bible *only*. Any doctrine that sidesteps Scripture must be considered man-made and rejected accordingly.

*   *   *   *   *

As with other literary works, the context of a biblical passage is important in determining what lesson we are to learn from the text. The literary context includes: the theme of a particular chapter or book; the circumstances behind the writing; and the identity of the recipient(s). For example, the main objective of the gospels (the books of Matthew, Mark, Luke, and John) is to acquaint us with Jesus' ministry as well as His death, burial, and resurrection. Additionally, Jesus often provided glimpses into the nature of the coming church age through His sermons and conversations that are recorded in these books. The Acts of the Apostles records the events surrounding the beginning of the church age and the introduction of the Holy Spirit into the lives of Christians. The epistles, which were written to various churches or individuals, were intended to provide instruction to Christians both in the first century and throughout the balance of the church age. The context of a chapter and/or book must always be given serious consideration if we are to fully understand its meaning.

*   *   *   *   *

We are quite often provided scriptural instruction through a method known as *direct command* or *assertion* by the author. For instance, there is little question about James' meaning when he speaks of bridling the tongue or caring for orphans and widows (James 1: 26-27). The words are simple and the meaning is clear. There are other times when we can legitimately use reason and logic to help us understand the message from a passage, a method known as *necessary inference*. Using this approach, we can often learn something from a passage even though it is not stated openly in the text. For instance, although we are not told the details of Philip's conversation with the Ethiopian eunuch, it is clear from the text that Philip directed him toward baptism since it was the eunuch who insisted on being baptized when they came upon water (Acts 8: 26-39).

Some men teach that Saul of Tarsus, who later became the apostle Paul, was instantly saved when he met the Lord on the Road to Damascus (Acts 9: 1-19). However, when men make this claim, they ignore the fact that Saul's sins were not forgiven until he met with Ananias three days later (Acts 22: 6-16). Since Scripture states that one cannot be saved without forgiveness of sins (Ephesians 1: 7; Colossians 1: 14), the argument that Saul was saved on the road is not supported by the facts provided in Luke's account of his conversion. This claim, then, fails the test of *reasonable* inference, much less the test of *necessary* inference.

Simply stated, we cannot draw honest conclusions about a passage of Scripture unless we approach it earnestly and avoid making unsupported assumptions. One cannot discover scriptural truth by abandoning or manipulating the words of the Bible in an effort to validate his/her own beliefs. We must always draw our beliefs from the Bible and the original intent of the author, and avoid claiming that the author meant something he did not say.

*   *   *   *   *

Occasionally, someone may develop a doctrine from a passage without considering what the balance of Scripture has to say on the subject. The best way to avoid doctrinal misunderstanding is to take into account *all* of God's Word. While certain passages speak broadly of God's will for mankind, no single verse reveals everything we need to know about God's message. John 3: 16 is a compelling passage, but without the history of the Old Testament and the support found in the gospels, we would have no insight into the meaning of this verse or what would be an appropriate response.

The message of Scripture is consistent in that it does not contradict itself. It does, however, complement itself. As a result, insight into one passage is often aided or clarified by another passage. The notion that the Bible does not contradict itself is founded upon the understanding that the totality of Scripture was inspired by God, and God would never disagree with Himself. This idea is well expressed in the adage – *the best commentary on the Bible is the Bible itself.*

It is often argued that, if the Bible really was its own best commentary, there would not be so many conflicting doctrines among men. In truth, however, these controversies exist only because many people do not look at what the Bible says – they look at what *part* of the Bible says. This approach has led to the development of many beliefs that do not fully harmonize with Scripture. Not only does God's Word fail to contradict itself but, taken in its entirety, it provides us with an unclouded understanding of His will. A doctrine may be formed based upon a single passage of Scripture; yet, if that doctrine challenges the theme of the Bible as a whole, or is in conflict with other passages, we would do well to question the reasonableness of that belief.

Paul cautioned Timothy to be a discriminating student of Scripture, *'rightly dividing the word of truth'* (2 Timothy 2: 15), in order to avoid being fooled by those who would misdirect him. Peter warned us that some men would distort Scripture, resulting in doctrine that would mislead (2 Peter 3: 16). We find that this is often achieved by isolating a passage and portraying it as complete instruction concerning a specific doctrine, without regard to what the balance of Scripture says, or by simply disputing plain biblical teaching. As an example, one sect has based their doctrine of baptism for the dead on the following words from Paul:

> Otherwise, what will they do who are baptized for the dead, if the dead do not rise at all? Why then are they baptized for the dead? (1 Corinthians 15: 29)

In this passage, Paul's words fall considerably short of endorsing a doctrine of baptism for the dead. As we take in all of God's Word, including additional statements by Paul himself, we cannot help but acknowledge that Scripture does not support this teaching (Luke 16: 19-31; 2 Corinthians 5: 10; Hebrews 9: 27). Paul does not sanction the doctrine of baptism for the dead, as some men claim, but merely recognizes that certain people are known to observe this rite. We can determine that Paul did not take part in the practice himself by his use of the word *they* when discussing those who were known to participate. Additionally, he does not suggest that their efforts provided any benefit for those who had died. As we consider the context of Paul's words, through a reading of the entire fifteenth chapter of 1 Corinthians, we find that this statement by Paul is simply a passing comment in a discussion about whether or not people are *raised* from the dead. The apostle is not attempting to legitimize baptism for the dead. It is best to avoid establishing doctrine from any passage without first weighing that teaching against the balance of Scripture.

* * * * *

At times in the New Testament, God involved Himself in the common lives of men in extraordinary ways as a matter of divine revelation and/or miraculous intervention. When God interacted with men in this way, the intended lesson or result was designed specifically for first century Christians in an effort to advance the work of the kingdom. We have no reason to believe that incidents of miraculous intervention were intended as a source of biblical doctrine. They are not doctrinal in character. In each case God's purpose was to affect the outcome of a situation (Acts 12: 6-10), influence certain decisions (Acts 9: 3-8), or shape the structure of the early church (Acts 10: 44-46). For instance, God granted the power of the Holy Spirit to the apostles so that they could perform miracles. He did this in order to demonstrate to the early church the special authority He had bestowed upon these men (Acts 2: 43; 2 Corinthians 12: 11-12).

The power granted the apostles is an example of miraculous intervention intended to profit the church in the first century. Its relevance to us lies in the fact that we can see exactly how God used the apostles to establish the church. Because God revealed, via the working of miracles, that these men were chosen vessels, we can also accept the teaching that their words were God's words (John 17: 1-21). However, we should not regard these miraculous powers as common in the church age, given the foundational role of the apostles in the kingdom (Ephesians 2: 20). On the contrary, it is evident that the power bestowed upon these men represents the greatest of exceptions as God intervened in order to affect the establishment of the body of Christ.

Ananias and Sapphira perished instantly when they *'lied to the Holy Spirit'* (Acts 5: 1-10). Once again we find an occasion of divine intervention. These deaths brought fear among the early believers (Acts 5: 11) as God demonstrated His hatred of sin and His total omniscience (complete knowledge) and omnipotence (complete power). Yet this was clearly an anomaly. This kind of punishment is not repeated in the New Testament and we do not anticipate God using this method of discipline today.

Through the deaths of Ananias and Sapphira, God revealed Himself to the early church in an extraordinary manner. Given the uniqueness of the event, we cannot develop biblical doctrine from this incident, nor do the apostles ever suggest that the episode holds any hidden doctrinal meaning. It does, however, provide further support for the authority of the apostles.

The Ethiopian eunuch submitted to baptism after Philip taught him the gospel message (Acts 8: 27-39). What is fascinating about this occasion is the fact that, after Philip had baptized the man, he disappeared from the eunuch's sight.

> And when they were come up out of the water, the Spirit of the Lord caught away Philip, that the eunuch saw him no more: and he went on his way rejoicing. (Acts 8: 39)

We are not told exactly why Philip was taken away in this manner, but the implication is that God had work for him in Azotus and Caesarea (v. 40).

If we could form doctrine from this kind of miraculous intervention we might determine that, for a man to be saved, the one administering his baptism must, like Philip, immediately vanish from sight. Of course, it would be foolish to draw that kind of conclusion from this incident. We have no reason to attempt to establish doctrine from such an exceptional case. Moments of miraculous intervention simply do not lend themselves to the establishment of biblical doctrine.

*   *   *   *   *

Finally, some men may form a spiritual view completely independent from scriptural instruction. Often a person's life experiences lead him/her to disregard biblical teaching when it comes to developing a belief system. In that case the written word is effectively abandoned as a source of doctrine. However, a belief that is founded upon experience that Scripture does not support is normally based upon what a person *wishes* to believe. In fact, it is often a camouflaged attempt to sidestep God's direction. This is frequently expressed in terms of, *'I have a relationship with God but I don't need the church'* or, *'God and I have an understanding.'* These remarks cannot be deemed sincere since they show no respect for the instructions God has provided in His Word. The way to Jesus is the church (1 Corinthians 12: 12-27; Ephesians 1: 22-23) and the way to the Father is through Jesus (John 14: 6). Any belief that proclaims a separate path to that relationship due to an earthly experience conflicts with God's own direction.

*   *   *   *   *

Little disagreement exists among believers when it comes to the salvation value of faith, confession, the deity of Christ, or a host of other creeds that are vital in our walk with God. Baptism, however, seems to be a subject that has the capacity to bring great division among those who believe in Jesus as the Son of God.

While this book is written to those who do not believe, or at least question, that water baptism is part of God's plan of salvation and for forgiveness of sins, it is also written to those who do believe baptism is essential, but have never understood it completely. If you have lacked the words or the Scripture to answer the arguments of men who dismiss baptism, this book will prepare you to make your belief clear through solid biblical teaching. The hope is that, upon reading this work, you will not only be able to defend your belief, but that you will boldly teach all that Scripture says about God's amazing covenant with man.

This book has been written with a single goal in mind. That goal is to discuss biblical instruction concerning baptism as honestly as possible. Honest presentation of God's teaching is essential if we hope to honor Him. In that same vein the assignment for you, the reader, is to hold this work to biblical scrutiny to assure that what is written here does not misrepresent the inspired words of Scripture.

*   *   *   *   *

The biblical passages cited in this book are from the New King James Version of the Bible. At times the author has italicized certain words in cited passages as a matter of emphasis. When this occurs, the highlighting is noted by the words *emphasis added* at the end of the passage. However, there are times in the NKJ and other versions of the Bible where the translators have enhanced the English text by inserting words, (e.g., pronouns and prepositions) that are not part of the original Greek. For instance, in the following verse, the words *'it is'* have been incorporated into the English translation.

> For *it is* not possible that the blood of bulls and goats could take away sins. (Hebrews 10: 4)

These words are italicized in recognition of the fact that they are not part of the original manuscripts. The reasons for these insertions are simply to aid in the transition to English and generally do not affect the meaning of the verse. In an attempt to be faithful to Scripture, these insertions will remain italicized in this work.

Table of Contents

Title	Page

Title	Page

Chapter I
Beliefs Regarding Baptism - In Brief

Few topics in the Bible rival baptism in stirring emotional debate among those who study God's Word and seek His ways. A host of scholars have penned countless books on the subject revealing a variety of beliefs about the method and purpose of baptism. Still, most views can be summed up in the few simple categories that follow.

Water Baptism Is Essential and by Immersion Only

A number of individuals believe that immersion in water is the only valid form of baptism, since this is the baptism portrayed within the pages of Scripture, and that it is necessary for salvation. Those who offer this view believe that the decision to submit to baptism is one that must be made by each person once he/she reaches an age when the decision is his/hers to make. It is at the time of baptism, accompanied by repentance, that forgiveness of sins and the indwelling of the Holy Spirit are received. According to this view, regeneration (renewal) of the one who submits to baptism is the main purpose of the ceremony. Of course, the water, in itself, has no power to purify someone spiritually. However, the work of the Holy Spirit is to apply the blood of Christ to the sins of the repentant man in the waters of baptism, cleansing him of all guilt.

A vast number of disciples chose to reject immersion as a condition of salvation beginning in the early to mid sixteenth century. Its revival can be found in the work and writings of Alexander Campbell[1] (1788-1866) and Barton W. Stone[2] (1772-1844) in the nineteenth century. These may be considered the fathers of what is known as the Restoration Movement in America. It was their belief that the church should be *restored* to the model that Jesus and the apostles established in Scripture. Their goal was to return, as closely as possible, to the design of the church that is presented to us in the New Testament, including both the structure of the church and the ordinances they observed.

Among those who believe that immersion is necessary for salvation, there are two distinct opinions when it comes to baptism with the Holy Spirit. Within this group, some believe that baptism with the Holy Spirit involved the miraculous outpouring of the

Spirit that we witness in the book of Acts. It is held that this occurred only twice in Scripture (Acts 2: 1-4; 10: 44-46) and that, once its mission was accomplished, God discontinued His use of that experience. Others contend that baptism with the Holy Spirit occurs at the time of immersion in water as the *gift* of the Holy Spirit is bestowed upon the obedient believer (Acts 2: 38).

Water Baptism Is Essential by Immersion, Pouring, or Sprinkling

Another view that finds support among men focuses on the mode of baptism. Some men believe that, although water baptism is essential, immersion is not its only acceptable form. They consider sprinkling or pouring water over a person to be legitimate methods of baptism. Many who hold this view teach that baptism can occur as early as infancy to cover what is known as *original sin* (the idea that men are born with the guilt of sin). In the case of an infant, no decision on the part of the child is needed. The parents may make a decision on the child's behalf and he/she can then be baptized (sprinkled).

An early work known as the Didache[3], also called The Teaching of the Twelve Apostles, suggests that alternate forms of baptism may have been accepted as early as the second century. Although the title suggests that the book contains the apostles' teachings, it is doubtful that they were involved in its writing since some of the instructions found there do not follow the example provided to us by the apostles in the New Testament. For instance, the Didache called for reciting the Lord's Prayer three times daily and also established ceremonial prayers that were to be said both before and after partaking of the Lord's Supper.

When it comes to baptism, the Didache teaches that both the individual administering a baptism and the person being baptized, as well as any others who are willing, should fast for two days leading up to the event. No similar teaching can be found in Scripture. The examples of the Day of Pentecost (Acts 2: 38-41), the Philippian jailer (Acts 16: 31-33), the Ephesian disciples (Acts 19: 1-5), and many others reveal that this was not a practice of the apostles. According to Scripture, the apostles immediately baptized those who wished to accept Jesus as Savior. While the apostle Paul fasted for three days before he was baptized, it was not in anticipation of baptism. He did not learn about baptism until the end of his fast (Acts 9: 1-18), at which time he received baptism immediately.

The <u>Didache</u> also suggests that sprinkling or pouring might be acceptable for baptism if there is not enough water available for immersion. However, if variations in the method of baptism were used in the second century, it must have been extremely rare since no such incidents are documented.

The earliest record of anyone using a form of baptism other than immersion is found more than two hundred years after the establishment of the church. In AD 251, a man by the name of Novatian[4] was ill and bedridden. Novatian wished to be baptized, but he was unable to rise and submit obediently to immersion in water. The church leaders decided that, given Novatian's condition, they would merely pour water over him in place of immersion. As time passed, more church leaders opted for either sprinkling or pouring water on an individual as a form of baptism. Finally, in AD 1311 at the Council of Ravenna[5], the leaders of the Roman Catholic Church officially approved these as acceptable forms of baptism.

This is the viewpoint that most closely resembles Martin Luther's[6] (1483-1546) idea of the role of baptism even as he opposed the many unauthorized rituals that were practiced by the church at the time. While Luther proclaimed a doctrine of salvation by *faith only*, he still believed baptism was necessary for salvation. Luther's differences with the church grew out of his concern that the Roman Catholics held dear many practices *not* established in Scripture. He did not dispute that baptism was essential. This is the belief held today by the Lutherans, those who follow closely the teachings of Martin Luther.

Water Baptism Is a Sign

While many accept that baptism, in one form or other, is essential for eternal life, others see it as a deed that is unrelated to salvation. Since this is a physical activity, it is believed that baptism is a human *work* and, therefore, can have no direct spiritual effect. Those who take this stand regard baptism as a *sign* of the covenant of grace – a sign commanded by God – arguing that one's submission to baptism is merely a demonstration to others that he/she has made a commitment to Christ. Salvation and the indwelling of the Holy Spirit, it is said, occur separately from water baptism. This viewpoint stems from the belief that water

20

baptism in the New Testament was intended to replace infant circumcision that was the *sign* of the Old Testament covenant. This is the view of baptism that is most popular today among evangelicals in America.

One well-known Bible scholar of Luther's time, William Tyndale[7] (1484-1536), who was an Englishman and an early translator of the Bible, seemed to hold views more in line with evangelicals than Lutherans. While he held baptism in high regard, he apparently saw it as a sign of salvation rather than a requirement.

John Wycliffe[8] (1324-1384) was the first man to translate the Bible into English and the first to use Olde English variations of the words *baptize* and *baptism* in reference to this ceremony. He was also one of the earliest to suggest that baptism was not intended to wash away original sin. Addressing the role of baptism, Wycliffe determined *'that baptism doth not confer, but only signify grace, which was given before.'* [9] He did, however, consider baptism essential for church membership and a prerequisite for partaking of the Lord's Supper.

Much of the discord surrounding the subject of baptism began during the Reformation Movement of the sixteenth century, which resulted in an amazing transformation of the religious community. A man by the name of Huldrych Zwingli[10] (1484-1531), a Swiss theologian and contemporary of Martin Luther, was the first person of sufficient standing to successfully promote the belief that baptism was simply an outward sign of salvation. This occurred around AD 1525. Zwingli considered infant baptism to be legitimate – not for the benefit of salvation, but as a matter of joining the child to the community of believers. Prior to the time of Zwingli, the universal understanding of the writings of the apostles was that baptism was the manner in which men could *attain* eternal life.

John Calvin[11] (1509-1564) believed baptism to be a manner of initiation during which men were admitted into the fellowship of the body of Christ. To an extent, he saw some spiritual value in baptism, although he essentially saw it as a new covenant sign, in the same fashion that circumcision was a sign of the Abrahamic covenant. He did not believe baptism was a *means* to receive salvation, but perceived it as a matter of an individual publicly *accepting* the promises of God.

John Wesley's[12] (1703-1791) perspective on baptism was very similar to Calvin's. Wesley, the founder of the Methodist denomination, did not consider one mode of baptism to be more or less scriptural than another. There is an impression in some of his sermons that he saw baptism as man's acceptance of grace in some sense, as well as the manner of initiation into the church; yet he denied that baptism was the *new birth* of which Jesus and the apostles spoke. Wesley considered baptism to be an outward covenant sign that separated believers from nonbelievers. He preached and taught in favor of infant baptism based on the belief that it represented a rite of admission into the church.

Water Baptism Is Immaterial

Baptism in water is considered insignificant by many others who confess Jesus as Lord. The fact that it is a command of Christ is apparently the only reason these people participate in baptism; that is, if they participate at all. They reject the notion that one is reborn at the time of baptism. To these men, participation in baptism is a work of man and, therefore, cannot be a matter of salvation. Like the teaching of baptism as a covenant sign, this belief developed from the teachings of Zwingli in the sixteenth century. Despite the fact that, prior to the time of Zwingli, baptism was understood by all men to be the moment of forgiveness of sins and salvation, the past few hundred years have seen his teachings grow in popularity.

Baptism with the Holy Spirit

Finally, there are those who insist that it is baptism with the Holy Spirit, rather than baptism in water, that is the moment of salvation. The claim is that the outpouring of the Holy Spirit that is depicted in the book of Acts is, by definition, baptism with the Holy Spirit, and that men can experience this same manifestation of the Spirit even today. Supporters of this view maintain that only through the outpouring of the Holy Spirit, as experienced on the Day of Pentecost, can a man receive the seal of salvation. As on the Day of Pentecost, this (Holy Spirit) baptism is accompanied by the presence of miraculous spiritual gift(s) in one's life – most notably the spiritual gift of speaking in tongues – as a sign of salvation.

This view of baptism with the Holy Spirit has risen in popularity among those in the Pentecostal movement, which had its beginnings within the United States in the early twentieth century. The most notable incident, often considered the birth of the movement, took place in Los Angeles in 1906. At that time, many claimed to have received baptism in the Spirit, along with the gift of tongues, just as it had occurred on the Day of Pentecost.

There are some in the Pentecostal movement, however, who do not argue that this experience signifies the time of salvation. To them the outpouring of the Spirit represents a second blessing that God bestows upon men as a matter of distributing miraculous gifts of the Spirit. They do not necessarily see this experience as a matter of redemption.

*   *   *   *   *

While these opinions summarize the most popular views on the subject, certainly a wide variety of beliefs have sprouted from these few, taking in an entire host of religious perspectives. Since Scripture is plainspoken in its instruction regarding baptism and its relationship with salvation, it is difficult to understand how these disputes have risen to such prominence in religious circles. Since some of the claims openly clash, it is *impossible* for all of these beliefs to be legitimate. Therefore, given the eternal consequences involved in the baptismal debate, seeking biblical guidance is critical for those who wish to honor God.

NOTES FOR CHAPTER 1

1. The notion that immersion in water is essential for salvation must, in a sense, be qualified. Campbell held that a Christian is anyone who obeys God's instructions to the extent that he/she is aware of those instructions. According to Campbell an individual is responsible, *"in all things according to the measure of knowledge of his will."* One who is unaware of the charge for immersion could clearly not be held accountable for disobedience to that charge. This, however, is not intended to be license to ignore a call once one is cognizant of God's direction. Campbell, Extract from **"Any Christians among Protestant Parties."** The Millennial Harbinger 8: (September 1837): 411; 33 (March 1862): 132. 2. Alexander Campbell.

2. Perhaps the most significant difference between Alexander Campbell and Barton W. Stone lies in the ultimate goal each sought to achieve. Campbell focused on the Bible as the single ultimate guide for Christianity and salvation. Stone, on the other hand, while he held the Bible as the single authority by which men might seek God, considered *unity* of the brotherhood his highest priority. Thus the greatest difference lies in their view of the un-immersed. While Campbell refused to fellowship with those who rejected immersion for the remission of sins, Stone did not. He refused to draw a line of distinction, as Campbell did, between immersed believers and those who had not been immersed. His

sentiment regarding these individuals is best expressed in his statement, *"I must believe that the household of Cornelius were made holy and received the Holy Spirit previous to their baptism yet before they were baptized they were not Christians nor united with the church of Christ."* This statement, of course, does not speak to fellowship with those who simply reject immersion, but it does reflect a softer perspective toward those who did not receive immersion for the forgiveness of sins. Stone, Christian Messenger 4: 235.

3. While the Didache was not discovered until 1873 in a monastery in Constantinople, its existence was never in doubt. The writings of the Didache were referenced by several other authors in the early church. The author, and even the date of the writing, are unknown. Few ever consider a date later than AD 200 while others suggest a possible date of writing as early as AD 50.

The notion that sprinkling or pouring of water for the purpose of baptism when immersion was not possible is first mentioned in this particular work confirming that immersion was certainly the form of baptism practiced and taught by the apostles. The teachings of this work, however, do not seem to follow absolutely the apostolic example (e.g., fasting a day or two prior to baptism) as can be seen in this excerpt regarding baptism:

> **On Baptism**. *7:1 But concerning Baptism, this is how you shall baptize. 7:2 Having first recited all these things, baptize in living water in the name of the Father and of the Son and of the Holy Spirit. 7:3 But if you do not have running water, then baptize in other water; 7:4 And if you are not able in cold, then in warm. 7:5 But if you have neither, then pour water on the head three times in the name of the Father and of the Son and of the Holy Spirit. 7:6 But before the Baptism, let him that baptizes and him that is baptized fast, and any others also who are able; 7:7 And you shall order him that is baptized to fast a day or two before.* The Didache, Chapter 7. This revision into English is based on the translation of J.B. Lightfoot.

4. Novatian was a schismatic of the third century, and founder of the sect of the Novatians; he was a Roman priest, and made himself antipope. His name is given as Novatus (*Noouatos*, Eusebius; *Nauatos*, Socrates) by Greek writers, and also in the verses of Damasus and Prudentius, on account of the metre.

> **Biography -** We know little of his life. St. Cornelius in his letter to Fabius of Antioch relates that Novatian was possessed by Satan for a season, apparently while a catechumen; for the exorcists attended him, and he fell into a sickness from which instant death was expected; he was, therefore, given baptism by affusion as he lay on his bed. The rest of the rites were not supplied on his recovery, nor was he confirmed by the bishop. "How then can he have received the Holy Ghost?" asks Cornelius. Novatian was a man of learning and had been trained in literary composition. Cornelius speaks of him sarcastically as "that maker of dogmas, that champion of ecclesiastical learning". His eloquence is mentioned by Cyprian (Ep. lx, 3) and a pope (presumably Fabian) promoted him to the priesthood in spite of the protests (according to Cornelius) of all the clergy and many of the laity that it was uncanonical for one who had received only clinical baptism to be admitted among the clergy. The story told by Eulogius of Alexandria that Novatian was Archdeacon of Rome, and was made a priest by the pope in order to prevent his succeeding to the papacy, contradicts the evidence of Cornelius and supposes a later state of things when the Roman deacons were statesmen rather than ministers. The anonymous work "Ad Novatianum" (x2i) tells us that Novatian, "so long as he was in the one

house, that is in Christ's Church, bewailed the sins of his neighbours as if they were his own, bore the burdens of the brethren, as the Apostle exhorts, and strengthened with consolation the backsliding in heavenly faith." The Catholic Encyclopedia, Volume XI.

5. Interestingly, the decision to accept forms of baptism other than immersion caused a rift between the Roman Catholic Church and her ally, the Greek Orthodox. The Greek Orthodox could not abide any form of baptism but immersion, realizing the meaning of the original Greek words used to define baptism.

In a history of the Baptist Church David Benedict, a contemporary of Campbell and Stone, noted the following regarding the work of a man by the name of James Basanage (date unknown) who wrote regarding the decision of Pope Stephen 21 to allow sprinkling in the case of infants in danger of death.

> "The learned James Basanage makes several very proper remarks on this canon: as that 'although it is accounted the first law for sprinkling, yet it doth not forbid dipping; that it allows sprinkling only in case of imminent danger: that the authenticity of it is denied by some Catholics: that many laws were made after this time in Germany, France, and England, to compel dipping, and without any provision for cases of necessity: therefore that this law did not alter the mode of dipping in public baptisms: and that it was not till five hundred and fifty years after, that the Legislature, in a council at Ravenna, in the year thirteen hundred and eleven, declared dipping or sprinkling indifferent.'" David Benedict, A General History of the Baptist Denomination in America, and Other Parts of the World, 1813.

6. Those who believe Luther was responsible for trivializing baptism misunderstand his view completely. Luther merely wished to rid the church of man-made traditions and rituals. His view is well defined in this excerpt from his work:

> In these words you must note, in the first place, that here stand God's commandment and institution, lest we doubt that Baptism is divine, not devised nor invented by men. For as truly as I can say, no man has spun the Ten Commandments, the Creed, and the Lord's Prayer out of his head, but they are revealed and given by God Himself, so also I can boast that Baptism is no human trifle, but instituted by God Himself, moreover, that it is most solemnly and strictly commanded that we must be baptized or we cannot be saved, lest any one regard it as a trifling matter, like putting on a new red coat. For it is of the greatest importance that we esteem Baptism excellent, glorious, and exalted, for which we contend and fight chiefly, because the world is now so full of sects clamoring that Baptism is an external thing, and that external things are of no benefit. But let it be ever so much an external thing here stand God's Word and command which institute, establish, and confirm Baptism. But what God institutes and commands cannot be a vain, but must be a most precious thing, though in appearance it were of less value than a straw. If hitherto people could consider it a great thing when the Pope with his letters and bulls dispensed indulgences and confirmed altars and churches, solely because of the letters and seals, we ought to esteem Baptism much more highly and more precious, because God has commanded it, and, besides, it is performed in His name. For these are the words, Go ye baptize; however, not in your name, but in the name of God. Luther, Large Catechism X2I, Part Fourth, Of Baptism. *Luther's Works,* 1551 edition, Vol. 2, p.76.

7. Regarding baptism, Tyndale wrote: *"If baptism preach me the washing in Christ's blood, so doth the Holy Ghost accompany it; and that deed of preaching through faith doth put away my sins. The ark of Noah saved them in the water through faith."* Tyndale, <u>Prologue to the Book of Leviticus</u>.

This view of baptism to forgive sins seems to be contradicted in the following work by John Christian unless it is understood that Tyndale believed that water alone could not bring forgiveness.

> Upon the subject of baptism he is very full. He is confident that baptism does not wash away sin. 'It is impossible,' says he, 'that the waters of the river should wash our hearts' (Tyndale, *Works* 2. 30. London, 1831). Baptism was a plunging into the water (Ibid, 25). Baptism to avail must include repentance, faith and confession (2I. 179). The church must, therefore, consist of believers (Ibid, 25). His book in a wonderful manner states accurately the position of the Baptists" Christian, <u>A History of the Baptists</u>, I, pp. 187-88).

8. Wycliffe held doctrinal views perhaps most closely associated with the Baptist denominational perspective. He wrote concerning the futility of infant baptism, though there does seem to be some confusion in his work concerning the fate of the un-baptized infant.

9. Walden, tom. ii. c. 98, 108.

10. Zwingli viewed Christian baptism as not only equivalent to, but identical to, the baptism of John. His assertion was that no new covenant was instituted and that the church age was merely a continuation of the old covenant. To Zwingli, the forgiveness of sins in baptism suggested in Scripture was symbolic in nature. He viewed Holy Spirit baptism as the baptism that saves. Baptism in water, to Zwingli, was perhaps more important to the feeble Christian who needed to do something as assurance of salvation. He expressed his view of baptism accordingly:

> …The inward baptism of the Spirit is the work of teaching which God does in our hearts and the calling with which he comforts and assures our hearts in Christ. And this baptism none can give save God alone. Without it, none can be saved – though it is quite possible to be saved without the baptism of external teaching and immersion. Zwingli, *Of Baptism, in Zwingli and Bullinger*, "Library of Christian Classics," Vol. 24. Ed. And tr. G.W. Bromiley (Philadelphia Westminster Press, 1953), p. 137.

11. It seems somewhat ironic that men such as Zwingli and Calvin, who saw no salvation value in baptism, fought so vigorously in favor of paedobaptism. The following excerpt from the work of Calvin depicts his position very well as he associates baptism with circumcision:

> At length they object, that there is not greater reason for admitting infants to baptism than to the Lord's Supper, to which, however, they are never admitted: as if Scripture did not in every way draw a wide distinction between them. In the early Church, indeed, the Lord's Supper was frequently given to infants, as appears from Cyprian and Augustine, (August. ad Bonif. Lib. 1;) but the practice justly became obsolete. For if we attend to the peculiar nature of baptism, it is a kind of entrance, and as it were initiation into the Church, by which we are ranked among the people of God, a sign of our spiritual regeneration, by which we are again born to be children of God, whereas on the

contrary the Supper is intended for those of riper years, who, having passed the tender period of infancy, are fit to bear solid food. Calvin, <u>Institutes of the Christian Religion, Book 4, Chapter 16, Section 30</u>.

12. Wesley understood baptism to be the *outward sign of an inward change* as is expressed in his words from Sermon 45:

> 1. And, First, it follows, that baptism is not the new birth: They are not one and the same thing. Many indeed seem to imagine that they are just the same; at least, they speak as if they thought so; but I do not know that this opinion is publicly avowed by any denomination of Christians whatever. Certainly it is not by any within these kingdoms, whether of the established Church, or dissenting from it. The judgment of the latter is clearly declared in the large Catechism: [Q. 163, 165. -- Ed.] -- Q. "What are the parts of a sacrament? A. The parts of a sacrament are two: The one an outward and sensible sign; the other, and inward and spiritual grace, thereby signified. -- Q. What is baptism? A. Baptism is a sacrament, wherein Christ hath ordained the washing with water, to be a sign and seal of regeneration by his Spirit." Here it is manifest, baptism, the sign, is spoken of as distinct from regeneration, the thing signified. Wesley, <u>Sermon 45, Part IV</u>.

Chapter II

Baptism and the First Covenant

The Shadow Covenant

The Bible offers us the opportunity to understand God's character as well as His perspective of man. In it He has established a covenant by which He hopes to reconcile us to Him. While the new covenant is established in the New Testament, the Old Testament provides the foundation for the development of the covenant of grace. The precursors for water baptism in the New Testament can be found in the old (first) covenant, which God made with Abraham and extended through Moses, so that the new covenant might be firmly grounded.

> 1. For the law, having a shadow of the good things to come, *and* not the very image of the things, can never with these same sacrifices, which they offer continually year by year, make those who approach perfect. 2. For then would they not have ceased to be offered? For the worshipers, once purified, would have had no more consciousness of sins. 3. But in those *sacrifices there is* a reminder of sins every year. 4. For *it is* not possible that the blood of bulls and goats could take away sins. (Hebrews 10: 1-4)

Through His servant Moses, God provided the Israelites with the Mosaic Law. This law, based upon God's covenant with Abraham, was the foundation upon which God established His relationship with the children of Israel. The Mosaic Law was also the predecessor to the covenant of grace that was instituted by Jesus' death, burial, and resurrection.

The apostle Paul addressed the idea of *shadows* found in the preceding passage (Hebrews 10: 1). In his letter to the Galatians, Paul identifies believers as those who had been freed from the bondage of sin by the blood of Christ and made heirs to the kingdom. Spiritually, he compares believers in the church age to the children of Abraham with whom God established His original covenant.

> 22. For it is written that Abraham had two sons: the one by a bondwoman, the other by a freewoman. 23. But he *who was* of the bondwoman was born according to the flesh, and he of the freewoman through promise, 24. which things are symbolic. For these are the two covenants: the one from Mount Sinai, which gives birth to bondage,

which is Hagar – 25. for this Hagar is Mount Sinai in Arabia, and corresponds to Jerusalem which now is, and is in bondage with her children – 26. but the Jerusalem above is free, which is the mother of us all. 27. For it is written:

Rejoice, O barren, you who do not bear!
Break forth and shout, you who are not in labor!
For the desolate has many more children than she who has a husband.

28. Now we, brethren, as Isaac was, are children of promise. 29. But, as he who was born according to the flesh then persecuted him who was born according to the Spirit, even so *it is* now. 30. Nevertheless, what does the Scripture say? *"Cast out the bondwoman and her son, for the son of the bondwoman shall not be heir with the son of the freewoman."* 31. So then, brethren, we are not children of the bondwoman but of the free. (Galatians 4: 22-31)

Elements of the First Covenant

Certain elements of the first covenant were intended to provide a mechanism for the Israelites to worship and honor God. These were not literally carried over to the new covenant; yet shadowy images of various elements of the new covenant can be found in the first covenant. As men inspired by God, including the author of the book of Hebrews, wrote the New Testament, they consistently drew comparisons between the two covenants. For instance, Scripture reveals in detail the offerings the Israelites were commanded to sacrifice to God continually in order to atone for the sins they had committed against Him. Who can doubt that the animal sacrifices performed under the old covenant were the *shadow* of Jesus' sacrifice on the cross? The earlier sacrifices that were offered by the priests on a daily basis were simply unable to afford men a clean conscience from the sins they had committed. Therefore, they were replaced by the one sacrifice (Jesus) that could offer what these priestly sacrifices could not.

Feasts of the First Covenant

In the first covenant, God employed a number of celebrations that involved specific feasts and foods. Some of these feasts were intended for the priests. For instance, only the priests were to partake of the sin offerings that were offered in the temple (Leviticus 6: 24-30). Other feasts, like the Feast of Weeks (Pentecost), the Feast of the Passover, and the Feast of the Tabernacles, involved the entire Israelite population. The people observed each of these festivals for reasons that were detailed by

Moses (Deuteronomy 16: 1-16). From Moses' writing we learn that the Passover Feast, also known as the Feast of Unleavened Bread, was celebrated in remembrance of the Israelites' release from slavery as death came to the firstborn of each household in Egypt. At that time those households who obeyed God's command were *passed over*, escaping this terrible plague. This was the final plague on the Egyptians, causing Pharaoh to decide to free the Israelites (Exodus 12: 17-23; Deuteronomy 16: 1-8).

The Feast of Weeks provided an opportunity for the children of Israel to recall their slavery in Egypt and, in turn, show their gratitude for the freedom they now enjoyed by giving free will offerings to God (Deuteronomy 16: 9-12). Through the Feast of Tabernacles the Israelites thanked God for their successful work in the field that produced bountiful crops (Deuteronomy 16: 13-17).

The new covenant also provides a feast in which we commemorate our relationship with God through Christ. Jesus established this feast, known to us as the Lord's Supper, during the Passover on the night prior to His crucifixion (Matthew 26: 26-29). As Jesus passed the loaf and the cup, He explained to the disciples that, like the feasts of the first covenant, they were to observe this feast as a memorial (Luke 22: 19-20). This new celebration was intended to remind them of His death – a death that had not yet occurred, but was imminent. It is fair to say that the disciples did not fully grasp the significance of this *breaking of bread* until sometime after Jesus' resurrection.

Conversion in the First Covenant

Scripture indicates that God provided a means by which Gentiles could convert to Judaism (Acts 2: 11; 6: 5). Apparently this included a ceremony involving water, historically referred to by some as *proselyte baptism*, that was comparable to the immersion performed by John the Baptist as well as Jesus' disciples. We have sufficient evidence in such writings as the Dead Sea Scrolls[1] and the Talmud[2] that various other ceremonies, also called baptisms, were employed prior to the time of Christ and John the Baptist for the purpose of purification.

While proselyte baptism is not mentioned in Scripture, it should be noted that this ceremony is addressed in neither a positive or negative manner. If the Israelites were utilizing a rite of conversion unacceptable to God, it is reasonable to believe that deed would have been highlighted in Scripture. If, however, God provided a means for Gentiles to be accepted into the Jewish faith, as we know He did, He would not necessarily need to communicate that in Scripture. Those who participated in that conversion process would simply become subject to the Jewish law once converted.

That having been said, we should consider proselyte baptism more of an *indirect* precursor to Christian immersion for two reasons. First of all, the fact that this practice is not communicated in Scripture as part of the old covenant is reason to dismiss it as a *direct* shadow of baptism. Secondly, Scripture records other purification ceremonies and events that *are* established in the Old Testament and seem more suited to this role. Still, we should not lose sight of the fact that, like other immersions, proselyte baptism was performed as a matter of conversion.

Purification in the First Covenant

While the Ten Commandments are delivered in the book of Exodus, many of the finer points of the Mosaic Law are revealed to us in the book of Leviticus. In fact, to a great extent it is in the book of Leviticus that God establishes water as a means of purification for religious purposes. Two different kinds of ceremonial washings were performed by the Israelites. The first is represented by the Hebrew word כבס (*kabac*). However, while this word denotes ritual washing, its use is generally limited to the washing of clothing as a matter of purification (Exodus 19: 10; Leviticus 11: 24-28). Occasionally this word is employed figuratively in passages like Psalm 51: 2 and Jeremiah 4: 14, but those references do not change the literal meaning of the word, which is to *wash*.

Another word in Leviticus also defines ritual cleansing by means of water – the Hebrew word רחצ (*rachats*), which is more often translated into English as *bathe*. While we find that there are certain times when רחצ refers to the washing of a man's hands and feet (Exodus 30: 19-21; 40: 31), it most often indicates a submergence (bathing) of the entire body as a matter of cleansing (Leviticus 15: 16; 16: 4; 22: 6; Numbers 19: 19). Occasionally it also refers to the washing of animal sacrifices prior to placing them on the altar (Leviticus 1: 2-23). This kind of washing, then, might reasonably be considered a *shadow* of Christian baptism. Yet we can conclude from Scripture that God's foresight with respect to baptism far surpasses specific ritual washings like these.

It is significant that God, beginning with the introduction of the Mosaic Law, has *always* relied on the combination of water and blood in the purification of His people. In the first covenant, those who offered sacrifices in keeping with the law, but failed to wash with water, were considered unclean despite the sacrifices that were made. While cleansing was not possible without the shedding of blood, water was also necessary for purification. Failure to bathe according to the law was even considered a breach of the covenant and grounds for separating that person from the general assembly (Numbers 19: 20). This principle applied directly to Gentile converts as they experienced a conversion involving both water (proselyte baptism) and blood (circumcision).

A number of Old Testament passages point to cleansing with water in order for the Israelites to be presentable to God. Various washings are noted throughout the book of Leviticus as well as passages such as Numbers 19: 7-8. In fact, the entire nineteenth chapter of Numbers demonstrates the emphasis God has placed upon cleansing by means of water.

Scripture speaks of a number of events that illustrate God's use of water as a means of purification. In the Red Sea He buried in water those who opposed Him, which also resulted in the liberation of the Israelites (Exodus 14: 1-31). Paul explained to the Corinthians that God's use of water in this instance could be viewed as an *image* of baptism (1 Corinthians 10: 2) as the Israelites were freed from that which enslaved them. Naaman, a commander in the Syrian army, was told to wash himself seven times in the Jordan River in order to be cleansed of his disease of leprosy (2 Kings 5: 1-14). Through the flood God destroyed all but Noah, who found favor in God's eyes, along with his family (Genesis 6: 5-8:22). The waters eradicated the evil of men. We are told that Christian baptism corresponds *directly* to the waters of the flood (1 Peter 3: 21).

These occasions illustrate the importance God placed upon the use of water in providing cleansing, both physical and spiritual, although mostly spiritual. Given the relationship between the Old and New Testaments, these should be considered *shadows* of the baptism that was to come. Similarly, the apostle John, acknowledging the divine role assigned to water, described it as an equal witness with the Holy Spirit and the blood to the eternal life we have in Jesus (1 John 5: 6-11).

The Old Reflected in the New

While many biblical writers discuss the bond between the old and new covenants, it is the writer of the book of Hebrews who truly captures the essence of that relationship. His examination of the two covenants offers us the opportunity to appreciate both the similarities and the differences between them. As he explores the old covenant, where the foundation for the new covenant was laid, the relationship between them becomes very clear. In fact, it seems that the very purpose of the first covenant was foundational. The elements comprising the first covenant were intended to be temporary. Throughout the Old Testament the focus is on the coming Messiah and the covenant of grace.

At times the *shadow* relationship between the covenants may seem a bit unclear. After all, we are seldom given any exact designations such as *ritual washings = baptism* or *the Passover Feast = the Lord's Supper.* In fact, there really are no equals between the covenants. The temporary images of the first covenant were replaced by the permanent features of the new covenant. Various ceremonies and ordinances formed the framework for the first covenant; however, these rituals were designed to be temporary. From the beginning God had in mind the covenant of grace in which we live.

After establishing the fact that Jesus is now the High Priest through whom we may approach the Father, the author of the book of Hebrews defines Jesus' role more precisely – He has risen to be with God and has established Himself as Mediator of the new covenant. We learn that it was not necessary for Jesus to fill the role of priest here on earth. Under the Mosaic Law the priests, descendants of Levi, performed the rites that served as *a copy and/or shadow of heavenly things.* Thus, the role of priests on earth had been fulfilled in the first covenant. Jesus' role was to take the position of High Priest in the new covenant, which was considered a more excellent ministry (Hebrews 8: 4-7).

In the new covenant, the significance of the temple and its design, including the many religious items that were located inside the temple, were no longer relevant (Hebrews 9: 1-5). Therefore, the ceremonies and items related to the temple were discarded. These included the various washings that served to provide purification as well as certain foods and drinks used in their frequent religious rituals (Hebrews 9: 6-10).

11. But Christ came *as* High Priest of the good things to come, with the greater and more perfect tabernacle not made with hands, that is, not of this creation. 12. Not with the blood of goats and calves, but with His own blood He entered the Most Holy Place once for all, having obtained eternal redemption. 13. For if the blood of bulls and goats and the ashes of a heifer, sprinkling the unclean, sanctifies for the purifying of the flesh, 14. how much more shall the blood of Christ, who through the eternal Spirit offered Himself without spot to God, cleanse your conscience from dead works to serve the living God? (Hebrews 9: 11-14)

There is a distinct directional shift when we reach verse eleven of this passage. While the first ten verses of the ninth chapter of Hebrews highlight the various aspects of the first covenant, in verse eleven the writer begins to feature the new covenant. The purpose of these verses is to portray the distinguishing characteristics of the covenant of grace. The weaknesses of the first covenant, established in verses one through ten, had been overcome through the blood of Christ. Although they had now been abandoned, certain aspects of the Mosaic Law (ritual sacrifices, etc.) were mirrored in the new covenant.

The temporary nature of these *shadows* (e.g., animal sacrifices, feasts, etc.) was exchanged for the permanence of those images instituted under the covenant of grace. Rather than a temple constructed of mortar and stone, Jesus entered a spiritual *'Most Holy Place'* where He would serve as the High Priest and *Intercessor* between mankind and God the Father (Hebrews 9: 12). Similarly, the animal sacrifices of the first covenant were obsolete once Jesus shed His own blood on our behalf (Hebrews 9: 13-14).

We find a comparable, but more in-depth, comparison of the covenants in the tenth chapter of Hebrews. The inadequacies of the Abrahamic covenant and the Mosaic Law failed to offer men true redemption. The blood of bulls and goats, which were central in covering man's sins under the law, could not offer men the *freedom* from sin that was necessary for mankind to be reconciled to God. Therefore, God replaced these with that which could accomplish the task – the sacrifice of Jesus (Hebrews 10: 1-11). Just as we discovered a transition in verse eleven of the ninth chapter of Hebrews, we once again notice a change in the writer's focus starting with the twelfth verse of chapter ten. While verses one through eleven address the weaknesses of the first covenant, beginning in verse twelve the author fully concentrates upon the characteristics of the new covenant in contrast with the old covenant.

The author identifies the new covenant as the means by which men may be reconciled to God (Hebrews 10: 12-14). With that in mind, the writer thoughtfully considers certain elements found within the new covenant (Hebrews 10: 12 – 11: 40). In considering the relationship between the two covenants, we discover that quite often God replaced a number of first covenant elements with a single component in the new covenant. For instance, we find that the one sacrifice in the new covenant replaced the many that were found in the first covenant. The *one sacrifice* for sin, in contrast to the numerous sacrifices required in the first covenant, can be found in Jesus' death on the cross (vs. 12-13). Through this one offering, *sanctification* was made possible (v. 14). The *Holy Spirit* stands as witness for those who would be saved (v. 15). True *remission of sins*, which was impossible in the first covenant, is now a reality (vs. 16-18). The role of *High Priest* has been assumed by Jesus, the only one truly worthy of that position (vs. 19-21). The combination of *faith, repentance,* and *one washing* (baptism), as opposed to the many washings of the first covenant, makes it possible for men to draw near to God (v. 22). *Confession* of Jesus as Lord is proclaimed by the faithful (v. 23). *Love* and *good works*, as well as the *assembly* of Christ's followers, offer exhortation and support to those who are members of Christ's body, which is the church (vs. 24-25). Certainty of *judgment* is in store for those who refuse to accept Jesus as Savior (vs. 26-31) while *eternal life* is the reward for those who partake in God's covenant of grace (vs. 32-39). Faith (chapter 11), then, is the manner in which men respond to this offer of grace.

The many feasts of the old covenant that were intended to honor God were insignificant when compared to the loaf and the cup (the one meal replacing the many) that represent the holiness and purity of the sacrifice of Jesus' body and blood. God also discovered a more suitable dwelling place among men in the repentant hearts of those who choose to submit to Him. No longer would God separate Himself from those who love Him.

The various purification practices (washings) of the first covenant, performed in conjunction with numerous blood sacrifices, were simply incapable of providing the children of Israel with the perfection God desired (Hebrews 10: 1). No amount of washings or sacrifices in the first covenant could offer what the one sacrifice and one washing in the new covenant were able to convey. God established a new and more powerful covenant, the covenant of grace, built upon the only sacrifice that could be considered worthy. The first covenant, and those elements comprising it, paled in comparison to the power of the new covenant made available to us through the blood of Christ.

Baptism and the Birthright of the First Covenant

In the first covenant there was a unique event that occurred at which time a child was recognized as a descendant of Abraham and heir to his covenant with God. It was the moment of childbirth. When an Israelite child was born, whether male or female, that child immediately inherited all the rights and privileges afforded anyone who was born into the lineage of Abraham, Isaac, and Jacob (Genesis 15: 17-21; 17: 1-8). This was an honor bestowed upon each Israelite; but it was not a result of anything the child had done. The inheritance was based solely upon the fact that the child was Abraham's descendant. Childbirth was the means by which one became heir. While Gentiles were allowed to participate in the Abrahamic covenant by converting to the Jewish faith, the normal manner through which the Israelites entered the covenant was childbirth.

In like manner there is a time, according to the New Testament, when a person becomes a child of God. It is a time understood to be the moment of regeneration as God cleanses a man or woman of his/her sins and that person is reborn. As with the covenant of Abraham, where participation was recognized as a right of birth, we are told in the New Testament that we enter the new covenant by being reborn by a Spiritual birth (John 3: 3-8; Titus 3: 5). As the Israelites were born of Abraham, we must be born of God. Thus, man's inheritance of the kingdom of God is received as a birthright for those who have been *born again* or *born of God* – by a spiritual birth (Galatians 4: 23-29; 1 Peter 1: 23; 2: 2; 1 John 2: 29; 3: 9) – into the family of God.

When the new birth, also called *new life* (Romans 6: 4), is presented in the New Testament, baptism is the time recognized as the moment of rebirth. As we consider the bond between the covenants, although the relationship between baptism and the ceremonial washings of old is easily established, its association with a child's birth into the Israelite family should not be ignored.

The Baptism of John – A Transition

Many view the water baptism that was introduced and administered in book of Acts as a temporary tool offered by God to help men transition from the old covenant to the new covenant. However, Christian immersion in water that is discussed throughout the New Testament would have ceased if God intended it to be temporary. The clear indication from the Great Commission is that Jesus meant for baptism to be permanent. At no time in the New Testament do the apostles suggest that baptism would come to an end.

It seems more reasonable that a baptism that was intended to provide a link between the two covenants would be found prior to the establishment of the new covenant in the book of Acts. We can rule out proselyte baptism since its role was to grant Gentiles access to the Mosaic Law. It is unlikely that a ritual such as proselyte baptism, which was not administered to the Israelites, would serve to join two washings (old covenant washings and new covenant baptism) that, at least initially, were applicable only to the Israelites.

Prior to the beginning of Jesus' ministry on earth, God specially selected John to fill the role of forerunner for Christ (Mark 1: 1-3). In fact, we could easily argue that God specially *created* John the Baptist, given the extraordinary circumstances surrounding his birth. Matthew gives us some insight into the life of John. He was a prophet who was sent to prepare the world for Jesus' coming.

> 7. As they departed, Jesus began to say to the multitudes concerning John: "What did you go out into the wilderness to see? A reed shaken by the wind? 8. But what did you go out to see? A man clothed in soft garments? Indeed, those who wear soft *clothing* are in kings' houses. 9. But what did you go out to see? A prophet? Yes, I say to you, and more than a prophet. 10. For this is *he* of whom it is written:
> *"Behold, I send My messenger before Your face,*
> *Who will prepare Your way before You.'*
> 11. "Assuredly, I say to you, among those born of women there has not risen one greater than John the Baptist; but he who is least in the kingdom of heaven is greater than he. (Matthew 11: 7-11)

John's ministry was marked by his emphasis on the rite of immersion in water. Baptism played such a predominant role in John's ministry that he eventually came to be called John the Baptizer, or John the Baptist. Yet John explained to his listeners that he did not baptize of his own volition, but that he was instructed by God to baptize with water (John 1: 33).

John's baptism was different from both proselyte baptism and the various washings of the old covenant. His was a baptism that offered forgiveness of sins (Mark 1: 4). Old covenant washings, which were unable to offer men God's desired effect of holiness, simply declared a man to be clean rather than unclean, or they prepared the priests to enter into the presence of God to perform sacrifices. Since John's baptism extended forgiveness prior to Jesus' death, it is most reasonable to view this as transitional, leading from the old covenant washings and/or childbirth to new covenant baptism in the name of Jesus.

One factor we must not overlook is the unique nature of John's ministry that is revealed through the prophets and the gospel writers. Isaiah prophesied that a man would precede the Messiah in order to make preparations for His coming, in essence, paving the road before Him (Isaiah 40: 3). Malachi also prophesied about a man who would be Christ's forerunner (Malachi 3: 1) whose role it would be to prepare the Israelites for the coming Messiah. Both Matthew (Matthew 3: 3) and Mark (Mark 1: 2-3) quote Isaiah's prophecy and apply it directly to John the Baptist.

Through the words of these inspired writers, the ministry of John the Baptist is seen and understood as preparatory for the appearance of the Messiah. If John and his ministry emerged in anticipation of Christ, the baptism he offered should be viewed in the same light. John's baptism provided forgiveness of sins – yet it was not baptism in the name of Jesus, nor did it involve the Holy Spirit. Accordingly, if the baptism of John was transitional between the covenants, water baptism in the name of Jesus that was instituted upon the establishment of the church in the book of Acts must be viewed with a sense of permanence.

The Nature of Water

When we consider the role of baptism, one thing we might take into consideration is the very nature of water itself. It would be shortsighted of us to believe that God's decision to use water in baptism was based solely upon its ability to cleanse. Water has life-giving and life-sustaining properties that nothing else in creation can claim. Tertullian, one of the early church fathers, pointed to these very characteristics of water as God's reason for using it as the means to enter His kingdom through immersion.

Although Tertullian apparently endorsed the problematic view of baptismal regeneration (the notion that the water itself held the power to regenerate), that does not diminish the symbolism of water found in the following statement:

> What *of the fact* that waters were in some way the regulating powers by which the disposition of the world thenceforward was constituted by God? For the suspension of the celestial firmament in the midst He caused by "dividing the waters;" the suspension of "the dry land" He accomplished by "separating the waters." After the world had been hereupon set in order through *its* elements, when inhabitants were given it, "the waters" were the first to receive the precept "to bring forth living creatures." Water was the first to produce that which had life, that it might be no wonder in baptism if waters know how to give life.[3]

The symbolism evident in the life-giving and cleansing properties of water, the ceremonial washings of the old covenant that were an early image of baptism, and the teachings of the apostles and Jesus concerning rebirth, provide us with substantial insight into the importance of the celebration of Christian baptism.

NOTES FOR CHAPTER 2

1. The Dead Sea Scrolls were discovered in the late 1940's in some caves in the hills west of the Dead Sea. They were hidden in these caves, located in an area known as Khirbet Qumran, presumably by a Jewish community of believers, who traveled to these hills as a manner of setting themselves apart from other men in favor of their pursuit of a relationship with God. These Essenes, as they were known, established a monastery-like community where the goal was the attainment of the highest level of Spiritual commitment.

The exact relationship between the Essenes and the Dead Sea Scrolls is the source of much debate, although the two seem to hail from roughly the same time period (second century B. C.) and location (Qumran). Still, some claim that this is merely coincidence. The likelihood, however, is that the Essenes either wrote or collected the writings, or a combination of these two possibilities.

The Dead Sea Scrolls address, to an extent, certain ritual washings for the purpose of purification. Unfortunately the mutilated condition of certain scrolls prohibited them from being read and translated. One particular scroll that fits this description was entitled *Baptismal Liturgy*. Still, this is not the only portion of the scrolls to deal with ritual washings. For instance, the following excerpt holds reference to such cleansing. Note the relationship in this passage between spirit, water, and sanctification.

> **88. Purification of Initiates at Qumran 6** ...For it is by the Spirit of the Counsel of Truth concerning man's ways that all his iniquities shall be covered, so he may look on the light of life. And by a holy Spirit for union with his Truth shall he be cleansed from all his injustices. And by an upright and humble Spirit will his sins be covered; and by humbling his soul toward all that God prescribes his flesh shall be cleansed for sprinkling with purifying waters,

and for sanctifying with cleansing waters. And he shall direct his steps to walk perfectly in all the ways of God, according to his command regarding the times appointed for his testimonies. And he shall deviate neither to the right nor to the left; and he shall not go beyond one of all his words. Then he shall be accepted by an atonement pleasing before God. And for him this will be for a covenant of Unity everlasting. – Dead Sea Scrolls, Community Rule (1QS) 3.6-12.

2. Throughout Old Testament times many oral rules were established by the scribes and priests of the Jewish faith. These rules became, for the most part, traditions of the Israelites that were often viewed as equal to the written law. The Talmud is a document dating back to the first century that stands as an attempt to form a written work of the oral laws that had been handed down over the centuries. Besides codifying these oral rules, the Talmud is also a source of commentary with respect to the Torah, offering the views of the scribes and priest regarding the writing of God's Word. These excerpts specifically address the ritual of proselyte baptism as a means of allowing entrance into the Jewish faith by Gentiles.

86. Essene Initiation - 137. There is no immediate initiation for those who are eager (to join the Essene) party. Rather, they give one a small axe, the loincloth mentioned above, and white garments, putting him under discipline for one year while he remains outside. 138. And during this examination period he gives evidence of his self-control, they lead him nearer to their discipline, letting him participate in cleaner waters for purification. But he is not yet received into their common life. For after proving his endurance, his character is tested for two more years. And then, if he appears worthy, he is admitted to the community. ---Josephus, Jewish War 2.137-138.

91. Rabbinic Proselyte Baptism I He who wants to be a proselyte is not received right away. They say to him:

--"Why do you want to be a proselyte? Have you not seen that this people is poorer and more oppressed and humiliated than all peoples? Troubles and trials come upon them, and they bury their sons and their sons' sons. They are killed on account of circumcision and immersion and all the rest of the commandments. And they do not behave in public like all the rest of the nations." **2** If he says, "I am not up to this!" they dismiss him and he goes his own way.

If he takes this on himself, they lead him down to the place of immersion (*beth tebilah*). **3** They cover him with water around the place of his nakedness, and they tell him some of the details of the commandments... **5** And they say good and comforting words to him:

--"Happy are you! Who have you joined? Him who spoke and the world was! The world was created only for the sake of Israel. Only Israel is called "sons of God" (cf. Deut 14:1), and there is none beloved before God except Israel. All the words that we spoke to you we told you only to increase your reward!" --- Babylonian Talmud (appendix), Gerim 1.1-5.

3. Tertullian, On Baptism, Chapter 21. Water Chosen as a Vehicle of Divine Operation and Wherefore. Its Prominence First of All in Creation.

Chapter III

God's New Covenant

The Blood of the New Covenant

Those of us who live in the church age live in the covenant of grace that God established through the death of Christ. This *new* covenant is strikingly different from the *first* covenant that God originally established with Abraham. In the Abrahamic covenant, men could not attain salvation (eternal life) due to some deep-seated weaknesses that were discussed in the previous chapter. Sin is the one thing that separates men from God. For men to be reconciled to God, those sins must be removed. Yet the sacrifices of animals that were performed under the Mosaic Law failed to eliminate the guilt of sin (Hebrews 10: 4). Additionally, men were unable to keep the law perfectly. The transgression of one law was still transgression of the law (James 2: 10) and could not be undone.

47. Most assuredly, I say to you, he who believes in Me has everlasting life. 48. I am the bread of life. (John 6: 47-48)

Jesus revealed to His disciples that He alone was the source of (eternal) life. Those who wished to participate in that life, eating His flesh, so to speak, would have the opportunity for eternal life (John 6: 53). Some of the Jews failed to understand His words. Since they did not understand, many were alarmed by the comment and began to argue about the prospect of literally eating a man's flesh. However, Jesus was speaking of spiritual things they were not ready to grasp – things related to the coming covenant of grace.

Participation in a covenant – any covenant – involves blood in some fashion. At times blood is a factor in the initial establishment of the covenant. For instance, we find that Noah sacrificed animals to God upon exiting the ark as the covenant was established between him and God (Genesis 8: 20). This is true even in a marriage where the mixing of the blood in marital relations is intended as a consummation of the covenant between a man and a woman. At other times it is blood that activates the covenant at a later date. Such is the case with a will where someone must die in order for the promises of the covenant to take effect. Death, or blood, is required for a will or covenant to take effect, and this was true of the first covenant as well (Hebrews 9:18). We are told that this is why the blood of animals was necessary in the first covenant.

In the new covenant Jesus has become the Mediator between God and men. He gained this position by dying on our behalf. In addition, through that same death, the promise of forgiveness of sins (Matthew 26: 28) and eternal life was made available (Hebrews 9: 15) to men. The New Testament contains the conditions of the new covenant (the testament or will of Jesus) while the blood (death) of Christ is the dedication, or stamp, of that covenant – that which activates the covenant. Christ's death was required in order for the new covenant to become effective (Hebrews 9: 16-17). Without His sacrifice the new covenant would not exist.

The New Ordinances

As James discusses the good works that men might accomplish due to their earnest relationship with God (James 2: 14-26), he is not concerned with men abiding by statutes in obedience to God's commands. Instead, James addresses the characteristics of Christ's followers. The more we learn about the character of God the more we realize that, like Him, we must be kind and loving and give of ourselves sacrificially to help others. These are traits that God wants to see in His people.

Repentance, confession, baptism, and partaking of the Lord's Supper are commands of God that are to be obeyed. They are distinct from the character traits mentioned by James. Repentance, to an extent, can occur as a natural human response when we realize how our sins affect God. For this reason repentance cannot really be classified as an ordinance *per se*. However, certain other commands of God do not occur quite so naturally and are, therefore, a matter of ordinance.

Who, simply because he/she wishes to have a relationship with God, would consider being immersed in water? It is not something that occurs instinctively – it is something that is taught. It is a rite that is performed. No one would even know to be baptized unless it was specifically commanded of us within the framework of the gospel message. Who would partake of the Lord's Supper? This ceremony would not occur naturally simply because we know God wants us to live lives that honor Him, or because we understand the golden rule. The only means available for us to understand these things is the fact that they are specifically explained in the pages of the New Testament. Therefore, these are not about character or good works, but about ordinance.

The fact that God did away with *fleshly ordinances* when Jesus died and rose again (Hebrews 9: 10) has resulted in the teaching that men can realize salvation without human activity. It is true that God did away with the ordinances of the first covenant. However, these were temporary in nature since they could not offer men true freedom from sins (Hebrews 9: 9). If, however, God intended to eliminate *all* ordinances for His people, He would not have established communion – or baptism. Since God removed fleshly ordinances, while at the same time establishing the Lord's Supper and baptism in the name of Jesus, we can conclude that He does not consider these to be fleshly, but spiritual ordinances.

Scripture is brimming with passages that reveal the need for men to honor God by keeping His commands (1 Corinthians 7: 19; 1 Thessalonians 4: 1-18; 2 Peter 3: 1-2; 1 John 2: 3-4; 5: 3; et al). Not only is it important for us to keep God's commands as a matter of honoring Him, but certain commands are required of man in his pursuit of salvation (Acts 2: 38; 3: 19; Romans 10: 9-10).

> Now I praise you, brethren, that you remember me in all things and keep the traditions just as I delivered *them* to you. (1 Corinthians 11: 2)

The word translated as *traditions* in this passage is the Greek word *paradosis*, which is also translated *teachings* (NIV), or *ordinances*[1] (KJV), in this same context. Paul urged the Corinthians to keep these traditions, or ordinances, precisely as he had taught them.

As the writer of Hebrews offers us insight into God's new covenant with man, he makes it very clear that the ordinances of the first covenant were no longer relevant. However, we find that he does not consider ordinances, in general, to be obsolete. On the contrary, according to the writer, God has provided a specific manner of purification in the new covenant.

> 19. Therefore, brethren, having boldness to enter the Holiest by the blood of Jesus, 20. by a new and living way which He consecrated for us, through the veil, that is, His flesh, 21. and having a High Priest over the house of God, 22. let us draw near with a true heart in full assurance of faith, having our hearts sprinkled from an evil conscience and our bodies washed with pure water. (Hebrews 10: 19-22)

The moment of baptism binds together man's faith and God's work as we are freed, by grace, from an evil past. Yet the sequence of events in this passage is significant in that baptism and a clean conscience with respect to our former life take place before we *'draw near to God.'* [2] The two phrases, *'having hearts sprinkled'* and *'having bodies washed,'* are written here in perfect participle form. This literally translates as *our hearts having been sprinkled* and *our bodies having been washed.* In other words, they occur prior to, or (at the very latest) at the same time that we draw near. Just as the priests of the first covenant did not enter God's presence prior to washing, so we prepare to enter His presence in baptism.

Man's responsibility in God's new covenant is a responsibility of faith. Man approaches God by faith, in baptism, as a matter of seeking forgiveness (Hebrews 10: 22). This teaching is confirmed in Peter's first epistle where the apostle identifies baptism as man's petition to God for a clean conscience (1 Peter 3: 21).

Paul wrote, in his letter to the Ephesians, about the nature of the abolished ordinances of the Mosaic Law and the first covenant that had so alienated the Gentiles (Ephesians 2: 15). Jesus' death eliminated these ordinances, offering reconciliation of both Jews and Gentiles *'to God into one body'* (Ephesians 2: 16), giving all men *'access to the Father by one Spirit'* (Ephesians 2: 18). Of particular interest in this passage is the fact that Paul ties together the Spirit and the body in much the same way that they are linked throughout the New Testament. Peter instructed the Israelites on the Day of Pentecost to repent and be baptized. Those who were obedient to these commands received the Holy Spirit (Acts 2: 38) and were added to the church body (Acts 2: 41). As a complement to Peter's remarks, Paul also stated that we are all admitted to the body *'by one Spirit'* (1 Corinthians 12: 13).

The Witness of the Spirit, the Water, and the Blood

The apostle John, in his first epistle, spends a considerable amount of time proclaiming and defending Jesus' identity as Savior. In that letter he discusses in detail the fact that God had given water the deliberate role of *witness* in the covenant of grace (1 John 5: 1-8).

1. Whoever believes that Jesus is the Christ is born of God, and everyone who loves Him who begot also loves him who is begotten of Him. 2. By this we know that we love the children of God, when we

love God and keep His commandments. 3. For this is the love of God, that we keep His commandments. And His commandments are not burdensome. 4. For whatever is born of God overcomes the world. And this is the victory that has overcome the world – our faith. 5. Who is he who overcomes the world, but he who believes that Jesus is the Son of God? 6. This is He who came by water and blood – Jesus Christ; not only by water, but by water and blood. And it is the Spirit who bears witness, because the Spirit is truth. 7. For there are three that bear witness in heaven: the Father, the Word, and the Holy Spirit; and these three are one. 8. And there are three that bear witness on earth: the Spirit, the water, and the blood; and these three agree as one. (1 John 5: 1-8)

Gnosticism had begun to take root even in the first century. Gnostics claim that Jesus' deity did not begin until He was baptized by John. They also insist that His Godly nature departed from Him prior to the crucifixion. John disputes this teaching, explaining that Jesus was and is the Son of God in every sense and for all time. In defense of this truth John noted the witnesses of the Holy Spirit (descending like a dove), the water (Jesus' baptism), and the blood (the crucifixion).

Most scholars agree that the witness of the Holy Spirit and water points to Jesus' baptism and the blood to His crucifixion, since these are considered the bookends of His ministry here on earth. Jesus began His ministry when John *baptized* Him in the Jordan River. When Jesus rose from the water, John witnessed the *Spirit* descending and alighting on Jesus like, or in the form of a dove. At that time God proclaimed, *'This is My beloved Son, in whom I am well pleased'* (Matthew 3: 16). Thus, the Holy Spirit and water provided witness before men to Jesus' role as God's Son. Finally, Jesus shed His *blood* on the cross, ending His earthly ministry.

The *witness of three* is directly related to the recognition, in the Mosaic Law, of the strength of two or three witnesses (Deuteronomy 19: 15). Such testimony gives weight and substance to a case. The rationale behind the witness of three is the notion that, if a man accuses another of wrongdoing it is simply one man's word against the other. However, on the witness of two or three men, a believable case can be made. Both Jesus and the apostles carried this same philosophy into New Testament teaching (Matthew 18: 16-20; 1 Timothy 5: 19).

If we can bank on the testimony of two or three witnesses, then we should absolutely trust the testimony of God's witnesses. His witnesses are more reliable than men because God is true. He has no inclination to deceive; and God's witnesses are the Holy Spirit, the water, and the blood. To what, then, are these three considered witnesses?

> 11. And this is the testimony: God has given us eternal life, and this life is in His Son. 12. He who has the Son has life; he who has not the Son of God does not have life. (1 John 5: 11-12)

The testimony of the Holy Spirit, the water, and the blood continues even today. While Jesus' baptism and death had occurred more than fifty years prior to the writing of John's letter, their testimony is regarded as contemporary with this work. The word *testify* (v. 7) appears in present tense as does the statement, *'this is the testimony'* (v. 11). John has in view not only the Spirit descending upon Jesus, but also the Spirit descending on us. He has in sight not only Jesus' baptism, but ours. The indwelling of the Holy Spirit is promised to all those who are obedient to Christ. Just as Jesus began His ministry here on earth with water baptism, to which the Holy Spirit bore witness, we begin our relationship with Christ in baptism.

It is not insignificant that the Spirit came upon Jesus as He rose from the water since it is at the time of baptism that we receive the promised presence of the Holy Spirit (Acts 2: 38). The Lord's Supper, then, continues to testify to the salvation we have through the blood of Christ. John closes this passage with a familiar thought, reminding us that, *'He who has the Son has life; he who does not have the Son of God does not have life'* (1 John 5: 12).

Admittedly, the connection with Christian baptism and the Lord's Supper in this passage must be considered secondary. The main focus is Scripture's identification of Jesus as the Messiah. Witness to that truth is offered through the Spirit, the water, and the blood. However, given the fact that these are the very elements by which we receive eternal life, their significance with respect to salvation cannot be ignored. John makes it very clear that these are witnesses to *our* eternal life and that life is attainable only through Jesus (v. 11).

As we consider the terms of the covenant of grace, the message is clear that those who *have* Christ and have been promised the indwelling of the Holy Spirit are those who have been obedient in water baptism (Galatians 3: 26-27; Acts 2: 38; 5:32; 1 John 3: 24).

Our opportunity for a relationship with God, which is revealed to us in the New Testament, is one where God is our Father and we are His children (Romans 8: 15-17; 1 John 3: 1). It is a relationship that is established when we are born of God. It is a covenant relationship of blood. The apostle John, writing this epistle in the sunset years of his life, identifies water as a witness that we have received eternal life.

Participation in the New Covenant

A covenant defines the nature of a relationship and governs that relationship forward from the time it is instituted. For this reason, it is customary that terms and conditions would apply in the implementation of a covenant. So it is with the covenant of grace as God revealed through the apostles exactly what He expects from those who wish to participate.

Just as childbirth offered the Israelite newborn participation in the first covenant, we understand that a man must be reborn (born of God, born of Spirit, regenerated) in order to share in the covenant of grace (John 3: 5; 1 Peter 1: 23). According to Paul, participants in the new covenant are considered the spiritual descendants of Abraham (Galatians 3: 7-9). Yet no one may be called a descendant of Abraham without first accepting the terms of the covenant that are spelled out in the New Testament.

Like the first covenant, where God incorporated various provisions, He has also established certain requirements for men in the covenant of grace. The person who fails to accept these conditions gives up his/her claim to the inheritance that is offered there. These conditions include belief in Jesus as the risen Messiah (Acts 16: 31), repentance of sins we have committed (Acts 3: 19), confession of Jesus as Lord (Romans 10: 8-10), and baptism in His name (1 Peter 3: 21). Finally, He calls upon each of us to live a life fully devoted to His holy ways in both worship and actions (Romans 12: 1-2).

Perhaps no passage identifies the role of baptism within God's covenant of grace more clearly than Paul's words to the Colossians, a commentary offering insight into the work that God performs at the time of baptism. While Paul spends much of his time in this book emphasizing proper doctrine, he has also filled the epistle with words of encouragement in order to uplift his readers. He accomplishes both goals as he reminds the Colossians of the first steps they had taken in their relationship with God.

11. In Him you were also circumcised with the circumcision made without hands, by putting off the body of the sins of the flesh, by the circumcision of Christ, 12. buried with Him in baptism, in which you also were raised with Him through faith in the working of God, who raised Him from the dead. 13. And you, being dead in your trespasses and the uncircumcision of your flesh, He has made alive together with Him, having forgiven you all trespasses, 14. having wiped out the handwriting of requirements that was against us, which was contrary to us. And He has taken it out of the way, having nailed it to the cross. (Colossians 2: 11-14)

In this passage, it is important to understand that the apostle is not equating baptism in the new covenant with circumcision in the first covenant. Paul mentions physical circumcision in verse thirteen, but not in connection with baptism. According to the apostle, the Colossians had faced two major barriers in their relationship with God. The first problem was that, like all men, they were sinners (*dead in their trespasses*). The second challenge they faced was the fact that they were Gentiles (*uncircumcision of their flesh*) and, therefore, they were prevented from participating in the first covenant. Paul's words here mirror his comments in Ephesians where he refers to the Gentile status of his readers as an obstacle in the first covenant (Ephesians 2: 11-12).

The apostle's point in verses thirteen and fourteen is that these challenges (their sins and their status as Gentiles) were no longer problems for the Colossians. Paul explained that these obstacles had been removed through Jesus' sacrifice of Himself, a point also made in his corresponding message to the Ephesians. They had not only been forgiven of their sins via the cross, but the requirements of the law, which had previously separated Jews from Gentiles, had been eliminated.

Paul's reference to circumcision in verse eleven is one that many people consider a declaration that baptism is meant to be a replacement for circumcision. Yet, Paul is not pointing to the ceremony of physical circumcision here, but to the manner in which God surgically removes sin from a person's heart, making him/her free from sin. It is replacement of the old man (flesh) with the new (spiritual) man. The gist of Paul's remark is that, as the Colossians submitted to Christ in baptism they were, in essence, spiritually circumcised. Similarly, when Paul taught the Galatians that they had clothed themselves with Christ at the time of baptism (Galatians 3: 27), he was not proposing that baptism was a substitute for the Galatians physically dressing themselves. Instead he offered a picture of men spiritually covering themselves with Christ in baptism. Neither, in his words to the Colossians, is he displacing physical circumcision with baptism. Paul simply offers the Galatians and Colossians an analogy. In each passage, the apostle's aim is to explain in familiar terms exactly what occurs spiritually as we submit to Christ in water baptism.

In much the same way that the word *circumcision* is used symbolically in other passages, so it is applied here. *Circumcision of the heart* is mentioned in the Old Testament as a reflection of a man's attitude toward God. Yet this kind of circumcision has no more relationship with physical circumcision than clothing ourselves with Christ is associated with a physical wardrobe. No one can mistake these writings of Moses and Jeremiah as a reference to literal physical circumcision. Neither should we make that mistake in Paul's letter to the Colossians.

> Therefore circumcise the foreskin of your heart and be stiff-necked no longer. (Deuteronomy 10: 16)

> Circumcise yourselves to the Lord, and take away the foreskins of your hearts, you men of Judah and inhabitants of Jerusalem...(Jeremiah 4: 4)

Scripture offers us an explanation of the meaning of Paul's phrase, *'made without hands'* in the Colossians passage (v. 11). The author of Hebrews mentions a *'tabernacle not made with hands, that is, not of this creation'* (Hebrews 9: 11). The passage depicts a temple existing on a purely spiritual plane. No one would deny that circumcision takes place in the physical realm, yet these words signify things that occur strictly in the heavenly arena. The circumcision of this Colossians passage is repeated in Paul's letter to the Romans. We experience *'circumcision of the heart, by the Spirit'* (Romans 2: 29 – NIV). Paul is not concerned with a *replacement* for physical circumcision in Colossians, but simply recognizes the *presence* of spiritual circumcision at the moment of baptism.

In the first covenant purification involved both the sprinkling of blood and washing with water (Leviticus 1: 5; 3: 2; 5: 9; Numbers 19: 7-21). Under the provisions of God's new covenant, a man is circumcised with the *'circumcision of Christ'* (Colossians 2: 11), which is His death. His shed blood is sprinkled upon (applied to) our sins as a purifying agent (Hebrews 10: 22; 11: 28;

Revelation 1: 5). A direct link is established between baptism and the timing of the spiritual circumcision (cutting off) of our sins and our past in the Colossians passage (Colossians 2: 12). The use of the perfect participle reveals that this circumcision is performed at the time of baptism, *having been buried with Him.* While this expression alone could suggest that spiritual circumcision (of our sins) takes place following baptism, the balance of the passage provides sufficient evidence that the two occur simultaneously. The passage does not offer the option of spiritual circumcision prior to baptism.

Man approaches God in the covenant of grace by having our hearts *'cleansed from an evil conscience'* and our bodies *'washed in pure water'* through submission to baptism (Hebrews 10: 22). One who has not yet received the circumcision of Christ is still dead in his/her trespasses (Colossians 2: 13). Therefore, if one has not received this *spiritual circumcision* (Colossians 2: 11), or has not yet clothed himself with Christ (Galatians 3: 27), then it stands to reason that, prior to baptism, he is still lost in his sin.

In his letter to the Romans, Paul elaborates on the relationship between baptism and Jesus' death, burial, and resurrection. He told the Romans that they had been buried with Christ in baptism as a matter of personal participation in Jesus' sacrifice of death. While for us it is symbolic, for Him it was true death. Imitating Jesus' resurrection from the dead, we rise symbolically from the watery grave (Romans 6: 4). A person begins his walk in a new life in Christ when he is raised from the waters of baptism. The spiritual circumcision that takes place at this time (the cutting away of sin) frees the believer from his sins. Any claim that one might be saved prior to baptism, the time when his sins are washed away, does not follow this biblical pattern.

> 25. Husbands, love your wives, just as Christ also loved the church and gave Himself for her, 26. that He might sanctify and cleanse her with the washing of water by the word, 27. that He might present her to Himself a glorious church, not having spot or wrinkle or any such thing, but that she should be holy and without blemish. (Ephesians 5: 25-27)

Once again we find water associated with God's new covenant in Paul's words to the Ephesians as he compares the relationship between Christ and the church with the covenant of marriage. The role of water in this context is significant. We learn that Jesus loved the church and that He sacrificed Himself for her (v. 25). If, however, Christ's sacrifice of Himself constitutes the whole of the equation, why is *water* mentioned here at all? In this instance, we find that we are not cleansed *directly* through Jesus' sacrifice, but by means of the water (v. 26). Christ's sacrifice does not automatically cleanse the bride. It does, however, provide the opportunity for cleansing through the washing of water.

The function of water, as it is assigned by Paul in this passage, is to *cleanse* – to *sanctify*. This is identified as the role of baptism in the New Testament. Without the sanctification that is imparted at the time of baptism no one would be added to the church. No church body would then be available to be presented holy. Without the forgiveness offered in baptism the body of Christ cannot exist. Cleansing and sanctification are accomplished *'with the washing of water... '*(v. 26).

Is it possible that the word *water*, in this context, might be representative of something other than baptism? While some may be inclined to hope that is the case, no Bible scholar of worthwhile repute would attempt it. Even John Calvin[3] and John Wesley[4], neither of whom was convinced of the spiritual efficacy of baptism, recognized that it is clearly depicted in this instance.

What can we make of the expression *'by the word'?* The use of this phrase on this occasion may be regarded from two possible perspectives. The most reasonable view is that it means *according to (or in accord with) the word of God.* In other words, the *message* concerning washing (baptism) is found *in* the Bible and the message of the gospel is the basis for baptism's effectiveness. This same word (*rhema*) represents the *word* (or message) of God in certain other passages (Romans 10: 17; Ephesians 1: 13; 6: 17). At other times it is also translated using such words as *spoken message* or *command*. The other view is that this could be a reference to the fact that it is in the name of Jesus that we are baptized. However, this is less likely since the word most often used to refer to the name of Jesus is the Greek word *logos*.

Salvation is offered to us through our faith in the death, burial, and resurrection of Christ. The work of the Spirit during our washing with water (baptism) makes us presentable (holy) in God's eyes. This is precisely why, when addressing various churches and individuals in the epistles, the apostles always presumed that Christians to whom they wrote had been baptized (Romans 6: 3-4; 1 Corinthians 12: 13; Galatians 3: 26-27;

Ephesians 4: 5; Colossians 2: 11-12; Titus 3: 5). The idea that someone who had not been baptized was a Christian is an idea never entertained by the apostles simply because he/she would not yet be considered a follower of Christ. Therefore, while the apostles did not always *speak* of baptism within the pages of Scripture, they did recognize that everyone whom they addressed in the epistles was an immersed believer. We should be very cautious about disregarding this fundamental apostolic principle.

NOTES FOR CHAPTER 3

1. Tertullian wrote regarding the fact that baptism was an ordinance, addressing those who would negate the rite.

> Here, then, those miscreants[137] provoke questions. And so they say, "Baptism is not necessary for them to whom faith is sufficient; for withal, Abraham pleased God by a sacrament of no water, but of faith." But in all cases it is the *later* things which have a conclusive force, and the *subsequent* which prevail over the antecedent. Grant that, in days gone by, there was salvation by means of bare faith, before the passion and resurrection of the Lord. But now that faith has been enlarged, and is become a faith which believes in His nativity, passion, and resurrection, there has been an amplification added w the sacrament, viz., the sealing act of baptism; the clothing, in some sense, of the faith which before was bare, and which cannot exist now without its proper law. For the *law* of baptizing has been *imposed*, and the formula prescribed: "Go," *He* saith, "teach the nations, baptizing them into the name of the Father, and of the Son, and of the Holy Spirit." The comparison with this law of that definition, "Unless a man have been reborn of water and Spirit, he shall not enter into the kingdom of the heavens,"[140] has tied faith to the necessity of baptism. Accordingly, all thereafter *who became* believers used to be baptized. *Then* it was, too, that Paul, when he believed, was baptized; and this is the meaning of the precept which the Lord had given him when smitten with the plague of loss *of sight*, saying, "Arise, and enter Damascus; there shall be demonstrated to thee what thou oughtest to do," to wit-be baptized, which was the only thing lacking to him. That point excepted, he had sufficiently *learnt and believed* "the Nazarene" to be "the Lord, the Son of God." Tertullian, <u>On Baptism, Chapter X2I. - Another Objection: Abraham Pleased God Without Being Baptized. Answer Thereto. Old Things Must Give Place to New, and Baptism is Now a Law.</u>

2. Gareth L. Reese notes the sequence of the two acts presented in Hebrews 10: 22.

> The Old Testament ceremony had the priests washing at the laver before entering the Holy of Holies. Just like the Levitical priest had to wash before drawing near to God, most commentators refer to the truth that baptism (immersion in water) is here identified as a second condition that must be met before men have free access to God's presence. Gareth L. Reese, <u>The New Testament Epistles – Hebrews</u>, Copyright 1992, page 178, Scripture Exposition Books.

3. http://www.ccel.org/ccel/calvin/calcom41.iv.i.html, John Calvin, <u>Commentary on Galatians and Ephesians</u>, Jun 2, 2007.

4. http://eword.gospelcom.net/comments/ephesians/wesley/ephesians5.htm, John Wesley, <u>Notes on the Bible</u>, June 2, 2007.

Chapter IV
When Is the Time of Salvation?

Man is saved by grace through faith (Ephesians 2: 8), a biblical principle upon which all believers agree. The question is not *if* man is saved by faith, but *at what time* in the journey of faith man initially receives salvation. Some people might suggest that knowing the moment of salvation is not significant. After all, it is the *fact*, and not the *time*, of salvation that is most important. However, if we do not know *when* we are saved, how can we know *if* we are saved? John noted, when writing about the respective roles of *the Spirit, the water, and the blood,* that the very purpose of his writing was so that people could know they had received eternal life (1 John 5: 13). If then, we can *know* that we have attained salvation, Scripture must be clear in explaining the time it is received.

> For we are to God the fragrance of Christ among those who are being saved and among those who are perishing. (2 Corinthians 2: 15)

> Therefore we do not lose heart. Even though our outward man is perishing, yet the inward man is being renewed day by day, (2 Corinthians 4: 16)

A key point concerning salvation, as these verses reveal, is that it is a process that span a person's life from the time he/she first accepts Christ as Savior to the moment of his/her death. That lifetime may last decades or days, depending on when one accepts Christ, but each of us continues to be saved daily by Christ's death and resurrection. While there is a moment of initial salvation, that instant when God bestows eternal life, each of us continues to be saved on a daily basis as we walk in the way of the Lord. The challenge we face, however, is determining the time at which salvation is initially bestowed upon the person who believes in Jesus.

Salvation by Grace

Some men seem to be offended by the idea that something other than grace[1] might have a place of importance within the covenant of grace. They reason that anything added to grace must somehow be seen as an insult to God. Their contempt is often expressed in the equation *'grace* equals *grace* plus *nothing.'* They insist that grace must stand alone since *grace* plus *anything else* is no longer grace. Actually, there is some legitimate reasoning behind this perspective. Just as *one* plus *anything* is no longer *one*, so *grace* plus *anything* is no longer *grace*. Where this view errs, however, is in the assumption that grace is equivalent to salvation. If *grace* equals *salvation*, we have no choice but to accept that all men are saved. After all, it is not God's will that anyone would perish but that everyone would be saved (2 Peter 3: 9).

Grace is the *offering* of eternal life that God has presented to men through Christ's sacrifice of Himself. It is a *gift* in that men are not expected to pay the cost that is required to receive it. Obviously, no man has the ability to pay such a price. If, however, grace is all that is required (if *grace* equals *salvation*), surely all men must be saved. However, God does not force His grace upon men, but merely offers it. Grace is not imposed upon those unwilling to receive it. Therefore, since it is not true that *grace* equals *salvation*, we can only conclude that salvation involves something beyond God's grace. No one, then, should be too offended by the proposition that, at the very least, *belief* must be added to *grace* for *salvation* to be realized.

Salvation by Belief

A considerable number of believers insist that a person receives salvation at the moment he/she first believes in the deity of Christ and His sacrifice for the sins of men. Those who take this position teach that, while obedience is not insignificant, belief alone is sufficient for salvation and is the *sole requirement* for eternal life according to the gospel message. This teaching finds its basis in those passages of Scripture that indicate that believers will, indeed, be saved.

> Those by the wayside are the ones who hear; then the devil comes and takes away the word out of their hearts, lest they should believe and be saved. (Luke 8: 12)

> For since, in the wisdom of God, the world through wisdom did not know God, it pleased God through the foolishness of the message preached to save those who believe. (1 Corinthians 1: 21)

> In Him you also *trusted,* after you heard the word of truth, the gospel of your salvation; in whom also, having believed, you were sealed with the Holy Spirit of promise. (Ephesians 1: 13)

It is important, as we study God's plan for the redemption of men, that we take the time to differentiate between the *method* of salvation and the *time* of salvation. Belief is essential for eternal life, as these passages indicate. Yet, while these verses confirm the necessity of belief, no verse points to belief as the time when we attain salvation. Teaching *that* believers are saved does not automatically identify the moment of belief as the time of salvation. In fact, according to Scripture, the moment of belief is clearly *not* the time of salvation.

Salvation by Faith

The purpose of God's new covenant is to point men toward forgiveness, righteousness, and eternal life. It is a bit misleading to claim that the passages cited above reflect belief alone as the means to salvation as they seem to imply. A single verse normally does not express the intentions of the author or speaker as fully as when the surrounding text is considered. Taken in context, belief is always qualified, at a very minimum, by the faith[2] of the believer. Paul told the Corinthians that belief, absent faithfulness to the gospel message, was hollow.

> 1. Moreover, brethren, I declare to you the gospel which I preached to you, which also you received and in which you stand, 2. by which also you were saved, if you hold fast that word which I preached to you – unless you believe in vain. (1 Corinthians 15: 1-2)

In his epistle, James discusses the fact that belief, unless it is accompanied by faith and works, has no power to save. When James notes that *'Even the demons believe'* (James 2: 19), he is highlighting the fact that no one is saved by belief alone. John mentioned certain rulers who also believed in Jesus, but they refused to confess Him for fear of the Pharisees (John 12: 42). The suggestion that those who refused to confess Christ, let alone the believing demons, should expect forgiveness or salvation at the mere moment of belief conflicts completely with teaching presented throughout Scripture.

For those who insist that men receive forgiveness and salvation at the moment of belief, it should now be clear that this is not the case. Such a view suggests that *belief* is the same as *faith*. Given these illustrations offered by James and John, this notion should now be put to rest. Additionally, Paul warned the Corinthians that it is possible to, *'believe in vain.'* Scripture teaches that, while it is necessary to believe, not *everyone* who believes will be saved. Belief, unaccompanied by faith, cannot affect salvation.

> 1. Therefore, having been justified by faith, we have peace with God through our Lord Jesus Christ, 2. through whom also we have access by faith into this grace in which we stand... (Romans 5: 1-2)

> 8. For by grace you have been saved through faith, and that not of yourselves; *it is* a gift of God, 9. not of works, lest anyone should boast. (Ephesians 2: 8-9)

Belief and faith are certainly closely associated with one another, but they are not the same. While a man can believe without having faith, he cannot have faith without belief. Therefore, the conditions for salvation have necessarily expanded to include *grace, belief, and faith.* Yet, certain fundamental elements of God's plan are still missing; therefore, even the moment of faith cannot be the time of salvation since more conditions of salvation must be fulfilled.

Salvation by Repentance

Few believers would ever deny the need for repentance[3] for those who seek salvation. Repentance lies at the very heart of God's plan of salvation. It is both a desire and a command of God that men should repent, turn from their wicked ways, and return to Him.

> ...but unless you repent you will all likewise perish. (Luke 13: 3)

> For godly sorrow produces repentance *leading* to salvation, not to be regretted; but the sorrow of the world produces death. (2 Corinthians 7: 10)

Who, then, can doubt that repentance is vital for a man to be reconciled to God and receive salvation? Scripture is absolutely clear that no man may be saved without repenting of his sins. Of course, repentance is not belief, nor is it faith. A man repents *as a result of* his faith. Therefore, since repentance is necessary for a person to partake in the grace of God, it must surely be considered a condition of salvation. Consequently, the components of God's plan of salvation must include *grace, belief, faith,* and *repentance.* Still, even though all of these elements of God's plan explain the *method* of salvation, the *time* of salvation continues to elude. Scripture indicates that even though one believes, has faith, and repents of his sins, not all conditions for attaining salvation have been met.

Salvation by Confession

A popular teaching among men today is that a simple private prayer asking God into your life is all that is necessary to attain salvation. However, the following passages reveal the need for a verbal confession[4] of Jesus as Lord – a confession spoken to others. God desires a confession from those who seek salvation as a matter of witnessing to other Christians the person's acceptance of Jesus as Savior. If God intended our confession of Jesus as Lord and Savior to take place privately (between the individual and God alone), no instruction for a vocal confession would be necessary. Paul confirms this very point in his letter to the Romans and his first letter to Timothy.

> 8. But what does it say? *"The word is near you, in your mouth and in your heart"* (that is, the word of faith which we preach): 9. that if you confess with your mouth the Lord Jesus and believe in your heart that God has raised Him from the dead, you will be saved. 10. For with the heart one believes unto righteousness, and with the mouth confession is made unto salvation. (Romans 10: 8-10)

> 12. Fight the good fight of faith, lay hold on eternal life, to which you were also called and have confessed the good confession in the presence of many witnesses. (1 Timothy 6: 12)

Some men may suggest that our confession of Jesus as Lord is more about a *way of life* (in both word and deed) than it is about a specific declaration before men. It is safe to say that confessing Jesus as Savior takes in both ideas. Nonetheless, Scripture does teach plainly that God expects each one of us, as a matter of salvation, to proclaim openly before Christian witnesses our belief in Jesus as God's risen Son and Lord of our life. The apostle Paul highlights the point that this verbal confession is to be *'made unto salvation'* (Romans 10: 10).

To this point we have seen that God has established a variety of conditions for those who would be saved. We have learned that belief is the first of these conditions. God has designed the plan of salvation such that, without belief in Jesus as the Son of God a man cannot be saved (Mark 16: 16). Paul indicated to Timothy, *'I have fought the good fight, I have finished the race, I have kept the faith'* (2 Timothy 4: 7). Belief is as important as the first step in a race. In fact, it *is* the first step in that race of which Paul wrote. No one can finish a race if he refuses to take that initial step. Faith, repentance, and confession cannot be present where belief is absent.

We also discover in Scripture that faith is essential to salvation. Furthermore, one who has not repented of his/her sins or confessed that Jesus is Lord will not be saved. Since Scripture is clear in its instructions regarding these various elements of the plan of salvation, it is only reasonable to accept and teach them as requirements in God's plan of salvation. Therefore, if we are to be true to Scripture we must consider *grace, belief, faith, repentance,* and *confession* all essential for *salvation*. However, even with all of this understanding about *how* men are saved, we have not yet determined the exact moment of salvation.

Salvation by Love

We must not overlook one very crucial element of God's plan of salvation. Jesus emphasized what is the *most* critical component in our relationship with both God and other men when one of the Pharisees attempted to challenge Him.

> 35. Then one of them, a lawyer, asked *Him a question,* testing Him, and saying, 36. "Teacher, which is the greatest commandment in the law?" 37. Jesus said to him, *"'You shall love the Lord your God with all your heart, with all your soul, and with all your mind.'* 38. This is the first and greatest commandment. 39. And the second is like it: *'You shall love your neighbor as yourself.'* 40. On these two commandments hang all the Law and the Prophets." (Matthew 22: 35-40)

Love for both God and man is the predominant theme in both the old and new covenants. Love is the basis upon which God has chosen to offer salvation to those who have turned away from Him; thus it is the reason Jesus gave His life on the cross. Love is not only God's motivation, but it is His character trait. As such, He expects love to be a character trait of all those who seek Him. Paul, in his first letter to the Corinthians, offered some especially touching remarks concerning the value of love with respect to the kingdom of God.

1. Though I speak with the tongues of men and of angels, but have not love, I have become sounding brass or a clanging cymbal. 2. And though I have *the gift of* prophecy, and understand all mysteries and all knowledge, and though I have all faith, so that I could remove mountains, but have not love, I am nothing. 3. And though I bestow all my goods to feed *the* poor, and though I give my body to be burned, but have not love, it profits me nothing. 4. Love suffers long *and* is kind; love does not envy; love does not parade itself, is not puffed up; 5. does not behave rudely, does not seek its own, is not provoked, thinks no evil; 6. does not rejoice in iniquity, but rejoices in the truth; 7. bears all things, believes all things, hopes all things, endures all things. 8. Love never fails...13. And now abide faith, hope, love, these three; but the greatest of these *is* love. (1 Corinthians 13: 1-8; 13)

While this chapter in 1 Corinthians is only a tiny fragment of the teaching on the subject of love that can be found in Scripture, it is an insightful commentary on the value that God places upon love. Paul notes that love lies at the very heart of Christianity. Without love Paul considered himself *a clanging cymbal* – a mere noise maker. Without love he saw himself as *nothing*. The love with which Paul is concerned is love for brother and sister, friend and foe. It is a love that involves both action and passion. It is the kind of love God showed to mankind that is revealed in His Word. Since it is all of these things and more, it is also a love God deems essential for the man or woman who would be saved.

Love unites us with God and with each other (in the body). God's promise is to those who love. While love is considered an element of Christian growth, we can determine from Scripture that a life void of love is a life that has not been converted. In fact, it is supposedly our love for Christ and His sacrifice that leads us to obedience and salvation. Therefore, we can reason that some degree of love for Christ must be included among those elements that are critical even to our initial redemption. Thus, each of the following – *grace, belief, faith, repentance, confession,* and *love* – are deemed essential when considering what man must *do* in response to the gospel message.

Salvation by Baptism

Beyond the grace that comes from God, a common thread runs through each of those conditions that have, so far, been determined to be critical in man's response to the gospel message. That common thread relates to time. These various terms of salvation reflect not only the manner by which we are saved, but the manner in which we are to live. Of course, there is a moment when a person *first* believes, but it cannot end there. Belief involves not just the initial moment of acceptance that Jesus is the Messiah, but a lifetime of commitment to that belief. So, too, faith and love must continue to grow throughout the life of the Christian. Additionally, while there is certainly a point at which a man first repents of his sins, God intends that each one of us should live a life that is directed by a repentant heart; and God forbid that any would ever cease to confess Jesus as Lord.

These conditions of salvation are simply that: *conditions of salvation*. They define *how* men are saved and, consequently, how we are to live in Christ. Yet we find no evidence that any one of them defines the moment salvation is received. That is because one element still remains. Interestingly, it is a part of God's plan that is characterized by its unique relationship with time.

Both Mark 16: 16 and 1 Peter 3: 21 point specifically to baptism as a condition for attaining salvation. In fact, Peter states in his letter that baptism is actually the manner in which we are saved. In Acts 2: 38 he told the Jews in Jerusalem that they were to be baptized in order to receive forgiveness of sins and the gift of the Holy Spirit. Baptism, then, must be united with all other *conditions* that are presented in Scripture as essential to salvation. While baptism is a matter of salvation, as these verses testify, much is also revealed about the *time* of salvation in a thorough study of this ceremony.

In his words to the Romans, Paul draws a vivid picture of the death of Christ by which He overcame our sins. Death itself was defeated (Romans 6: 1-18). Jesus' death on the cross, we are told, is the very means by which we are able, ourselves, to die to our own sins. It is the *source* of our salvation. Having offered, in the first few chapters of Romans, a thorough examination of the grace of God, Paul now stirs his audience both emotionally and psychologically by reminding them of the precise moment they knew salvation. In this walk down memory lane he makes some interesting points regarding baptism. Paul regards baptism as a burial *with* Christ. Who, then, should be buried but one who is dead. During baptism, upon death to the sinful life, men are buried with Christ. According to the apostle, it is at the time of baptism that men die with Christ (Romans 6: 8) to sin (Romans 6: 2).

Baptism is the moment established by God in which we die *to* sin and are buried *with* Christ. Additionally, Paul characterizes it as a symbolic act, representing Jesus' death, during which we are united together (Romans 6: 5). Therefore, baptism is more than simply dying to sin and being buried with Christ. It is an action that provides unity between the new convert and Christ as well as among the body of believers as each person experiences this same death and burial.

Paul's portrayal of baptism in this instance does not end with a person's death to sin and burial with Christ. We discover that, after we have been buried, we rise to a new existence as Christ had done when He rose from the grave (Romans 6: 4). Just as we are united together in a symbolic death, we rise from the water so that we can live a new life characteristic of His resurrection (Romans 6: 5). It is precisely at the point of rising from the waters of baptism that, like Christ, each man begins his new life. It is the rebirth that Jesus explained to Nicodemus. It is a new life in that it is no longer dominated by sin since that man no longer exists (Romans 6: 17-18).

In his epistle to the Colossians, Paul confirmed the fact that baptism is the time of salvation. He explained to the Colossians that they had received spiritual circumcision, the removal of their sins, in baptism through faith (Colossians 2: 11-14). Note that this was an act God performed rather than a work credited to these disciples. It was a time when, according to Paul, they were buried with Him and raised with Him. Once this was accomplished they were made alive (v. 13), their sins having been forgiven.

Baptism, like belief, faith, repentance, and confession, is a part of the *method* of salvation. What clearly differentiates baptism from the rest, however, is that it is also the *time* of salvation. Certainly, baptism is pointless unless it is accompanied by all precepts discussed here. Baptism cannot stand by itself. Not one of these *conditions* can, alone, lead to salvation – not even belief or faith. Yet, of all the requirements God has set for us, baptism is designated as the moment when a person's sins are forgiven, he is freed from the law, and the new life that is promised is received. This is the reasoning behind Peter's claim in his epistle that baptism saves (1 Peter 3: 21).

Baptism is set apart from all other commands in God's plan of salvation by its uniqueness with respect to time. While God has designated all of these as fundamental in His design for men to attain salvation, baptism is the specific time He has chosen for the death of the old life and the resurrection of the new. Baptism, like childbirth, occurs at one point in time, never to be repeated. No other time has been appointed to accomplish what is completed in baptism, which is salvation.

What About the Sinner's Prayer?

What are we to do with the Sinner's Prayer? Is this not the time of salvation? After all, countless American evangelists insist that the way to salvation is through what they call the Sinner's Prayer. Of course, the greatest problem we face with this teaching is that it cannot be found in Scripture. Still, there are those who plead the case that such a prayer can be inferred from various passages.

It is certainly true that the Sinner's Prayer, as we know it, is absent from Scripture. Whether it is on the Day of Pentecost or Paul teaching the Philippian jailer, or any other time when the apostles explained the manner whereby men might be saved, the Sinner's Prayer is not found. In the post-Pentecost era prayer is never taught in Scripture as a matter of salvation for those outside of Christ. Men who seek to derive the Sinner's Prayer from the pages of Scripture claim that, while it is true that this teaching is not explicitly found in the Bible, surely this must be the intent of certain passages.

> 13. "And the tax collector, standing afar off, would not so much as raise his eyes to heaven, but beat his breast, saying, 'God, be merciful to me a sinner!' 14. "I tell you, this man went down to his house justified..." (Luke 18: 13-14)

The prayer of the tax collector (above) is perhaps the closest thing Scripture has to the Sinner's Prayer. Yet, there is no mention here of salvation through Jesus Christ or forgiveness through His blood. This man did not ask Jesus *into his heart*, which is the essence of the Sinner's Prayer.

Actually, what Jesus has provided for His disciples, in this illustration, is an example of the humility God wishes to see in every man. Jesus' focus is not on the method of salvation in the new covenant. Rather, He wanted His disciples to truly understand the humility a man must show if he expects God to take notice of him. The passage simply portrays the repentant heart that is essential for those who wish to seek forgiveness.

> As for me, I will call upon God; and the LORD shall save me. (Psalm 55: 16)

The LORD is nigh unto all them that call upon him, to all that call upon him in truth. (Psalm 145:18)

These words from the book of Psalm would seem to indicate that salvation might be found by simply *calling upon God.* Yet, we are not told exactly *how* this might be done or what it really means to call on God. It is important to recognize that these words were written while the Israelites lived under the Mosaic Law, prior to Pentecost. Given that fact, the suggestion that verbally calling on the name of the Lord, in itself, leads to salvation ignores the requirements of the law itself. Considering the many details of the Mosaic Law that are spelled out in Exodus and Leviticus, with the continuing sacrifices and rituals, it was understood that the calling of which the Psalmist wrote would go well beyond a mere verbal declaration. In the Old Testament, the notion of calling on the name of the Lord would have involved so much more. Faithfulness to God's law was, no doubt, the manner in which men called upon Him.

Exactly what does it mean to '*call on the name of the Lord*'? Some men teach that this expression, when it is used on or after the Day of Pentecost in the New Testament (Acts 2: 21; 22: 16), implies something akin to the Sinner's Prayer. It seems, however, that we should view these passages in an even broader sense. On the Day of Pentecost, as Peter addressed the crowd gathered in Jerusalem, he explained, citing the prophet Joel (Joel 2: 32), that those who call on the name of Jesus will be saved (Acts 2: 21). Interestingly, a few short sentences later, as members of the audience were convicted by the message they heard, they asked Peter and the other apostles what they should *do* (Acts 2: 37). Since Peter had just explained to them that those who call on Jesus' name would be saved, exactly what is the point of this question? Why did not those who sought salvation on that day simply cry out to Jesus for salvation, offering a Sinner's Prayer?

The fact of the matter is that they did not know *how* to call on His name. This is the reason for the question, '*what shall we do?*' They needed further direction from Peter and the other apostles so that they might know exactly what God expected from them as a response. In reply, Peter instructed them to *repent and be baptized.* This was, according to the apostles, the manner in which men were to *call* on Him. Therefore, the *calling* of which Peter spoke points to the obedient manner in which men respond to the gospel message rather than an allusion to the Sinner's Prayer, which was actually unknown at the time.

> 16. And now, why are you waiting? Arise and be baptized, and wash away your sins, calling on the name of the Lord." (Acts 22: 16)

In the famous exchange between Ananias and Saul of Tarsus (Acts 22: 16), we find another example where baptism is identified as the manner in which men *call on the name of the Lord*. Remember that Ananias spoke these words after Saul had fasted and (by implication) prayed for three days, no doubt repenting and seeking direction from the Lord. For this reason there was no need for Ananias to command Saul to repent. He had spent three days repenting. It is safe to assume that his prayer was much more intense, and his repentance more grief-stricken, than most men who cite the Sinner's Prayer today. Yet, as intense as this time must have been, Saul's repentant prayer did not satisfy the provision of *calling upon Him* since, as Ananias met with him, Saul's sins had not been forgiven. He was not saved despite his change of heart. His prayer was not the manner by which Saul *called on the Lord*, otherwise Ananias would not, after this three day period, explain to him that he must *now* call on the Lord.

> 19. Those whom I love I rebuke and discipline. So be earnest, and repent. 20. Here I am! I stand at the door and knock. If anyone hears my voice and opens the door, I will come in and eat with him, and he with me." (Revelation 3:19-20)

This verse, written by the apostle John, is often cited by those who seek to dismiss Scripture's portrayal of baptism as a matter of forgiveness. The passage is considered an evangelistic appeal to men everywhere, suggesting that by simply opening up their hearts to Jesus, they can commune with Him and be saved. Of course, the greatest irony concerning this passage is the fact that it is not written to the lost multitudes of John's time. Instead it is a plea to the church at Laodicea where they were *'neither hot nor cold'* (Revelation 3: 15). It is not an appeal to a lost and dying world, but a petition to members of the body of Christ who, while they had at one time been faithful, were now unenthusiastic about their service to the Lord. The passage does not suggest that prayer might be used as a means of communing with Christ by those outside the church. In order to derive authority for the use of the Sinner's Prayer from this passage, scriptural context must be abandoned.

The truth is that the Sinner's Prayer developed out of necessity as a result of the Reformation Movement that occurred in the sixteenth century. At that time men first began to deny that salvation occurred at the time of baptism, which was a staple of Christian doctrine. This caused a void within the plan of salvation that was taught among Protestant denominations. For a long time after the Reformation Movement, many men were confused concerning the time of salvation. As more and more men surrendered to the teaching that baptism is not the moment of salvation, the confusion broadened and it became necessary to replace baptism with something else – some occasion that could identify the time of salvation.

Relying heavily on passages like Revelation 3: 20, evangelists in the seventeenth and eighteenth centuries sought vigorously to establish some other moment that might be considered the time of salvation. During the 1700's some ministers developed a time of confession that was considered the moment of salvation. They established what was called the Mourners Seat, although other names were used. Their custom was to spotlight certain men and women during the worship service with the challenge for them to accept Christ. Those who then admitted their sins and confessed Jesus as Lord were saved. They were not required to cite the Sinner's Prayer since it did not yet exist.

This practice continued for approximately two centuries as the *path* to salvation. It was the plea for *salvation without activity on man's part* that drove these doctrinal changes. Still, it is interesting that every event later developed to pinpoint the moment of salvation ultimately laid the responsibility at the feet of the sinner, requiring him to *do* something in response to the gospel message. So it is with the Sinner's Prayer.

The Sinner's Prayer, as we know it today, actually began to develop late in the nineteenth century. Various men, including a minister by the name of Dwight Moody (1837-1899), a converted baseball player named Billy Sunday (1863-1935), and others were responsible for its widespread acceptance. Some even began to teach that it was a prayer *'for the forgiveness of sins'*. Today, despite the absence of biblical support, the Sinner's Prayer is predominantly preached and accepted as the time of salvation.

While this is an abbreviated history of the development of the Sinner's Prayer, we must consider it honestly. The fact that it did not exist for the first 1,800 years of the church age, along with its complete lack of biblical support, gives us reason to fully reject the Sinner's Prayer as the time of salvation. It seems we may more aptly consider the Sinner's Prayer to be one of the *traditions of men* against which Paul offered the Colossians solemn warning (Colossians 2: 8).

Salvation by Obedience

Jesus ended the well-known Sermon on the Mount with some interesting comments concerning exactly what it is that separates the saved from the unsaved (Matthew 7: 21-29). Hailed as one of the most fascinating passages in the New Testament, this is also arguably one of the most puzzling sections of all Scripture. Apparently at the time of judgment, many who had seemingly accomplished great things in the Lord's name will stand before Christ wishing to receive their eternal reward. Yet Jesus' response will be that He never knew them. Who could be so passionate for the cause of Christ and, in the end, not see heaven? While the answer is given, in that these have not *'done the will of the Father'*, it is not initially clear exactly how or where they had fallen short. What is even more intriguing is that, given Jesus' remark, *'I never knew you'* (Matthew 7: 23), we can conclude that they had never been saved.

Given the astonishment found in their response to Christ's words, we can determine that disbelief was not the issue. Jesus' remark, *'everyone who hears these sayings of Mine, and does not do them'* (Matthew 7: 26) indicates that, while these believers may have been active and passionate in their efforts, there was something they had been commanded to do but, for some reason, simply had not.

Perhaps the point of greatest significance in this hypothetical exchange between Jesus and these lost men is the fact that there is a difference between *activity* on behalf of the kingdom and *obedience* to the Father. It is a distinction so critical that works are hollow without the obedience of which Jesus speaks. As He further explains the nature of the gulf that exists between activity and obedience, the meaning becomes clear. The word *'Therefore'* in the twenty-fourth verse indicates that Jesus was about to give His explanation of the judgment of these individuals.

Like the foolish builder, because of their disobedience the foundation for their relationship with Christ had never been properly laid. Jesus explains this fully as He concludes His comments with the parable of the wise and foolish builders (Matthew 7: 24-27). The wise man was representative of those who were obedient, laying the proper foundation. Consequently, when we consider the meaning of the statement, *'whoever calls on the name of the LORD shall be saved'* (Romans 10: 13), we must remember that, *'Not everyone who says to Me, 'Lord, Lord,' shall enter the kingdom of heaven, but he who does the will of My Father in heaven.'* (Matthew 7: 21). *Calling on Him* evidently involves much more than simply speaking His name or saying a prayer. It encompasses obedience to the will of the Father.

Certainly other inferences can be found in this passage. It is reasonable to conclude that Jesus' words suggest obedience to more than just the precepts of belief, repentance, confession, and baptism. Still, the foundational aspects of the passage cannot be overlooked. The proper foundation can help keep one's faith from crumbling. Ignatius, a church leader who had studied under the watchful eye of the Apostle John, wrote, *'Let your baptism endure as your arms*[5], suggesting that submission to baptism can offer some protection from distractions or attacks upon our faith.

God has established a covenant of grace; however, salvation does not come by grace alone despite the claims of men. The precepts of God are clear, and we know that no one may enter the kingdom without doing the will of the Father. That suggests activity – not the activity of good works, but the response of obedience. No one may be saved without initially laying the necessary foundation for a relationship with Christ. How that foundation is to be laid is established and explained to us in God's Word. The words of Christ concerning obedience make it clear that man's salvation is contingent upon obedience to the precepts that God has established.

NOTES FOR CHAPTER 4

1. Justification and sanctification are available to man only by grace through the blood of Christ. Campbell addresses the essence of the bestowing of these as a matter of mercy in that man cannot achieve them on his own.

> What, then, is justification, the first fruit of this heavenly cluster of Divine graces? It is, indeed, a trite but a true saying, that the term justification is a forensic word; and, therefore, indicates that its subject has been accused of

crime, or of the transgression of law. It also implies that the subject of it has not only been accused and tried, but also acquitted. Such, then, is legal or forensic justification. It is, indeed, a sentence of acquittal announced by a tribunal, importing that the accused is found *not guilty*. If convicted, he cannot be justified; if justified, he has not been convicted.

But, such is not justification by grace. Evangelical justification is the justification of one that has been convicted as guilty before God, the Supreme and Ultimate Judge of the Universe. But the whole world has been tried and found guilty before God. So that, in fact, "there is none righteous; no, not one." Therefore, by deeds of law, no man can be justified before God. "For should a man keep the whole law, and yet offend in one point, he is guilty of all." He has despised the whole authority of the law and the Lawgiver. It is, then, utterly impossible that any sinner can be forensically or legally justified before God, by a law which he has in any one instance violated. Alexander Campbell, Christian Baptism, with Its Antecedents and Consequents, Chapter 2, Justification (1851).

In a specific, evangelical sense, sanctification is the act of separating a person or thing from a common to a special and spiritual use. In the following chapter on Sanctification, we have dilated, in a discursive way, on the whole subject of spiritual influence, in illumination and conversion, as terminating in sanctification. These, indeed, are concurrent means of self-consecration and of Divine sanctification or separation to God. But, in strict reference to our specific object, here, we have only to state, that the Christian is contemplated, not merely as adopted into the family of God, not merely as pardoned or justified, but, as also sanctified or consecrated to [285] God, both in state and character. Of this separation or sanctification to God, the Holy Spirit,--which, in the Christian, is the Holy Guest, commonly called the Holy Ghost, is the personal agent and author, his word the instrument, and the blood of Christ, apprehended and received by faith, the real, cleansing, purifying means. Alexander Campbell, Christian Baptism, with Its Antecedents and Consequents, Chapter 2I, Sanctification (1851).

2. According to Campbell, there is a difference between mere belief (mental ascent or acceptance) in God and the leap to faith when the conviction of that belief leads to an alteration of one's lifestyle.

Every faculty of man has its proper object and its proper use. Has he the faculty of vision? There are objects to be seen, and advantages to be gained from seeing them. Has he the faculty of hearing? There are the harmonies and the melodies of nature and of the human voice to be heard and to be enjoyed. Has he the faculty of reasoning? There are objects to be compared, and conclusions of practical utility to be deduced from them. Has he the faculty of believing? There is the testimony of men, and there is the testimony of God, to be believed and appropriated. Now, as this is the noblest faculty which man possesses, conversant with things past, present, and future, proximate and remote, God has ordained that he shall walk by faith, physically, intellectually, and morally. Hence man is obliged to walk through his whole life more by faith than by his five senses, his own observations, or his own experience--probably more than by these all combined. This being a very fundamental fact, we shall be at some pains to develop it. Alexander Campbell, Christian Baptism, with Its Antecedents and Consequents, Chapter IV, Faith (1851).

3. While few would ever challenge the precept of repentance for salvation, nonetheless, the role of a repentant heart should be kept in perspective. Belief and faith have their respective roles, but it is sin that separates man from God. Clinging to a life of sin will continue to separate an individual from Him. It is necessary, then, to separate oneself from sin in order to draw close to God.

> It is specially worthy of notice in this investigation that in the first and last communications of the Messiah we find an imperative *repent*. His harbinger, also, introduced his personal advent with the command, "Repent, for the reign of heaven approaches." In the commencement of his own personal ministry, his first discourse was, "Repent, for the reign of heaven approaches." His twelve Apostles, under their first commission, we are informed by Mark, went abroad proclaiming repentance to people. The same proclamation was made by the seventy evangelists sent to the lost sheep of the house of Israel. Indeed, the ministry of John is characterized as the proclamation of "the baptism of repentance for the remission of sins."[4] So that during the personal ministry of the Lord Jesus, and that of his harbinger, repentance was the burthen of every discourse to the people. Alexander Campbell, Christian Baptism, with Its Antecedents and Consequents, Chapter V, Repentance (1851).

4. B. W. Johnson views Romans 10: 10 as a call, not only for confession of Jesus as Lord, but as a confession to others in the brotherhood rather than a personal conversation between an individual and the Lord.

> The faith of the heart must be openly confessed. This is a test of the faith. Unless Christ had provided such tests as confession and obedience we could not know whether ours was really a belief of the heart. That our faith moves us to confession is to us an assurance of salvation. The whole Christian life is a confession. B. W. Johnson, People's New Testament (1891), Romans 10: 10

5. Ignatius, Anti-Nicene Fathers, Vol I, Chapter VI.—The duties of the Christian flock.

Chapter V
Must I Be Baptized?

The question, *'Must I be baptized?'* which has plagued men through the ages and brought bitter division among believers, lies at the heart of the debate over baptism. The writings of Martin Luther, John Wesley, Alexander Campbell, John Calvin[1], and various other well-respected men of the religious community reveal passionate reflection on every side of this issue. How could men so knowledgeable in the things of God take such conflicting stands with respect to something that seems so basic? A thorough examination of every book, essay, or letter written by these men would still fail to explain what causes some to draw from Scripture one belief about baptism while others come away with a completely different point of view.

The views of these men, however, should not be considered the foundation for biblical doctrine, despite the fact that they may offer appealing arguments. The many intriguing schools of thought proposed by men on the subject of baptism must not be allowed to displace God's own perspective. How can we know God's view of baptism? This can be accomplished only when we are willing to accept what the Bible teaches on the subject.

Interpretation of the Word

Men often feel compelled to interpret the Bible in a manner that causes them to drift from the straightforward teaching contained within its pages. Peter wrote that even the men who authored the Bible avoided their own personal interpretations of the Holy Spirit's guidance (2 Peter). When an apostle or other author of Scripture interjected his personal thoughts, he always made it known that the thoughts were his own (1 Corinthians 7: 12).

The truth is, we have been called to *study* God's Word, not to *interpret*[2] it (2 Timothy 2: 15). While it may seem there is a fine line between interpretation and study, it is reasonable that we should, at the very least, embrace those teachings found in Scripture that are presented in a plain and direct fashion. For those who are prepared to devote the necessary time, God has delivered His Word in a manner that makes clear those things He desires for us to know. Those who are willing to apply themselves will find the words of the Bible relatively easy to understand and sufficient to deliver God's message.

That is not to say that interpretation may be completely dismissed since, at times, the Bible demands it. Certainly the parables call for interpretation. However, when we must rely on interpretation, it is important that we apply legitimate interpretive principles methodically and consistently. The same standards used to understand other literature should be applied to Scripture. It is critical that we consider the context of the passage under consideration, the original intent of the author or speaker, and the meaning the hearers would have reasoned at the time a statement was made. We must never allow our own beliefs to lead the way in interpretation.

Furthermore, we have no reason to *force* interpretation upon the straightforward teaching found in the instructive writings of the apostles. While Jesus spoke mystically at times (Matthew 13: 10-12), that mystique was relevant only for those who lived prior to the church age. We have been offered a much better understanding of Jesus' teaching than were those who listened to Him during His life here on earth. Jesus' teachings are fully explained to us by the apostles.

Through the words of the apostles we have considerable insight into the make-up of the kingdom of heaven about which Jesus spoke. Unlike Jesus, the apostles' words are ordinarily presented in a straightforward manner. When an apostle employs symbolic language in Scripture, as with other works of literature, its figurative character is evident to the reader (Romans 11: 17-21; 1 Corinthians 3: 5-9; Galatians 4: 21-31). After all, God had placed upon their shoulders the task of revealing the kingdom to all nations. While Paul's epistles bear deep spiritual overtones, they are not written in cryptic code that few can understand, especially concerning matters of salvation.

Corinthians, Galatians, Ephesians, and certain other epistles, were written to the general membership of the church body rather than a privileged group of theologians, and should be received with that in mind. They do not contain secret messages that only the most elite scholars can understand. God is an incredible communicator who has provided the Bible as our map to eternal life. He would not covertly hide His real message from us. Therefore, unless the context offers commanding evidence to the contrary, we should always embrace the apostles' words in the candid manner in which they are written.

The Principles of Baptism

If we accept that God is the ultimate author of the Bible, we should equally recognize that He has not thrown it together haphazardly. Scripture is designed, in a systematic manner, to provide us with God's instructions. Through His Word He intends to direct us on a path that will restore us to Him. Within that structure there is an order to the teaching of baptism.

The seeds of the baptismal discussion within the pages of the New Testament are planted in the four gospels (Matthew, Mark, Luke, and John). In each of these books the dialogue begins with a look at the baptism that was performed by John the Baptist. While it is not discussed at length, we learn from Scripture that John's baptism was performed in water (Matthew 3: 11); it had a purifying nature (John 3: 25); it was combined with repentance for forgiveness of sins (Luke 3: 3); and it would eventually be replaced by a baptism offered by the coming Messiah (Mark 1: 8). Each of these authors cites John's prophecy concerning a future baptism.

> I indeed baptize you with water unto repentance, but He who is coming after me is mightier than I, whose sandals I am unworthy to carry. He will baptize you with the Holy Spirit and with fire. (Matthew 3: 11)

> I indeed baptize you with water, but He will baptize you with the Holy Spirit. (Mark 1: 8)

> John answered, saying to all, "I indeed baptize you with water; but One mightier than I is coming, whose sandal strap I am not worthy to loose. He will baptize you with the Holy Spirit and fire." (Luke 3: 16)

> "I did not know Him, but He who sent me to baptize with water said to me, 'Upon whom you see the Spirit descending and remaining on Him, this is He who baptizes with the Holy Spirit.'" (John 1: 33)

Looking forward to the coming church age, John the Baptist prophesied about a baptism that would eclipse the water baptism that he was performing. It would be a baptism that involved none other than the Holy Spirit Himself. John's prophecy concerning baptism with the Holy Spirit raises some rather intriguing questions as to the character of this future baptism. What does it mean to be baptized with the Holy Spirit? Who would perform this baptism? How would it differ from John's baptism?

Each book of gospel also provides us with insight into the time Jesus spent with His disciples after His resurrection. As a complement to John's prophecy about baptism, two of the authors, Matthew and Mark, also touch on Jesus' remarks concerning this coming baptism.

18. And Jesus came and spoke to them, saying, "All authority has been given to Me in heaven and on earth. 19. Go therefore and make disciples of all nations, baptizing them in the name of the Father and of the Son and of the Holy Spirit, 20. teaching them to observe all things I have commanded you, and lo, I am with you always, even to the end of the age." *Amen* (Matthew 28: 18-20)

15. And He said to them, "Go into all the world and preach the gospel to every creature. 16. He who believes and is baptized will be saved; but he who does not believe will be condemned." (Mark 16: 15-16)

While these statements may provide answers to certain questions concerning John's prophecy, in that this new baptism would be performed by men under Jesus' authority, these passages raise still other questions. First of all, exactly what is the relationship between baptism and making disciples? These men were commanded to baptize men from all nations in the *process* of making disciples. Secondly, what does baptism have to do with eternal salvation? After all, this is the startling message from the passage in Mark. It is those who believe and are baptized who, according to Jesus, will be saved.

Having planted the seeds of baptismal instruction in the ministry of John the Baptist, and having watered that seed in Jesus' remarks to the disciples after His resurrection, God finally provides answers after Jesus' ascension as crowds were gathered together in Jerusalem.

38. Then Peter said to them, "Repent, and let every one of you be baptized in the name of Jesus Christ for the remission of sins; and you shall receive the gift of the Holy Spirit"...41. Then those who gladly received his word were baptized; and that day about three thousand souls were added to them." (Acts 2: 38, 41)

We now have a fuller explanation of the discussion in the gospels concerning baptism. This new baptism is performed as a matter of receiving forgiveness of sins and is accompanied by the presence of the Holy Spirit in our lives. Additionally, we are, at the time of baptism, counted among those who belong to Christ. In baptism we are *'added to them.'* That is how baptism relates to becoming disciples. That is how baptism relates to salvation.

These three passages (Matthew 28: 18-20; Mark 16: 15-16; Acts 2: 38-41) set the stage for the lessons on baptism that are found in the balance of the New Testament. They help us to better understand the core principles for baptismal discussions in the book of Acts and the epistles. While Paul adds much to our understanding of baptism, including the symbolism upon which the act of baptism is based, these three passages help to identify the reasons for, and significance of, baptism. Therefore, a deeper examination of these passages would be wise so that we might better understand the nature of baptism in the New Testament.

Baptism in Matthew 28: 19

Jesus commanded certain things of His disciples in His final days on earth. Upon their shoulders He laid the burden of establishing His following among all nations.

> 18. And Jesus came and spoke to them, saying, "All authority has been given to Me in heaven and on earth. 19. Go therefore and make disciples of all nations, baptizing them in the name of the Father and of the Son and of the Holy Spirit, 20. teaching them to observe all things I have commanded you, and lo, I am with you always, even to the end of the age." *Amen* (Matthew 28: 18-20)

Baptism appears here as a *product* of initial instruction. Essentially what Jesus told them is that they were to *'make disciples...baptizing them....'* Both discipleship and baptism are defined in terms of establishing men as Christ's followers. Additionally, baptism was to be performed under the authority of Jesus (v. 18) and in the name of the Father, Son, and Holy Spirit (v. 19). Once a person is established as Christ's follower, further instruction concerning *'all things...commanded'* is necessary.

Two distinct kinds of teaching are proposed by Jesus. It seems a fundamental understanding of certain basic instruction (Greek: *matheteuo*) is necessary for someone to become a disciple - instruction that would result in baptism for those who wished to respond. However, *becoming* a follower of Christ is one thing. Living a life that meets the high expectations of one of His followers would require teaching well beyond simple belief in the Lordship of Christ and submission to baptism. Therefore, once the elements of basic instruction and baptism have been accomplished, further *teaching* (Greek: *didasko*) concerning the Christian way of life would be necessary. From the moment of baptism each disciple should seek to understand what is expected of those who would follow Jesus. They were to learn of His commands – His way of life.

Of course, we understand that these instructions concerning discipleship, baptism, and teaching are aimed equally at us. Therefore, it is upon us, as Christ's followers, to continue the tradition that Jesus established on that day. We are to disciple, baptize, and teach.

Baptism in Mark 16: 16

As we consider whether or not a person *must* be baptized as a matter of salvation, we find in Jesus' own words a clear-cut statement concerning the link between baptism and redemption.

> 15. And He said to them, "Go into all the world and preach the gospel to every creature. 16. He who believes and is baptized will be saved; but he who does not believe will be condemned." (Mark 16: 15-16)

Some men question whether the final verses of Mark's gospel (Mark 16: 9-20) should have been included in the Bible since they question his authorship. Without going into much detail, the truth is Scripture provides ample support for the material presented in these verses (Luke 8: 2; 24: 35-51; John 20: 1-23) even if it could be proved that Mark was not the author.[3] In addition, the text appears in *virtually* all early Greek and Latin manuscripts. Of the countless manuscripts available, only a few omit this section. While respect for those particular manuscripts is significant, they still stand alone in excluding the passage. Furthermore, the fact that these verses were widely recognized as Scripture by many of the early church fathers of the second and third centuries speaks volumes concerning their legitimacy.

Interestingly, the discussion surrounding the ending of Mark is not really focused on the accuracy of the verses. The debate primarily centers upon Mark's authorship rather than the substance of the writing. Most scholars agree that the contents of these verses should be considered reliable. Also, those men who ultimately made the decision regarding inclusion saw fit to incorporate them into God's Word. Given the biblical support for the validity of the material as well as God's undeniable influence upon scriptural content, they will be treated as divinely inspired in this book.

For those who prefer to disregard this longer ending for the book of Mark, it is important to note that the redemptive role of baptism does not rely upon Mark 16: 16. Scripture offers conclusive testimony concerning the principles of baptism even in the absence of this passage. Still, this section does offer us some insight into the function of baptism in God's plan of salvation.

Men often deny that Mark 16: 16 links baptism to salvation simply because Jesus failed to say *he who is not baptized will not be saved.* The absence of these words leads many to reject the view that Jesus is presenting baptism as a redemptive matter. Yet the passage clearly maintains that, to be saved, we are to believe *and* be baptized. Those are unambiguous instructions that are offered considerable support from many other passages of Scripture.

Following this statement of simple instruction, Jesus explains that those who do not believe will not be saved. Logically, what unbeliever would consider being baptized to be saved? The unbeliever is lost regardless of his baptismal status. In fact, an unbeliever *cannot* be baptized – he can only become wet. Once it is determined that an individual does not believe, baptism is irrelevant. There would be no reason for Jesus to declare the lost state of an unbeliever who was not baptized since, by his disbelief, he is already lost.

Furthermore, when Jesus spoke of belief, He *presumed* a person's submission to baptism. Just as belief, in this context, presumes repentance (Acts 3: 19) of sins and confession of Jesus as Lord and Savior (Romans 10: 9-10), baptism is a given. Consequently, it would be pointless for Him to account for those who *believed and were not baptized.* Those who believed *were* baptized. The prospect that believers were not baptized is given no consideration since their baptism is understood.

The fact that believers were baptized, and that their baptism was presumed, finds support in Acts 2: 41 and Acts 8: 12 when those who believed *were* baptized. It was those who did not believe who were not baptized. Additionally, Peter offered no one exemption from baptism in his sermon on the Day of Pentecost as he commanded, *'let every one of you be baptized'* (Acts 2: 38).

If Jesus considered baptism unrelated to salvation, why has He interjected it at this time while neglecting the principles of repentance and confession? If baptism is unessential, no reasonable explanation can be offered for its inclusion either here or in the commission given in Matthew's gospel (Matthew 28: 19).

Some may ask the question, *if belief includes baptism, why has Jesus identified belief and baptism individually in this verse*? The fact is that, in Scripture we are provided with only a small sample of the instruction Christ offered to the apostles. While Jesus had surely explained to them the significance of baptism in the coming kingdom prior to this occasion, these are some of His final words before His ascension. Here, and in Matthew 28: 19, the purpose is to openly identify baptism as a critical component of the gospel message. No other reasoning seems to explain His mention of baptism at this time.

Of course, these words are meant for us at least as much as they were meant for the apostles. While the apostles surely understood the significance of baptism, prior to this point in Scripture *we* have only read about the baptism performed by John and Jesus' disciples (John 4: 1-2). Until now there have only been allusions to a baptism that was to come (Matthew 3: 11; John 3: 5). However, in Mark 16: 16 baptism is presented as a critical element of salvation in the church age. Jesus singles out baptism prior to His ascension in order to eliminate any question about the significance of the ceremony.

The combination of belief and baptism mentioned here also addresses another fundamental issue. While disbelief, by itself, is enough for someone to be eternally lost, Jesus' words teach us that it takes more than mere belief to *attain* salvation. Those who charge that the phrase concerning unbelief somehow nullifies the call to be baptized fail to appreciate the fact that Scripture does not recognize any claim of faith in God that disregards His commands (1 John 2: 4), including commands that lead to salvation. Certain other New Testament authors have provided us with a clearer understanding of the kind of belief that Jesus and the apostles taught. These authors inform us that the opposite of belief in Jesus – the belief that saves – is disobedience to His commands. Consequently, the belief that saves is belief that embraces obedience.

18. And to whom did He swear that they would not enter His rest, but to those who did not obey? 19. So we see that they could not enter in because of unbelief. (Hebrews 3: 18-19)

7. Therefore, to you who believe, *He is* precious; but to those who are disobedient,
> *"The stone which the builders rejected*
> *has become the chief cornerstone,"*
8.   and
> *"A stone of stumbling*
> *And a rock of offense."* (1 Peter 2: 7-8)

It is most fascinating the role that belief plays in Mark 16: 16 and how cleanly it matches up with conversion examples in the book of Acts. This speaks to the complementary character of Scripture. Upon learning about Jesus, the eunuch asked to be baptized. Philip told him he could receive baptism *if he believed* (Acts 8: 37). Rather than portraying belief as the solitary means to salvation, Philip depicted it as a prerequisite to baptism. The same is true concerning the Samaritans (Acts 8: 12-13). We are not told that they were saved when they believed, but that they were baptized when they believed. Likewise, we discover that the Philippian jailer was baptized *when he believed* (Acts 16: 33). So it is in this context as Jesus told His followers that those who believe are candidates for baptism and salvation. However, those who do not believe are unqualified for baptism.

Baptism in Acts 2: 38

Convincing support for the necessity of baptism within God's plan of salvation can be found in the initial proclamation of the gospel message to mankind.

> 38. Then Peter said to them, "Repent, and let every one of you be baptized in the name of Jesus Christ for the remission of sins; and you shall receive the gift of the Holy Spirit." (Acts 2: 38)

On the Day of Pentecost, the crowds in Jerusalem asked Peter and the other apostles what they should do in response to the message they had just heard. The answer, given by Peter, is the first time within the church age where the path to forgiveness, and ultimately salvation, is identified. How can men be saved? Forgiveness/redemption comes by repentance and baptism. The teaching is clear whether read in the Greek or English.

This verse, alongside certain other passages, offers us clarification concerning God's design for salvation. First, men must believe that Jesus is the Messiah (Mark 16: 16; John 3: 16) and that His death offered mankind the opportunity to be reconciled to God (2 Corinthians 5: 21). Secondly, realizing that separation from God came about because of our own sins, it is our responsibility to repent (Acts 2: 38; 2 Peter 3: 9) of the sins that have so dishonored Him. Finally, we are to proclaim Jesus as Savior (Romans 10: 9-10) and receive immersion in water. At that time, according to God's promise, He will forgive the penitent believer (Acts 2: 38; 1 Peter 3: 21).

Those who claim that Mark 16: 16 and Acts 2: 38 should not be accepted at face value argue that taking their meaning literally would contradict the message of the gospel that is portrayed in the balance of Scripture. Yet Mark 16: 16 does not infringe upon Peter's message of Acts 2: 38 or vice versa. These verses, in turn, do not violate the instructions offered in either 1 Peter 3: 21 or Matthew 28: 19-20. Nor do they interfere with the teaching found in Romans 6: 1-5, 1 Corinthians 12: 13, Galatians 3: 26-27, Colossians 2: 12, Titus 3: 5, or Hebrews 10: 22. Neither do these passages encroach upon those that speak of salvation through belief (Galatians 3: 22) and/or faith (Romans 3: 28), when we remember that those being addressed were baptized believers. The authors of these letters always presumed the believer's submission to baptism in water. In all honesty, the literal meaning of the words in these verses fully complements *all* New Testament instruction concerning salvation.

The Fallacy of Negative Inference

Occasionally men will appeal to what is known as the *fallacy of negative inference* theory in an effort to dispute passages that speak of a direct relationship between baptism and salvation. The basic premise of this philosophy is that, although a statement may be true, that fact does not necessarily mean that the negative inference of that same statement is also true. If we attempt to apply this theory practically, we might make the statement that *a man who lives in Detroit lives in Michigan.* However, while the statement is factual, we cannot automatically infer from it that *a man who does not live in Detroit does not live in Michigan.* Indeed, it is very possible that a man who does not live in Detroit may still live in the state of Michigan

Often men attempt to apply this same theory specifically to the passages of Mark 16: 16 and Acts 2: 38. The claim is, while it is true that Jesus stated, *'He who believes and is baptized will be saved,'* this does not necessarily mean that *He who believes and is not baptized will not be saved.* Likewise, Peter's command to *repent and be baptized* in Acts 2: 38, does not necessarily disqualify those who are not baptized from receiving that same forgiveness.

However, rather than simply claiming that one statement does not *necessarily* suggest the negative, men have developed a teaching that fully equates two unequal statements. Thus they teach that, *'He who believes and is baptized will be saved'* is the same as saying *He who believes and is not baptized will be saved.* Similarly, *'Repent, and let every one of you be baptized in the name of Jesus Christ for the remission of sins'* is no different than saying, *Repent for the remission of sins.*

The attempt to apply this theory to passages such as these, however, is fundamentally flawed. The factual statements used to develop the argument are simply incompatible with those remarks to which they are being compared. The statement, *a man who lives in Detroit lives in Michigan,* is merely an observation of the man's status. This cannot be reasonably applied to verses that are clearly directional in nature, intended to guide us to a destination, any more than it can apply to other passages that provide us with redemptive instruction. The following verses teach us what *will be* the outcome of obedience.

Repent therefore and be converted, that your sins *may be* blotted out...
Acts 3: 19) - emphasis added

...if you confess with your mouth the Lord Jesus and believe in your heart that God has raised Him from the dead, you *will be* saved. (Romans 10: 9) - emphasis added.

Can a man repent without being truly converted and still anticipate salvation? Does the one who refuses to either believe in or confess Jesus as Lord have any reason to be hopeful about his eternal existence? Of course, he does not. These verses are directional, intended to guide us to the goal of salvation.

When a man offers directions to someone it is customary to provide the clearest, shortest route to the desired destination. A person's failure to follow those directions, as they are given, would prevent him/her from reaching the desired location. So it is when God gives directions in order for men to realize a specific outcome. His directions are very straightforward. In Mark 16: 16 we discover what *will be* the status of those who believe and are baptized. Peter proclaimed in Acts 2: 38 that all who accept the invitation to repentance and baptism *will receive* forgiveness of sins and the gift of the Holy Spirit. These verses do not focus on where a man *is* (e.g., Detroit), but where he *will be* if he follows the directions he has been given. They tell us what we must do to attain eternal life. In these passages we are shown the pathway to salvation.

Recognizing the instructive nature of these verses, as well as the failure of this method to refute the teaching found there concerning baptism, some men have altered their approach to challenging these verses by taking into account their directional character. Therefore, the argument has shifted from *a man living in Detroit* to the suggestion that, if Jesus had said, *He who believes and reads his Bible every day will be saved*, it would not necessarily mean that daily Bible reading was essential to salvation.

In this case, *negative inference* is offered to challenge the need for Bible reading, and subsequently baptism, as a matter of salvation. In short, the argument states that, if daily Bible reading is not a matter of redemption, the same must be true of baptism. No reason is given for replacing baptism with Bible reading. Those making the claim apparently assume that what is true of Bible reading is equally true of baptism, biblically speaking. Yet, at no time in Scripture is Bible reading equated with baptism.

Two noticeable flaws immediately surface with respect to this proposal, especially relative to Mark 16: 16. The first, and perhaps the most obvious flaw, is the fact that those are not the words spoken by Jesus in this verse. Jesus did not say *He who believes and reads his Bible every day will be saved*. The point of the substitution is to try and discredit what Jesus actually said. It provides no legitimate insight into the teaching that Jesus offered at this time. The fact that daily Bible reading is not assigned redemptive status in Scripture is undoubtedly a key reason Jesus did not declare it here.

Additionally, if we should consider this a proper means of biblical analysis, why is it that, in all of Scripture, this methodology is applied *only* to these two passages? Imagine the potential biblical doctrine we could develop if we were to use this same logic through the balance of Scripture (tongue-in-cheek). Yet honest biblical examination demands that we accept God's Word *as it is written*.

The second flaw, which is perhaps not quite so obvious, is that, had Jesus made the statement as proposed – inserting *Bible reading* rather than *baptism* – and Scripture supported this teaching as it does baptism, we would need to recognize daily Bible reading as a redemptive matter. The instructive nature of the statement would demand it.

Ultimately, this attempt to disprove scriptural teaching concerning baptism challenges the very heart of legitimate biblical analysis. The entire proposition of negative inference, when applied to Mark 16: 16 or Acts 2: 38, contends that both Jesus and Peter mistakenly included baptism in their instructions concerning what men must do to attain eternal life. Yet, Jesus has already explained to his disciples those things He considered immaterial when it comes to following Him.

> 21. Then another of His disciples said to Him, "Lord, let me first go and bury my father." 22. But Jesus said to Him, "Follow Me, and let the dead bury their own dead." (Matthew 8: 21-22)

Not only does Jesus not mince words, but He also does not give commands frivolously. He considered taking the time to bury one's father, an apparent representation of anything that might delay or hinder our calling, as insignificant for the person who really cares to be a disciple. He does not view baptism in that same light. The New Testament offers consistent instruction about the redemptive value of baptism (Matthew 28: 19-20; Romans 6: 1-4; Galatians 3: 27; Ephesians 4: 5; Hebrews 10: 22; Titus 3: 5). Applying the negative inference philosophy in an effort to refute that teaching is, at the very least, an irreverent approach to understanding God's Word.

The Divine Inspiration of the Word

The premise that was established in the Preface of this book, that the Bible is the inspired Word of God, is a most significant one. Based upon that truth, we need to fully appreciate the fact that these passages were written the *way* they were written for a reason. The truth is, Jesus did say, *'He who believes and is baptized will be saved...'* (Mark 16: 16). Peter did proclaim, *'Repent, and let every one of you be baptized in the name of Jesus Christ for the remission of sins; and you shall receive the gift of the Holy Spirit'* (Acts 2: 38). The responsibility of any translator, beyond simply converting words from one language to another is, first and foremost, to ensure that the meaning of the words is not lost in the translation process. The message from these two statements regarding baptism is unmistakable and undeniable. Yet, the failure of many to accept God's message has been, and continues to be, the source of considerable disagreement in the religious community.

Paul explained to Timothy, whom he called his *'son in the faith'* (1 Timothy 1: 2), the high value that God has placed upon Scripture (2 Timothy 3: 16). He told Timothy that all Scripture comes from God and is to be treated as a reliable source of doctrine, reproof, correction, and instruction. Note that *all* of Scripture, not just those points with which we agree, is given with this in mind. Therefore, this is just as true for Mark 16: 16 and Acts 2: 38 as it is for any other passage. That means that the teaching concerning baptism in these verses should be understood as significant rather than immaterial. The apostle John offers a serious warning against the altering of the Scripture of the book of Revelation (Revelation 22: 18-19). Given God's view of the value of His inspired Word, it is safe to say that He would frown upon our attempts to modify any Scripture to fit our own beliefs.

Of course, few, if any, would ever suggest that we could legitimately remove the phrase *'and is baptized'* from Jesus' words in Mark 16: 16. Surely no one would dare rewrite the verse to say, *He who believes and is not baptized will be saved.* Yet, without eraser or pen in hand, these changes are made verbally every day by those who willfully deny the fact that Jesus, in this passage, proclaims the need for baptism.

The Baptism of the Ethiopian Eunuch

The Bible is filled with testimony concerning baptism and its central role in God's plan of salvation. Numerous biblical examples of people being baptized reveal the emphasis that was placed upon this ceremony. Perhaps one of the most persuasive accounts depicting the importance of the role of water baptism in the New Testament is found in the episode of Philip and the Ethiopian eunuch (Acts 8: 26-39). Because the eunuch did not understand the Scripture he was reading, God arranged for Philip to meet with him and teach him. We must first acknowledge the fact that Philip was sent by an angel of God to minister to this man. If God would send Philip in this way, He surely would not send him with a false message. Additionally, since he was sent by God, He must have been confident that Philip had no misconception concerning that message.

As Philip taught the eunuch (Acts 8: 35), he evidently revealed within his teaching the significance of immersion in water. When they came upon some water it was the eunuch who insisted on being baptized (Acts 8: 36). His words suggest that he was not asking *if* he should be baptized, since he had obviously settled on that decision. Instead, he asked Philip what would keep him from being baptized *now*. Just as Peter had proclaimed on the Day of Pentecost, the eunuch must have understood from Philip's teaching that forgiveness of sins and the gift of the Holy Spirit were granted at the time of immersion in water (Acts 2: 38). He understood baptism to be a matter of salvation. The eunuch sought baptism in water as a direct response to the teaching he had received from Philip.

Philip baptized the eunuch – in water. Once this was accomplished, *'the Spirit of the Lord caught Philip away, so that the eunuch saw him no more; and he went on his way rejoicing'* (Acts 8: 39). Based upon what we have already read concerning the effects of baptism, the eunuch's rejoicing can rightfully be viewed as his recognition from Philip's instruction that he had received salvation. He seems to fully appreciate Philip's teaching. There is no record here of a miraculous outpouring of the Holy Spirit, so he would not have been rejoicing over that; although the eunuch would have received the *gift* of the Holy Spirit described by Peter (Acts 2: 38) upon his obedience in water baptism. He was not ecstatic due to a miraculous spiritual gift granted to him; nor did he rejoice prior to baptism. The eunuch's enthusiasm was, without a doubt, a result of his understanding of the redemptive power of immersion in water (Mark 16: 16) as taught by Philip. This episode is consistent with *instruction* concerning salvation in the New Testament and harmonizes fully with the initial instruction God has provided concerning baptism in the New Testament (Matthew 28: 18-20; Mark 16: 15-16; Acts 2: 38-41).

The Baptism of Cornelius

One of the more familiar accounts of conversion in the New Testament is that of Cornelius, a Gentile who was directed by an angel of God to send for Peter so that he might receive instructions concerning the things of God.

44. While Peter was still speaking these words, the Holy Spirit fell upon all those who heard the word. 45. And those of the circumcision

who believed were astonished, as many as came with Peter, because the gift of the Holy Spirit had been poured out on the Gentiles also. 46. For they heard them speak with tongues and magnify God. Then Peter answered, 47. "Can anyone forbid water, that these should not be baptized who have received the Holy Spirit just as we *have?*" 48. And he commanded them to be baptized in the name of the Lord. Then they asked him to stay a few days. (Acts 10: 44-48)

Cornelius, joined by his companions in Caesarea, was the first Gentile to be converted to Christianity. Luke explains that he was a devout and God-fearing man (Acts 10: 1-2). Yet, despite his faithfulness, he lacked knowledge that was *essential* to his salvation (Acts 11: 14) – the message of the gospel. Through His death, burial, and resurrection, Jesus had blazed the only trail that could lead to eternal life (Acts 4: 12). An important point found in this narrative is one that is too often overlooked – acceptance of the gospel is reliant upon a person's response to that message (Acts 10: 35). As the events of the day unfolded in Caesarea, we discover that Cornelius did respond to the message Peter brought. When Peter realized that salvation was also meant for Gentiles, as he witnessed the unmistakable work of the Holy Spirit, he commanded that they should be baptized in water.

Men are divided as to exactly *when* these Gentiles were saved. Those who claim that water baptism is insignificant to salvation commonly offer the account of Cornelius in an attempt to make their case. They maintain that the manifestation of the Holy Spirit upon Cornelius preceding his baptism proves that he was saved prior to immersion. In fact, they often claim that this episode with the Gentiles proves that baptism with the Holy Spirit, and not water baptism, is the path to salvation. This belief is based upon the assumption that Holy Spirit baptism and water baptism *may* take place at two distinct times and that baptism with the Holy Spirit manifests itself in the gift of tongues. Since these Gentiles spoke in tongues, the argument is made that they were baptized with the Holy Spirit at that time and, consequently, saved prior to water baptism.

Others maintain that Cornelius and those with him received salvation at the time they were immersed in water (v. 48), a belief that is founded upon the principles that were discussed earlier concerning baptism in the New Testament (Matthew 28: 18-20; Mark 16: 15-16; Acts 2: 38-41).

Both points of view can find some support within the pages of Scripture. The baptismal instruction found in the gospels and on the Day of Pentecost offers support for the proposal that salvation for these Gentiles accompanied their baptism in water. Since baptism is defined as the time of forgiveness (Acts 2: 38) and salvation (Mark 16: 16), this is a reasonable conclusion. However, Peter's words later in the book of Acts could be interpreted to suggest that these men *may* have been redeemed as the Spirit came upon them. In a discussion centering on the relevance of the Mosaic Law to Gentiles in the new covenant, Peter states:

> 7. "...Men and brethren, you know that a good while ago God chose among us that by my mouth the Gentiles should hear the word of the gospel and believe. 8. So God, who knows the heart, acknowledged them by giving them the Holy Spirit, just as He did us, 9. and made no distinction between us and them, purifying their hearts by faith." (Acts 15: 7-9)

Did God purify (regenerate) their hearts prior to their immersion in water? No one may speak from either side of the aisle with complete confidence. It is possible; however, no absolute conclusion can be drawn from the text. Peter does not say exactly *when* God purified their hearts – only *that* He did so. On the other hand, Jesus explained to His disciples, while He was with them, that men of this world - that is to say, those who are of flesh rather than spirit - cannot know the Spirit (John 14: 17). Based on this verse it is not unreasonable to suggest that, as the Spirit came upon these Gentiles, God saw them as *men of Spirit* rather than *men of flesh*. Still, no exception is made at this time with respect to water baptism. These men were immersed in water.

Peter certainly recognized the uncommon nature of the events that he witnessed at the house of Cornelius. He remembered only one other time[4] when the Spirit manifested Himself in this way. Now God had once again poured out His Spirit in a mysterious and miraculous way – to the Gentiles. He had revealed His plan for the Gentiles in a manner that Peter acknowledged could only come from God. This was unquestionably a sign to Peter, and those with him, that salvation was not limited to the Israelites, but was intended for all men everywhere. This objective is revealed in the passage cited above as Peter explained the *reason* for the Spirit falling on the Gentiles in such a phenomenal manner. He stated that this was the means by which God acknowledged them.

In this case, the word for *acknowledged* (v. 8), which is μαρτυρεω (*martureo*), reveals that God was *bearing witness* to Peter and those with him concerning His acceptance of Gentiles into the kingdom. According to <u>The New Strong's Exhaustive Concordance of the Bible</u> the word means: 'to be a witness, i.e., *testify*...give testimony, (be, bear, give, obtain) witness.'[5] Indeed, various other Bible translations plainly bear this out.

> And God, which knoweth the hearts, *bare them witness*, giving them the Holy Ghost, even as he did unto us (Acts 15: 8, KJV) – emphasis added.

> And God, who knoweth the heart, *bare them witness*, giving them the Holy Spirit, even as he did unto us (Acts 15: 8, ASV) – emphasis added.

> God, who knows the heart, *showed that he accepted them* by giving the Holy Spirit to them... (Acts 15: 8, NIV) – emphasis added.

> And God, who knows the heart, *testified to them* giving them the Holy Spirit, just as He also did to us (Act 15: 8, NASB) – emphasis added.

The work of the Holy Spirit upon these Gentiles is an example of God's divine intervention, which was discussed in the Preface of this book. Through this miracle He revealed to Peter and the Jews His intention to offer salvation to the Gentiles. This was the *purpose* of the occasion. It was not God's intention to establish a *new path* to salvation that ignores or alters the role of baptism, but to establish salvation for a *new people*. The focus of the episode is not on the *manner* by which men are saved, which has already been established (Mark 16: 16; Acts 2: 38), but on those to whom salvation was now made available. This narrative contains no instruction that would challenge the principles of baptism that were discussed earlier. According to Peter, the extraordinary nature of the event, as the Holy Spirit was poured out in an exceptional manner, was simply God's way of acknowledging His approval of Gentiles as part of the kingdom.

It is clear from his words that Peter understood the importance of baptism for the Gentiles. As on the Day of Pentecost and Philip's encounter with the eunuch, baptism was the obvious course of action (Acts 10: 47). His call for baptism for the Gentiles was undoubtedly founded upon the principles of discipleship (Matthew 28: 19), forgiveness and the Holy Spirit (Acts 2: 38), and salvation (Mark 16: 16) to which Peter was a witness. He saw no reason to make any exception to the principles of baptism simply because of the unusual circumstances involved.

Baptism – Duty or Privilege?

In a real sense, there is a subtle tone of resistance hidden within the question, *'Must I be baptized?'* that is the title of this chapter and is, today, asked by so many. When men were instructed concerning baptism in the New Testament the response was not, *'Must I be baptized?'* as though it was a burden, but rather, *'When can I be baptized?'* as those who submitted to immersion in water did so with a sense of hope. Peter stated, concerning Cornelius and the other Gentiles, *'Can anyone keep these people from being baptized with water?'* (NIV - Acts 10: 47) The Ethiopian eunuch asked Philip, *'What hinders me from being baptized?'* (Acts 8: 36). Similarly, the apostle Paul (Acts 9: 18), Lydia (Acts 16:14-15), and the Philippian jailer (Acts 16: 33), as well as many others anxiously participated in baptism. In fact, they were baptized immediately – apparently recognizing that time was of the essence.

Disciples in the New Testament seemed to view baptism not as a burdensome obligation, but as an honor and opportunity eagerly anticipated. Perhaps this transformation in our approach to baptism can be traced to the disparity that exists between the respect awarded this ceremony in the first century versus the manner in which it is trivialized in modern times. During the Reformation Movement, as men began to call baptism a *work* rather than a spiritual experience, much of the appeal it had once known slowly began to fade. Yet, if we will allow the Bible to be our teacher, baptism can and should be a time of excitement and renewal today just as it was in the days of the apostles.

NOTES FOR CHAPTER 5

1. Martin Luther believed in Spirit regeneration at the time of baptism, *The Large Catechism by Martin Luther, X21 Part Fourth of Baptism*; yet he also held to the belief of infant baptism and sprinkling or pouring of water as acceptable, *The Large Catechism by Martin Luther, X21A Part Fourth of Baptism*. John Wesley, founder of Methodism, fell short of considering baptism a means of regeneration, but believed it was a sign equivalent to circumcision in the OT. Wesley also believed infant baptism was not only acceptable to God, but deemed it absolutely necessary for the salvation of a child, *Wesley's 25 Articles Of Religion, Article 15, Of The Ordinances*. John Calvin, along with Wesley, believed water baptism to be a sign of the new covenant as circumcision was of the old. For this reason he also believed infant baptism acceptable. Calvin believed in predestination and, therefore, only those whom God had chosen would be baptized. *John*

Calvin - The Institutes of Christian, Book IV, Chapter XV. Alexander Campbell believed both in the regeneration effects of baptism and the necessity of immersion. He denied any scriptural basis for infant baptism. *Christian Baptism With Its Antecedents and Consequents, By Alexander Campbell.*

2. Campbell wrote of the misinterpretation of the Bible by scholarly men, noting that God's intent was for men to simply read the worth of the words rather than seek a hidden meaning. His reasoning was that if special rules apply to Biblical interpretation that apply nowhere else, how should man ever understand what God expected of men?

> *God has spoken by men, for men.* The language of the Bible is, then, *human* language. It is, therefore, to be examined by the same rules which are applicable to the language of any other book, and to be understood according to the true and proper meaning of the words, in their current acceptation, at the times and in the places in which they were originally written and translated.

> If we have a *revelation* from God in human language, the words of that volume must be intelligible by the common usage of language; they must be precise and determinate in signification, and that signification must be philologically ascertained--that is, as the words and sentences of other books are ascertained by the use of the dictionary and grammar. Were it otherwise, and did men require a new dictionary and grammar to understand the Book of God,--then, without that divine dictionary and grammar, we could have no *revelation* from God; for a revelation that needs to be revealed is no revelation at all.

> Again, if any *special rules* are to be sought for the interpretation of the sacred writings, unless these rules have been given in the volume, as a part of the revelation, and are of divine authority;--without such rules, the Book is sealed; and I know of no greater abuse of language than to call a *sealed book* a revelation. [54]

> But the fact that God has clothed his communications in human language, and that he has spoken by men, to men, in their own language, is decisive evidence that he is to be understood as one man conversing with another. Righteousness, or what we sometimes call *honesty,* requires this; for unless he first made a special stipulation when he began to speak, his words were, in all candour, to be taken at the current value; for he that would contract with a man for any thing, stipulating his contract in the currency of the country, without any explanation, and should afterwards intimate that a *dollar* with him meant only *three francs,* would be regarded as a dishonest and unjust man. And shall we impute to the God of truth and justice what would blast the reputation of a fellow-citizen at the tribunal of political justice and public opinion! Campbell, Christian Baptism, with Its Antecedents and Consequents, Chapter 21, THE BIBLE-PRINCIPLES OF INTERPRETATION, (1851).

3. David Miller addressed the legitimacy of Mark 16: 9-20 writing for Apologetics Press.Org. After extensive exegetical discussion concerning evidence for both omission and inclusion, his findings are as follows:

> For the unbiased observer, this matter is settled: the strongest piece of internal evidence mustered against the genuineness of Mark 16:9-20 is **no evidence at all**. The two strongest arguments offered to discredit the inspiration of these verses as the production of Mark are seen to be lacking in substance and legitimacy. The reader of the New Testament may be confidently assured that

these verses are original—written by the Holy Spirit through the hand of Mark as part of his original gospel account. Apologetics Press: Reason and Revelation - Is Mark 16: 9-20 Inspired?

4. That this particular manifestation of the Spirit had occurred on one other occasion is clear from Peter's words in Acts 11: 15. Gareth Reese addressed the truth of this statement as follows:

> The reference in the word "beginning" is to the day of Pentecost, Acts 2; and the "us" is limited to the apostles. It is strongly implied that there had been no common reception of the baptism in the Holy Spirit since Pentecost, for if it were something that all Christians were expected to and did receive, Peter could have simply pointed to the numerous other incidents and not have had to go back to Pentecost for an example. Gareth L. Reese, New Testament History – Acts, page 414, Scripture Exposition Books, 2002.

5. James Strong, LL.D., S.T.D., The New Strong's Exhaustive Concordance of the Bible, Greek Dictionary of the New Testament, p. 46, 1990, Thomas Nelson Publishers.

Chapter VI

Baptism and the Gospel

The Message of the Gospel

The gospel (good news) is the message of Christ through which the opportunity of salvation is made available to men. That message is revealed to us through the words of the Bible. Although the Bible was written by men, we understand that these men were guided by the Spirit of God as they penned the words of Scripture. While the message of salvation is made known to us through God's Word, the redemption of any individual is still dependent upon his/her response to that message in the manner established in the teaching of the apostles – the men through whom Jesus introduced His church on earth (Ephesians 2: 20).

Each aspect of the gospel message, according to the apostles, is considered critical to our salvation. For instance, without Jesus' death, burial, and resurrection, no man could receive salvation (eternal life in heaven). Additionally, without accepting (believing) the teaching that Jesus is the Son of God, that He died in our place for the sins we have committed, and that He rose again as a matter of conquering death and paving the way for our resurrection (Romans 10: 1-13), no one could be redeemed. Other elements of the gospel message include repenting of the sins we have committed against God and other men (Acts 3: 19), confessing Jesus as Lord and Savior before witnesses (Romans 10: 9-10), and submitting to immersion in water as a matter of remittance of sins (Acts 2: 38). Obedience to these fundamentals of the gospel is considered vital for anyone to attain salvation, but the message does not end there.

Once a person has attained salvation by following the instructions offered in God's Word, he/she must make every effort to honor God by living a life that exemplifies faithfulness to Christ (Matthew 28: 20; John 5: 23). The kind of life we ought to live is also taught in Scripture. Jesus, along with the apostles, offers us considerable insight into the attributes of a life that honors Him.

Those passages where the principles of baptism are initially discussed (Matthew 28: 18-20; Mark 16: 15-16; Acts 2: 38-41) indicate that it is intended to be presented as an element of the gospel message. As we mentioned earlier, in Matthew's account of Jesus' proclamation of the Great Commission, he notes two different kinds of teaching that Jesus commanded of His followers. First they were to *disciple* men from every nation – *'baptizing them'* (Matthew 28: 19). This kind of instruction is markedly different from *'teaching them to observe all things that I have commanded...'* (Matthew 28: 20). It is the initial instruction that is meant to bring men to a belief in Christ. It is teaching that will hopefully result in baptism for the person who hears that message.

The fact that Jesus had the salvation value of baptism in mind in Mark 16: 16, is evident from the immediate context of His words that men so often overlook. Jesus links belief *and* baptism directly to the gospel message in this instance. He instructed the disciples to, *'Go into all the world and preach the gospel to every creature'* (Mark 16: 15). Immediately following this command to preach the gospel, Jesus explained who would be saved as a result. The saved were those who were obedient to that gospel message – a teaching echoed by both Peter (Acts 2: 38; 1 Peter 3: 21; 4: 17) and Paul (2 Thessalonians 1: 8). If, in response to hearing the gospel message, Jesus anticipated that people would believe and be baptized, we must recognize baptism as an element of that message.

The Day of Pentecost is the first time in the covenant of grace that the complete message of the gospel is revealed to mankind (Acts 2: 5-40). As Peter and the other apostles preached on that day, their words drew an exclamation from those who believed as they asked, *'what shall we do?'* (v. 37). In his response, Peter directed them toward repentance and baptism (v. 38). While it should be obvious from these passages that the message of the gospel focuses on leading men to Christ through baptism, it is a point that many men are simply unwilling to accept despite clear biblical instruction.

Approaching the Bible

It is generally accepted among those who profess Jesus as Lord, that belief in Jesus as the risen Son of God is a basic principle of the gospel message. This broad consensus is primarily based on the many biblical passages that candidly call for belief in Christ as a matter of salvation.

> For God so loved the world that He gave His only begotten Son, that whosoever believes in Him should not perish but have everlasting life. (John 3: 16)

So they said, "Believe on the Lord Jesus Christ, and you will be saved, you and your household." (Acts 16: 31)

Many similar passages can be found throughout the New Testament maintaining belief in Jesus as a condition of salvation. Therefore, few would ever argue against it. However, the reading of verses such as these has led some men to conclude that belief alone (or faith alone, where belief and faith are deemed to be equivalent) is all that is necessary to attain salvation. Single verses, however, usually fail to provide us with a full view of God's plan as it is presented in Scripture. For those who wish to pursue true scriptural doctrine, honest consideration must be given to all that the Bible teaches about a doctrinal matter, as well as the context of that teaching. If only certain passages regarding salvation are examined, while others remain ignored, we may end up misunderstanding God's instructions. In fact, selective use of Scripture such as this may be adopted to demonstrate biblical support for virtually any belief we may wish to embrace. For instance, by applying God's Word in such a discriminating fashion, we could conclude that belief is, in fact, *not* necessary to secure salvation.

38. Then Peter said to them, "Repent and let every one of you be baptized in the name of Jesus Christ for the remission of sins; and you shall receive the gift of the Holy Spirit." (Acts 2: 38)

There is also an antitype which now saves us–baptism… (1 Peter 3: 21)

By eliminating those passages that address the principle of belief in Jesus, we could actually conclude that salvation is attainable simply through repentance and baptism, as these verses suggest. However, applying Scripture in such a restrictive manner denies God the opportunity to fully instruct the reader. In like manner, if we wish we could use this same technique to advocate a path to salvation that sets aside repentance.

He who believes and is baptized will be saved; but he who does not believe will be condemned. (Mark 16: 16)

Then Crispus, the ruler of the synagogue, believed on the Lord with all his household. And many of the Corinthians, hearing, believed and were baptized. (Acts 18: 8)

If we are to learn from Scripture the things God wants us to know, we must be honest in our approach to His Word. The first thing we must do, if we are to be honest, is allow Scripture to complement itself. We will not gain understanding by pitting God's Word against itself. The fact that belief is presented in the Bible as essential to salvation does not mean that belief *alone*, exclusive of repentance or baptism, is sufficient. If we are intended to consider belief alone as sufficient to salvation, what are we to do with those passages that depict baptism as essential? The concepts are contradictory. This could explain why we do not find the phrase *belief alone* anywhere within the pages of God's Word.

Ironically, while the term *belief alone*, or *belief only*, does not appear in the pages of Scripture, the phrase *faith only* can be found there. However, *faith only* is not presented as the means to salvation.

> You see then that man is justified by works, and not by faith only.
> (James 2: 24)

While this remark from James is not necessarily addressing one's initial salvation, this is the only time in the Bible when we find these words joined together in this manner. That means that any other use of the terms *faith only* or *belief only*, when taught as a matter of redemption, has developed from the teaching of men rather than from biblical instruction.

The Philippian Jailer and the Message of the Gospel

The Philippian jailer was a man in search of answers. When he asked what he must do to be saved, Paul explained to him that he must believe in Jesus (Acts 16: 30-31). However, contrary to the claims of men, belief in Jesus was not the complete message that Paul delivered on that day; it was merely the introduction to his message. An honest examination of the narrative reveals that baptism was taught to the jailer (Acts 16: 33) just as it had been taught to the eunuch (Acts 8: 36). As we read the story of the apostle's conversation with the jailer, in order to conclude that Paul's entire message consisted only of belief in Jesus as a matter of salvation, we must ignore the rest of the account as told by Luke.

30. And he brought them out and said, "Sirs, what must I do to be saved?" 31. So they said, "Believe on the Lord Jesus Christ, and you will be saved, you and your household." 32. Then they spoke the word of the Lord to him and to all who were in his house. (Acts 16: 30-32)

After explaining to his listeners that they must believe, Paul *'...spoke the word of the Lord to him...'* Those words (*the word of the Lord*) resulted in baptism. Of course, the jailer and those with him also undoubtedly repented of their sins and confessed Jesus as Lord (though these last two are not specifically cited). On this occasion, Paul's teaching would have been consistent with that of both the apostle Peter (Acts 2: 38) and Philip (Acts 8: 36-38). In a review of the entire apostolic age, beginning with the Day of Pentecost, we discover that conversions reported in Scripture consistently involved water baptism. In fact, in *every* case where details of the conversion are offered, baptism is present.

Expressions such as *the word of the Lord* or *preach the word*, when they appear in the New Testament, pertain to the gospel message that was preached (Acts 8: 4; 11: 19; 15: 35-36; 19: 10) by the apostles and evangelists in the first century. The New Testament writers used terms like *'preached the word of God'* (Acts 13: 5), *'preach the word'* (Acts 14: 25), *'preach the gospel'* (Acts 15: 7), *'preach the word of the Lord'* (Acts 15: 36), and similar phrases interchangeably (Acts 8: 25). We even discover, as Philip taught the Ethiopian eunuch, that the gospel message is represented simply by the name of Jesus as Philip, *'preached Jesus to him'* (Acts 8: 35).

The *word of the Lord* was, and still is, the gospel message of salvation through Jesus that is to be preached to all. It is true that, today, many men teach a strict message of *belief only*. Yet we find that, once Paul had explained to the Philippian jailer that he must *believe* in Jesus in order to be saved, *'they continued to teach this man and others in his house concerning the word of the Lord.'* Since Paul continued to speak the *'word of the Lord'* (the gospel), having already explained the need for belief, we can conclude that the substance of that message involves considerably more than mere belief. Of course, most will concede this point given the scriptural support for repentance of sins (Acts 3: 19) and confession of Jesus as Lord (Romans 10: 9-10), along with the fact that the *good news*, in itself, is the story of the death, burial, and resurrection of Jesus Christ (1 Corinthians 15: 3-5).

However, this narrative confirms that the *'word of the Lord'* that Paul taught included instruction about baptism since the jailer, along with his family, was baptized that very night in response to Paul's teaching. Furthermore, while Paul would have undoubtedly introduced the entirety of the gospel message concerning salvation, we are not told that his listeners repented or confessed, but that they were baptized. This omission suggests that their participation in baptism was the key point Luke intended to convey to his readers as a matter of importance.

Some who seek to challenge the role of baptism in the plan of salvation have brought to our attention the fact that the episode with the jailer is the only time in Scripture when the question concerning salvation is actually framed, *'What must I do to be saved?'* Pointing to Pentecost, they note that, at that time the question asked of Peter and the other apostles was simply, *'What shall we do?'* Since the jailer asked what he should do *to be saved*, these men maintain that Paul's answer in this context is the only one we should consider relevant for those who seek salvation. In addition, they claim that only the first sentence spoken by Paul at this time, which was, *'Believe on the Lord Jesus Christ, and you will be saved'*, can be considered legitimate in determining God's plan of salvation. Thus, only one sentence in all of Scripture (Acts 16: 31) is relevant to our salvation in the church age.

Of course, the sole objective of this kind of scrutiny is to force personal doctrine upon the text. The question on the Day of Pentecost was clearly asked by men seeking salvation. Indeed, Peter's single aspiration on that day was to present to the Israelites the opportunity to be saved. Additionally, numerous other statements made by Jesus (Matthew 7: 21; Mark 16: 16), Paul (Romans 6: 1-4; 10: 9-10), and Peter (Acts 3: 19; 1 Peter 3: 21) are equally focused on redemptive instruction. These passages are no less relevant when it comes to conversion than the incident with the jailer.

A Profile of the Gospel in the Book of Acts

In their relentless effort to challenge the redemptive role of baptism, some men have suggested that Scripture simply does not mention baptism frequently enough for it to be considered vital (apparently compared to belief). Interestingly, this same logic is not offered with respect to confession. Yet, upon the founding of the church in the book of Acts, the narrative touches on confession in only a handful of passages (Acts 2: 21; 8: 36-37; 22: 16). The word *confess*, as a part of the plan of salvation, is absent from the book of Acts. Still, the examples of Peter's words on the Day of Pentecost (Acts 2: 21), the confession offered by the Ethiopian eunuch (Acts 8: 37), and Paul's *'calling on the name of the Lord'* (Acts 22: 16) provide evidence of its significance. Additionally, Jesus regarded the proclamation of the good confession made by Peter (Matthew 16: 16) as the basis (rock) upon which the church would be built (Matthew 16: 18).

In order to avoid any misrepresentation of Scripture, it should be noted that Acts 8: 37 may have been a late addition to the text. For that reason, it is not included in certain versions (e.g., the NIV and NASB) of the Bible. If, however, this text is eliminated, we are left with only two verses in the book of Acts that could be cited as references to confession; and those passages (Acts 2: 21; 22: 16) are portrayed as *'calling on the name of the Lord.'* Whether or not this may be deemed a literal verbal declaration is perhaps a matter of opinion. For the sake of argument we will grant that this is the case, although, as we discussed earlier, it seems apparent from Scripture that confession of Jesus as Lord would only be one element of the *calling* mentioned here.

The command to r*epent*, in some form, appears in the book of Acts eleven times. Twice reference is made to John's *'baptism of repentance'* (Acts 13: 24; 19:4). The remaining nine incidents speak either directly or implicitly of forgiveness and/or salvation.

Some derivative of the word *baptize* occurs twenty-seven times in the book of Acts. Some claim that Acts 1: 5 and Acts 11: 16 each carry specific reference to baptism with the Holy Spirit occurring separately from water baptism. Setting aside those passages, twenty-five of these instances specifically denote baptism in water. Of these twenty-five occasions, seven refer to the baptism performed by John the Baptist. Twice it is commanded as a matter of forgiveness of sins (Acts 2: 38; 22: 16). In sixteen other references to water baptism in the book of Acts, it is portrayed as an element of conversion as various men and women accepted Christ.

Some form of the word *belief* appears in the book of Acts forty-four times. Four of these may be viewed as identifying belief specifically as a matter *leading to* salvation (Acts 10: 43; 13: 39; 13: 48; 16: 31). At certain other times belief is depicted simply as a prerequisite for baptism (Acts 8: 12-13, 37; 18: 8). Four instances are concerned with those who failed to believe in Jesus (Acts 9: 26; 13: 41; 19: 9; 28: 24). Three occasions mention belief in something or someone other than Christ (Acts 24: 14; 27: 11; 27: 25). Beyond these instances, ordinarily when *belief* appears in any form in the book of Acts, it is a general reference to *belief, believing,* or *believers* regarding those who were considered followers of Jesus.

The principle of *faith* is either written or spoken in the book of Acts on fifteen occasions. At times it speaks of the faith exhibited by men as they were physically healed (Acts 3: 16; 14: 9). Often it simply expresses general reliance on the gospel message and/or Jesus (Acts 6: 5-8; 11: 24; 13: 8; 14: 22-27; 16: 5; 20: 21; 24: 24). Twice faith is depicted as having a purifying or sanctifying effect (Acts 15: 9; 26: 18).

A Profile of the Gospel in the Epistles

The third through the fifth chapters of Romans are often cited as Paul's declaration of the gospel of Christ and all that it involves. However, in the epistles the message of the gospel is not necessarily presented in a way that explains the manner in which men are saved. The gospel message that is discussed in the epistles is normally given in the form of a review since these letters were written to those who were already part of the body of Christ. Rather than people seeking salvation, these men and women had already *put on* Christ, a fact that Paul frequently mentions (Romans 6: 4, 17; 1 Corinthians 12: 13; Galatians 3: 27). The men and women addressed in the epistles had already accepted Jesus as their Savior, repented of their sins, and been baptized in obedience to His commands. Therefore, it would be unnecessary, even redundant, to teach the conditions of salvation to those who had already been faithful to God in that respect.

Within the book of Acts we do not find the explicit *command* to openly confess Jesus as Lord as a matter of salvation. However, we do find Paul teaching this as a matter of salvation in his letter to the Romans.

9. that if you confess with your mouth the Lord Jesus and believe in your heart that God raised Him from the dead, you will be saved. 10. For with the heart one believes unto righteousness, and with the mouth confession is made unto salvation. (Romans 10: 9-10)

While the passage drives much discussion, it is difficult to ignore the straightforward character of Paul's words. It seems that God expects from each one of us, as a matter of salvation, open confession before men that we accept Jesus as Savior. This is an act – a word spoken – fashioned after the words of Peter when he proclaimed his belief in Jesus as the Son of God (Matthew 16: 16), also known as the *good confession*. Paul mentions this profession of belief later, in his letter to Timothy, recalling that the young man had made his confession *'in the presence of many witnesses'* (1 Timothy 6: 12). Public confession of Jesus as Lord is also touched upon in other passages (John 12: 42; 1 John 4: 15), but none as explicitly, or as boldly, as Paul's directive to the Romans.

While the word *repentance* appears thirteen times in the epistles, it is considered a matter of a man's initial salvation on only four of these occasions (Romans 2: 4-5; 2 Corinthians 7: 10; 2 Timothy 2: 25; 2 Peter 3: 9). Water baptism is mentioned seventeen times in the epistles. Four of these occasions link baptism directly to forgiveness of sins, newness of life, and salvation (Romans 6: 3-4; Galatians 3: 27; Colossians 2: 12; and 1 Peter 3: 21). Two other verses point to baptism as a matter of unity (1 Corinthians 12: 13; Ephesians 4: 5). Four passages discuss baptism as a matter of cleansing or regeneration without explicit use of the words *baptize* or *baptism* (1 Corinthians 6: 11; Ephesians 5: 26; Titus 3: 5; Hebrews 10: 22). From the apostle Paul we learn about baptism's connection to the crossing of the Red Sea (1 Corinthians 10: 2) and the custom of baptism for the dead (1 Corinthians 15: 29). Certain other instances simply discuss baptism in relation to the various passages already mentioned here.

The abundant teaching in the Pauline and general epistles concerning belief (it appears more than eighty times), as opposed to baptism, which occurs seventeen times, has lead many to suggest that it carries with it greater significance. This is one of the reasons so many men have concluded that belief alone is sufficient for salvation. Of course, belief is the most important precept of all since it is the initial step toward God. Without it no man would repent or be baptized. However, most fail to realize that the majority of instances in the epistles that speak of belief simply use the word *believing* or *believer* as a means of identifying Christians. Only a dozen or so passages actually teach belief as a direct matter of salvation, and even certain of those, such as Galatians 3: 22-27, appear in conjunction with the teaching of baptism. Following are some common examples of the use of *belief, believing*, etc., in the epistles. These are not actually references to salvation. Quite often the writer either uses the word to simply identify Christians or speaks of general belief in God/Christ.

> Therefore tongues are for a sign, not to those who believe but to unbelievers; but prophesying is not for unbelievers but for those who believe. (1 Corinthians 14: 22)

> For to you it has been granted on behalf of Christ, not only to believe in Him, but also to suffer for His sake. (Philippians 1: 29)

> ...so that you became examples to all in Macedonia and Achaia who believe. (1 Thessalonians 1: 7)

> This is a faithful saying, and these things I want you to affirm constantly, that those who have believed in God should be careful to maintain good works. These things are good and profitable to men. (Titus 3: 8)

> Therefore, to you who believe, *He is* precious; but to those who are disobedient... (1 Peter 2: 7)

Faith is the central theme of the epistles with well over one hundred fifty references. Oftentimes faith is defined as the path by which we are justified and, therefore, saved (Romans 5: 1; Galatians 2: 16). Not only are we saved by faith, but we are also told repeatedly that we must live by faith. Indeed, one who does not actively live by faith is not saved by faith (Hebrews 10: 38; James 2: 24).

Those who claim that we are saved at the earliest twinkling of our faith apparently do not fully understand the concept of the faith of Scripture. Faith does not sprout in an instant. Certainly there is an initial moment of awareness when we choose to place our trust in the message of the gospel (Romans 10: 17), but faith involves growth over time (2 Corinthians 10: 15; 2 Thessalonians 1: 3) as our knowledge of and trust in God increases. Faith identifies our *journey* with God (2 Corinthians 5: 7; Colossians 1: 23) rather than the moment of our salvation. That is how the writers of the epistles describe faith to us. By faith we believe that Jesus was crucified for our sins (Romans 10: 14-17). It is by faith in Christ that we repent of our sins (Acts 20: 21) and confess Him as Savior

(Romans 10: 9-11). It is also by faith that the Spirit removes our sins from us in Christian baptism (Colossians 2: 11-12; Titus 3: 5).

The Relationship of Belief, Repentance, and Baptism

Baptism is intimately linked with belief and repentance within the pages of Scripture. In fact, the Bible portrays them as inseparable when it comes to salvation (Mark 16: 16; Acts 2: 38). Those who teach that belief/faith alone is sufficient for salvation refuse to acknowledge the role of baptism in the redemption process. However, numerous passages force us to reject salvation by belief/faith only (2 Thessalonians 1: 8; John 12: 42). In truth, there is so much Scripture to challenge this claim – much of it involving baptism – that it is difficult to see how we can ignore it and still honor God.

Quite often a passage or verse declares openly the redemptive value of baptism (Mark 16: 16; Acts 2: 38; Romans 6: 3-4; Colossians 2: 12; 1 Peter 3: 21). The claim that baptism is not required for salvation ultimately denies that these passages may be taken literally. After all, if baptism is really necessary for salvation, that contradicts what many men consider overwhelming evidence that salvation comes through belief only or faith only. If then, Scripture does state on occasion that those who believe are saved (Acts 10: 43), or that we are saved by faith (Romans 3: 28) while, at the same time, presenting baptism as a matter of salvation, how can such an inconsistency be reconciled? This dilemma can only be resolved by acknowledging the role of baptism in the plan of salvation.

The prospect of an unrepentant Christian in the first century was as foreign to those who penned the words of the epistles in the New Testament as it is to us today. Similarly, anyone who had not confessed Jesus as Lord and Savior would not have been considered saved (Romans 10: 9-10). So it is with baptism. The undeniable understanding of those who wrote the letters of the New Testament was that the *believers* to whom they were writing had been obedient to apostolic instruction concerning *all things* necessary to attain salvation (Romans 6: 3; 1 Corinthians 12: 13; Galatians 3: 27; Colossians 2: 12; 1 Peter 3: 21). When Paul wrote of believers being saved, it was with this in mind. Believers were, to Paul, those who had grieved to the Lord over their sins, confessed Jesus as Savior, and had been baptized in His name.

The apostles taught *the things concerning the kingdom of God'* (Acts 19: 8). Variations of this theme, as noted earlier, can be found throughout Scripture in reference to the gospel message that was preached by the apostles and evangelists. Although we are not told the specifics of each conversion portrayed in the book of Acts, the message must have been very consistent since the results were always the same (Acts 2: 38-41; 8: 12, 35-36; 9: 17-18; 10: 44-48).

In Luke's account of Philip's ministry, he offers us a great deal of insight into the relationship between belief and baptism. One incident involved the Samaritans who, having heard the teaching from Philip about Jesus, believed and were baptized.

> 12. But when they believed Philip as he preached the things concerning the kingdom of God and the name of Jesus Christ, both men and women were baptized. 13. Then Simon himself also believed; and when he was baptized he continued with Philip... (Acts 8: 12-13)

We find no specific mention of repentance as Philip preached the gospel message to the Samaritans. However, we understand from Scripture that this would have been a basic part of the message Philip delivered and that his listeners would have repented in response to that message.

In like manner, we can assume with confidence that those who listened and responded to the gospel message on the Day of Pentecost believed in Jesus as the Messiah. While their belief is not explicitly stated in Scripture, we understand from other passages that, absent their belief, they would not be saved (Mark 16: 16; Romans 10: 9-10). The question that was asked of Peter and the other apostles, *'Men and brethren, what shall we do?'* allows us to simply take their belief for granted.

Interestingly, among the conversion examples in the book of Acts, while we are often left to assume the presence of belief and repentance, we have no need to assume anyone's baptism. In each example of conversion the believer's submission to baptism is openly discussed in the narrative. The only exceptions are the twelve apostles and Apollos (Acts 18: 24-28), both of whom had received the baptism of John the Baptist.

Like repentance, baptism is presented in Scripture as the expected and immediate response of those who believe the gospel message. Note that, when the Samaritans believed, they were baptized. Simon was also baptized when he believed. We are not told that these people opted to be baptized once they were saved, but that the decision to be baptized was the obvious and anticipated outcome of their belief. Luke's phrase, *'when they believed,'* suggests that belief presumably leads to baptism. That is to say, when men believed the gospel message they were baptized. In each detailed account of conversion in the book of Acts, baptism is portrayed, not as an afterthought for the person who had already been converted, but the juncture to which the gospel message directs those who choose to believe.

Lydia was a woman who listened to the gospel and responded (Acts 16: 14-15). In keeping with all other conversions, her immediate response to the message of the gospel, as spoken by one of God's teachers, involved her submission to baptism. The only credible explanation, the *necessary inference*, is that Paul directed her to submit to baptism in his presentation of the gospel. She apparently considered baptism an act of faithfulness to God. She told Paul and his companions that they could judge her faithfulness by her response to their teaching. Narratives such as these provide us with practical examples of the principles of baptism that are discussed more thoroughly in certain other passages of Scripture (Mark 16: 16; Acts 2: 38; 1 Peter 3: 21).

Just as we recognize that the Samaritans would have repented of their sins, even though repentance is not mentioned in the narrative, we can presume that Lydia also repented of her sins and confessed Jesus as Lord as she accepted Him as her Savior. The apostles portray both repentance and confession as vital elements in God's plan of salvation (Acts 2: 38; 3: 19; Romans 10: 9-10). Philip and Paul would have taught nothing less than the full gospel of Christ on these occasions and those who believed would have followed their instructions. This is also true of baptism. Although baptism might not be cited specifically in a passage that teaches belief as a means to salvation, like repentance, the presence of baptism is always couched within the message.

What is apparent in the many accounts of conversion in the New Testament is that, in each case, the initial instruction given by the apostles and other teachers was dependent on the circumstances of the listener. It was unnecessary to explain to the Jews in Jerusalem on the Day of Pentecost that they must first believe since it was clear to the apostles that these people already believed (Acts 2: 37). However, when the Philippian jailer asked Paul what he must do to be saved, Paul's first response was that he must believe in Jesus. Since the jailer did not yet believe, Paul met him at his level and explained what would be the first step on his journey of salvation. That first step was belief. It was not, however, the final instruction the jailer received from Paul. The apostle continued to teach the man until he understood sufficiently so that he could accept Jesus, repent of his sins, and receive baptism for the forgiveness of those sins.

> 1. And it happened, while Apollos was at Corinth, that Paul, having passed through the upper regions, came to Ephesus. And finding some disciples 2. he said to them, "Did you receive the Holy Spirit when you believed?" So they said to him, "We have not so much as heard whether there is a Holy Spirit." 3. And he said to them, "Into what then were you baptized?" So they said, "Into John's baptism." 4. Then Paul said, "John indeed baptized with a baptism of repentance, saying to the people that they should believe on Him who would come after him, that is, on Christ Jesus." 5. When they heard *this,* they were baptized in the name of the Lord Jesus. (Acts 19: 1-5)

In his encounter with certain Ephesian disciples, Paul asked them if they had received the Spirit when they first believed. This question might appear to validate the claim that belief alone is sufficient for salvation, if it were not for the conversation that followed. In the very next verse the passage is very telling as Paul clearly assumes that, if these men believed, they must have been baptized. He did not ask *if* they had been baptized, but *into what* they had been baptized. Paul recognized a direct connection between submission to Christian baptism and receiving the Holy Spirit, a doctrine consistent with the principles of baptismal instruction (Acts 2: 38). Paul's words, indicating an intimate link between belief, baptism, and the Holy Spirit, convey his regard for the role of baptism in God's grand design.

As we noted earlier, it is often taught by men that the third through the fifth chapters of the book of Romans contain the complete gospel message. Interestingly, at no time in that section of Scripture does Paul teach that baptism is critical to salvation – a point upon which the teaching of salvation by *belief only* relies heavily. We find that this is also true of John's proclamation of life through Christ (John 20: 30-31) and Paul's reminder to the Corinthians concerning the gospel he had preached when he was among them (1 Corinthians 15: 1-11). Many men turn to these passages to demonstrate scriptural support for their doctrine of salvation by belief only. It is said that, if baptism was really essential, Paul would have mentioned it in these instances. Yet, we find that repentance is not mentioned in these passages either. Can we equally conclude that repentance is unnecessary? Of course we cannot. We understand from other passages that a man must repent in order to be saved (Acts 2: 38; 3: 19). Therefore, even when repentance is not mentioned, we recognize it as part of the gospel message based on other Scripture. Like baptism, it is implicitly present in relation to belief.

If we are to consider these writings of Paul as *complete* with respect to the gospel message, even though they fail to mention repentance, we must recognize that the belief of which he writes involves considerably more than acknowledgement of, or trust in, Jesus as Lord. Belief, as a response to the gospel, encompasses all that Scripture teaches as essential in our acceptance of Christ.

When addressing the various churches, groups, and individuals in the epistles, at no time did the apostles ever distinguish between believers and *baptized* believers, specifically because they saw no such distinction. All believers were baptized believers just as all believers were repentant believers. The words *believe, believer,* or *belief* refers to those who had been obedient to apostolic instruction concerning the gospel message. Those who were not fully submissive to these teachings were not considered believers. Therefore, these apostles simply identified the acceptance of, and obedience to, the gospel message as *belief,* and those who responded accordingly as *believers.*

Who among the Corinthians remained un-immersed? When Paul wrote about how they were wrongfully identifying themselves with the one who had baptized them (1 Corinthians 1: 1-17), there is no allusion to those who had not been immersed. He also recognized that the Galatians were *'all sons of God through faith,'* because they had been *'baptized into Christ'* (Galatians 3: 26-27). If we can accept that believers addressed by Paul had repented of sins and confessed Jesus as Savior, despite the fact that these are rarely mentioned in conjunction with belief, we can easily presume their baptism. In that case, we can consider belief – obedient belief – as sufficient for salvation.

Paul's Alleged Disclaimer Concerning Baptism

In a hasty reaction to certain comments Paul made in his first letter to the Corinthians, many men claim that his objective was to condemn the Corinthians' overemphasis on water baptism. As they began to wrongly identify their own Christianity with the person who had baptized them, Paul accused the Corinthians of straying from the true gospel message that focused on Jesus as Savior. He did not write to them about the insignificance of baptism, but about the irrelevance of the one who performed the baptism. He expressed relief that he personally had baptized few, thus avoiding claims of baptism in the name of Paul.

> 14. I thank God that I baptized none of you except Crispus and Gaius,
> 15. lest anyone should say that I had baptized in my own name. 16.
> Yes, I also baptized the household of Stephanas. Besides, I do not
> know whether I baptized any other. 17. For Christ did not send me to
> baptize, but to preach the gospel.... (1 Corinthians 1: 14-17)

Paul seems unsure of exactly how many he had baptized in Corinth, and uncertain whether there may have been some he had forgotten (1 Corinthians 1: 14-17). In a life marked by many baptisms in a variety of locations (Acts 16: 15, 33; 19: 5), his failure to remember exactly whom he had baptized at one location is understandable. If Paul had only performed a few baptisms, it is likely he would be able to recall them more clearly.

A number of modern-day teachers take considerable liberty with Paul's statement about his role as a preacher. They say that, in his remark, *'For Christ did not send me to baptize, but to preach the gospel,'* Paul was clearly dismissing baptism as a component of that gospel message. However, this is neither a fair nor honest assessment of Paul's words since the content of the gospel message is not under examination at this time. What Paul is addressing is his role as a preacher/teacher in contrast to his physical participation in baptizing others. In keeping with that theme, his remark simply distinguishes between *baptizing* and *preaching*.

Those who seek to challenge the salvation value of baptism insist that Paul, in this statement to the Corinthians, is contrasting baptism and the gospel. Thus they place the emphases of the statement on the words *baptize* and *gospel*. This leaves us with, 'For Christ did not send me to *baptize*, but to preach the *gospel*.' This approach to the text ignores the point Paul is making. He is not distinguishing between an action (baptism) and a thing (the gospel message), but between two specific actions. In that case, we read, 'For Christ did not send me to *baptize*, but to *preach* the gospel.' Thus he contrasts the *action* of baptizing against the *action* of preaching. Given the context of the statement, this is the most reasonable understanding of the remark. Paul's focus on the insignificance of the person performing the baptism says nothing about the merit of baptism or its relationship to the gospel message he taught. Furthermore, since Scripture fully supports baptism as part of the gospel (Mark 16: 15-16; Acts 2: 38; Romans 6: 1-4; 1 Peter 3: 21), we have no basis for concluding that Paul is setting it aside here.

Paul's point about his assigned role of preaching is a perfect example of an elliptical statement, a form of Greek syntax that is used occasionally in Scripture to stress a significant point. More specifically, the speaker/writer uses the phrase '*ου...αλλα*' (*not...but*), as we find in this passage, to emphasize one matter over another. Paul's remark, *'For Christ did not (ου) send me to baptize, but (αλλα) to preach...'* simply underscores his primary role. This would not prevent Paul from baptizing, which he clearly did, but highlights his role as a teacher. Similar use of the ellipsis can be found in a number of passages in the New Testament.

> Do not labor for the food which perishes, but for the food which endures to everlasting life. (John 6: 27)

> You have not lied to men but to God. (Acts 5: 4)

> Little children, let us not love in word or in tongue, but in deed and in truth. (1 John 3:18)

By suggesting that men *'should not labor for their food,'* Jesus was not suggesting that working for physical food is irrelevant, but was simply stressing the importance of laboring for spiritual food. When Ananias and Sapphira lied to Peter, they had *'not lied to men but to God.'* While they had certainly lied to men, Peter was emphasizing the fact that, in doing so, they also had lied to God. Could John possibly be teaching that we should not love each other *'in word or in tongue?'* He was, of course, promoting the need to love each other in deed and in truth since love expressed in words is revealed in deeds. He had no intention of devaluing the verbal expression of love.

Elliptical statements can provide a powerful message as the writer seemingly overshadows a significant principle (labor for food, lying to men, or loving words) with the one where emphasis is placed. The point is not to discount the importance of the first principle, but to accentuate the second. We can reject the claim that Paul was dismissing baptism as part of the gospel since the elliptical nature of his comment – accenting one element without excluding another – is confirmed by the very fact that Paul baptized many during his ministry. Evidently God did send him to baptize.

Some men also insist that Paul's thankfulness for personally baptizing only a few at Corinth suggests a lesser role for baptism; but this view ignores the explanation Paul himself offers for this statement. He was relieved that the Corinthians could not look to him as their savior simply because he had baptized them. In fact, if Paul was concerned that members might look to him as savior based purely upon his incidental participation in baptism, it seems that both Paul and these Corinthian converts considered this rite to be a key moment in their conversion experience. Therefore, rather than suggesting a fading role for baptism, the passage actually reveals the exceptional relevance placed upon its observance in the early church. A man who regards baptism as trivial is unlikely to be overly impressed with the person performing the rite. To place such great emphasis on that person, baptism itself must have been held in high esteem.

It is evident from the narrative that the Corinthians understood baptism to be a matter of identification or association. Unfortunately, they had linked baptism to identification with other men rather than with Christ. They boasted about being *'of Paul...of Apollos...of Cephas'* as a result of baptism. Pointing to the fact that Christ, not Paul, was crucified for them, he presses the Corinthians to remember that, having been baptized in the name of Christ, they were *of Christ.* They were not baptized in, and could not be saved by, Paul. Thus he assigns his concerns, not to baptism's irrelevance, but to its worth, hoping to avoid claiming for himself the glory that was meant for Christ alone.

The Bible offers no evidence of a change in Paul's teaching on baptism. Had such a transformation taken place it would necessarily have occurred in the period of time that is discussed in Acts 19: 8-10. In the nineteenth chapter of Acts, verses one through seven, Paul met with the men from Ephesus who had received the baptism of John. He in turn baptized those men in the name of Jesus. Following this incident Paul remained in Ephesus for a while.

Over a period of somewhere between two and three years Paul remained in Ephesus teaching in the synagogue and in the school of Tyrannus. Scholars agree that he wrote his first letter to the Corinthians near the end of his time there. As we have noted, it is his statements in the first chapter of 1 Corinthians that are most often quoted to suggest a diminishing role for water baptism. Yet Luke offers nothing in his narrative that would give us reason to believe Paul's message was altered in any way. On the contrary, we find that *'...this continued for two years'* (Acts 19: 10) arguably indicating that his message remained consistent. A reading of the entire nineteenth chapter of Acts will provide many of the details of Paul's stay in Ephesus. No change of doctrine and no declining role for water baptism are indicated. His teaching *continued* throughout his ministry.

Paul's role in the early church must be given full consideration. His chief responsibilities, as revealed throughout the epistles, involved teaching the unsaved while enriching the lives of those who were already converted to Christ through praise and discipline. When he explained to the Corinthians that God did not send him to baptize (1 Corinthians 1: 17), it is most reasonable to conclude that, while Paul certainly baptized many believers, physically baptizing new converts was not the primary task to which God had set his hand. Others could baptize, but few could teach in the bold and persuasive manner for which Paul was known. His was a role of instruction. In the twelfth chapter of this same letter to the Corinthians, Paul told these very same people that different Christians performed different functions within the body of Christ. Scripture reveals, however, that Paul continued to teach the significance of water baptism consistently through the end of his ministry.

Scholars estimate that Paul wrote the book of 1 Corinthians around AD 55, toward the end of his ministry in Ephesus, as previously noted. He also penned numerous other passages on the subject of baptism at various times throughout his ministry. For instance, his letter to the Romans was written in or around AD 57. Colossians is dated approximately AD 60 and he wrote to Titus in AD 63.

3. Or do you not know that as many of us as were baptized into Christ Jesus were baptized into His death? 4. Therefore we were buried with Him through baptism into death, that just as Christ was raised from the

dead by the glory of the Father, even so we also should walk in newness of life. (Romans 6: 3-4)

11. In Him you were also circumcised with the circumcision made without hands, by putting off the body of the sins of the flesh, by the circumcision of Christ, 12. buried with Him in baptism, in which you were also raised with *Him* through faith in the working of God, who raised him from the dead. (Colossians 2: 11-12)

4. But when the kindness and the love of God our Savior toward man appeared, 5. not by works of righteousness which we have done, but according to His mercy He saved us, through the washing of regeneration and renewing of the Holy Spirit. (Titus 3: 4-5)

The passages cited from Romans and Colossians, which were written years after the book of 1 Corinthians, reveal a man who positively believed baptism to be a critical step in our walk with God. In his letter to Titus, Paul wrote about a cleansing (washing) that involves regeneration and renewal by or through the Holy Spirit. The word translated *washing* in this instance is the Greek word *loutrou* (λουτρου), which literally means *bath*.[1] Given the New Testament teaching identifying water baptism as the moment of rebirth (John 3: 5; Acts 2: 38; 1 Corinthians 6: 11), this *washing* should be seen as water baptism as Paul again ties together washing (with water) and the Holy Spirit, much as Peter did on the Day of Pentecost. This view is reinforced by Paul's comments to the Romans as he explained that the moment of burial and resurrection in baptism is when we begin life anew. His view of baptism throughout his ministry is amazingly consistent.

In Luke's account of Paul's journeys in the book of Acts, we find that he encountered the Jews in Jerusalem in or around AD 58. As he reflected upon his own conversion, Paul described, from personal experience, the direct relationship between baptism and forgiveness of sins. He understood from Ananias' instructions that baptism was the time God forgave him of his sins (Acts 22: 16).

No passage in the Bible that reflects the life and teachings of Paul, whether written before or after 1 Corinthians, suggests that he ever regarded water baptism as unnecessary for the forgiveness of sins. Given the support found in Scripture for the importance of baptism, it is difficult to understand how the debate has reached such an elevated level.

Paul's View of the Relationship Between Baptism and Faith

It is generally believed that Paul's letter to the Galatians was written about the time he wrote 1 Corinthians, although it could arguably be dated earlier. Since many evangelicals today insist that Paul, at some point in time, changed his position on baptism's significance, and since Galatians *may* have been written early in Paul's ministry, the book is not really a suitable tool to combat the misconceptions about Paul's statements to the Corinthians. Nevertheless, his writing here does offer us a pretty clear view of Paul's perspective on baptism:

> 21. *Is* the law then against the promises of God? Certainly not! For if there had been a law given which could have given life, truly righteousness would have been by the law. 22. But the Scripture has confined all under sin, that the promise of faith in Jesus Christ might be given to those who believe. 23. But before faith came, we were kept under guard by the law, kept for the faith which would afterward be revealed. 24. Therefore the law was our tutor *to bring us* to Christ, that we might be justified by faith. 25. But after faith has come, we are no longer under a tutor. 26. For you are all sons of God through faith in Christ Jesus. 27. For as many of you as were baptized into Christ have put on Christ. 28. There is neither Jew nor Greek, there is neither slave nor free, there is neither male nor female; for you are all one in Christ Jesus. 29. And if you *are* Christ's, then you are Abraham's seed, and heirs according to the promise. (Galatians 3: 21-29)

Paul places a great deal of emphasis on baptism in this passage even though it is faith that is recognized as the means of justification. While modern men try to isolate baptism from faith, Paul does not. Instead, he thoughtfully binds them together. Baptism is relevant, according to Paul, even in the presence of faith. We learn that prior to faith men were kept under guard by the law. However, when it comes to faith, baptism is a vital part of God's plan.

Noting that we are baptized into (the body of) Christ, Paul saw baptism as a passageway through which a person could find his/her way into Christ. Actually, rather than portraying baptism as merely *a* passageway, Paul states that it is *the* passageway to Christ. He points out that *putting on* Christ is limited to *'as many of you as were baptized',* (Galatians 3: 27). In a message where faith is the focus, recognizing that the law was a thing of the past, Paul is firm in his presentation of baptism as a step *into* Christ.

Having explained that we are justified by faith (vs. 23-26), Paul begins verse twenty-seven with an interesting word. It is the word *for*, which is translated from the Greek word *gar* ($\gamma\alpha\rho$). According to <u>Strong's Exhaustive Concordance of the Bible</u> this word *assigns a reason*[2] to the statement(s) made. Note the careful manner in which Paul designed his remarks: *'But before faith came, we were kept under guard by the law...Therefore the law was our tutor to bring us to Christ...But after faith has come, we are no longer under a tutor. For (the reason is) you are all sons of God through faith in Christ Jesus. For (the reason is) as many of you as were baptized into Christ have put on Christ.'*

It is extremely difficult to miss the apostle's point if we consider his words honestly since the bond he establishes between baptism and our relationship with God is unmistakable. According to Paul, the reason we have been justified *by* faith (v. 24) and are no longer under a tutor (v. 25) is that we are sons of God *through* faith (v. 26). The reason we are deemed to be sons of God *through* faith is that we, having been baptized *into* Christ, have *put on* Christ (v. 27).

While Scripture always supports itself, God only needs to identify an element's salvation value once for it to be true. Consequently, if we are told in Scripture that we must repent to be saved (Acts 2: 38; 3: 19), then we must humble ourselves and repent. While confession is mentioned only briefly as a matter of salvation (Romans 10: 9-10; 1 Timothy 6: 12), we must still recognize that, *'with the mouth confession is made unto salvation'* (Romans 10: 10). Therefore, since baptism is identified as an essential ingredient of the gospel message and a condition of salvation (Mark 16: 16; Acts 2: 38; 1 Peter 3: 21), who are we to argue? If we are to accept Scripture as God's message to mankind, we must embrace baptism as part of the gospel message.

NOTES FOR CHAPTER 6

1. *Loutron, on, to, (louw)*, ...a bathing, bath...used in the N.T. and in eccles. writ. of baptism. <u>Thayer's Greek-English Lexicon of the New Testament</u>, p. 382, 1977, Baker Books House.

2. James Strong, LL.D., S.T.D., The New Strong's Exhaustive Concordance of the Bible, Greek Dictionary of the New Testament, p. 20, 1990, Thomas Nelson Publishers.

Chapter VII

What Is the Purpose of Water Baptism?

Men hold a variety of views about the reasons for baptism. Some believe that the value of baptism is purely ornamental and that its only real benefit lies in the witness to others that a man has made a commitment to Jesus. Others believe that baptism does have a greater purpose than simply its outward appearance since it is a command of God. Baptism to them is an act of submission to God's will. Still others teach that the function of baptism goes well beyond the more obvious activities of witness and obedience. For these people baptism is a spiritual act that offers spiritual blessings. Those who respect the promises that are associated with baptism understand that it is at the time of immersion that one's sins are forgiven. According to this view, baptism actually has salvation value since, according to Scripture, no one may be saved without first being holy (1 Corinthians 3: 17; Hebrews 12: 14) and no one may be holy without first having his/her sins cleansed by Christ's blood (Colossians 2: 11-12; Hebrews 10: 22).

Baptism as an Outward Sign of an Inward Change

A favorite saying among those who deny the salvation value of baptism is this – *baptism is an outward sign of an inward change* – a phrase made popular by John Wesley[1] and others. Of course, no reasonable person can dispute the fact that there is an obvious physical aspect to baptism. However, the Bible does not portray it as an outward sign whose worth is limited to its physical nature. When the Bible does address the purpose of baptism, its value is *never* confined to its physical characteristics. Admittedly, it is one facet of a person's faithfulness to which we can attest since men are able to witness baptism, but that is not its primary role as defined in God's Word.

> Then Peter said to them, "Repent, and let every one of you be baptized in the name of Jesus Christ for the remission of sins; and you shall receive the gift of the Holy Spirit." (Acts 2: 38)

> And now why are you waiting? Arise and be baptized, and wash away your sins, calling on the name of the Lord. (Acts 22: 16)

Or do you not know that as many of us as were baptized into Christ Jesus were baptized into His death? (Romans 6: 3)

For as many of you as were baptized into Christ have put on Christ. (Galatians 3: 27)

There is also an antitype which now saves us - baptism... (1 Peter 3: 21)

The truth is no passage of Scripture teaches that the early church practiced baptism as an outward sign of conversion. Despite the modern view that baptism is a sign of the covenant of grace, the word *sign* is never applied to baptism by Jesus or the apostles.

The Efficacy of Baptism

Since the time of the Reformation Movement in the sixteenth century, men have taught boldly that the rite of Christian baptism has no real force. It is said that the changes that take place in a man's relationship with God occur prior to his immersion in water. It has even been proposed that, unless one *has been redeemed,* he/she cannot legitimately submit to baptism. Our participation in the rite of baptism is simply considered obedience to a command of God whose role is to provide testimony to others of the change that has already taken place within us. This, however, is not the manner in which baptism is presented to us in Scripture.

In the normal course of events, men tend to confess Jesus as Lord and submit to immersion in water before a number of witnesses (Acts 2: 41; 1 Timothy 6: 12). However, that is not always true. In the case of Paul, or the Ethiopian eunuch, or even the Philippian jailer, baptism was administered rather privately. Apparently no other believers were present when Philip baptized the eunuch. He confessed his belief to Philip alone (Acts 8: 37). Just as Peter told the crowd on the Day of Pentecost, Ananias instructed Paul to be baptized in order to have his sins washed away. These men submitted to baptism immediately. They did not wait for a group to congregate. The immediacy with which baptism was administered in the early church suggests that its more significant value can be found in its effect on the person's relationship with God. Even the baptism offered by John the Baptist prior to Christ's death was considered much more than a mere exhibition of personal commitment. It was joined with repentance *'for the forgiveness of sins'* (Luke 3: 3)

As we consider the biblical uses of the word *baptize*, something significant stands out. Baptism is efficacious. That is to say, the thing or person being baptized is altered *during* baptism. This is true whether the subject is Christian baptism or any of a variety of other baptisms that are mentioned in God's Word. Indeed, a distinguishing feature of baptism is that it changes the person or thing that is being baptized. According to Strong's Concordance, '*baptising...results in permanent change.*'[2]

Numerous incidents in Scripture are identified as baptism. Peter explained that baptism should be associated with the flood of Noah's day (1 Peter 3: 21). In his depiction of the relationship between the two, the apostle indicates that the waters of the flood are reflected in the waters of baptism. God destroyed the world via the flood. Water was God's *agent* of destruction and its power was realized as evil men of the world were destroyed *in the water*. It was a baptism of the earth that *resulted* in permanent change. This change did not take place prior to, but at the time of the flood.

Paul taught the Corinthians that baptism could also be pictured in the crossing of the Red Sea. He explained that the Israelites had been '*baptized into Moses*' (1 Corinthians 10: 2) at that time. Like the flood, this baptism was also effective as the evil of the Egyptians was destroyed *in the water*. The episode exhibits two noticeable characteristics of Christian baptism: first, the Israelites crossed *through* the sea (on dry land), exiting the other side where they would begin a *new life*; and second, the threat from the world they had known was overcome *in the sea* as they left their life of slavery behind them. While some may suggest that Pharaoh had actually freed the Israelites prior to the incident at the Red Sea, there is a considerable difference between Pharaoh's proclamation, which meant nothing, and the actions of God as the Israelites were baptized into Moses. Their freedom was realized in the sea.

Baptism with the Holy Spirit is a challenging subject. Many believe this experience was limited to the early church while others insist that Christians of every age and time must realize baptism with the Spirit in some form. While the definition of baptism with the Spirit is one that divides many men, everyone appreciates the fact that a spiritual change takes place at that time. Who would deny that this baptism, at the very least, identifies the *moment* that a man receives the Holy Spirit in some manner? It is a time of change. Men do not receive the Spirit prior to, but *at the time of,* baptism with the Spirit. The man who has experienced baptism with the Spirit is not the same as he was prior to that moment of encounter.

As Jesus considered the path He knew He must take, He questioned whether His disciples could endure the *baptism* He Himself faced (Mark 10: 38). Jesus was, of course, contemplating the death, burial, and resurrection He would experience in order to save mankind. It was the sacrifice He must make. This, too, was a baptism filled with power. Indeed, this should be considered the most powerful, most life-altering baptism of Scripture. It is the baptism (death, burial, and resurrection) of Christ that provides worth to Christian baptism (1 Peter 3: 21). It was a baptism that resulted not in mere change, but in the establishment of an entirely new covenant – the covenant of grace.

Change takes place *during* baptism. That is a constant principle of baptism, whether it is the rite of Christian baptism in water or any other baptism mentioned in Scripture. Baptism always results in some kind of transformation. Men of earth remained evil until the waters of the flood arrived. The Israelites were not free of their former life until their enemies were overcome in the waters of the sea. Men could not be saved by the blood of Christ prior to His experiencing the baptism of which He spoke. It was specifically *through* His baptism of sacrifice that the opportunity of *life* came to men.

Whether it was the purification of the baptism performed by John the Baptist (John 3: 25), or the ritual baptisms of the Pharisees as they attempted to purify themselves from the defilement they experienced from being among Gentiles in the marketplace (Mark 7: 4), the understanding has always been that change (cleansing) would occur during baptism.

The Purpose of John's Baptism

The groundwork for Christian baptism, which is seen in the ministry of John the Baptist, provides us with a better understanding of the effects of this ceremony. Luke's narrative reveals that forgiveness of sins was closely linked to the repentance and baptism over which John presided. We can gain a better appreciation for the power of John's baptism by reviewing a conversation he had with his disciples concerning purification.

25. Then there arose a dispute between *some* of John's disciples and the Jews about purification (καθαριμος). 26. And they came to John and

said to him, "Rabbi, He who was with you beyond the Jordan, to whom you have testified—behold, He is baptizing (βαπτίζει), and all are coming to Him!" (John 3: 25-26)

It is not surprising that the subject of purification would focus on baptism for these men of Jewish descent. In Old Testament Israel, purification was often associated with the various ritual cleansings that were commanded by God in the first covenant (Numbers 8: 7, 21; 19: 9; 31: 23; Ezra 6: 20). The view that water baptism was an instrument for purification was clear to these men since God's use of water for religious cleansing was well known. Indeed, Scripture teaches, in the various passages where John's baptism is discussed, that it was for the forgiveness of sin – a baptism providing purification (Mark 1: 4; Luke 3: 3).

Beyond the obvious feature of obedience (Luke 7: 29-30), purification (forgiveness) seems to be the primary function of the baptism of repentance offered by John. The numerous promises allied with Christian baptism, such as membership in the body of Christ, were simply not available during the time John was baptizing.

Christian Baptism for the Forgiveness of Sins

It was through the work of the apostles that Christian baptism was first introduced. While there are undeniable similarities between the baptism of John and Christian baptism, some very pronounced differences do stand out. The distinctions between the two were announced on the Day of Pentecost. As people gathered together in Jerusalem to celebrate Pentecost (Feast of Weeks), the account provides Peter's answer in response to the question, *'Men and brethren, what shall we do?'*

Then Peter said to them, "Repent, and let every one of you be baptized in the name of Jesus Christ for the remission of sins; and you shall receive the gift of the Holy Spirit." (Acts 2: 38)

As with John's ministry, repentance and baptism are closely associated on the Day of Pentecost. These two acts are joined at the hip, leading the believer toward forgiveness of sin and a new relationship with Jesus Christ. Christian baptism, like the baptism performed by John, continued to provide forgiveness of sins, but the basis for baptism along with the promises associated with it appear to have been expanded. The converts in the book of Acts were baptized *'in the name of Jesus'* and promised the *'gift of the Holy Spirit.'* Scripture does not mention John's baptism being performed in a specific name; nor was the Holy Spirit promised as a result of baptism prior to Pentecost as Peter proclaimed on that day.

During the ministry of John the Baptist, God's new covenant - which was established through the death, burial, and resurrection of Jesus - was not complete and the Holy Spirit had not yet presented Himself to men. On the Day of Pentecost, His indwelling presence was made available to those who were willing to repent of their sins and be baptized. The Day of Pentecost must be viewed from a proper perspective. It was intended as a critical juncture in man's relationship with God – a day when the new covenant of grace was instituted, offering men the promise of true and permanent cleansing from sins committed.

Despite the frankness of Peter's words, two primary trains of thought are offered to counter the apostle's teaching of baptism as a matter of forgiveness that is presented in this verse (Acts 2: 38). The first argument is that the promises of forgiveness and the gift of the Holy Spirit (in the Greek text) refer only to the command to *repent.* This view is based on the fact that *repent* and *you shall receive* are each written in second person plural while *be baptized* appears in third person singular form. This shift, however, is simply intended to personalize submission to baptism. It is a method found occasionally in the New Testament that is intended to stress personal responsibility (Acts 3: 26; 11: 29-30; 1 Corinthians 7: 24; Revelation 20: 13). The fact that Greek scholars recognize that forgiveness is joined to both repentance and baptism in this verse should settle the issue.[3]

Concern over the link between baptism and forgiveness that this verse offers has led many men to argue that Peter's words have actually come to us broken and in need of mending. Their answer is to focus on the singular-plural blend found within Peter's statement. In essence, their solution is to surgically fracture the verse, ever so gently, and reset it so that it reflects the meaning they believe the apostle *intended* to convey, despite what he actually said. Having treated the statement to heal according to their own beliefs, we now find men teaching the more modern version illustrated as follows:

Then Peter said to them, "Repent (and let every one of you be baptized in the name of Jesus Christ) for the remission of sins; and you shall receive the gift of the Holy Spirit."

The restated text depicted here, which shows the command to be baptized as a side comment, is essentially what evangelicals teach today concerning this verse. Of course, the transformed reading conveys a far different message than the original Spirit-breathed version. That being the case, perhaps we should consider closely the consequences of rewriting Scripture to validate our own beliefs.

The basis for this approach to Acts 2: 38 is the assumption that Peter actually intended to separate baptism from the receiving of forgiveness. If that was Peter's goal he has disguised it well. In this critical passage that was inspired by the Holy Spirit and designed to lead men to eternal life, it is difficult to imagine Peter unintentionally distorting a key element of the message. Yet men insist that he was presenting repentance alone as the means to forgiveness while portraying baptism as a minor ceremony performed after the fact. This is not merely a strained interpretation, but a serious mishandling of the text.

In truth, Peter's words openly reject the position stated above as he establishes a solid bond between baptism and forgiveness. The fact that he meant to include baptism as an element of forgiveness is confirmed in his first epistle where he states that *baptism saves* (1 Peter 3: 21). That is the sum and substance of his portrayal of baptism in this sermon on the Day of Pentecost. The foundation of Scripture upon which Acts 2: 38 is built fully supports Peter's command that these men and women should repent and be baptized in pursuit of forgiveness.

Criticism of Peter's portrayal of baptism on this day continues with a focus on the prepositional phrase, *for the remission of sins,* with specific emphasis on the word $\varepsilon\iota\varsigma$ (*eis*), which is pronounced *ice* and is translated in this passage as *for*. Claiming that $\varepsilon\iota\varsigma$ could be interpreted *because of* or *with respect to,* many insist that baptism is not performed for the *outcome* of forgiveness, but is practiced *as a result of* forgiveness that has already occurred. If that is the case, however, Peter was telling the crowd that they must also *repent* because they had already received forgiveness. This view places forgiveness ahead of repentance when, in reality, repentance always precedes forgiveness – a formula that is taught consistently within the pages of Scripture (Luke 3: 3; 17: 3; 24: 47; Mark 1: 4; Acts 3: 19; 5: 31; 2 Peter 3: 9). Of course, some men teach that forgiveness occurs somewhere between repentance and baptism, but that is not the way it is depicted here. The commands to *repent* and *be baptized*, in this passage, both fall squarely ahead of the receiving of forgiveness.

A great deal of confusion is created by those who maintain that one need not be *'baptized for the remission of sins.'* Much time and energy has been spent as men attempt to deny what is spoken plainly in Acts 2: 38. Since it lies at the heart of the debate over the need for baptism, a thorough examination of the translation of the word εις is very important.

1519 εις ice – a primary preposition; to or into (indicating the point reached or entered), of place, time, or (figuratively) purpose (result, etc.); also in adverbial phrases:--(abundant-)ly, against, among, as, at, (back-) ward, before, by, concerning, + continual, + far more exceeding, for (intent, purpose), fore, + forth, in (among, at, unto, -so much that, -to), to the intent that, + of one mind, + never, of, (up-)on, + perish, + set at one again, (so) that, therefore(-unto), throughout, til, to (be, the end, -ward), (here-)until(-to), ...ward, (where-)fore, with. Often used in composition with the same general import, but only with verbs (etc.) expressing motion (literally or figuratively).[4]

1519 εις, Prep governing the Accusative, and denoting entrance into, or direction and limit: in, to, towards, *for, among.*[5]

The meaning of the word εις throughout the Bible, as with the word *for* in the English language, is largely dependent upon the context in which it is used. The word appears more than 1,750 times in the New Testament. In most of these cases it holds the meaning *to* or *into* while referencing a time or place. Of course, there are obviously instances when it is translated into various other words, such as *for.* Quite often when this occurs the meaning can be most closely associated with the definition of *purpose.* Occasionally, however, the text does suggest another meaning.

For what does the Scripture say? *"Abraham believed God, and it was counted to him for (εις) righteousness."* (Romans 4: 3)

Paul, explaining to the church in Rome the futility of seeking salvation through deeds of merit, portrayed Abraham as *being in a state of* righteousness as his belief was credited to him. This passage is probably not the best example, however, since we understand that Abraham's belief *led to* righteousness, thus supporting the position that baptism *leads to* forgiveness.

Those who argue that εις may be interpreted *because of* in Acts 2: 38 claim to find support for that view in the following words spoken by Jesus:

> The men of Nineveh will rise up in the judgment with this generation and condemn it, because they repented *at* (εις) the preaching of Jonah... (Matthew 12: 41).

Reading that the people of Nineveh repented *at* (*in response to* or *because of*) Jonah's preaching that had already taken place seems to offer an opportunity for men to declare that we are baptized in response to forgiveness that has already taken place in Acts 2: 38. It should equally be noted, however, that the repentance of the Ninevites, while it was certainly in response to Jonah's preaching, was done *with a view to* his message and/or brought them *into* compliance with that message. This is the view many Greek scholars prefer.[6] Still the translation *because of the preaching of Jonah* seems to fit the context well enough that we should consider its possible impact on the purpose of baptism proposed by Peter.

While this treatment (Matthew 12: 41) of the word εις can be found, it is extremely scarce not only in Scripture, but also in Greek literature generally, and is considerably less common than those times when the meaning of *purpose* is clearly intended. Nonetheless, the word appearing infrequently in this form still does not resolve the argument for or against this meaning in Acts 2: 38. Given this fact, we must determine Peter's intent on the Day of Pentecost based upon the context of the passage and the apostle's choice of words.

Interestingly, a significant characteristic can be found in Peter's sermon that plainly separates his use of εις from passages like this one from Matthew. In this instance, Peter uses the imperative commands for the people to *repent* and *be baptized.* While the word εις may be translated with various meanings depending upon the context, we know that this setting involves directives, in the form of imperatives, from Peter as he sought a decision from the crowd. That fact demands the translation of *purpose* and is the very thing that distinguishes this statement from others. In fact, if the translation, *because your sins have been forgiven,* was legitimate, given the imperative statements involved, it would apparently be the single instance in the whole of Greek literature where this was the case. The ειϛ spoken by Jesus in Matthew 12: 41 is simply not comparable to the ειϛ found in Acts 2: 38. The vain attempts to equate the two stem from a refusal to accept scriptural teaching concerning baptism.

In the first chapter of Mark, Jesus encountered a leper as He traveled in Galilee. The man begged Jesus to heal him, which Jesus did willingly. This is a very telling episode since, once healed, Jesus provided the man with some instruction.

> And saith unto him, See thou say nothing to any man: but go thy way, shew thyself to the priest, and offer for (περι) thy cleansing those things which Moses commanded, for (ειϛ) a testimony unto them. (Mark 1:44 - KJV)

As on the Day of Pentecost, in this passage ειϛ follows an imperative as Jesus directed the man to *go* to the priests and make an offering according to the law. What makes this incident so appealing is the fact that the man was told to go to the priests and *offer* (imperative) *for* (in response to) a healing that had already taken place. The problem for those who claim that baptism is offered for forgiveness that has already been received is that the word here translated *for* is not the word ειϛ, but rather the word *peri (περι).* Even more challenging is the realization that the healed man was to make this offering *for* (ειϛ), or *for the purpose of,* a testimony to the priests. This is the effect an imperative has on the meaning of the word ειϛ.

If we are to gain understanding from Acts 2: 38, we must give honest consideration to the context of Peter's words. He was responding to the Israelites' question regarding what they must *do* in order to alter their current condition. Had these Israelites, standing before Peter, already attained a state of righteousness, Peter surely would have responded by telling them that nothing was required of them. Such was not the case, however. A specific response was necessary for them to be forgiven so that God might view them as holy.

> For this is My blood of the new covenant, which is shed for many for (ειϛ) the remission of sins. (Matthew 26: 28)

Jesus told His disciples that His blood was to be shed *'for the remission of sins.'* Supporting passages throughout Scripture (Ephesians 1: 7; Colossians 1: 13-14) offer undeniable evidence that the phrase *'for the remission of sins'* in this setting suggests *purpose.* Jesus indicated that He would *do* something (shed His blood), and that the *goal* of that action was to provide forgiveness of sins. The meaning *because* is simply inapplicable or Jesus would have shed His blood *because men had been forgiven.*

Among believers there is no real dispute with respect to Matthew 26: 28. Most men agree that the phrase *'for the remission of sins,'* as it is written here, speaks to the *effect* of the shedding of Jesus' blood. In like manner, John the Baptist offered *'a baptism of repentance for remission of sins'* (Mark 1: 4; Luke 3: 3). The only reasonable conclusion is that this combination of repentance and baptism was also intended to bring about remission of sins. The same phrase used by Jesus, *εις αφεσιν αμαρτιων*, which defined the shedding of His blood for the forgiveness of sins, is found in connection with the baptism and repentance associated with John the Baptist. In each instance, action was taking place where forgiveness of sins was the intended outcome.

In Acts 2: 38, the only reasonable understanding of the word *εις* is *for the purpose of* (or *with a view to).* As with the texts from Matthew 26: 28, Mark 1: 4, and Luke 3: 3, the context demands this meaning. The statement made by Peter on the Day of Pentecost, while inserting terms that personalize baptism and forgiveness, is the exact same terminology found in each of the other passages. If Jesus' death was meant to affect forgiveness (Matthew 26: 28) so, too, are the repentance and baptism discussed in Mark 1: 4 and Acts 2: 38. The people on that day were to repent and be baptized with remission of their sins in view.

Had Peter *intended* to teach that the men and women on the Day of Pentecost should be baptized *because they had received* forgiveness of sins, he had a much better option than the word *εις*. He had available to him the word in *περι* (Mark 1: 44). This would have portrayed participation in baptism as a *response to* forgiveness received rather than the means to receive that forgiveness. There can be no question that this rite of baptism was presented to those in the early church as the path necessary to receive forgiveness of sins.

What is so fascinating about the controversy over the meaning *because of* in Acts 2: 38 is the fact that translator error is not alleged in any other passage of Scripture where this word is used. This suggests that out of nearly 1,800 instances where εις appears in the New Testament, the translators got it right – save one. In fact, challengers to the translation of *for* in Peter's sermon often point to the accuracy of those instances where a different meaning is understood (e.g., Matthew 12: 41) in an effort to persuade us that, in this passage, it is wrongfully translated. Yet, if εις is misinterpreted in Acts 2: 38, what can we say about the reliability of the nearly 1,800 other times when it is used in the New Testament (e.g. Matthew 12: 41)? Even more unsettling is the fact that the challenge to the translation of *for* (purpose) in this case is not built on a foundation of linguistics or Greek scholarship, but on theological exception to God's Word. Therefore, if we can trust that εις is translated correctly in all other passages, regardless of what that translation might be, we should equally trust the translation, *for the remission of sins.*

Peter fully rejects forgiveness of sins (and salvation) prior to repentance and baptism on the Day of Pentecost. He concludes his sermon in verse forty with a call to salvation, appealing to the crowd to *'Be saved...'* or, as it is stated in the NIV, *'Save yourselves from this corrupt generation.'* Of course, Peter was not proposing that they had the capacity to actually save themselves from sin. Yet as long as they stood guilty of Jesus' death, the very crime (sin) of which Peter had just accused them, they would remain lost. They could, however, choose to be obedient to the commands given by Peter, leading to their salvation. In that sense the decision as to whether or not they would be saved ultimately rested upon the shoulders of each man and woman.

Some men claim that the word *saved,* in this instance (v. 40), could hold one of a variety of meanings – perhaps *healing* or *deliverance* - but the truth is that this is an obvious call to salvation. Peter did not close his sermon with a scant one-sentence plea for salvation. His entire address focused upon the decision his listeners faced. We are told that, *'With many other words he testified and exhorted them, saying, "Be saved..."'* encouraging them to choose in favor of salvation. After all, this is the Day of Pentecost. This is the day salvation has come to earth. To suggest that *saved* holds any meaning other than spiritual salvation, when this has been the sum and substance of his entire message, does great injustice to the text. Peter's plea, spoken on the heels of his command to repent and be baptized, is for his listeners to decide in favor of salvation.

Through the centuries it is very significant that interpreters have been ever consistent in their translation of the word εις in this passage. The relationship established in Acts 2: 38 is one of cause and effect. Repentance and baptism *resulted in* forgiveness of sins. We have further support for this treatment of εις from scholars around the world . Over the pages of time the Bible has been translated into numerous languages. In every language and translation the interpreters have been remarkably consistent with this passage. A review of the word εις as it has been translated into various languages in the context of Acts 2: 38, reveals uniform handling of this word by translators in various parts of the world.

Language	Trans.	Definition
French	pour	/pur/ prep **(a)** (in order) to; ~ **faire** to do; in order to do; **pour ne pas faire** so as not to do; **c'etait ~ rire** or **plaisanter** it was a joke; ~ **que** so that; ~ **ainsi dire** so to speak[7]
Latin	in	prep. (1) with acc., *into on to, towards, against,* of time, *until;* in omne tempus, *for ever;* in diem vivere, *to live for the moment.* **of tendency or purpose,** *for;* in adverbial phrases, indicating manner or extent: in universum, *in general;* in vicem, in vices, *in turn.*[8]
Polish	na	prep. –2. [czas, termin] for[9]
Portugese	para	[para] prep –2. [indica motivo, objectivo] (in order) to; **cheguei mais cedo ~ aranjar lugar** I arrived early (in order) to get a seat.[10]
Russian	для	*prep+gen* for; for the sake of; …in order to[11]
Spanish	para	prep. 1 : for 2 HACIA : towards 3 : (in order) to[12]

Scripture itself, however, effectively counters the suggestion that the word εις might be translated *because your sins have been forgiven* in Acts 2: 38. In fact, we need not travel far to determine the meaning of εις in this context. One day, as Peter and John approached the temple, a man who had been lame his entire life asked them for money. Rather than giving him money, Peter reached out and lifted the man to his feet, healing him on the spot. As people gathered in reaction to this miracle, Peter began to preach. The following excerpt is taken from Peter's sermon on that day:

> Repent therefore and be converted, that (*eij*) your sins may be blotted out... (Acts 3: 19).

Once again, $\varepsilon\iota\varsigma$ is used in connection with forgiveness of sins, although some Greek texts use $\pi\rho o\varsigma$ (*hopos*) in its place. Yet, in this setting, the argument that repentance and conversion take place *because of prior forgiveness* is not offered, not because the circumstances are different, but because this passage does not encroach upon a specific belief about baptism. Repentance and conversion affect forgiveness of sins in this setting. The text as well as the context leave no other options and provide us with undeniable confirmation that forgiveness comes *as a result of* obedience to the commands given. Peter's words allow no alternative translation. If, in Acts 3: 19, forgiveness is defined as the outcome of obedience, it must be that this is also true in Peter's first sermon (Acts 2: 38). Peter was telling the crowd to repent and be baptized with their eyes fixed on the goal of forgiveness.

It may actually be a bit misleading to suggest that we repent *in order to receive forgiveness* – a point we should address before continuing. It is true, of course, that forgiveness does not come without repentance (Acts 3: 19) and, therefore, forgiveness always follows repentance; but repentance for our sins is more like the pain of separation we experience with the death of a loved one. Repentance before God arises out of our regret when we realize that we have separated ourselves from God via our own sins. It is not a matter of presuming that God will forgive *because* we have repented, but repenting *because* we realize we have wronged Him.

This is what we saw in King David. He repented, not because he thought this was the only way to forgiveness, but because he realized that his own actions had saddened God. David was sorrowful because of his awareness that he had separated himself from God. This painful knowledge was the source of his repentance. In this sense, if our motive behind repentance is to simply *seek* forgiveness, we have an unfortunate misunderstanding of the repentance of Scripture. True repentance comes only when we humble ourselves before God *because* we are distressed over the realization that our sins have grieved Him. The heartache we experience from our recognition that we have caused God pain must be the source of *our* repentance. If this is not the motivating force then we dare not call it repentance. While God's Word does tell us that remission of sins is not possible without repentance, if we do not *honestly* repent we should not anticipate forgiveness.

Accepting responsibility when we have wronged someone, coupled with our sorrow for what we have done, is not quite the same as asking forgiveness. It is true that the two walk hand in hand, but unless we truly repent, asking for forgiveness would be meaningless. First then, we repent and turn from what we have done. Only when we have honestly repented are we in a position to actually ask forgiveness. In fact, what man, having refused to repent, would even expect to be forgiven?

As we consider the teaching about repentance and baptism in Acts 2: 38, it is significant to note that we do not repent *in Jesus' name* (or in the name of the Father, Son, and Holy Spirit as in Matthew 28: 19). Yet, quite often we are taught to *be baptized* in the name of Jesus (Acts 8: 16; 10: 48; 19: 5; 1 Corinthians 1: 13; Galatians 3: 27). That fact helps us to understand that it is specifically baptism *in Jesus' name* that is performed in order to receive forgiveness. Repentance simply sets the stage for forgiveness. Like belief, repentance is necessary for one to qualify for baptism. First Peter told the crowd to *repent* of their sins. He then commanded that each one should *'be baptized in the name of Jesus Christ for (with a view to) the remission of sins.'* Baptism has been established by God, upon a foundation of repentance (Acts 3: 19) and belief (Mark 16: 16; Acts 8: 37), as man's request for forgiveness (1 Peter 3: 21). After calling upon these men and women to repent of their sins against God and receive baptism as a matter of seeking cleansing from those sins, Peter explained to them the additional benefit of the gift of the Holy Spirit.

Until recently no Bible translation has ever seen fit to interpret Acts 2: 38 any differently than it has been translated for centuries, precisely because the text allows no other reading. Recently, however, the original translation of the International Standard Version (v1.1.0) stated that Peter told the crowd on the Day of Pentecost to *'repent and be baptized...since your sins are forgiven.'* It is interesting that, in a later version of this translation

(v. 1.3.0), the passage was modified to read '...for the forgiveness of sins.' When asked about the rephrasing of this verse, Dr. William Welty responded:

> The change in the ISV text was made to correct an inadvertent divergence in that passage from our Principles of Translation... Our reading of Acts 2:38 in v1.1.0 is accurate in that baptism follows acknowledgment of forgiveness: hence our rendering originally read: "Be baptized, since your sins..." However, strictly speaking, the Gk. text does read "for the forgiveness". We elected to go back to a more literal reading of the Gk. text.[13]

The impact from these words should cause men and women everywhere to reconsider seriously what they have been taught concerning the purpose of baptism in this passage. Having originally set aside the countless historical translations of this verse, evidently the writers reconsidered their work, ultimately deciding that their version of the text failed the test of unblemished interpretation. It is only fair to mention that Dr. Welty does consider the meaning of the passage somewhat blurred since, when translated properly, it does not mix well with his beliefs concerning baptism. In fact, he is to be commended for his forthrightness in abiding by honorable principles despite this obvious internal tug-of-war. Yet the fact that the translation is founded upon unbiased standards rather than personal ideology only helps to reinforce the legitimacy of the statement *for the forgiveness*. Therefore, for the thousands of scholars who for decades – even centuries – have hoped upon hope that εις might be interpreted *because*, it seems that door of opportunity should be considered permanently closed.

Those assembled in Jerusalem on the Day of Pentecost clearly believed the gospel message the apostles preached; yet this belief was inadequate, on its own, for them to receive God's grace. The question asked of the apostles, *'Men and brethren, what shall we do?'* demonstrates that the crowd was seeking direction from these men as to what they might do in order to change their current state of sinfulness. Peter explained the means by which they could escape that condition. His response is clear and sure. In full support of Peter's teaching at this time, this promise of forgiveness of sins at the time of baptism is also taught by the apostle Paul in his Colossians letter (Colossians 2: 11-14). The undeniable theme from this passage is that God made the penitent man alive, having forgiven his sins. Exactly who has been forgiven? It is the man who has died to sin and been *buried in baptism.* For those who would have us believe that men are saved prior to baptism, we must ask, why would we bury someone who is alive in Christ? Baptism is defined as the moment of our death to sins and burial with Christ. It is the dead man, not the living (renewed), who is buried in the water. It is the dead man, not the living, who is made alive. This is done *through our faith in the work of God.*

B. W. Johnson authored <u>The People's New Testament</u>, a commentary dating back to 1891. In it he provides one of the most thorough and reasonable explanations ever afforded this passage (Acts 2: 38), giving the author, Luke, and the Spirit of God due respect by expressing the meaning of the words of the passage as they were intended to be understood.

> 38. Repent, and be baptized. For the first time the terms of pardon under the New Covenant and the Great Commission are given; given once for all time, and always the same. The convicted, broken-hearted, sorrowing sinner, believing that Jesus is the Christ, is to repent and be baptized. Repent. Not sorrow. They already sorrowed; but a change of purpose; the internal change which resolves to serve the Lord. The Greek term rendered repent, means a change of mind. The act of obedience in baptism is an outward expression of both faith and repentance. In the name of Jesus Christ. "Upon the name" (Revised Version). Upon the ground of the name. In submission to the authority of Jesus Christ. For the remission of sins. Thus, by complying with the conditions just named, they shall receive remission of sins. No man can receive pardon without faith and repentance, nor can he without submission to the will of Christ. "Eis (for) denotes the object of baptism, which is the remission of the guilt contracted in the state before metanoia (repentance)."--Meyer. "In order to the forgiveness of sins we connect naturally with both the preceding verbs. This clause states the motive or object which should induce them to repent and be baptized."--Prof. Hackett. The gift of the Holy Spirit. Promised as a comforter to all who obey Christ, but whom "the world cannot receive."[14]

Christian Baptism for the Purpose of Regeneration

Baptism is the *time*[15] when we are regenerated. A sinful person enters the water and a new creature rises from the water. This new creature is now heir to the kingdom of God.

> Therefore we were buried with Him through baptism into death, that just as Christ was raised from the dead by the glory of the Father, even so we also should walk in newness of life. (Romans 6: 4)

4. But when the kindness and the love of God our Savior toward man appeared, 5. not by works of righteousness which we have done, but according to His mercy He saved us, through the washing of regeneration and renewing of the Holy Spirit, 6. whom He poured out on us abundantly through Christ Jesus our Savior, 7. that having been justified by His grace we should become heirs according to the hope of eternal life. (Titus 3: 4-7)

The teaching that baptism is a time of regeneration calls for an understanding of what it means to experience regeneration. We should make an effort to realize the spiritual changes that take place at the time of baptism. Scripture points to three distinct principles of regeneration, none of which is necessarily more significant than the others.

The first principle of regeneration that we will examine is justification (1 Corinthians 6: 11). Justification is viewed by most men as forgiveness of sins but, to an extent, it is more than that. It is the means by which we are separated from our old self and made a new creature (Romans 6: 3-6). Justification, which involves the application of Christ's blood to our sins, surpasses the mere pronouncement that we are *no longer* guilty of sins committed and suggests that, by faith and the grace that is offered to us through the blood of Christ, God bestows a sinless condition upon the obedient believer. He replaces our old carnal being with a new life (Galatians 6: 15). God is able, in His omnipotence, to offer the new Christian a life that is absolutely free of sin. While we certainly recall our previous sins, God does not. To Him it is as if those sins never occurred.

Justification is what Paul was talking about when he suggested what it is that man is unable to achieve through works (of the law). Man cannot, through any human deed, blot out sins committed. No feat performed by man reaches the level of righteousness necessary to earn justification. Only God has that capability. This is not to say that our active participation in responding to the gospel message plays no part in justification. According to Scripture it is at the time of baptism, as we willfully submit to Him, that God has chosen to grant justification (Romans 5: 1 - 6: 7).

Sanctification (1 Corinthians 6: 11), the setting apart of an individual, is the second aspect of regeneration that occurs at the time of baptism. Sanctification alone is not necessarily salvation-related. We discover that there are times in Scripture when sanctification is recognized without the automatic bestowal of salvation (1 Corinthians 7: 14). Yet, in relation to baptism, sanctification is directly linked to redemption and forgiveness. Within the design of salvation we are sanctified, just as we are justified, as we are washed in baptism (1 Corinthians 6: 11; Ephesians 5: 26).

Finally, regeneration is the time when a person is adopted as a child of God (Romans 8: 15; Galatians 4: 5). In truth, no one may be saved without experiencing the adoption process. It is through adoption that we are able to become heirs of God – heirs to the kingdom of God. Like justification and sanctification, adoption is available to us by our faith, through the blood of Christ, at the time of baptism (1 Peter 1: 17-25).

Regeneration, and all that it involves, is essential to salvation. No one may be saved without experiencing the new birth of which Jesus spoke in His conversation with Nicodemus (John 3: 1-6). No one may be saved without first becoming a true child of God (Romans 8: 14-17). While there is considerable disagreement among men as to the moment at which regeneration occurs, Scripture is filled with testimony that God has set aside the ceremony of baptism for that very purpose.

Christian Baptism for the Purpose of Salvation

Salvation (eternal life) is a result of baptism so closely associated with forgiveness and regeneration that it is difficult to separate them. Without forgiveness and regeneration one cannot be saved and, for the forgiven/regenerated man or woman, the promise of salvation is instantly fulfilled. The new and eternal life of the Christian, which he receives during baptism (Romans 6: 4-5), is the ultimate destination of faith (1 Peter 1: 9) and, therefore, a legitimate motive for baptism. Jesus proclaimed that it is those who satisfy the commands to believe and be baptized who would be saved (Mark 16: 16). Peter echoed this sentiment, stating plainly that salvation is found in baptism (1 Peter 3: 21). If salvation is the *goal* of our faith, salvation may reasonably be viewed as the *primary* purpose of baptism.

The gospel leads to salvation. Baptism is *for* the forgiveness of sins and regeneration. These, in turn, are *for* the purpose of salvation. Belief (John 3: 16), repentance (2 Corinthians 7: 10), and confession (Romans 10: 9) are all identified in Scripture as leading to the goal of salvation/eternal life. Even Jesus' life, death, burial, and resurrection were designed so that man might receive salvation by God's grace through faith (Ephesians 2: 8). Essentially everything God has done on earth from the time of man's fall has been focused on nothing else. If we consider honestly the apostles' words, the only reasonable conclusion concerning baptism is that it is for the purpose of receiving salvation.

The Gift of the Holy Spirit Bestowed in Christian Baptism

The benefits received by those baptized in Jesus' name go beyond the biblically stated *purpose* of baptism. Forgiveness of sins (Acts 2: 38), regeneration (Titus 3: 5), and salvation (1 Peter 3: 21) are stated as reasons for baptism. However, intimacy with God through the Holy Spirit is portrayed in Scripture as more of an honor, perhaps even a divine blessing bestowed upon the man or woman who is obedient in water baptism. Peter did not tell the people on the Day of Pentecost to be baptized *for the purpose of the gift of the Holy Spirit.* Instead, the promise of the Spirit seems to be added as a point of additional privilege for those who believed (Acts 2: 38).

Often called the *indwelling* of the Holy Spirit, the gift of the Holy Spirit is portrayed in Scripture as a one-on-one relationship with God the Father through the work of the Holy Spirit. The fact that the gift of the Spirit (Acts 2: 38) is the *presence* of the Spirit rather than a gift *from* the Spirit is easy to determine from a variety of New Testament passages where we learn of the role of the Spirit in our lives (2 Corinthians 1: 22; 1 Thessalonians 4: 8). We are told that the Holy Spirit rests upon us (1 Peter 4: 14) and lives in us (Romans 8: 9). He resides in our inner being (Ephesians 3: 16). It is by His presence that we are able to exhibit the fruit of the Spirit (Galatians 5: 22). The Holy Spirit abides with us to help us in our daily walk. He provides *unity* among the members of the body (Ephesians 4: 4), *hope* for eternal life (Romans 15: 13), *sanctification* (Romans 15: 16), *discernment* (1 Corinthians 2: 14), *joy* (1 Thessalonians 1: 6), *spiritual sustenance* (2 Corinthians 3: 6) and a host of other spiritual advantages. Occasionally, within the context of His indwelling presence, the Spirit is even able to intercede for us when necessary (Romans 8: 26-27). In essence, the Spirit walks with us as we serve the Lord daily in order to enhance our relationship with God and with each other.

Christian Baptism and Membership in the Body

Beyond the role of baptism to provide forgiveness, regeneration, salvation, and the gift of the Holy Spirit, an additional benefit is revealed to us on the Day of Pentecost following Peter's words to the assembly. Having explained what the Jews in Jerusalem must do to receive redemption, many of them responded in obedience.

> Then those who gladly received his word were baptized; and that day about three thousand souls were added *to them.* (Acts 2: 41)

The connection between baptism and souls being *'added to them'* is stated plainly enough; but to what, or to whom, were they added? When we consider this verse in connection to other Scripture (Acts 2: 47; 1 Corinthians 12: 13; Colossians 1: 18), we understand that those who believed the gospel message and were baptized on that day were added to the church, also called the body of Christ.

Baptism is portrayed as a means by which men are added to the body of Christ for fellowship and support, identifying this as an additional benefit of baptism. It is one of the steps involved in the process through which one is added to the church, thus *putting on* Christ (Galatians 3: 27), offering endorsement for what Luke penned in Acts 2: 41 regarding those who were added to Christ's body.

The Unifying Mettle of Christian Baptism

Paul, in his letter to the church at Ephesus, offered them a lesson about unity in the body of Christ (Ephesians 4: 4-6). He asked them to keep hold of the unity that had been taught by the apostles. Within this lesson, baptism, along with various other unique elements of the faith, is identified as a source of unity. This is a fundamental teaching of Scripture. Not only is baptism considered a matter of unification within the body, but it is also a matter of oneness with Christ. Paul offered detailed instruction to the Romans concerning the manner in which they were unified with Christ at the time of baptism.

> 4. Therefore we were buried with Him through baptism into death, that just as Christ was raised from the dead by the glory of the Father, even so we also should walk in newness of life. 5. For if we have been united

together in the likeness of His death, certainly we also shall be in the *likeness* of *His* resurrection. (Romans 6: 4-5)

The unifying nature of baptism goes beyond mere harmony within the body. These words to the Romans reveal that unity with Christ is central in our participation in baptism. It is the time a person is united with Christ, not just in this earthly life, but for all eternity. From Paul's words we learn that it is those who have *experienced unity in His death through baptism* who will ultimately experience *unity in His resurrection,* offering support for Jesus' own claim discussed earlier (Mark 16: 16).

Whether in the gospels, the book of Acts, or the many epistles where it is discussed, the significance of baptism in the New Testament is undeniable (though many deny it). In baptism men acknowledge and, in a symbolic manner, participate in the sacrifice of Jesus as a matter of experiencing death from sin, burial in water, and resurrection to a new life (Romans 6: 3-5). We must not take lightly the value Scripture places upon this rite as a key moment in Christian conversion. Baptism, an act commanded by Jesus, is intended to draw men closer to God and to each other. It is in baptism that we are cleansed from sin and become a part of the body of Christ. In baptism, we are regenerated by the Spirit and able to begin a new life. It is also at this time that the Holy Spirit begins to take an intimate active role in the life of a convert. There can be no doubt that submission to baptism is vital for those who wish to be united with Christ.

Effects of Baptism with Errant Motivation

As we consider the purpose of baptism, that study naturally gives rise to one especially engaging question. If one is baptized but refuses to accept the biblical reasons of forgiveness-regeneration-salvation, is baptism beneficial for that person? In other words, will that man or woman receive the promises associated with baptism even though he/she does not accept that these things actually occur at that time? After all, Jesus did tell His disciples that one who believes and is baptized would be saved (Mark 16: 16) without qualifying the remark in any way. So then, does baptism received in the name of Jesus make one eligible for the spiritual benefits ascribed to the rite regardless of what he/she believes concerning its value or purpose?

It is important to realize that the act of immersion in water in itself has no built-in power or spiritual value. The changes in our relationship with God that do occur at the time of baptism take place based fully upon two factors. First, it is up to the believer to have faith in the promises of God at the time of baptism. Second, God works directly in response to the personal faith of the one who submits to baptism. Paul states that we are resurrected with Him through faith (Colossians 2: 12). Therefore, the assurance of salvation is *dependent* upon the person's faith concerning God's fulfillment of His promise.

There exists a theme in Paul's letters to Timothy that focuses specifically on the importance of following acceptable doctrine. Sound scriptural doctrine is *vital* to a healthy relationship with God (1 Timothy 1: 3; 6: 1-5). Salvation itself, according to Paul, is dependent upon the teaching of, and adherence to, biblical doctrine (1 Timothy 4: 16). Sincere belief in false doctrine is given no standing in Scripture with respect to salvation. Paul warned the Corinthians that their belief could be *in vain* unless they *hold fast* to the gospel message (1 Corinthians 15: 2). We learn from Scripture that false doctrine misleads (2 Peter 3: 16) and that any gospel other than that taught by the apostles is no gospel at all since it comes from men rather than God (Galatians 1: 6-9).

Apostolic instruction about baptism involves not only the necessity of the act itself, but also the reasoning and motivation intimately linked to baptism. In fact, the apostles taught the people about the need for baptism based upon the promises associated with it (Acts 2: 38; Romans 6: 1-4; Titus 3: 5). Consequently, if we are to abide by the apostles' doctrine, we cannot separate baptism from the foundational reasons for which God has established it (Acts 2: 38; Romans 6: 1-4; Galatians 3: 26-27; 1 Peter 3: 21-22).

From Paul's words to the Romans we learn that our walk as a new creature not only follows, but is dependent upon, our unity with Christ in the baptismal waters (Romans 6: 5-8). This is a truth of which Paul acknowledges these disciples were fully aware (Romans 6: 6). Emphasis is placed upon an understanding of the spiritual activity that is found within the act of baptism.

5. For if we have been united together in the likeness of His death, certainly we also shall be in the *likeness* of *His* resurrection, 6. knowing this, that our old man was crucified with Him, that the body of sin might be done away with , that we should no longer be slaves of sin. 7. For he who has died has been freed from sin. 8. Now if we died with

Christ, we believe that we shall also live with Him, 9. knowing that Christ, having been raised from the dead, dies no more... (Romans 6: 5-9)

Paul's subject matter here is, of course, baptism in water (Romans 6: 1-4). The observant reader will undoubtedly notice that in each of these remarks we find an *'if'* statement. In addition, the outcome in each case appears to be dependent upon the proposition found within the *'if'* statement. Those who *will share in the likeness of His resurrection* are those who *have participated with Him in the likeness of His death* (v. 5), which is baptism (v. 4). However, Paul does not stop there. He highlights the fact that the Romans were aware of these things, stating that there is a *knowing* (γινωσκοντες), or recognition, of these truths.

Similarly, it is those who have died with Him (v. 8) in baptism (v. 4) who will (eternally) live with Him. Paul explains that, *'...if we died with Christ, we believe...knowing that Christ...dies no more'* (vs. 8-9). Here the word *knowing* (ειδοτες) is a perfect active participle, plural in number, and it is linked directly to the verb *'believe.'* This suggests that our *belief* that death with Christ (v. 4) will ultimately allow us to live (eternally) with Him hinges, at least partially, upon our understanding His victory over death in relation to baptism.

It would be wise to concede a certain amount of flexibility when it comes to our comprehension at the time of baptism. For instance, in verse eight above it is most likely that Paul is simply offering these converts greater insight into the meaning of baptism rather than reviewing things they understood fully when they accepted Christ. It would be a bit much to expect anyone to have full understanding of all the intricacies of baptism at the time he/she submits to this rite. Many scholars who have studied the Bible for years often find themselves discovering some truth in Scripture that previously had escaped them. It is certainly possible that the Philippian jailer did not fully comprehend *all* the benefits the night he was baptized even though Paul surely taught him well (Acts 16: 32-33). We find that Paul spent much time and effort in his epistles educating immersed believers concerning the deeper meaning(s) of baptism (Romans 6: 1-4; Colossians 2: 11-12). Yet Scripture does seem to stress a basic understanding that baptism is the time God has chosen to redeem the repentant sinner and grant the gift of the Spirit (Acts 2: 38; 19: 2). Other benefits, such as membership in the body, often appear to be explained after submission to baptism (Acts 2: 41).

Through the words of the apostles God has fully demonstrated the purpose for which baptism was designed (forgiveness, regeneration, et al). If we are, in the spirit of discipleship, to observe all that Jesus has commanded (Matthew 28: 20), and it was He who commanded baptism, as a matter of honoring God we must regard it appropriately. What, then, is to become of someone who insists that forgiveness and other benefits assigned to baptism will not occur as God has promised, assuming that salvation has somehow already been attained despite biblical instruction? If the reality of God's work is subject to our faith in God's promise that this will occur, and we have not that faith, in His omniscience, God will know it. Therefore, men and women who disregard God's purpose for baptism have no assurance, and are in no position to presume, that God will overlook personal doctrine and grant baptismal benefits to those who are fixed on denying them.

The Purpose of Baptism for the Gentiles

Our study of the purpose of baptism provides an excellent opportunity to address an ongoing debate over baptism – one that specifically zeroes in on the baptism of Gentiles. Some men have proposed that, while water baptism may have been essential for the Jews in the first century, this is not necessarily true for those of us who are not direct descendants of Abraham. After all, those passages that *directly* link forgiveness to baptism seem to be aimed specifically at the Jews (Acts 2: 38; 22: 16). At least they appear to be uttered in defined Jewish settings. Gentiles, it is said, never really received the command to be baptized *for the remission of sins.*

Of course, this view completely disregards Paul's teaching on the subject including his re-baptism of the disciples he met at Ephesus (Acts 19: 1-7). He emphasized to the Romans *newness of life* and *freedom from sin* in baptism (Romans 6: 1-7) and explained to the Galatians that this was the moment when they *'put on Christ'* (Galatians 3: 27). Additionally, Peter, when writing to the Christians scattered throughout Asia, proclaimed that *baptism saves* (1 Peter 3: 21). He also commanded the immediate baptism of the Gentiles in Caesarea (Acts 10: 48).

In His final instructions to the apostles, Jesus suggested no limit to the significance or value of baptism among Gentiles. He commanded them to *'...make disciples of all nations, baptizing them...'* (Matthew 28: 19). This statement concerning the salvation of men through belief and baptism is offered without qualification as Jesus told them to, *'Go into all the world'* (Mark 16: 15-16). Later, through the book of Acts and the epistles (many of which were written to Gentiles) we gain much of our insight into the meaning of baptism. Scripture simply does not discriminate between the baptism of Jews and the baptism of Gentiles. Jesus' inclusion of baptism in His all-encompassing final command speaks volumes concerning its effect for *all* men.

NOTES FOR CHAPTER 7

1. John Wesley, credited as the founding father of Methodism, was previously a priest in the Anglican Church. Adapting the Thirty-nine Articles of Religion from the Anglican Church, Wesley developed his own Twenty-five Articles of Religion. Viewing the sacraments as signs of faith he penned the following regarding first, the sacraments in general, and then baptism specifically.

Article 16—Of the Sacraments
Sacraments ordained of Christ are not only badges or tokens of Christian men's profession, but rather they are certain signs of grace, and God's good will toward us, by which he doth work invisibly in us, and doth not only quicken, but also strengthen and confirm, our faith in him.

There are two Sacraments ordained of Christ our Lord in the Gospel; that is to say, Baptism and the Supper of the Lord.

Those five commonly called sacraments, that is to say, confirmation, penance, orders, matrimony, and extreme unction, are not to be counted for Sacraments of the Gospel; being such as have partly grown out of the corrupt following of the apostles, and partly are states of life allowed in the Scriptures, but yet have not the like nature of Baptism and the Lord's Supper, because they have not any visible sign or ceremony ordained of God.

The Sacraments were not ordained of Christ to be gazed upon, or to be carried about; but that we should duly use them. And in such only as worthily receive the same, they have a wholesome effect or operation; but they that receive them unworthily, purchase to themselves condemnation, as St. Paul saith. Wesley, Twenty-five Articles of Religion, Article 16 – Of the Sacraments.

Article 17—Of Baptism
Baptism is not only a sign of profession and mark of difference whereby Christians are distinguished from others that are not baptized; but it is also a sign of regeneration or the new birth. The Baptism of young children is to be retained in the Church. Wesley, Twenty-five Articles of Religion, Article 17 – Of Baptism.

2. Strong's Concordance
http://cf.blueletterbible.org/lang/lexicon/lexicon.cfm?Strongs=G911&Version=KJV, Accessed January 15, 2005.

3. Just a few of the scholars who speak with confidence concerning the link between forgiveness and both repentance and baptism in Acts 2: 38 include the following:

Bruce Metzger was the editor of the *Textual Commentary on The Greek New Testament,* published by the United Bible Societies.

Arthur L. Farstad was the chairman of the New King James Executive Review Committee and general editor of the *NKJV New Testament.*

John R. Werner is the International Consultant in Translation to the Wycliffe Bible Translators. He was also a consultant to Friberg and Friberg with the *Analytical Greek New Testament.*

Barclay Newman and **Eugene Nida** edited *The Translator's Handbook On The Acts Of The Apostles.*

Dr. H. B. Hackett and Dr. Alvah Hovey, both of these are Baptist theologians.

Dr. C. B. Williams, a long-time professor of Greek in Union University, Jackson, Tennessee.

4. James Strong, LL.D., S.T.D., The New Strong's Exhaustive Concordance of the Bible, Greek Dictionary of the New Testament, p. 26, Thomas Nelson Publishers, 1990.

5. Joseph Henry Thayer, D.D., Thayer's Greek-English Lexicon of the New Testament , p. 183, Baker Book House, 1977.

6. http://www.isv.org/musings/musings 15.htm [Online] May 5, 2007.

7. Marianne Chalmers and Martine Pierquin, Pocket Oxford Hachette French Dictionary Second Edition, p. 337, Oxford University Press, 2000.

8. D. P. Simpson, Cassell's Latin English Dictionary, p. 111, Hungry Minds, Inc., Macmillan Publishing, 1987.

9. Stownik Kieszonkowy, Larouse Polish English Pocket Dictionary, p. 116, Larousse/SEJER, 2004.

10. Luzia Araujo and Valerie Grundy, Larouse Portuguese English Pocket Dictionary, p. 233, Larousse/VUEF, 2003.

11. Della Thompson, The Oxford Russian Dictionary, p. 43, The Berkley Publishing Group, Oxford University Press, 1997.

12. Webster's Everyday Spanish - English Dictionary, p. 129, Federal Street Press, 2002
13. http://www.sermoncentral.com, "The Preposition "eis" in Acts 2:38" [Online] May 7, 2007.

14. B. W. Johnson, , The People's New Testament, Volume 1, The Acts of the Apostles, Christian Publishing Company, 1891.

15. That regeneration occurs at the time of baptism is addressed thoroughly by Alexander Campbell.

I. The change which is consummated by immersion, is sometimes called in sacred style, "*being quickened,*" or "*made alive,*" "*passing from death to life,*" "*being born again,*" "*having risen with Christ,*" "*turning to the Lord,*" "*being enlightened,*" "*conversion,*" "*reconciliation,*" "*repentance unto life.*" These, like the words propitiation, atonement, reconciliation, expiation, redemption, expressive of the various aspects which the death of Christ sustains, are expressive of the different relations in which this great change, sometimes called a "new creation," may be contemplated. The entire change affected in man by the Christian system, consists in four things:--a change of views; a change of affections; a change of state; and a change of life. Alexander Campbell, The Christian System, page 62.

We have the phrase "*washing of regeneration*" once, in contradistinction from the "renewal of the Holy Spirit," (Titus 2i. 5) but never, by itself, as indicative of this four-fold change. Alexander Campbell, The Christian System, page 63.

Chapter VIII
What is the Mode of Baptism?

The mode of baptism, where *mode* speaks of the physical manner by which men administer the rite, is certainly the source of a great deal of dissension in the religious community. A variety of forms of this ceremony have been passed down from one generation to the next. While immersion is preferred by many, some men also recognize either sprinkling or pouring water as acceptable methods of baptism. However, the Bible has much to say about the mode of baptism that was established by Jesus for those who would enter His kingdom.

The Baptism of John

Immersion in water was first introduced through the life of John the Baptist as it is portrayed in the four gospels. In the New Testament we find many passages that demonstrate the fact that water was the instrument used by John to perform baptism (Matthew 3: 6-13; Mark 1: 5-8; Luke 3: 16; John 1: 26; Acts 1: 5).

John the Baptist was designated as the forerunner of Christ. His role was to prepare the people (more specifically, the Israelites), through teaching and baptism, for Jesus' ministry on earth. The fact that John's baptism involved water is essentially an undisputed point among scholars and laymen alike. The real challenge is seeking the biblical *method* of baptism. This involves careful consideration of the original Greek since the meaning of the word *baptism* in the English language has become somewhat diluted.

The Meaning of Bapto, Baptizo, and Baptisma

We will begin our investigation with the Greek word βαπτω (*bapto*), from which we derive other words such as βαπτιζω (*baptizo*)[1] and βαπτισμα (*baptisma*). βαπτω indicates that some sort of dipping or submersion is taking place, but not *just* dipping. It is a dipping that results in permanent change.

βαπτω 1) to dip, dip in, immerse. 2) to dip into dye, to dye, colour. The clearest example that shows the meaning of baptizo is a text from the Greek poet and physician Nicander, who lived about 200 B.C. It is a recipe for making pickles and is helpful because it uses both words. Nicander says that in order to make a pickle, the vegetable should first be 'dipped' (βαπτω) into boiling water and then 'baptised' (βαπτιζω) in the vinegar solution. Both verbs concern the immersing of vegetables in a solution. But the first is temporary. The second, the act of baptising the vegetable, produces a permanent change.[2]

In one form or other this word appears four times in the New Testament, each time depicting the act of someone dipping something in liquid and then removing from the liquid what was dipped.

One story with which most people are familiar is the one about Lazarus and the rich man. Upon his death, a wealthy man found himself in Hades where he was in torment in the fire. Lazarus, a beggar who was mistreated by the rich man while they were both alive, also died and was taken to Abraham's bosom, which is presumably Paradise. In his agony, the rich man begged Abraham to allow Lazarus to *dip* (βαψη) his finger in water (Luke 16: 24). He hoped that Lazarus, with just that drop of water on the tip of his finger, might cool the rich man's tongue.

In the account of the Last Supper (John 13: 26), a form of the word βαπτω appears twice, both referring to Jesus *dipping (βαψας)* the bread in the dish, which must have contained some kind of dressing or wine. When Jesus removed the bread from the dish He passed it to Judas, His betrayer.

The apostle John witnessed a robe that was *dipped,* literally *having been dipped (βεβαμμενον),* in blood and then removed so that it could be worn (Revelation 19: 13). The word *dip* in our English language implies the action of immersion in, and removal from, some kind of liquid or container. While the use of the word *bapto* depicts the act of *dipping* or *immersion,* its transformation into *baptizo,* according to the definition provided above, results in some kind of permanent change taking place.

The words *baptize, baptism,* etc., were actually fabricated by those men who were responsible for translating the Bible from Greek into English. Interpreters formed these words from their Greek counterparts for use in the English Bible. These words appear a number of times in the New Testament, usually in connection with the water ritual performed by John and his disciples, Jesus' followers (John 4: 1-2), and men in the church age beginning on the Day of Pentecost. Occasionally, however, those men who converted the Bible into English actually did translate this word rather than falling back on their manufactured word, which was *'baptize.'* In those instances the translation is normally found to be some form of the word *wash* (e.g., wash, washed, washing, etc.).

> 9. It *was* symbolic for the present time in which both gifts and sacrifices are offered which cannot make him who performed the service perfect in regard to the conscience – 10. *concerned* only with foods and drinks, various washings *(βαπτισμοις)*, and fleshly ordinances imposed until the time of reformation. (Hebrews 9: 9-10)

A number of ceremonies and rituals in the first covenant were performed on a regular basis by the Israelites (Hebrews 9: 9-10). The function of these ordinances varied depending on the circumstances involved. Feasts were generally intended as a manner of celebration – a means of honoring God. The various washings commanded under the first covenant provided a means of religious purification – sometimes for the priests prior to entering the temple and other times for any person (Israelite) who, for some reason specified in the Mosaic Law, found himself/herself in an unclean state.

> 1. Then the Pharisees and some of the scribes came together to Him, having come from Jerusalem. 2. Now when they saw some of His disciples eat bread with defiled *(κοιναις)*, that is, with unwashed *(νιψωνται)* hands, they found fault. 3. For the Pharisees and all the Jews do not eat unless they wash *(νιψωνται) their* hands in a special way, holding the tradition of the elders. 4. *When they come* from the marketplace, they do not eat unless they wash *(βαπτισμος)*. And there are many other things which they have received and hold, like washing *(βαπτισμος)* of cups, pitchers, copper vessels, and couches. 5. The Pharisees asked Him, "Why do Your disciples not walk according to the tradition of the elders, but eat bread with unwashed *(κοιναις)* hands?" (Mark 7: 1-5)

> 37. And as He spoke, a certain Pharisee asked Him to dine with him. So He went in and sat down to eat. 38. When the Pharisee saw *it*, he marveled that He had not first washed *(βαπτιςο)* before dinner. 39. Then the Lord said to him, "Now you Pharisees make the outside of the cup and dish clean, but your inward part is full of greed and wickedness. 40. Foolish ones! Did not He who made the outside make the inside also?" (Luke 11: 37-40)

These passages from Mark and Luke are rather popular among those who deny the significance of immersion since the text seems to address the washing of a man's hands or inanimate objects such as pots and pans. In all honesty, however, these statements shine an exceptionally favorable light on the doctrine of baptism by immersion.

The reference to the *'tradition of the elders'* did not represent Old Testament commands as we might suspect. Quite often Jesus scolded the religious leaders of His day for demanding rituals that God had not ordained (Matthew 12: 1-13; 15: 1-20). Men had established the washing of the *fists* mentioned here, not in search of physical cleanliness at the table, but as an artificial religious ceremony developed by men. Appropriately νιψωνται, a form of νιπτω (*nipto*), is used specifically acknowledging the washing of a portion of the body such as the hands or the face.

It is important to recognize the difference between the custom of hand washing (νιψωνται) discussed in verses two and five, where the topic is the Pharisaic practice of ceremonially washing their hands prior to eating, and the washing[3] (βαπτιζο) mentioned in verse four. Mark detours slightly, touching briefly on certain other ritual washings that were practiced by the Pharisees but not condoned by God. The ceremonial washing of hands was just one of many counterfeit rituals, but it brought to mind a practice that was truly despicable, one that concerned their interaction with Gentiles.

In the minds of the Pharisees, contact with Gentiles by a Jew must certainly pollute the entire body. Therefore, when returning from a public setting like the marketplace, where they would have encountered Gentiles, the Pharisees ritually *bathed* (βαπτιζο) prior to eating so that they might be considered clean. The reference to washing in verse four is not to the hands or face or another *part* of the body, nor is that implied. Hand washing (or unclean hands) is not cited in reference to βαπτιζο but is linked to νιψωνται and κοιναις (vs. 3 and 5). The change from νιψωνται to βαπτιζο is not only intentional, but significant, since verse four suggests an immersion of the entire body similar to the way dishes are submerged (βαπτισμος) in water for washing. The passage suggests that even the washing of dishes had taken on a ritual-like personality for the Jews.

The same reasoning must also apply to Luke 11: 37-40. Having come from a place where *'the crowds were thickly gathered together'* (Luke 11: 29), the Pharisee did not question Jesus about

His failure to ceremonially wash His hands, nor is hand washing mentioned here. Instead the man asked Him why He did not *bathe* (βαπτιςο) His body since He had been among Gentiles. Jesus' response in verses thirty-nine and forty frustrates the claim that this washing is a reference to the hands alone. Thus the Pharisees had developed two types of washing that were required. The first involved washing (νιψωνται) the hands or fists (though some perhaps legitimately claim that it was a cleansing *of* or *up to* the wrists). The second (βαπτιςο) was required for those who had been in the company of Gentiles (v. 4).

If the word *couch* in the passage in Mark causes any confusion, an explanation must be given. Does this suggest that these Pharisees *dipped* a piece of furniture into water as a means of washing? This word indeed identifies the so-called dining couches that were present in homes of that day. It is reported that the Pharisees had carried their ceremonies to such an extreme that they did actually dip some of their furniture as a matter of ritual cleansing.

While many evangelicals accept that *bapto (βαπτω)* does indeed mean to *dip* or *immerse*, they deny that this meaning must apply to derivatives such as *baptizo (βαπτιςο)*. Yet this meaning is difficult to escape given the fact that, in Strong's own definition, we find straightforward acknowledgement that the person or object being *baptized* is presumed to be *fully wet*.

> 907. βαπτιςο baptizo, bap-tid'-zo; from a der. of *911*; to make whelmed (i.e., *fully wet*); used only (in the N.T.) of ceremonial *ablution*, espec (techn.) of the ordinance of Chr. *baptism*:-baptist, baptize, wash.[4]

Occasionally in Scripture when the word *wash* appears in English it is translated from Greek wording that is not a form of βαπτω. One such instance recalls the time when Jesus washed the feet of the disciples (John 13: 5-9).

The English word *wash,* appearing twice in this passage, is translated from two Greek words, each a derivative of the root word νιπτω, which was encountered previously with respect to Mark 7: 3, meaning *to cleanse*. More precisely, they are used in connection with washing *especially the hands or the feet or the face.*[5] Given the context in this passage, their use seems most suitable.

Further support for this translation of the word νιπτω is found in the book of John where this same word is once again translated as *wash*. Early in His ministry Jesus encountered a man who had been blind from birth (John 9: 1-7). Forming clay from a mixture of dirt and saliva and placing the clay upon the man's eyes, Jesus told him to go and *wash* his eyes in the Pool of Siloam. Having obeyed, he then returned to Jesus with his eyesight fully restored. As we can see, Jesus told the man to *'Go, wash....'* The word νιπτω, translated as *wash* in these passages, accurately depicts the kind of washing that was taking place. God's Word is very consistent in its use of language as His will is disclosed through the writing of men inspired by Him. No doubt God was painstakingly vigilant as, through the hands and minds of men, He knitted together the books through which His plan would be revealed.

> 37. And behold, a woman in the city who was a sinner, when she knew that *Jesus* sat at the table in the Pharisee's house, brought an alabaster flask of fragrant oil, 38. and stood at His feet behind *Him* weeping; and she began to wash (βρεχειν) His feet with her tears, and wiped *them* with the hair of her head; and she kissed His feet and anointed *them* with the fragrant oil. (Luke 7: 37-38)

> 1. So it was, as the multitude pressed about Him to hear the word of God, that He stood by the Lake of Gennesaret, 2. and saw two boats standing by the lake; but the fishermen had gone from them and were washing (επλυνον) their nets. (Luke 5: 1-2)

The word βρεχειν (*brechein*) comes from βρεχω (*brecho*), which means: *to moisten (espec. by shower): - (send) rain*[6], while επλυνον (*eplunon*), a form of αποπλυνω (*apopluno*), renders a meaning: *to rinse off.*[7] The honesty with which these words describe the actions involved in these passages only goes to strengthen the position that the verbiage of Scripture is both intentional and precise. So it is when βαπτω, βαπτιςο, or βαπτισμα, appear in Scripture. These words were undoubtedly chosen because they accurately portray the events of the scene to the reader.

Baptism – The Antitype

The countless arguments offered by men in their efforts to contest immersion in water as the baptism of the church age simply fall short. Scripture is not only filled with instruction concerning immersion in water (Romans 6: 1-4; Colossians 2: 12), but it is noticeably void of any evidence that the first century church practiced baptism in any other form. We find that immersion as the method of baptism is fully supported by the apostle Peter in his first epistle where he provides rather conclusive evidence about the baptism that was practiced in New Testament times.

> 18. For Christ also suffered once for sins, the just for the unjust, that He might bring us to God, being put to death in the flesh but made alive by the Spirit, 19. by whom also He went and preached to the spirits in prison, 20. who formerly were disobedient, when once the Divine longsuffering waited in the days of Noah, while *the* ark was being prepared, in which a few, that is, eight souls, were saved through water. 21. There is also an antitype which now saves us--baptism (not the removal of the filth of the flesh, but the answer of a good conscience toward God), through the resurrection of Jesus Christ... (1 Peter 3: 18-21)

In Noah's day God chose water as the instrument by which He would cleanse the world of the evil that had overtaken mankind. According to Peter, baptism in the church age is a counterpart to the waters of the flood. Translated as *antitype,* the word αντιτυπον (*antitupon*) reveals a great deal more about the relationship between baptism and the waters of the flood. The best way for us to understand the relationship that this word depicts is by considering the two Greek words from which this one word is formed. The prefix αντι (*anti*), in colloquial English, is usually understood to mean *against* or *opposed to*. However, Funk & Wagnals renders a meaning of *opposite to or reverse*.[8] Strong's defines it as *opposite...Often used in composition to denote contrast....* [9] The second half of the word *antitupon* finds its origin in the Greek word τυπος (*tupos*) which, while it has many synonyms, essentially refers to *form* or *manner*.[10] Thus the English word *type* helps to form the word *antitype.*

We can have a better grasp of the meaning of the word *antitype* if we understand both the means of Noah's salvation and the relationship between the testaments. New Testament baptism is a counterpart to the waters of the flood in much the same fashion that a mirror reflects the image before it in an opposite manner. Drue Freeman describes this reverse effect in the following excerpt from his work:

> There is a distinct vocabulary found in the New Testament that references the Old Testament. The Greek word HUPODEIGMA means that which is shown privately as an example or pattern. TUPOS is an impression that is left from the blow of a hammer... An ANTITUPON is a counterpart like an echo. [11]

The hammer leaves an impression that is opposite in nature. The result of the hammer's strike is a depression while the hammerhead protrudes. Noah was saved through water, in that this was the device used by God to separate him from the evil by which he was surrounded. So it is in baptism as God has again chosen water as the instrument in which He separates a man from the evil of sin. Yet, Noah was saved as God lifted him above the water – the antitype of immersion. Today we are saved, not through escaping the water, as was Noah, but by the *opposite ($\alpha\nu\tau\iota$) form* or *manner ($\tau\upsilon\pi\varsigma$)*. We are immersed. Concerning this verse, one popular commentary states:

> Opposite of imagery which pictures those who floated safely above the waters within the ark is that of a complete immersion which "saves us."[12]

In reality, given God's choice of water to purge the earth of evil via the flood, nothing short of total immersion would do. A slight sprinkle or even torrential rains would ultimately fail to provide the cleansing that God desired. A complete flooding of the earth was needed to accomplish the task at hand. Since Peter claimed that baptism corresponded to the flood, where we find immersion was essential, perhaps we should consider closely the importance we place upon the mode of baptism we use.

The History of Baptism in the Church

The Roman Catholic Church deserves recognition for their passion for history, having spent incredible amounts of time and money to assure that accurate records of the history of the church are available to us. For this reason the Catholic Encyclopedia is a valuable source of information for those in search of the history of religion. The following excerpt from the Catholic Encyclopedia regarding baptism provides helpful insight into the history of baptism from the earliest times.

> Scripture is so positive in its statements as to the use of true and natural water for baptism that it is difficult to see why it should ever be called in question...The remote matter of baptism, then is water, and this taken in its usual meaning...The proximate matter of baptism is the ablution (cleansing) performed with water. The very word "baptize", as we have seen, means a washing. Three forms of ablution have prevailed among Christians, and the Church holds them all to be valid because they fulfill the requisite signification of the baptismal laving. These forms are immersion, infusion, and aspersion. The most ancient form usually employed was unquestionably immersion. This is not only evident from the writings of the Fathers and the early rituals of both the Latin and Oriental Churches, but it can also be gathered from the Epistles of St. Paul, who speaks of baptism as a bath (Ephes, v, 26; Rom., vi, 4; Tit., 2i, 5). In the Latin Church, immersion seems to have prevailed until the twelfth century. After that time it is found in some places even as late as the sixteenth century. Infusion and aspersion, however, were growing common in the thirteenth century and gradually prevailed in the Western Church.[13]

Immersion was recognized from the beginning of the church as the form of baptism by water. Through much of history we learn that *'immersion seems to have prevailed.'* It was long after the time of the apostles that church leaders began accepting other forms of baptism.[14]

Essentially all scholars agree that the water baptism of the New Testament took the form of immersion. The general consensus among theologians is that βαπτιςω, βαπτισμα, and βαπτισμος depict the act of immersion. We can conclude from an abundance of evidence that sprinkling and pouring of water were never used in Scripture with respect to the ceremony of baptism. Had these methods been in use we can be confident that words portraying sprinkling or pouring would have been used to identify baptism. Ραντιςω (*rhantizo*) and εκχεω (*ekcheo*) are Greek for sprinkling and pouring, respectively. Yet, in the pages of Scripture these words are never used in conjunction with this ceremony of baptism. Had they been accurately descriptive no doubt they would have been utilized where appropriate, but they are not. For this reason immersion is universally viewed as the water baptism taught in the Bible. It seems a bit bold that we should take it upon ourselves to modify this ceremony that God has established.

The International Standard Bible Encyclopedia offers these thoughts about the Greek use of the words that form our English words of baptize and baptism – root word *βαπτο*. This is a passage that offers us considerable insight into the method of baptism:

> The Greek language has had a continuous history, and Greek [baptizo] is used today in Greece for baptism. As is well known, not only in Greece, but all over Russia, wherever the Greek church prevails, immersion is the unbroken and universal practice. The Greeks may surely be credited with knowledge of the meaning of their own language.[15]

As we read or hear the words *baptize* or *baptism* in the English language, each one develops a picture in his/her own mind as to what these words mean. To some it would mean immersion while others may envision sprinkling or pouring. Yet, when the people of the first century heard these words spoken, they would have heard and pictured the following:

> Go therefore and make disciples of all the nations, *immersing* them in the name of the Father and of the Son and of the Holy Spirit. (Matthew 28: 19)

> He who believes and is *immersed* will be saved. (Mark 16: 16)

> Repent, and let every one of you be *immersed* in the name of Jesus Christ for the remission of sins... (Acts 2: 38)

> Or do you not know that as many of us as were *immersed* into Christ were *immersed* into His death? (Romans 6: 3)

> For as many of you as were *immersed* into Christ have put on Christ. (Galatians 3: 27)

> There is also an antitype which now saves us – *immersion*... (1 Peter 3: 21)

Paul's Portraiture of Baptism

While the Greek terminology used to define baptism is strong evidence of its form, even more support is found in Paul's vivid portrayal of this ceremony (Romans 6: 3-4; Colossians 2: 11-12). It seems baptism is intended to be representative of the death, burial, and resurrection of Christ. One method alone offers this symbolism as Paul described it.

We discover from the apostle's words that when God designed baptism it was with this specific symbolism in mind. Sprinkling or pouring water on an individual simply fails to exhibit the characteristics that Paul has presented here. The symbolism in baptism (immersion) should be obvious since one who is baptized is buried into death and raised to a new life. In Colossians 2: 12 the word συνθαπτω (*sunthapto*), which translates as *buried with Him,* suggests a joint burial with Christ. Once again, the words from which this one is formed offer additional insight into Paul's teaching. The first of these is συν (*sun*), which means *with* or *together.*[16] The second portion, θαπτω (*thapto*), means *to bury* or *to celebrate funeral rites.*[17] Paul's emphasis here indicates that the representation of Christ's death and resurrection in baptism may not be as insignificant as many claim.

Paul pleads with the Colossians asking them to remain faithful to God (Colossians 2: 1-23). Through his insight into human character he recognized that, if these men and women could psychologically and emotionally return to that moment of decision and conversion, their commitment to God could be strengthened. His strong portrayal of the attributes of burial and resurrection is undoubtedly an effort to awaken a precious memory in the minds of his readers. Paul's discussion of these characteristics of baptism continues well into the third chapter of Colossians. Had these men and women not actually participated in a symbolic burial and resurrection, Paul's words would certainly not provide the emotional spark that he sought in order to refresh their faith.

Interestingly, it is not Paul's intent to focus on the mode of baptism in these passages. The heart of his message centers on the significance of baptism to the Christian life. The picture of immersion (burial) that Paul offers is present by default as he discusses the symbolism found in the act of baptism. Immersion was understood by his readers and simply reflected that symbolism. There was no need for Paul to dwell on the mode of immersion for two reasons. First of all, the wording in the Greek language depicts immersion. Secondly, those to whom he penned these words had experienced the very baptism (immersion) of which he wrote.

God's Word plainly binds the form of baptism to its very purpose. If regeneration occurred prior to baptism, a persuasive argument could be made that the form of baptism is really unimportant. Forgiveness and salvation prior to baptism would truly relegate it to the role of a superficial ceremony. However, given Paul's explanation of the symbolism and the labors of God that are involved, the mode and purpose of baptism may not be separated without destroying completely the role of baptism as it is presented in Scripture.

Challenges to immersion as the baptism of Scripture rely mostly upon the claim that baptism does not need to mean immersion, and/or that the biblical examples or teaching about baptism are unconvincing in determining the method used. After all, could not Philip and the eunuch have entered the water together where Philip then poured water over him as a matter of baptism (Acts 8: 38)? Did John baptize where there was *much water* because he required it for immersion or because the many who came out to see him would simply need water for personal use (John 3: 23)? Is Paul's reference to burial in connection with baptism purely symbolic with no real reference to the mode of baptism (Romans 6: 4; Colossians 2: 12)? If we ignore the meaning of $\beta\alpha\pi\tau\iota\zeta\omega$ in the Greek and the historical records depicting baptism as immersion in the first century, these questions might be considered reasonable. However, ignoring Greek terminology and historic records is a questionable approach to understanding Scripture.

The Bible offers an abundance of evidence not only that the form of baptism was by immersion, but that this form was meaningful for its characterization of the death, burial, and resurrection of Christ. If Paul considered significant the manner in which people were baptized, perhaps we would do well to consider its significance today. The meaning of the words employed in the original Greek, as well as the symbolism expressed in the baptism of which Paul wrote, point specifically to immersion as the form of baptism that was used in New Testament times. Therefore, it seems only reasonable that the burden of proof for another mode must lie with those who profess it. Since Scripture offers no evidence for any other form of baptism, we should teach and practice immersion in keeping with God's Word.

NOTES FOR CHAPTER 8

1. Alexander Campbell addressed well the meaning of the word baptizo as *immersion* or *dipping*. He makes the important point that the origin of a word, in this case bapto, must not be ignored when determining a word's intended meaning. Citing a multitude of

independent historically authoritative works, he notes that *all* consider the word baptizo, unless a figurative use is explicit in the text or implicit in the context, should always be understood as immerse, dip, or plunge. Following are examples of those references as found in Alexander Campbell, <u>Christian Baptism, with Its Antecedents and Consequents,</u> (1851).

> We shall first hear the venerable Scapula, a foreign lexicographer, of 1579. On *bapto,* the root, what does this most learned lexicographer depose? Hear him: "*Bapto*--mergo; immergo, item tingo (quod sit immergendo)." To translate his Latin--To dip, to immerse; also, to dye, *because that may be done by immersing.* Of the passive *baptomai* he says, "Mergor, item lavor--to be immersed, to be washed." Of *Baptizo*--"Mergo seu immergo, item submergo, item abluo, lavo--To dip, to immerse; also, to submerge or overwhelm, to wash, to cleanse."

> Next comes the more ancient Henricus Stephanus, of 1572. *Bapto* and *baptizo*-- "Mergo seu immergo ut quae tingendi aut abluendi gratia aqua immergimus-- To dip or immerge, as we dip things for the purpose of dyeing them, or immerge them in water." He gives the proper and figurative meanings as Scapula gives them.

> Schleusner, a name revered by orthodox theologians, and of enviable fame, says, (Glasgow ed. 1822,)--"1st. Proprie, immergo ac intingo, in aquam immergo. Properly it signifies, I immerse, I dip, I immerse in water. 2d. It signifies, I wash or cleanse by water--(quia haud raro aliquid immergi ac intingi in aquam solet ut lavetur)--because, for the most part, a thing must be dipped or plunged into water that it may be washed." Thus he gives the reason why *baptizo* figuratively means to wash, because that it is frequently the effect of immersion. Alexander Campbell, <u>Christian Baptism, with Its Antecedents and Consequents,</u> (1851).

2. Strong's Concordance
http://cf.blueletterbible.org/lang/lexicon/lexicon.cfm?Strongs=G911&Version=KJV, Accessed January 15, 2005.

3. T. J. Conant offers insight into the separation of these two washing ceremonies that were performed by the Pharisees.

> The unvarying sense of the word (baptizo) is expressly distinguished from the application of water to some portion of the body denoted by other words. In Mark 7: 3, it is said that the Pharisees "eat not" (i.e., never eat) "except they wash their hands," these being always liable to ceremonial defilement; and that when they come from a public place, as the market (the whole body having been exposed), "except they IMMERSE (BAPTIZE) THEMSELVES, they eat not." In the former case, the writer uses the appropriate word (NIPTEIN) for washing any portion of the body; as the *face* (Matt. 6: 17), the *hands* (Matt. 15: 2), the *feet* (John 13: 5). In the latter case he uses, in distinction from it, the word BAPTIZEIN, which by constant usage expressed an entire submersion of the object spoken of. As there is here no limitation ("they IMMERSE THEMSELVES"), the whole body of course is meant. Conant, <u>The Meaning and Use of Baptizein,</u> Published by The Wakeman Trust 2002, page 119.

Alexander Campbell also addresses quite effectively this particular episode between Jesus and the Pharisees.

These washings before dinner, reported by Mark and Luke, contain the only two instances in which any part of *baptizo* is ever translated by *wash,* in the New Testament. And, fortunately, the antithesis between the washings here mentioned, indicated by the words employed in the original, and the facts stated, not only does not sustain the common version in translating both words by the same word, *wash;* but clearly intimates that the latter term, *baptizo,* ought here to have been rendered immerse. In verse 3d, it is *nipto* with *pugmee,* a word already shown to mean washing the hands, face, or feet, always when applied to the human person. This is true in every case in the Bible. Moreover, it has *pugmee,* the fist, in construction with it; that is, as Lightfoot and others interpret it, to the wrist, or so far as the fist extends. When the hand is shut, says Pollux, as quoted by Carson, the outside is called *pugmee.*[1] Now, as this limits the first washing, the second, being expressed by *baptizo,* and having no part of the body mentioned as its peculiar regimen, according to the usage of the Greeks, (and the Romans, in the case of *lavo,*) the whole body is meant. Hence, they dip or bathe themselves after being to market; whereas, ordinarily, they wash their hands only up to the wrist. [166] Alexander Campbell, Christian Baptism, with Its Antecedents and Consequents, Book Second, Chapter 10 (1851).

4. James Strong, LL.D., S.T.D., The New Strong's Exhaustive Concordance of the Bible, Greek Dictionary of the New Testament, p. 18, 1990, Thomas Nelson Publishers.

5. James Strong, LL.D., S.T.D., The New Strong's Exhaustive Concordance of the Bible, Greek Dictionary of the New Testament, p. 50, 1990, Thomas Nelson Publishers.

6. James Strong, LL.D., S.T.D., The New Strong's Exhaustive Concordance of the Bible, Greek Dictionary of the New Testament, p. 19, 1990, Thomas Nelson Publishers.

7. James Strong, LL.D., S.T.D., The New Strong's Exhaustive Concordance of the Bible, Greek Dictionary of the New Testament, p. 15, 1990, Thomas Nelson Publishers.

8. Funk & Wagnals Desk Dictionary Volume 1 A-M, p. 27, 1980, Lippincott & Crowell, Publishers.

9. James Strong, LL.D., S.T.D., The New Strong's Exhaustive Concordance of the Bible, Greek Dictionary of the New Testament, p. 12, 1990, Thomas Nelson Publishers.

10. James Strong, LL.D., S.T.D., The New Strong's Exhaustive Concordance of the Bible, Greek Dictionary of the New Testament, p. 73, 1990, Thomas Nelson Publishers.

11. http://www.realtime.net/~wdoud/topics/hermeneutics.html, Lesson 11, Types, Symbols, and Parables.

12. The General Epistles: A Practical Faith, Practial Christianity Foundation, L. L. Speer, Founder, Green Key Books, p. 174.

13. The New Advent Catholic Encyclopedia, Volume 2; Matter and Form of the Sacrament (1) b.

14. *A GENERAL HISTORY OF THE BAPTIST DENOMINATION IN AMERICA, AND OTHER PARTS OF THE WORLD* was written by David Benedict in 1813. In this work is found the following excerpt with respect to the history of the various modes of baptism. "The Council of Ravenna, 1311, legalized the baptism of sprinkling, but the

155

practice of 'clinical,' or bedside baptism had long been in use and spread from the sickroom into the churches." David Benedict, <u>A General history of the Baptist Denomination in America and Other Parts of the World</u>, 1813.

15. *International Standard Bible Encyclopedia*.

16. James Strong, LL.D., S.T.D., <u>The New Strong's Exhaustive Concordance of the Bible, Greek Dictionary of the New Testament</u>, p. 68, 1990, Thomas Nelson Publishers.

17. James Strong, LL.D., S.T.D., <u>The New Strong's Exhaustive Concordance of the Bible, Greek Dictionary of the New Testament</u>, p. 35, 1990, Thomas Nelson Publishers.

Chapter IX
One, and Only One, Baptism

The Baptism the Apostles Taught

Bible scholars do not completely agree on the date that the book of Ephesians was written. In fact, some even question whether Paul was the author of the book of Ephesians. However, it is difficult to attribute this work to someone else given the initial greeting in chapter one and Paul's reference to himself in chapter three. It is possible that the letter was dictated to one of Paul's companions, but authorship ultimately falls upon Paul.

Ephesians was written at some point in time after Paul's ministry in Ephesus. We can draw this conclusion from their personal concern about Paul's welfare, which he discusses in his closing remarks. He was obviously addressing people who knew him and cared a great deal about his well-being. Paul twice alludes to the notion that he was a prisoner at the time he wrote the epistle. While some believe he may have been a prisoner in Ephesus, it would have been for a very short period of time. He was also imprisoned in Caesarea for a while around A. D. 58-60. Yet we get a sense from the narrative of the book that it had been a while since Paul had seen these friends.

While pinpointing the exact date of this epistle is difficult, it is likely that the book was written between A. D. 61–62 when Paul was a prisoner in Rome, roughly four or five years after he had completed his ministry in Ephesus. Paul finds no fault with the faith or works of the Christians at Ephesus. This letter is Paul's proactive effort to guard this group of believers against things that might lead them to fall from grace and cause division within the body.

Paul explained to the Ephesians that baptism should be considered one of the unique unifying elements of the body of Christ (Ephesians 4: 5). Logic tells us that this baptism must be the same water baptism he taught while he was among them. It is the very baptism he administered in Ephesus in the nineteenth chapter of Acts. He does not suggest to the Ephesians that the *one baptism* mentioned here is anything other than what they had already been taught – by him.

Peter's lesson that baptism in water is the *'antitype which now saves us'* (1 Peter 3: 21) is confirmed by the many baptisms in which Paul participated and about which he wrote. Baptism, as it is presented in Paul's words to the Romans, is an occasion when we are buried and raised (Romans 6: 3-8). This can only be the same water baptism experienced by the Ethiopian eunuch (Acts 8: 38), Cornelius (Acts 10: 48), Lydia (Acts 16: 15), the Philippian jailer (Acts 16: 33), and Paul himself (Acts 22: 16). It is the very moment, as Paul told the Galatians, that we *put on Christ* (Galatians 3: 27). Two apostles, writing by the inspiration of the Holy Spirit, would not – could not – contradict each other by teaching about two separate baptisms, each of which held the capacity to save.

The Baptism of Rebirth – John 3: 5

Each of the apostles whose works were included in the Bible wrote about the ceremony of water baptism. Paul's letters are filled with lessons about the meaning and redemptive value of immersion in water (1 Corinthians 6: 11; Galatians 3: 27; Ephesians 4: 5). His writings teach us that baptism is a time of renewal and rebirth (Romans 6: 1-4; Titus 3: 5). Peter identifies baptism as a significant matter when it comes to forgiveness of sins and salvation (Acts 2: 38; 1 Peter 3: 21). Each one recognized the work and gift of the Holy Spirit that are associated with water baptism (Acts 2: 38; 19: 1-3).

The apostle Matthew wrote about the ministry of John the Baptist in his gospel letter and recorded John's prophecy about baptism with the Holy Spirit (Matthew 3: 11). Much of the apostle John's writing concerning baptism also deals with that performed by John the Baptist. Mark and Luke, who were not apostles, identified the baptism of John the Baptist as a *'baptism of repentance for the remission of sins'* (Mark 1: 4; Luke 3: 3) and the apostle John revealed its purifying nature (John 3: 25-26).

In his opening remarks in the first chapter of the gospel that bears his name, the apostle John mentioned the concept of spiritual rebirth (John 1: 12-13). He said that those who have received Christ had been *'born of God.'* The topic resurfaces in John's account of a conversation that took place between Jesus and a Pharisee by the name of Nicodemus. Jesus explained to Nicodemus that a man must be *'born again'* or he could not *'see the kingdom of God'* (John 3: 3). When Nicodemus asked Him exactly how a man could be born again, Jesus answered him plainly.

Jesus answered, "Most assuredly I say to you, unless one is born of water and the Spirit, he cannot enter the kingdom of God." (John 3: 5)

Many men have vigorously argued that Jesus' use of the word *water* in this setting is simply a reference to physical childbirth, since amniotic fluid surrounds the fetus in the womb, and that being born again is what Jesus meant by *born of Spirit*. Others believe this is either a figurative use of the term *water*, as it occasionally appears in the New Testament, or a reference to the Spirit Himself. Still others maintain that Jesus is highlighting a direct connection between immersion in water and salvation as God has defined it in His plan. The dilemma this presents can only have one true answer. For the sake of the salvation of many, we cannot afford a mistake in determining what that answer is.

It is a bit awkward to suggest that Jesus would teach Nicodemus that he must experience physical childbirth in order to enter the kingdom of God. Yet, this is what many claim He was saying to Nicodemus. Instruction regarding childbirth would be completely irrelevant in a discussion about salvation since all men were brought into the world through childbirth. Additionally, this approach to Jesus' remark effectively breaks up a statement, *'born of water and the Spirit,'* that is too tightly woven to allow it. The answer Jesus gave Nicodemus was in direct response to his question regarding what it means to be born again. Jesus explained that a person must be *'born of water and the Spirit.'* This statement is intended to offer Nicodemus clarification of the phrase *born again.*

When the subject arises in Scripture, childbirth is consistently referred to as *'born of flesh'* (John 3: 6; Galatians 4: 23) *or 'born of woman'* (Job 14: 1; 15: 14; 25: 4; Matthew 11: 11). The phrase *'born of water'* is not used to identify childbirth, nor is that the case here. On the other hand, *water* often refers to baptism and/or being born again or renewed (Acts 8: 36; 10: 47; Hebrews 10: 22; Titus 3: 5; 1 Peter 3: 21). In His explanation of how a man might be *'born again,'* Jesus links *'born of water'* with *'born of Spirit,'* indicating that the two are inseparable and that neither may be ignored by those who wish to *'see the kingdom of God'* (v. 5). In fact, His words indicate that this is not two births, one *'of water'* and one *'of the Spirit,'* but one birth involving *both* water and Spirit.

In His remark immediately following the words *'born of water and the Spirit,'* Jesus actually notes the difference between being *'born of flesh'* (childbirth) and *'born of Spirit'* (v. 6). He would not bind these two births so tightly in verse five only to distinguish between them in His next breath. Therefore, *'born of water'* must indicate something other than childbirth – something that is an element of rebirth (v. 3).

Men often fail to consider the relevance of the Jewish culture to this conversation. The truth is that Nicodemus, raised as an Israelite, had always understood that the relationship between God and the children of Israel was established as a (physical) birthright. In His response to Nicodemus that a man must be born again, Jesus knew the perspective from which this Pharisee viewed his relationship with God. Rather than suggesting that childbirth was somehow a condition of salvation, Jesus explained in verse six that a man's relationship with God was *no longer* a matter of human heritage. For that reason Jesus could not be presenting childbirth as a condition of salvation. On the contrary, in the new covenant childbirth was removed as a matter of participation in the covenant and replaced with a new birth – a *birth of water and Spirit.* Therefore, despite insistence by many that the terminology reflects childbirth, this is not a viable option in identifying the meaning of the phrase *'born of water.'*

Others insist that the water about which Jesus spoke figuratively represents either the Word of God or the Spirit or some kind of spiritual symbolic water we might *drink* in order to receive eternal life. Certainly, there are other times when the word *water* is used symbolically in the New Testament. On a number of occasions in His ministry Jesus spoke of quenching a spiritual thirst with *'living water'* (John 4: 7-10). Later the apostle John also wrote about the *'waters of life'* (Revelation 21: 6; 22: 1, 17).

What is evident in instances where water is applied in such a figurative manner is that the author or speaker always makes it clear that the word is being used symbolically. Jesus does not suggest, in His conversation with Nicodemus, that He was speaking of anything but *bona fide* water. Here the word *water* stands on its own without any reference to *'living water'* or *'waters of life.'* Each time Jesus spoke of water without direct figurative application, He was referring to the physical substance of water (Matthew 10: 42; Mark 9: 41; 14: 13; Luke 5: 4; 7: 44; 13: 15;

16: 24; 22: 10; John 2: 7; Acts 1: 5). We have no reason to make an exception in this case.

Despite overwhelming evidence, many continue to insist that Jesus could not have been referring to Christian baptism in His conversation with Nicodemus. After all, while both proselyte baptism and John's baptism were available at the time, Christian baptism was still to come. This fact has led men to suggest that Jesus would not have instructed Nicodemus about baptism in the church age since it had not yet been introduced. Yet Jesus stated that in order to enter the kingdom, a man must be born of water and the Spirit. This raises the question, could Nicodemus have been *'born of Spirit'* at this time? Exactly what does it mean to be *'born of Spirit'*? Was this an element of the baptism of John? Did the forgiveness offered through John's baptism constitute spiritual birth, or does this phrase have something more in view?

Jesus undoubtedly knew that a Pharisee such as Nicodemus would recognize *'born of water'* as the baptism of John. This would have been a reference point for Nicodemus. Furthermore, forgiveness was available through John's baptism. Therefore, it makes sense that Jesus was pointing Nicodemus toward baptism as a matter of forgiveness. That is certainly Jesus' most immediate meaning for the Pharisee, despite the fact that he lived under the Mosaic Law. While baptism was not yet commanded as a matter of salvation, it was recognized as ordained by God. Those who refused John's baptism were deemed to have *'rejected the will of God'* (Luke 7: 30). Therefore, Jesus was telling Nicodemus that he should be baptized with the baptism of John.

It is also important to recognize that Jesus' conversation with Nicodemus, like most of His teaching, is equally meant for those of us who live in the covenant of grace. Messages about the coming kingdom were often embedded within Jesus' words. The beatitudes (Matthew 5: 1-11) and the parables were certainly reflective of the new covenant. He also alluded to the Lord's Supper before introducing it to the disciples (John 6: 49-58). A feature of Jesus' role on earth was to speak of things yet to come. Because of this, His listeners did not always fully grasp the deeper meaning of His words (Matthew 13: 13; Mark 4: 11-12), nor did Jesus expect them to understand.

As we consider John the Baptist's prophesy concerning *baptism in the Holy Spirit* (Matthew 3: 11), it seems reasonable to conclude that birth of Spirit about which Jesus spoke involves the gift of the Spirit that was reserved for the church age (Acts 2: 38). John the Baptist realized that the baptism he performed could not offer men the kind of relationship with God that they would experience through the Spirit in the new covenant. Furthermore, from Jesus' own lips we learn that the Holy Spirit would not be given to men until after He had ascended to heaven (John 7: 39). The view that *'born of water and the Spirit'* reflects *Christian* baptism also fits perfectly with Paul's words to Titus concerning *'the washing of regeneration and the renewing of the Holy Spirit'* (Titus 3: 5). The two phrases, one by Jesus and one by Paul, appear to express the very same thought.

If being born of Spirit is limited to the church age, Nicodemus could not, at this time, be born of Spirit in the Christian sense (with the gift of the Spirit). Such a rebirth would not be available to men until the new covenant was established. Thus, Jesus' words point to a time when it would be possible to be *'born of water and the Spirit.'* The fact that those Ephesians who had received John's baptism were later baptized in the name of Jesus (Acts 19: 5) indicates that John's baptism was not sufficient once the new covenant was established, and that being *born of Spirit* is intended to direct us to Christian baptism.

Consequently, if the water in this passage reflects immersion in water, Jesus is solidly placing upon mankind the specific condition of baptism in water as a key element of rebirth, stating that short of baptism a man *'cannot enter the kingdom of God'* (John 3: 5). Later in this book we will examine some of the writings of the early church fathers. In their works we find that they viewed Jesus' conversation with Nicodemus as a clear directive for water baptism.

The logical conclusion from a biblical standpoint is that the water in this conversation points to immersion in water since it is the view that harmonizes with the balance of Scripture. This is hardly the only instance where baptism is portrayed as the time of the new birth. Paul calls it, *'newness of life,'* (Romans 6: 4). He told the Corinthians that they had been, *'washed...in the name of the Lord Jesus and by the Spirit of our God'* (1 Corinthians 6: 11). Additionally, Peter stated that being born again occurs as a result of purification, which in turn comes through obedience to the truth (1 Peter 1: 22-23) - a comment that is offered just prior to his claim that baptism saves (1 Peter 3: 21). He also identifies baptism as the time of forgiveness (Acts 2: 38). Jesus' words to Nicodemus are in complete accord with various other instructive passages concerning baptism, including His own words to His disciples (Matthew 28:19; Mark 16: 16).

The fact that Jesus had baptism in mind in His discussion with Nicodemus is also supported by the apostle John, who happened to record this episode. Like Jesus, John substituted the word *water* for the word *baptism*. In challenging the Gnostics of his day in his first epistle, John taught that water (a direct reference to Jesus' baptism by John the Baptist) stands as a witness of Christ's deity and, hence, our salvation (1 John 5: 6-11). John must have understood, given his use of the word *water* to indicate *baptism*, that when Jesus spoke of being *born of water and the Spirit*, His focus was baptism.

Men are often very persistent as they insist that the water of John 3: 5 *might* be considered *childbirth, the Holy Spirit, symbolic water*, or even limited to the baptism performed by John the Baptist. Most consider the meaning of water in this passage unimportant as long as it is *not* Christian baptism; therefore, any of these viewpoints is believed to be acceptable. Of course, these same men cannot verify its absolute meaning; they can only tell us what they are convinced it does not mean. However, if men can only guess about its meaning, how can those very same men say with any confidence that it does not mean baptism? Since a man's failure to be *born of water and the Spirit* not only can, but will keep him from heaven, it seems rather careless to be unconcerned with the meaning of the phrase. Yet the reason men remain uncommitted about the meaning of the expression *'born of water'* is simply an unwillingness to accept the only meaning that suits the message, which is baptism.

Paul wrote about one baptism that was unique within the kingdom (Ephesians 4: 5). This one baptism, so vital that Paul went out of his way to note its significance, can be none other than the baptism identified in other works of Peter and Paul. In speaking to Nicodemus, Jesus talked about a birth of water so meaningful that failure to experience it would disqualify an individual from entering God's kingdom (John 3: 5). Peter stated boldly that baptism saves (1 Peter 3: 21). The connection between baptism and salvation in the New Testament leaves no room for maneuvering. The birth of water mentioned in John 3: 5 can be nothing other than the one baptism of Ephesians 4: 5 – Christian immersion in water for the remission of sins.

God has sewn a thread throughout Scripture that is undeniable. Through the use of this thread the Bible always explains itself fully, at least on those issues that are of greatest significance. Quite often we receive clarification by such elementary means that an accompanying verse escapes us. Such is the case with the account of the discussion between Jesus and Nicodemus. Their conversation begins in the second verse of the third chapter of John and continues through the twenty-first verse. It is the twenty-second verse that provides a wake-up call regarding this account.

> After these things Jesus and His disciples came into the land of Judea, and there He remained with them and baptized. (John 3: 22)

Jesus not only explained to Nicodemus that being born again involved being baptized; but He followed that teaching by example.

Baptism with the Holy Spirit and with Fire
Paul stated that there is *one baptism* (Ephesians 4: 5). Despite that fact, two additional baptisms are prophesied by John the Baptist. In his role as forerunner to Christ, John the Baptist took every advantage of the opportunities available to him as he prepared the people for Jesus' coming. In seeming contrast to the water baptism he offered, John points to baptism with the Holy Spirit and baptism with fire (Matthew 3: 11) as two baptisms that were yet to come. His words suggest that, in New Testament times, certain kinds of baptism may, in fact, surpass his own water baptism. (Since an entire chapter is dedicated to *baptism with the Holy Spirit*, details concerning it will not be discussed here.)

While this episode in Matthew, and its corresponding passage in the gospel of Luke (Luke 3: 16), is the only reference specifically to a *baptism* with fire in the New Testament, it is not a particularly encouraging picture. The image of fire as a means of *purification* and/or *punishment* was not a new concept for the Israelites to whom John was speaking. Sacrifices in the Old Testament were burned on an altar as a means of cleansing the people from their sins. It is possible that Abel, the son of Adam and Eve, offered burnt offerings to God, but fire is first mentioned in the Old Testament when Noah and his family exited the ark (Genesis 8: 20).

We know that Abraham offered burnt offerings to God (Genesis 22: 8) and, in like manner, the Israelites were commanded to provide burnt offerings for their sins (Leviticus 9: 8-10). These animal sacrifices were central among the rituals commanded by God. Records of these offerings are scattered through the Old Testament and provide us with testimony as to God's use of fire for the purpose of purification.

Occasionally, however, God used fire as a more direct means of purging evil. When God destroyed the cities of Sodom and Gomorrah, He did it with fire (Genesis 19: 24). As Joshua was leading the Israelites, God had him destroy the enemy cities with fire (Joshua 6: 24; 8: 8-19; 11: 11). Elijah called down fire from heaven to destroy those who opposed God (2 Kings 1: 9-14). In several other instances we discover that God used fire to rid the earth of evil. These accounts suggest that baptism with fire is something we should avoid. An expanded look at the excerpt from Matthew will reveal additional relevant information concerning baptism with fire (Matthew 3: 10-12).

Baptism with fire, as the phrase implies, seems to point to a future judgment. The fire will apparently consume sinners at the time of judgment in much the same way that men are overwhelmed by water in baptism. This baptism, then, is one that should be feared, but only by those who are unfaithful to God. Whether the fire is literal or figurative in nature, it offers a frightening portrait of the wrath of God (Hebrews 12: 29).

The baptism with fire prophesied by John the Baptist cannot be mistaken for the one baptism taught by Paul and the other apostles. At no time in the New Testament epistles do the apostles ever even discuss baptism with fire. It is certainly not identified as a matter of salvation. On the contrary, it seems to be more a matter of condemnation.

Baptism – A Once-in-a-Lifetime Experience

Paul's reference to *one baptism* in the book of Ephesians is often hotly contested. Some view it as confirmation of immersion in water as the one baptism that is endorsed by Paul. Others have claimed, and perhaps justifiably so, that it may not be completely fair to assume that Paul is pointing specifically to the *method* of baptism in his words to the church at Ephesus. After all, any reference to the *one Lord's Supper* among this grouping is conspicuously absent. The argument is that *one baptism* is not meant to suggest a single mode of baptism, but the fact that this event is intended to take place only once in the life of each Christian.[1] The same cannot be said of the Lord's Supper. The rite of Communion was never intended to be a one-time observance. Instead it is a continuing celebration of the sacrifice of Jesus' body and blood. Baptism is a single ceremony through which our sins are forgiven. One who has been baptized need not be baptized a second time. The Christian's sins are forgiven, once and for all, through the one baptism. The author of the book of Hebrews uses this very reasoning in the ninth and tenth chapters as he contrasts the old and new covenants. Of course, forgiveness of future sins of the immersed believer is still dependent upon a life of continual repentance.

This view of *one baptism* does not change the fact that, throughout his ministry, Paul taught immersion in water as the baptism of entrance into the kingdom. The claim is merely that the method of immersion in water may not be the primary focus of Paul's words in this instance. Still, it is in the one-time immersion in the waters of baptism that each man is cleansed permanently from a guilty conscience of sin and presented, pure and holy, to Christ.

NOTES FOR CHAPTER 9

1. Tertullian was a strong advocate of the teaching that immersion in water was essential for an individual's salvation. Nonetheless, his view regarding the one baptism mentioned in Ephesians takes the perspective that this passage more accurately denotes the once in a lifetime occasion of the rite rather than the singular method in which it is administered.

Chapter X

When Does Baptism Mean Water?

As we study what the Bible has to say on the subject of baptism we become keenly aware that some scriptural accounts utilize the words *baptize* or *baptism* in a context where it cannot possibly mean immersion in water. This is a source of confusion for many. Certain other passages mention baptism without clearly explaining exactly what is involved. Still other New Testament texts describe in detail the type of baptism being addressed. This apparent inconsistency has fostered a number of thoughts regarding biblical teachings with respect to baptism. A thorough examination of the many references to baptism throughout the Bible does, however, provide answers to the concerns raised by this seeming disparity.

When Baptism Obviously Means Water

There are times when we can, with absolute certainty, conclude that water is involved in the baptism being discussed. This is easily determined in a number of passages in the gospels where baptism is the topic. Often the message is crystal clear in that the use of water as a vehicle for baptism is plainly stated (Matthew 3: 5-16; Mark 1: 4-9; Luke 3: 16; John 1: 25-33).

...for John truly baptized with water... (Acts 1: 5)

The baptism performed by John the Baptist was unquestionably a baptism in water. Nowhere in Scripture do we find the slightest suggestion that John used any instrument other than water for baptism. Since we know that John baptized in water we can reason that when the baptism being addressed is that performed by John, it is *always* baptism in water. Consequently, in certain other passages where baptism is the topic of discussion, the vehicle must be water even though the author or speaker does not specifically mention it (Matthew 21: 25; Mark 11: 30; Luke 3: 2-12, 21; 7: 29-30; 20: 4; Acts 1: 21-22; 10: 37; 13: 23-24; 18: 25; 19: 3-4).

Given the fact that John baptized with water, and by applying some simple reasoning, we can conclude that several other times when baptism is mentioned, water is certainly the instrument of reference. For example, the baptism performed by Jesus' disciples was undoubtedly baptism in water since the Bible mentions no difference between the kind of baptism administered by John the Baptist and that performed by Jesus' followers (John 3: 22-26). A careful examination of the gospels (the books of Matthew, Mark, Luke, and John) reveals that the baptisms performed there always involved water.

While the baptisms performed by John the Baptist and Jesus' disciples were significant, the baptism in which people participated after Jesus' resurrection and ascension must be given consideration. It is this baptism that is relevant to the church age. Several examples from the book of Acts depict water as the device in which men and women were baptized. These include the account of Philip teaching the gospel to the Ethiopian eunuch (Acts 8: 36) and Peter's visit to the house of Cornelius (Acts 10: 46-48). The conclusion that both the Ethiopian eunuch and those present at the house of Cornelius were baptized in water is plainly stated in the text. However, at other times the Bible is not quite so explicit in identifying the vehicle of baptism.

Before we endeavor to probe passages that may be in question, let us consider another baptism that is cited in the Bible so that we might gain better insight.

Death, Burial, and Resurrection - The Baptism of Jesus

In addition to baptism with fire and baptism with the Holy Spirit (Matthew 3: 11), which John the Baptist contrasted with water, the gospels indicate another occasion that is justifiably called baptism. The mother of James and John, as a matter of pride, asked Jesus to grant her sons positions of prominence in the kingdom that is to come. Jesus responded with the following remarks directed toward her sons:

> But Jesus answered and said, "You do not know what you ask. Are you able to drink the cup that I am about to drink, and be baptized with the baptism that I am baptized with?" (Matthew 20: 22)

Luke addresses this same baptism in a somewhat different setting, but there can be no mistaking the unique event of which Jesus is speaking.

> But I have a baptism to be baptized with, and how distressed I am till it is accomplished! (Luke 12: 50)

168

We can all agree that the baptism mentioned by Jesus in this setting was not water, fire, or Holy Spirit baptism. While the use of the word *baptism* may be considered somewhat symbolic in this instance, the event of which Jesus was speaking was all too real as He was looking forward with great anguish to His own death, burial, and resurrection. The significance of Jesus' words lies in the fact that these are the very elements after which water baptism was designed (Romans 6: 3-4).

When Water Is Not Intimated

While baptism with water and fire, as well as Jesus' death and resurrection, to which He refers as a baptism, may be easily explained, we must now contend with those passages where some form of the word *baptize* is used without specifying a medium (water, fire, etc) for that baptism. These passages are often at the heart of the discord that persists among believers when it comes to baptism. A thorough study of each of these instances should provide us with the insight we need to make a determination about the kind of baptism to which each passage points.

Jesus spoke the Great Commission (Matthew 28: 19-20), as it is so often called, to His followers after His resurrection. His apostles were to go into the world and lead people to follow Him, *baptizing them.* The baptism discussed in this passage must be seen as a baptism that was to be performed by men since it is something Jesus clearly commanded them to do. A study of the prophecies of Jesus (Acts 1: 5) and John the Baptist (Matthew 3: 11) regarding baptism with the Holy Spirit and baptism with fire suggests that these were not to be performed by men, but by God. As we sift through the book of Acts, we discover that the baptism performed by those whom Jesus had commanded to baptize was indeed baptism in water. Based on the evidence available to us in Scripture, the baptism commanded in the Great Commission was unquestionably baptism in water.

15. And He said to them, "Go into all the world and preach the gospel to every creature. 16. He who believes and is baptized will be saved; but he who does not believe will be condemned." (Mark 16: 16)

The final chapter of Mark, like the last chapter of Matthew, is a brief summation of Jesus' resurrection and ascension. Included here are some of Jesus' final instructions to His followers prior to

His ascension. On this occasion Jesus told His disciples that men must believe and be baptized while declaring the consequences for those who refused. Since baptism is linked here with belief, and since belief is a responsibility of man, we can see that this baptism is also a duty of man. It is something men are commanded to do. The only baptism that is taught in Scripture as man's responsibility is baptism in water (Matthew 28: 19; Acts 2: 38).

The Day of Pentecost

When the Day of Pentecost arrived, Peter called upon those who wished to follow Christ to *'repent and be baptized'* (Acts 2: 38). Since water is not mentioned in this passage, the greater landscape of Scripture must be considered so that we can determine the kind of baptism about which the apostle was speaking.

Those who believed their teaching about Christ asked the apostles a question that carries with it a sense of timelessness. It is a question that is asked in one form or other by everyone who comes to the realization that they are lost in their sins. They asked, *'...what shall we do?'* (Acts 2: 37) In his answer that they should *'repent and...be baptized,'* Peter placed the responsibility to accomplish these tasks squarely on the shoulders of his listeners. Peter obviously believed they had the capacity to *obey* his instructions. They could not choose to be baptized with the Holy Spirit or with fire since these were to be administered by God. Given this, along with the fact that only days had passed since Jesus had commanded His followers to go and baptize *with water*, the only possible conclusion is that Peter was speaking of baptism in water. A review of Cornelius' conversion (Acts 10: 47) reveals that the baptism commanded by Peter at that time was also water baptism. Although Peter had witnessed the Holy Spirit being poured out on these Gentiles, he still commanded water baptism just as Jesus had ordained it. He would have done no less on the Day of Pentecost.

A significant element of baptism on the Day of Pentecost is that it was united together with repentance. The only baptism prior to this that was tied to repentance was the baptism of John the Baptist and, by association, the baptism performed by Jesus' disciples. No other determination can be made, then, but that the baptism commanded by Peter on the Day of Pentecost was baptism in water.

Baptism in Samaria

When Philip was in Samaria preaching to the crowds we are told that *'both men and women were baptized'* (Acts 8: 12). Once again Luke tells us of an incident involving baptism where no specific instrument for that baptism is identified. Yet, we are provided with clear scriptural evidence that the baptism in Samaria was baptism in water.

While Philip was teaching in Samaria an angel of the Lord told him to head south toward Gaza. Philip obediently left Samaria and traveled south where he joined with the Ethiopian eunuch. As the story unfolds we find Philip teaching the eunuch the gospel, to which the eunuch responded, *'See, here is water. What hinders me from being baptized?'* (Acts 8: 36) Once again Philip's teaching resulted in baptism – in water. Given this corresponding text we can, with confidence, conclude that the baptism performed in Samaria was also baptism in water.

The Baptism of Saul

Saul of Tarsus was a man who waged war against Christianity. Miraculous intervention by Jesus turned him from an enemy of the church into Paul, an apostle who spent the remainder of his life teaching others about Christ. Luke records the events surrounding Saul's conversion, first in a narrative (Acts 9: 1-19) and later in Paul's own words as he took the opportunity to reflect personally on his conversion experience (Acts 22: 6-16).

As in other situations, the mode and instrument for baptism are not mentioned. Still, we find in this text a recurring scenario. As was true concerning baptism on the Day of Pentecost, in Samaria, and with the eunuch, Saul appears to have control over the decision to be baptized. He was not told that if he believed God would baptize him with the Holy Spirit. Baptism is a matter of response by Saul. Ananias' instruction is that *he should not hesitate*, but that he should, *'Arise and be baptized.'* Once again God's Word offers abundant support for the determination that this was, indeed, a baptism in water.

For those who insist that *'calling on the name of the Lord'* (Acts 22: 16), aside from baptism, was the means by which Saul's sins were washed away, Scripture simply offers no support for that view. Peter, on the Day of Pentecost, instructed the people that they must be baptized *for forgiveness of their sins.* Interestingly, the circumstances surrounding Saul's conversion are actually quite similar to the events surrounding Peter's meeting with Cornelius. Each man (Saul and Cornelius) was advised what he must *do*. Peter instructed Cornelius just as Ananias directed Saul regarding how he should respond to the gospel. In these two cases, one of the first instructions provided was that each of these men should be baptized – in water. This is the same instruction Peter gave to the Jews on the Day of Pentecost, Philip offered to the Samaritans and the eunuch, and Paul taught to Lydia and the Philippian jailer. This same instruction is no less important for us today.

Through some simple deductive reasoning we can easily determine that several other incidents also involve baptism in water (Acts 16: 15; 33; 18: 8; 19: 5). In each case, it is evident that believers made the decision to receive baptism and that humans administered the rite. No legitimate debate can be raised that these were not accounts involving water.

The Symbolism of Baptism

A number of scholars claim that, in his writings, Paul never specifically stipulated water as a vehicle for baptism. When he does broach the subject, they say he refers to it simply as baptism. Of course, this view ignores those passages where Paul does regard the cleansing of God's people through the washing of water (Ephesians 5: 26; Titus 3: 5) and those times that Paul administered baptism. We can, however, determine what Paul means when he discusses baptism in his epistles. The answer, as always, lies in the study of God's Word.

When Paul wrote to the church in Rome he had not yet journeyed there. Most likely none of the apostles had yet been to Rome. Others (e.g., Ananias and Sapphira) had carried the gospel message to the people there and a church body was formed.

> 3. Or do you not know that as many of us as were baptized into Christ Jesus were baptized into his death? 4. Therefore we were buried with Him through baptism into death, that just as Christ was raised from the dead by the glory of the Father, even so we also should walk in newness of life. 5. For if we have been united together in the likeness of His death, certainly we also shall be *in the likeness* of *His* resurrection, 6. knowing this, that our old man was crucified with *Him*, that the body of sin might be done away with, that we should no longer be slaves of sin. (Romans 6: 3-6)

The imagery of baptism here is captivating, providing what G. R. Beasley-Murray calls *'...the most extensive exposition of baptism Paul has given....* [1] His instruction concerning baptism begins with a simple question to his readers, *'Or do you not know that as many of us as were baptized into Christ Jesus were baptized into His death?'* (Romans 6: 3). This question is rhetorical in the same vein as Jesus' question to Nicodemus in the third chapter of John when He asked, *'Are you a leader of Israel, and do not know these things?'* (John 3: 10). Paul was not seeking an answer, but was reminding these disciples of those things about which they were fully aware.

The apostle Paul was the kind of man who selected his words very deliberately and efficiently. In this passage his aim is to portray baptism as representative of the death, burial, and resurrection of Christ. The *only* baptism found in Scripture that embodies this imagery is immersion in water. The New Testament never suggests that another baptism (Holy Spirit, fire, etc.) might reflect this symbolism. This likeness is specific to immersion in water.

It is during our immersion in water, as defined by Paul in the sixth chapter of Romans, that we are united together with Christ (Romans 6: 5), being *buried with Him.* He also identifies the Romans' submission to baptism as obedience in the following verses (vs. 16-18). This is the same kind of baptism in which Paul participated throughout the book of Acts, whether in submission as he was baptized by Ananias, or as one who administered baptism to others. Therefore, we have no reason to speculate that Paul was speaking of any baptism other than the one he experienced in Damascus and had administered to Lydia and the Philippian jailer, which was water baptism.

Baptism in Corinth

Paul's discussion of baptism in the book of 1 Corinthians is considered critical in the debate surrounding this topic. As the apostle addresses the issue that the Corinthians faced, the narrative provides us with considerable insight into the baptism of which he wrote. He scolded the Corinthians for associating themselves too strongly with the person who had performed their baptism, thus taking the focus off of Christ. Men who were baptized by Paul claimed to be disciples of Paul. Those baptized by Cephas identified themselves with him. Apollos faced the same problem with those whom he had baptized. Given the fact that they were placing on a pedestal those men who had performed these baptisms, we can be confident that the baptism being discussed was administered by men. Paul even acknowledges that he had baptized some of those at Corinth. Reference is specifically made to the conversion of Crispus, whom Paul claims to have baptized. We have already determined that his baptism could be nothing other than immersion in water (Acts 18: 8).

Paul's rebuke of the Corinthians for their error in judgment does not end with the first chapter. In the third chapter we find him still teaching on the same topic and still addressing their claims that they are *'of Paul'* or *'of Apollos.'* He continues his teaching with an illustration of two men, one who plants (preaches) and one who waters (baptizes), recognizing that even with their efforts, no crop can grow without God (1 Corinthians 3: 4-7). In this setting, the *planting and watering* are the *preaching and baptism* mentioned in the first chapter.

Even if nothing more was written, we already have conclusive evidence that baptism in the first chapter of 1 Corinthians is baptism in water, but Paul has not yet finished. In the sixth chapter we discover yet another statement about the baptism of the people at Corinth. Explaining that they could no longer be identified with their former sinful life, Paul defines the reason they were now separate from the world of sin.

> ...But you were washed, but you were sanctified, but you were justified in the name of the Lord Jesus by the Spirit of our God. (1 Corinthians 6: 11)

According to Scripture, we are sanctified (Ephesians 5: 26) and justified (Romans 5: 1 - 6: 7) by the Spirit as we are immersed in water in Jesus' name. Some men try to distinguish between the *washing* that is addressed in the sixth chapter of 1 Corinthians and the *baptism* of the first chapter, but the writing simply will not allow it. Paul binds the teaching together too methodically in these chapters for us to even imagine that they are distinct. Thus, not only does baptism in the first chapter speak of water baptism, but the *watering* and *washing* of the third and sixth chapters point to the same.

Later in the same letter, in the tenth chapter, Paul draws a connection between the Israelites' baptism in the sea, as they escaped the Egyptians by crossing the Red Sea on dry land (1 Corinthians 10: 2), and Christian baptism. He notes at that time how these Israelites of old yielded to temptation even after they had been freed (baptized) in the sea. His warning to the Corinthians was, in their freedom, to avoid the same mistakes. Here the word *baptized* is used in a somewhat figurative sense since the Israelites obviously were not, themselves, immersed in the Red Sea. It was, however, the evil of men (Egyptians) that was immersed, similar to the flood of Noah's day. Furthermore, we should recognize that the Israelites found their freedom through the instrument of water. Like the flood, this baptism could also be considered an *antitype* of Christian baptism.

As we continue through the book of 1 Corinthians, we find that the subject of baptism surfaces two more times. In one instance it is mentioned in response to doubt about resurrection of the dead by some in the church at Corinth. Paul, in response to that doubt, noted that some people were even being *baptized for the dead* (1 Corinthians 15: 29) in search of the resurrection.

Various thoughts have been proposed regarding this passage. Some believe this statement is an indication that one might be discharging a promise made to a loved one who has already passed from this life, thus being *baptized for them*. This suggests that prior to death, a believer may have offered a plea to a close friend or family member, that they might be converted and, thus, see them beyond the grave. Others wonder whether some men might have been baptized out of deep respect for a deceased friend or relative. Still others see this simply as a statement about the Corinthians' own baptism as they anticipated their own resurrection from the dead. This is unlikely, however, given the third person reference to those who participated in baptism for the dead. It is most likely that Paul is talking about a man making a decision to be baptized *on behalf of* one who had died in an effort to save that person's soul.

Regardless of the exact motivation behind the deed, if we consider this passage honestly we must recognize that this is baptism that consists of water since it is, once again, decided upon and administered by men. It is obviously something men *chose* to do. Additionally, other than its objective of salvation for those already deceased, Paul draws no distinction between their participation in this baptism and that discussed in the first chapter of 1 Corinthians. The only baptism to which Paul could be referring is water baptism, even if it was for a purpose he could not endorse.

These remarks to the Corinthians about baptism for the dead also reveal an undeniable link between water baptism and eternal life. While he may not have condoned the practice of baptism for the dead, Paul recognized that the ceremony was being performed in an effort to attain salvation, even if it was for those who had already passed on. This lesson of salvation in baptism is taught throughout Scripture, although clearly the goal of the New Testament is to apply that lesson to those who are living.

The Baptism of 1 Corinthians 12: 13

The Bible consists of many man-made divisions such as chapters and verses that were developed centuries after the apostles penned these works. While these are often beneficial, they can occasionally obscure the intended message. They certainly make it much easier to locate various passages, but they should since this is the very reason they were developed.

Those who designed the divisions in Scripture must have done their best to avoid interfering with the flow of any passage. Yet, there are times when these divisions can be a little distracting. If we view 1 Corinthians simply as a letter that Paul wrote to a church, we find a much clearer picture of the baptism discussed in this epistle.

> For by one Spirit we were all baptized into one body—whether Jews or Greeks, whether slaves or free—and have all been made to drink into one Spirit. (1 Corinthians 12: 13)

The work of Holy Spirit, at the time of water baptism, involves the regeneration of that person who has decided to submit his/her life to God. This is a lesson we have already covered at length. Despite the simplicity of this biblical principle (Acts 2: 38; Colossians 2: 12; Titus 3: 5), many believe that when Paul wrote these words in 1 Corinthians 12: 13, he was talking specifically about baptism with the Holy Spirit, claiming that this occurs separately from water baptism.

Six times in this letter Paul mentions baptism (1 Corinthians 1: 11-17; 3: 1-9; 6: 11; 10: 1-5; 12: 13; 15: 29). Everyone accepts that the baptism discussed in the first through the sixth chapters involves water. This is also true of baptism for the dead in the fifteenth chapter. The tenth chapter holds an allusion to a figurative Old Testament baptism at the crossing of the Red Sea. Now we come to the baptism of the twelfth chapter. Many men have determined from Paul's words at this time that he is discussing baptism with the Holy Spirit *instead of* immersion in water. After all, it does say baptism comes *'by one Spirit'* with no apparent reference to water.

The point was made in the Preface of this book that the context of a word or text might be critical when attempting to determine its true meaning. That is the case here. Just as Paul was not giving approval for baptism for the dead when he wrote concerning it, neither is he distinguishing between immersion in water and baptism with the Holy Spirit in this case.

In the <u>New International Version of the Bible</u>, the twelfth chapter of 1 Corinthians is introduced by a heading just above the first verse. It is titled *Spiritual Gifts*. This is one of those man-made labels that can distract us from the main focus of the text. This subtitle suggests that Paul's aim is to teach his readers about the meaning and purpose of spiritual gifts. Even his opening remarks of the twelfth chapter, as he states, *'Now concerning spiritual gifts...'* (1 Corinthians 12: 1), may lead the reader to believe this is his point.

While the topic of spiritual gifts is addressed, the focus of Paul's lesson is not on the gifts themselves, but on the lack of unity among the church at Corinth due in part to the distribution of these gifts. Indeed, the Corinthians' lack of unity is the theme of the entire letter beginning with Paul's concern in the first chapter over their discord with respect to baptism. Paul now applies this lesson of disharmony to the difficulties that have surfaced among the people, perhaps out of jealousy or confusion, from the distribution of spiritual gifts. Paul is not so concerned with the details of the gifts themselves, but with the fact that they should be an opportunity for unity rather than division within the church.

As we come to the twelfth verse of the chapter, the NIV inserts another heading which is, *One Body, Many Parts,* a title that better defines the topic being discussed. Having addressed in the first several verses the friction that exists with respect to spiritual gifts, Paul turns his focus toward the bigger picture of unity in what he calls the body of Christ. The lesson taught is that, while men have many differences, believers are bonded together through unity in Christ. As Paul considers more deeply the subject of unity, he highlights the assorted roles of the members of the body that help men complement each other's work in Christ. This notion of oneness in Jesus is the subject that is being discussed in verse thirteen; and it must be read and understood in the light of this theme of unity.

Paul's instruction to the Corinthians is that members of the church must be unified in Christ. This is the framework upon which 1 Corinthians 12: 13 rests. The topic of discussion in the first eleven verses is on singleness of purpose rather than on the significance of spiritual gifts. It is this theme that leads us to Paul's comment concerning baptism. If, as Paul suggests, Christians are *'baptized into one body,'* it stands to reason that the baptism of which he speaks is baptism that offers membership in that body. Since the issue here is unity, we can also conclude that this is the baptism that unites the members of that body not only with each other, but with Christ (Romans 6: 5). It is the same baptism Paul addressed earlier when he stated, *'But you were washed, you were sanctified, you were justified, in the name of the Lord Jesus Christ and by the Spirit of our God'* (1 Corinthians 6: 11). Luke wrote, in the book of Acts, that water baptism is the mechanism through which men receive cleansing from sin, fulfillment of the promise of the Holy Spirit, and membership in His body (Acts 2: 38-47). The church, then, is unquestionably the body of Christ to which Paul refers in his letter to the Corinthians (see Colossians 1: 24).

The claim that Paul's words suggest a doctrine of baptism with the Holy Spirit that somehow replaces immersion in water is not supported by the context of this passage within the epistle. In this letter, with the single exception of Paul's reference to the Red Sea (1 Corinthians 10: 2), the apostle has in mind immersion in water (1 Corinthians 1: 13-15; 3: 6; 6: 11; 15: 29). If the baptism found in 1 Corinthians 12: 13 was anything other than the baptism in water that is addressed in the rest of this letter, we could reasonably expect Paul to make that distinction. Yet he does not. There is no need to differentiate between them since they are one and the same.

Two serious mistakes are made by those who consider the baptism of 1 Corinthians 12: 13 to be a lesson regarding baptism with the Holy Spirit, independent from the act of water baptism. The first, quite obviously, is the belief that this is a baptism without water. In his words Paul simply recognizes the association with, and work of, the Holy Spirit during water baptism that is noted at various times in the New Testament (Colossians 2: 11-12; Titus 3: 5). Furthermore, in order to establish this baptism as one that does not involve water we must somehow separate this discussion from Paul's comments in the sixth chapter. There he similarly indicates a washing that takes place *'in the name of Jesus and by the Spirit of our God'* (I Corinthians 6: 11). Yet any attempt to disconnect the two statements proves impossible. Paul unites purification *'by the Spirit'* with a washing that takes place *'in the name of Jesus.'* The only cleansing that is offered in any given name is immersion in water (Matthew 28: 19; Acts 2: 38). If the washing of the sixth chapter *'by the Spirit'* represents water baptism, which it surely does, it is inconsistent with the context of the passage to claim that 12: 13 represents something else.

Many fail to notice the connection between Paul's portrayal of baptism in 1 Corinthians 12: 13 and the baptism of the first chapter. He begins the letter by chastising the Corinthians for making baptism an issue that divides (1 Corinthians 1: 10-17). Now, in the twelfth chapter, he explains the gravity of their mistake. They have become divided over something that is intended to unite men in Christ.

The other error in judgment made by those who insist that Paul is not citing water baptism is the assumption that there exists a baptism other than immersion in water that grants membership into the church. This is a teaching foreign to Scripture. Since the members of the body will inherit the kingdom (Ephesians 3: 6), we must apply to this passage the scriptural principle that the promises of membership in the body (Acts 2: 41) and unity with Christ are fulfilled when one is baptized in water (Romans 6: 5). This occurs in unison with forgiveness of sins and the gift of the Holy Spirit (Acts 2: 38). That is why Paul identifies baptism as a crucial unifying element of Christianity (Ephesians 4: 5). The leap to a separate baptism with the Spirit is a leap made by modern men rather than Paul.

The Baptism of Galatians 3: 27

> For as many of you as were baptized into Christ have put on Christ. (Galatians 3: 27)

In this verses surrounding this one we learn that baptism is accompanied by faith and justification (v. 25), linking it directly to the forgiveness granted at the time of baptism (Acts 2: 38; 1 Corinthians 6: 11). It is also the time when we become sons (children) of God (v. 26), offering a direct connection to the teaching about rebirth found throughout the New Testament (John 3: 3-5; Galatians 6: 15).

Baptism is identified as the time when the Galatians' effectively *put on* Christ Jesus. If this text was discussing an unforeseen act from God, as with Cornelius (Acts 10: 44), Paul might have said that Christ *had been put on them* but, instead, they *had put on Christ.* It was something the Galatians had done. That fact indicates that the decision belonged to each man or woman. Baptism is portrayed here as a response of faith. If it is a response of faith, it is once again baptism initiated and administered by men as opposed to baptism that is involuntary and is not administered by men, but by God (e.g., baptism with fire). Paul's claim that there is but one baptism only confirms that this is water baptism.

The Baptism of Colossians 2: 12

More than once Paul compares baptism to the death, burial, and resurrection of Christ. In his letter to the Colossians, the lesson on baptism is expanded as the apostle offers teaching about the work that God performs on an person at the time of baptism. Similar to his instructions to the Romans, Paul once again portrays this as a baptism where we are *buried* and *raised.*

> 11. In Him you were also circumcized with the circumcision made without hands, but putting off the body of the sins of the flesh, by the circumcision of Christ, 12. buried with Him in baptism, in which you were also raised with *Him* through faith in the working of God, who raised Him from the dead. (Colossians 2: 11-12)

Immersion in water is the only form of baptism that is truly representative of Jesus' death, burial, and resurrection. Therefore, it must apply to Paul's writing to the Colossians. It is true that baptism is a physical act of faith. However, it is through this physical act that God does some of His most magnificent work. Through the sacrifice of Jesus, whose death, burial, and resurrection are symbolized in baptism, God accomplishes some very specific things. He forgives us of our sins. We are provided the promised indwelling of the Holy Spirit. Each one is then added to the body of believers. Finally, we are presented with eternal life.

The Baptism of 1 Peter 3: 21

> 18. For Christ also suffered once for sins, the just for the unjust, that He might bring us to God, being put to death in the flesh but made alive by the Spirit...20. when once the Divine longsuffering waited in the days of Noah, while the ark was being prepared, in which a few, that is, eight souls, were saved through water. 21. There is also an antitype which now saves us—baptism (not the removal of filth from the flesh, but the answer of a good conscience toward God), through the resurrection of Jesus Christ... (1 Peter 3: 18, 20-21)

Many men teach that the *baptism that saves* is not baptism in water, arguing that Noah was not saved through water (as the passage claims) but that he was saved in the ark as he rose above the water. In truth, Noah was saved by faith, a point on which we can all agree; but the connection between baptism and the flood of Noah's day is found specifically in the substance of water. That is why Peter could claim that Noah and his family really *'were saved through water.'*

The apostle's words are not vague. The baptism mentioned by Peter in the twenty-first verse is openly compared, not to the ark, but to the water. Those on the ark *'were saved through water.'* This is not a timid suggestion that baptism *might* be likened to the waters of the flood, but a bold proclamation of that fact. God saved Noah and his family *through water*, and it is the antitype of that water – baptism – through which men are saved today.

The side comment that is offered in verse twenty-one is actually intended to provide further clarification about the main thought of the text, which is that water baptism saves. Peter remarks concerning baptism, *'not the removal of the filth of the flesh, but the answer of a good conscience toward God.'* The claim that this comment signifies a baptism that does not have the *ability* to cleanse the flesh completely ignores the substance of Peter's words. A return to the original Greek text will help us identify the true meaning of this statement. Evidence that this passage points directly to water baptism, in addition to Peter's comparison of baptism to the waters of the flood, is found in a single word – the word translated into English as *but*.

Various words in the Greek language can be translated into English as *but*. Most often the word δε (*de*) is used. This word carries the meaning of *now, therefore, then, verily,* or *in truth*[2], etc. Occasionally it is the word και (*kai*), which tends to mean *and,*

181

also or *even*.[3] However, Peter uses the word αλλα (*alla*) in this instance. The use of this word points to a limitation to a general rule or an exception to a particular thought. Some of the primary definitions of the word are *objection, exception,* or *restriction*.[4] Strong defines it as *contrariwise*.[5] Peter's statement, '*not the removal of filth,*' is intended to differentiate between the water of baptism and the type of cleansing for which water was normally used – physical cleansing. This statement, identifying the function of baptism (*the answer of a good conscience toward God*), is completely out of place unless the baptism about which Peter is writing is immersion in water.

> Not everyone who says to Me, 'Lord, Lord,' shall enter the kingdom of heaven, but (αλλ) he who does the will of My Father in heaven. (Matthew 7: 21)

> But He said to them, "All cannot accept this saying, but (αλλ) only *those* to whom it has been given." (Matthew 19: 11)

> Peter said to Him, "Even if all are made to stumble, yet (αλλ) I *will* not be." (Mark 14: 29)

> 59. So it was, on the eighth day, that they came to circumcise the child; and they would have called him by the name of his father, Zacharias. 60. His mother answered and said, "No; (but) (αλλα) he shall be called John." 61. But they said to her, "There is no one among your relatives who is called by this name." (Luke 1: 59-61)

At the time Elizabeth gave birth to John the Baptist it was customary to name a son after his father or one of his ancestors. John's parents, Zacharias and Elizabeth, broke with tradition when they named their son John, following the instructions given by the angel of the Lord. This was truly an *exception* to the perceived, although unwritten, rule. The norm was that a son would be named after a relative, but *(αλλα)* John was not. Peter clarifies that it is not the *physical cleansing value* of the water of baptism but *(αλλα)* its *spiritual worth* that is important. Thus, he clearly identifies the baptism of the passage as baptism in water.

As we ponder the teaching of 1 Peter 3: 21, we must take into account the greater context of the entire epistle. The work is addressed, at least in part, to those who were new in Christ. This may even be considered an understatement since Peter indicates that members of his audience had *most recently* accepted Christ as Savior (1 Peter 2: 1-2). In fact, some men have speculated that this entire epistle is actually a sermon offered at a baptismal service that was later sent in written form to provide greater instruction concerning baptism. Therefore, in order to fully grasp the meaning of Peter's words we must recognize the fact that he was addressing newly converted Christians. As he addressed these babes in Christ, Peter noted that they had been *obedient children* (1 Peter 1: 14). Indeed, he states that they had actually *purified their souls through obedience* and, as a result, were *born again*, a rebirth through which they were granted new (eternal) life (1 Peter 1: 22-23).

Through the second and third chapters Peter continues his instructions to these *babes* in Christ, explaining the kind of challenges they could anticipate in their Christian walk as well as what God expected of them as disciples. This eventually leads to Peter's words in the third chapter where he identifies baptism as the antitype that saves. He follows this in the fourth chapter with instruction about Christian attitudes and accountability. The fifth and final chapter is a plea to those more mature members of the body, especially the elders, to care for those who are new in Christ and for each other.

As we consider the kind of baptism to which Peter is referring in 1 Peter 3: 21, it may help to recognize not only the context of this epistle, but also the greater context of the works of Peter. We cannot ignore Peter's reason for sending the letter. The apostle's goal in writing both 1 Peter and 2 Peter is one and the same and is explained clearly in his second epistle.

> Beloved, I now write to you this second epistle (in *both of* which I stir up your pure minds by way of reminder), 2. that you may be mindful of the words which were spoken before by the holy prophets, and of the commandment of us, the apostles of the Lord and Savior...
> (2 Peter 3: 1-2)

Peter wrote his epistles to help his readers recall 1) the words of the prophets and 2) the commandments given to them by the apostles. If this was not the original intent of the first epistle, which is possible given its context as well as Peter's parenthetic remark here, he certainly recognizes the first work as having that effect. Thus, it only makes sense that Peter was addressing the baptism that was commanded by the apostles. It is the very baptism he had proclaimed on the Day of Pentecost and at the house of Cornelius.

It is the baptism Paul administered to the Corinthians and the Ephesians. It is immersion in water.

Multiple Baptisms – Hebrews 6: 1-2

Faced with the fact that some were not growing spiritually simply because they were stuck on some of the simple doctrinal principles from the teaching of the apostles, the author of the book of Hebrews wrote:

> 1. Therefore, leaving the discussion of the elementary *principles* of Christ, let us go on to perfection, not laying again the foundation of repentance from dead works and of faith toward God, 2. of the doctrine of baptisms, of laying on of hands, of resurrection of the dead, and of eternal judgment. (Hebrews 6: 1-2)

Often, when we consider the word doctrine, it brings to mind the notion of *thou shalt do this* or *thou shalt not do that*. The Greek word for doctrine is διδαχη (*didache*), which simply means *teaching* or *instruction*. While it is possible that the *doctrine of baptisms* suggests the vast number of men and women who had been baptized, it is most likely a reference to instruction that had been given by the apostles regarding various types of purification in much the same way that they have been portrayed in this chapter. Paul wrote about the baptism of the Israelites in the Red Sea. The gospels address baptism with the Holy Spirit and baptism with fire as well as the full account of Jesus' death, burial, and resurrection, also called a baptism, not to mention the ceremonies of the first covenant. Were the Hebrews taught about different kinds of baptisms? Certainly they were. This passage is evidence of that fact. The *baptisms* mentioned in this passage, then, must refer to the host of baptisms, both figurative and literal, about which we have already learned.

* * * * *

Many look to the baptism discussed in the epistles of Paul, Peter, and others, believing that it is most certainly a Spirit baptism *rather than* water baptism, insisting the two are distinct from one another. Most will concede that certain passages refer to the act of water baptism (e.g., 1 Corinthians 1: 10-17). However, other passages (Romans 6: 3-4; 1 Corinthians 12: 13; Galatians 3: 27;

Ephesians 4: 5; Colossians 2: 12; 1 Peter 3: 21) are thought to identify *baptism with the Holy Spirit* as a baptism that does not involve the use of water.

What few people realize is that it was not until the nineteenth century that men first speculated about a spiritual baptism taking place separately from immersion in water. The doctrine originated with an Anglican clergyman by the name of E. W. Bullinger (1837-1913). Until that time, unless the scriptural context demanded another explanation, the word *baptism* was generally regarded as a direct reference to the rite of water baptism. Therefore, in order to be true to apostolic doctrine, we are compelled to regard Paul's use of the word baptism in that same vein. Of course, the word is used figuratively at times, as we have discussed. Nonetheless, it is difficult to credit Paul with a baptismal doctrine that was established nearly two thousand years after his death.

The New Testament consists of many incidents or narratives where some form of the word *baptism* is mentioned. In each case, the use of water can be easily determined by reviewing either the context or other corroborating passages. Still, there are those who deny that Paul taught water baptism, even rejecting the claim that his references to baptism in his epistles represented water baptism. Yet the only way to reach the conclusion that certain passages, such as 1 Corinthians 12: 13, do not involve water is to dismiss much of what the Bible teaches us about baptism.

NOTES FOR CHAPTER 10

1. G. R. Beasley-Murray, Baptism in the New Testament, William B. Eerdmans Publishing Company, 1994, p. 126.

2. Thayer's Greek-English Lexicon of the New Testament, p. 131, 1977, Baker Books House.

3. James Strong, LL.D., S.T.D., The New Strong's Exhaustive Concordance of the Bible, Greek Dictionary of the New Testament, p. 39, 1990, Thomas Nelson Publishers.

4. Thayer's Greek-English Lexicon of the New Testament, p. 27, 1977, Baker Books House.

5. James Strong, LL.D., S.T.D., The New Strong's Exhaustive Concordance of the Bible, Greek Dictionary of the New Testament, p. 10, 1990, Thomas Nelson Publishers.

Chapter XI
Not of Works!

Perhaps the most well-known argument that is offered in opposing water baptism as essential element of God's plan of salvation is that it is a *work*[1] and, in Paul's own words, a man cannot earn salvation through works (Ephesians 2: 8). This is a topic that deserves considerable discussion since it is critical to the debate, but first we should review exactly what Scripture teaches us about the *works* of a righteous man.

Works in the New Covenant

Contrary to what many men teach today, we learn from the inspired words of Scripture that no one can be saved without works. Peter told Cornelius that God would not accept the man who does not perform righteous works (Acts 10: 35). He also stated that our works are the means by which other men will recognize us as God's children and, consequently, give glory to God (1 Peter 2: 11-16). Paul explained to King Agrippa that repentance must be joined with works according to the *heavenly vision* (Acts 26: 19-20). James pointed out that the person who is not full of good works is spiritually dead (James 2: 20). Hence, he who has no works has no faith (James 2: 14). We cannot escape the conclusion that works are a part of the character of a faithful person. Since no one can be saved without faith, we can presume that no one can be saved without works. These statements about the relationship between faith and works are not meant to substantiate the need for baptism, but to dispel the myth that works are not necessary for salvation. Man is not justified by faith only, but by faith and works (James 2: 24). In fact, according to Scripture, our faith will ultimately be judged, or measured, by our works (1 Peter 1: 17; Revelation 20: 12-13).

Known as the faith chapter of the Bible, the eleventh chapter of Hebrews defines faith in terms of works. God respected Noah, Abraham, Jacob, Joseph, Moses, and others for their *works* of faith. Their actions reflected the intimate relationship each one had with God. That kind of relationship with Him naturally produces actions. If there are no deeds it is because there is no relationship and there is no faith. It is those who *do* the work of the Father who will be saved (Matthew 7: 21). Consequently, we can determine that those who have no works *will not be saved*.

Certainly works, or acts of righteousness, cannot be dismissed when it comes to a person's devotion to Christ. In fact, immediately following Paul's instruction that men are not saved by works (Ephesians 2: 8-9), he wrote that we as men were created for the purpose of performing good works (Ephesians 2: 10). During a study of the book of James a dear friend named Debbie stated that she believed God expects His children to have a *deedful heart,* a phrase that has stuck with this author since that day. It illustrates the kind of character a child of God will have with respect to deeds. He/she will desire to perform works of righteousness.

Obedient Faith Vs Works

While we may now have a better understanding about the relationship between faith and works, we must still address the proposition that baptism is an act during which men are saved, even though the Bible clearly teaches that no one can earn salvation. The question that must be answered is this: *Is baptism a deed of merit whereby men attempt to earn salvation, or is it an act of faith in obedience to God's instruction without which one cannot be saved?* Those who believe baptism is a work of merit often turn to the following verse in an effort to combat the numerous passages of Scripture that speak of the redemptive value of baptism:

> 8. For by grace you have been saved through faith, and that not of yourselves; it is a gift of God, 9. not of works, lest anyone should boast. (Ephesians 2: 8-9)

Despite the fact that Paul, in this instance, is writing to men and women who had already been converted to Christianity, it would be insincere to suggest that he is not speaking here of one's initial salvation. As we take in the context of this passage, it is clear that Paul is, in hind sight, addressing the time of conversion as a man is transformed from spiritual death to spiritual life (Ephesians 2: 5). Paul is addressing not only man's continuing daily salvation as cited in other epistles (2 Corinthians 4: 16), but the manner in which the Ephesians first received the grace of God, which was through faith.

In James' letter to the Israelites, where the blending of faith and works is the focus, his remarks are really about a person's enduring relationship with God where faith inspires works and works reflect faith. The inseparable link between true faith and righteous works is at the very heart of our walk with God. This is reinforced in Paul's letter to Titus when he explained that we must maintain our life in Christ through good works (Titus 3: 8).

These things having been said, the passage in Ephesians that teaches salvation *not of works* does not contradict scriptural teaching concerning the redemptive role of baptism, despite the fact that Paul is talking about man's initial salvation. As we take in the whole of Scripture, just as we must be sincere in acknowledging that Ephesians 2: 8 has the sinner's conversion in view, we must approach all of Scripture as honestly as possible. It is the only way we can truly honor God with respect to His Word. The truth is that the scriptural backdrop against which Paul wrote these words does, indeed, teach that, while salvation cannot be earned, when it comes to atonement the Bible consistently teaches the need for both faith and obedience on the part of men.

Those who see no difference between works and obedience face a basic dilemma in Scripture. This dilemma is found in what appears to be a contradiction between the words of Paul and the words of Jesus. While Paul teaches that no one can earn salvation (Ephesians 2: 8-9), Jesus equally emphasizes the teaching that men and women who fail to obey the commands of God will not be saved (Matthew 7: 21; John 14: 21). Additionally, both Peter and John recognize obedience as a matter of *attaining* initial salvation (1 Peter 4: 17; 1 John 2: 3-4). Adding to the confusion is the fact that Paul also remarks on the necessity of keeping God's commands and obeying the gospel message (1 Corinthians 7: 19; Thessalonians 1: 8-9).

How can such seemingly incompatible statements within Scripture be reconciled? The only reasonable conclusion is that these various teachings are not contradictory. The obedience addressed in these verses is not the righteous works of which James wrote, but the obedient faith by which we receive grace. In his letter to the Thessalonians, Paul ties together the notion that those who do not know God are those who have failed to obey the gospel. Jesus echoed this view regarding the importance of keeping His commands.

10. If you keep My commandments, you will abide in My love, just as I have kept My Father's commandments and abide in His love. (John 15: 10)

In the covenant of grace, the separation between Jew and Gentile that had existed under the Mosaic Law was now eliminated. Man's observance of the rules and regulations that made up the Old Testament law no longer defined man's relationship to God. In the new covenant men could only approach God by means of the blood of Christ. As we read Paul's letters to the Romans and Galatians, we discover additional teaching about works, similar to what he taught the Ephesians.

And if by grace, then *it is* no longer of works; otherwise grace is no longer grace... (Romans 11: 6a)

This only I want to learn from you: Did you receive the Spirit by the works of the law, or by the hearing of faith? (Galatians 3: 2)

Many other passages also teach this same principle concerning works (Romans 4: 4-5; 9: 30-32; Galatians 2: 15-16). The main distinction between the covenant of the law and the covenant of grace is clear. The manner in which man reached out to God under the Mosaic Law, with the many continuing rituals and sacrifices, was phenomenally different from how men would reach out to Him in the covenant of grace. In his epistles, Paul does not suggest that men have no responsibility to follow the teachings of Christ and the apostles in order to be saved. He simply teaches that no one was saved by means of the law. Many passages in the Bible call for each one to act upon his faith by responding appropriately to the gospel message. Paul would teach nothing less.

Circumcision is nothing and uncircumcision is nothing. Keeping God's commands is what counts. (1 Corinthians 7: 19)

Neither circumcision nor uncircumcision means anything; what counts is a new creation. (Galatians 6: 15)

According to the apostle Paul, it is *'keeping God's commands'* that is vital to our Christian walk. That is what counts. Yet the passage in Galatians reveals that the principles of *keeping God's commandments* and *being reborn* are actually interchangeable. Circumcision is once again deemed unimportant, while that which really matters is whether one is a *new creation* (Galatians 6: 15). Can we say that Paul placed more emphasis on *obedience* or on a *new creation*? It appears the two are considered equals here as obedience in Corinthians is rephrased in terms of rebirth/renewal in the Galatians text. The two thoughts are one. Who can deny, then, that short of obedience to the commands of God, there is no rebirth?

The apostles have taught us through their writings that salvation is not possible for those who do not obey the gospel message (2 Thessalonians 1: 8; 1 Peter 4: 17). Thus, if the gospel message is to be obeyed, there must be something within that message that *can* be obeyed. The gospel, as taught by the apostles, calls for action on the part of the believer in response to that message. Those actions (as opposed to works of merit) include repentance, confession, and immersion – in water. What separates these actions from deeds that do not have salvation value? It is faith in the death, burial, and resurrection of Jesus. The meritorious works mentioned by Paul (Ephesians 2: 8-9) are distinct from those that fall under the umbrella of faith. Salvation by merit has no relationship to salvation through faithful obedience to God's commands. Eternal life is not earned through baptism any more than it is earned through belief, repentance, or confession. Unlike obedience to the gospel that we perform within the arena of faith, meritorious works are performed outside that realm are simply irrelevant to God's plan of salvation.

The Christians in Rome lived in a state of grace in contrast to living under the law[2] (Romans 6: 14). A man cannot reside in both camps. He may either live under the law or under grace. Those who lived under the law were identified as *slaves of sin* while those living in grace were viewed by Paul as *slaves of righteousness* (Romans 6: 16). At one time, however, even those who now lived under grace had been under the law as slaves of sin. The fact that they no longer dwelt there can only lead us to conclude that at some point in time a transformation had occurred.

Despite his clear teaching that earning salvation through works was impossible (Ephesians 2: 8-9), Paul explained to the Romans that salvation *did* come through obedience (Romans 6: 1-18). He told them that it was specifically through their obedience (in this instance he is specifically citing obedience in baptism) that they had escaped the law and found themselves within the fold of grace.

Furthermore, they were under the law and slaves of sin *until* they obeyed the doctrine they were taught (v. 17), at which time they became slaves of righteousness (v. 18). Therefore, if this state of grace can be attained by obedience, but not by works, these two principles cannot be considered equals. Thus, if we honestly consider these principles, as they are taught in Scripture, we have no choice but to acknowledge the difference that exists between them. For this reason the apostles consistently taught obedience to the gospel as essential to salvation (Romans 6: 16-18; 10: 16; 2 Thessalonians 1: 8; 3: 14; Hebrews 5: 9; 1 Peter 1: 2; 4: 17) despite their insistence that salvation can never be earned.

In his first epistle, Peter provides penetrating insight into the value of baptism (1 Peter 3: 18-21), a passage we have already discussed at length. While Peter's discussion on the redemptive benefit of baptism is compelling, perhaps his most revealing statement is his explanation of *how* baptism provides salvation. Rather than describing the rite of baptism as a deed of merit through which we can earn our salvation, Peter explains that the salvation we receive at the time of baptism is granted to us *'through the resurrection of Christ'* (1 Peter 3: 21). Yet the point of seeking salvation through meritorious deeds, as characterized by Paul (Ephesians 2: 8-9), is to bypass the grace that is offered through Christ's death. That is what Paul condemned. Salvation in baptism achieves what meritorious works cannot since the entire focus in baptism is the death, burial, and resurrection by which grace is made available. Beasley-Murray, addressing Peter's proclamation that baptism saves (1 Peter 3: 21), recognizes the fact that the saving power of baptism is drawn directly from the resurrection of Christ:

> The chief lesson of this passage is its emphatic denial that the external elements of baptism constitute either its essence or its power. The cleansing in baptism is gained not through the application of water to the flesh but through the pledge of faith and obedience therein given to God, upon which the resurrection of Jesus Christ becomes a saving power to the individual concerned.[3]

One of the most meaningful metaphors in Scripture concerns the woman who touched the hem of Jesus' garment so that she might be healed (Luke 8: 43-48). While we have no reason to doubt the authenticity of Luke's account, there is no denying the lessons that can be drawn from the story. The woman represents a lost world full of sickness – hemorrhaging with sin. Jesus is the *only* means by which healing (forgiveness/salvation) is possible. Just as the woman fought through the crowd to reach Jesus we, too, must overcome obstacles that would prevent us from turning to Him. When the woman reached out and touched Him (His garment) she was restored to a life without the sickness that had tormented her.

In like manner, when we reach out to Jesus we are given newness of life absent the sins that had enslaved us. Yet, Jesus did not tell the woman that touching His garment (*an action*) had healed her, but that her faith had made her whole. The effort she put forth, fighting through the crowd in her weakened state and reaching out to touch Him despite the challenges she faced, does not change the fact that she was saved/healed by faith. On the contrary, her actions were the very means by which she was healed through faith. It was not the touching of the garment, but the work of God at that moment that healed her. So it is with baptism. Rather than undermining salvation by grace through faith, our response in baptism demands the utmost of faith and it is the work of God at that moment by which we are saved.

Baptism Vs Works

Scripture itself distinguishes between baptism and the good deeds of a faithful man or woman. In His words to the disciples, prior to His ascension, Jesus told them to, *'Go therefore and make disciples of all the nations, baptizing them in the name of the Father and of the Son and of the Holy Spirit'* (Matthew 28:19). Once they had accomplished these tasks of going, teaching, and baptizing, they were to instruct those who had been taught and baptized to *'observe all things that I have commanded you'* (Matthew 28:20). Jesus separates baptism from all other *things commanded* (works). Even repentance and confession, as important as these may be, are missing from Jesus' final instructions. Baptism is presented, not in relationship with *all things commanded*, but as a distinct critical matter in the *making of disciples*. The apostles faithfully followed Jesus' lead in distinguishing between baptism and works. In that vein, Paul wrote to the Ephesians about the uniqueness of baptism that sets it apart from what may be considered righteous works.

4. *There* is one body and one Spirit, just as you were called in one hope of your calling; 5. one Lord, one faith, one baptism; 6. one God and Father of all, who *is* above all, and through all, and in you all. (Ephesians 4: 4-6)

Certain components of God's covenant are considered by Paul to be vital in providing a sense of unity within the brotherhood. These include *one baptism* as well as *one body* (church), *one* (Holy) *Spirit, one hope, one Lord* (Jesus), *one faith*, and *one Father*. Such close association with these foundations of the faith offers some pretty impressive credentials for the significance of baptism in God's plan. The notion that works are incapable of helping someone attain salvation, a point made clear earlier in the epistle (Ephesians 2: 8-9), does not prevent Paul from pointing to the importance of baptism in the same letter.

Baptism is portrayed as different from the righteous works of the faithful Christian. The apostle essentially elevates this rite to a place of prominence that eclipses the good deeds of the Christian life to which we are called. At some point Scripture identifies each of these unique figures as vital to our salvation. For instance, Jesus is Savior specifically for those who are members of His (one) body (Ephesians 5: 23). We are told that the (one) Holy Spirit is the seal of our salvation (2 Corinthians 1: 22). It is through (one) faith in Jesus that we accept God's offer of grace (Ephesians 2: 8). Additionally, Paul explained to the Romans that we are saved by (one) hope of things yet unseen (Romans 8: 24). God the (one) Father sent His (one) Son as sacrifice for our sins (John 3: 16). Finally, (one) baptism is the time appointed by God for us to receive forgiveness of sins (Acts 2: 38). Paul distinguishes baptism here as an elite matter in man's reconciliation to God.

A clear contrast between meritorious deeds and faithful obedience in baptism is established in Paul's letter to Titus as he provides teaching about how men are saved. He told Titus, in a deliberate reference to baptism, *'...not by works of righteousness which we have done, but according to His mercy He saved us, through the washing of regeneration and renewing of the Holy Spirit.'* (Titus 3: 4-5). Bible scholars who teach that baptism is a *work of righteousness* struggle heavily with this verse. Most will (reluctantly) acknowledge the reference to baptism, but still emphatically deny that *'He saved us, through the washing of regeneration (baptism).'* Yet cleansing through baptism is a principle completely in line with New Testament teaching. The abundance of other Scripture identifying the redemptive role of baptism (Matthew 28: 19; Mark 16: 16; Acts 2: 38; 22: 16; Romans 6: 1-5; Galatians 3: 27; Colossians 2: 12; Hebrews 10: 22; 1 Peter 3: 21; et al) simply confound the view that it is in any way a meritorious work.

Baptism is a command of God that is linked to two specific promises – forgiveness of sins and the gift of the Holy Spirit – which, in turn, are tied to salvation throughout the New Testament. Peter reinforced Jesus' words from the Great Commission concerning baptism (Matthew 28: 19-20) when, on the Day of Pentecost, the Jews in Jerusalem heard and responded to the message that was being preached. The people asked what they should do in response to Peter's words (Acts 2: 37). It is fascinating that these people so long ago, as the gospel was first being declared, understood that they must *do* something in response to the message. Two thousand years later, with their account readily available to us, many stubbornly insist that no such response is necessary. Even more interesting is Peter's answer in that he actually does tell them what they must do: first they must repent, and then they are to be baptized (Acts 2: 37-38).

Peter's instructions on the Day of Pentecost are not only valuable regarding what he explained were necessary steps to salvation, but with respect to what he so noticeably omitted. He did not say, *'You do not need to do anything, since Jesus already took care of everything on the cross.'* Nor are statements such as, *'If you believe you are already saved,'* or, *'Ask Jesus into your life and say a prayer, and you will be saved,'* part of the gospel message delivered on that day. Yet these are the instructions offered by many teachers in our modern age when identifying what we must do to attain salvation. Peter, however, responded to these men based upon Jesus' command. He told them to repent and be baptized.

Baptism – An Act of Man or God?

In contrast to work performed by us, Paul identifies the work that is performed in baptism as work that God accomplishes specifically through our faith. Writing to the Colossians, he teaches that baptism is not an act of man, but a spiritual act in physical form through which God does *His* work (Colossians 2: 11-12). We are buried and raised with Christ in baptism. It is something that occurs *'through faith in the working of God.'* Our sins are washed away in baptism. That washing away of sins is an act of God, not man. Baptism, then, is an act of God to which men submit (passively) and cannot be considered a meritorious work of man.

A special point should be made about Paul's letter to the Colossians. While he spends some time reviewing baptism and the role it plays in God's plan, his statements just prior to these remarks are just as important.

> 4. Now this I say lest anyone should deceive you with persuasive words. 5. For though I am absent in the flesh, yet I am with you in spirit, rejoicing to see your *good* order and the steadfastness of your faith in Christ. 6. As you therefore have received Christ Jesus the Lord, so walk in Him, 7. rooted and built up in Him and established in the faith, as you have been taught, abounding in it with thanksgiving. 8. Beware lest anyone cheat you through philosophy and empty deceit, according to the tradition of men, according to the basic principles of the world, and not according to Christ. 9. For in Him dwells all the fullness of the Godhead bodily; 10. and you are complete in Him, who is the head of all principality and power. (Colossians 2: 4-10)

This lesson on baptism provides a clear sense that, if there are *'persuasive words that are deceiving'*, or a *'philosophy through which they may be cheated,'* or *'traditions of men,'* or *'basic principles of the world,'* baptism is not among them. These *'traditions of men,'* whether of drinks or festivals or Sabbaths, are discussed through the balance of the chapter. They do not include baptism. Furthermore, it is our symbolic death in baptism that is defined as the moment that we are separated from rules of the law (Colossians 2: 20-22). The claim that baptism is a work of man is clearly rejected as Paul explains the obvious difference between the *'traditions of men'* and the celebration of the death, burial, and resurrection of Christ in baptism.

Man cannot earn salvation. Those who teach salvation by works teach a false doctrine. It is a doctrine that contradicts the biblical teaching of salvation by grace, insinuating that a man could actually offer to God something of sufficient value that he might be worthy of eternal life. Yet nothing within the design of baptism suggests that God is indebted to us in any way. We bring nothing to baptism but a repentant heart and a desire to have our sins forgiven. This does not mean that we are entitled to forgiveness. Still, Scripture teaches us that God has promised to forgive the repentant believer at the time of baptism (Acts 2: 38) – and we know that God keeps His promises.

The debate concerning whether baptism is a human work or a spiritual act of obedience bears an uncanny likeness to a discussion between Jesus and the chief priests and elders about the baptism that was being performed by John the Baptist. Jesus asked them, *"The baptism of John – where was it from? Was it from heaven or from men?"* (Matthew 21: 25). We would do well to ask ourselves this same question as we consider the role of water baptism today. If we could honestly answer that Christian baptism is of human design, a much more reasonable defense could be offered that it is man's blatant attempt to somehow *earn grace* (an obvious oxymoron). If, however, baptism is of heavenly design, it is not our prerogative to abandon or devalue a ceremony that Scripture ties directly to our salvation (1 Peter 3: 21).

Faith – Man's Responsibility

Man is saved by grace. However, Scripture makes it clear that grace alone is not the fullness of God's plan. Each one of us is called upon to take specific steps to accept this grace. That response involves faith. Grace is God's part of the plan of salvation while faith is that portion that man must fulfill. Therefore, the question is not whether man has any role in the salvation process, since a man clearly must have faith; the real question that must be answered is, *'Exactly what is involved in this faith that is man's charge in God's plan?'* This is where men have differing ideas and opinions. Those who would have us accept that faith means men must only believe Jesus is the Son of God will cite the following Scriptures in support of this view:

> And this is the will of Him who sent Me, that everyone who sees the Son and believes in Him may have everlasting life. (John 6: 40)

> So they said, "Believe on the Lord Jesus Christ, and you will be saved, you and your household." (Acts 16: 31)

Apostolic doctrine cannot be determined by singling out passages such as these and teaching that they represent the complete message of salvation. This is why the Psalmist stated, *'The entirety of Your word is truth'* (Psalm 119: 160). The NASB puts it a little more precisely by stating, *'The sum of Thy word is truth.'* We must consider the *sum* of God's Word if we are to understand His ways. The call to obedience as a matter of salvation that is presented throughout Scripture is no less relevant than biblical instructions regarding the necessity of faith, and cannot be ignored. Indeed, we find that the gift of the Holy Spirit, promised to us through faith, is conferred specifically upon the obedient.

> And we are His witnesses to these things, and *so* also *is* the Holy Spirit whom God has given to those who obey Him. (Acts 5: 32)

> Now he who keeps His commandments abides in Him, and He in him. And by this we know that He abides in us, by the Spirit whom He has given us. (1 John 3: 24)

God bestows the gift of the Holy Spirit upon those who obey Him. The Holy Spirit abides in those who keep His commandments. It is clear from these passages that obedience to God influences whether we will receive the gift of the Holy Spirit. To what obedience does God call us in order to be given such an honor? We can determine that it is obedience to the very precepts He has commanded us to keep in order for us to receive the promised Holy Spirit – repentance and baptism (Acts 2: 38).

Another Gospel

The teaching that baptism is a deed of merit is relatively new, historically speaking. While the church has been in existence for nearly two thousand years, this view has become popular only within the last five hundred years. Yet, it is a view that has led many to take a rather belligerent attitude toward both baptism and those who teach that it does have redemptive value. In fact, many openly proclaim that any teaching that ties baptism to salvation is essentially *another gospel*. Consequently, those who teach that baptism is necessary for salvation are, according to Scripture, eternally condemned.

> 6. I marvel that you are turning away so soon from Him who called you in the grace of Christ, to a different gospel, 7 which is not another; but there are some who trouble you and want to pervert the gospel of Christ. 8. But even if we, or an angel from heaven, preach any other gospel to you than what we have preached to you, let him be accursed. 9. As we have said before, so now I say again, if anyone preached any other gospel to you than what you have received, let him be accursed. (Galatians 1: 6-9)

Later in this same epistle Paul identifies baptism as the time when the Galatians had *'put on Christ'* (Galatians 3: 27). It seems that if this was what he taught at the time of this writing, and then later changed his doctrine concerning baptism, he would be condemning himself by his very own words in verse eight above.

Still others argue that if baptism is really necessary for salvation, it means that millions of believers are lost; therefore it must not be a requirement. This, however, is not a view based upon scriptural teaching, but is a complaint that the requirement of immersion would be unfair if many are lost for failure to submit to baptism. Yet, biblical doctrine is to be determined from the words of Scripture and not our own personal wishes. Still, it will not hurt to give these views respectful consideration.

Throughout the first fifteen hundred years of the existence of the church, the general understanding from the teaching of the apostles was that baptism was the moment a man received forgiveness of sins and the gift of the Holy Spirit. This was a doctrine handed down by the apostles and understood by believers everywhere. The first view stated above, which claims that teaching baptism as a path to forgiveness of sins and salvation is equivalent to *preaching another gospel,* assumes that until the early sixteenth century no man actually taught the true gospel of Christ. Consequently, we must accept, if this view is correct, that no one prior to Huldrych Zwingli, in the 1520's, really comprehended the teaching of the apostles when it comes to baptism, including those who received their teaching directly from the lips of the apostles. As a matter of fact, Zwingli made this very claim, stating boldly that all previous teachers were wrong in their assessment of the role of baptism and that he alone had come to a true understanding of the apostles' doctrine.

> "In this matter of baptism -- if I may be pardoned for saying it -- I can only conclude that all the doctors have been in error from the time of the apostles. . . . All the doctors have ascribed to the water a power which it does not have and the holy apostles did not teach."[4]

Those, then, who deny the teaching that baptism is for the forgiveness of sins find the basis for their beliefs not in Scripture, but in the works and writings of Huldrych Zwingli nearly fifteen hundred years after the establishment of the church.

If it is true, as the Bible teaches, that baptism is essential for salvation, no doubt millions of believers, those who have not been baptized, are sadly lost. However, if we accept the premise that teaching baptism as a matter of salvation is *another gospel*, and if those who willingly teach another gospel are condemned, we are faced with another serious dilemma. The only reasonable conclusion is that from the beginning of the church until the time of the Reformation Movement, a period spanning roughly fifteen hundred years, none were saved.

We know that Peter acknowledged a parallel between the waters of the flood and the waters of baptism (1 Peter 3: 21), stating that baptism is the *antitype* of the flood. The NIV states that the waters of the flood *symbolized* baptism. In truth, Peter's words may be considered as prophetic as they are insightful. Given the general view of baptism in modern times, its connection with the waters of the flood may be even considered a bit disturbing. Within the world of religion today the vast majority strongly deny the necessity of immersion even though it is plainly taught in Scripture. According to Peter, in the days of Noah it was not the modest number who would be saved (eight) or the multitudes that would be lost that determined God's actions (2 Peter 2: 4-5). Noah and his family were saved due to their faithful obedience to the clear commands of God. Men today will undoubtedly be saved in the same manner.

Keeping God's Commandments Is Essential

For those who are vigorously opposed to the idea that some kind of response, or *action*, may be required from someone in order for him/her to attain salvation, please consider the following verses. These communicate to us the fact that one *cannot be saved* without keeping God's commandments.

> Not everyone who says to Me, 'Lord, Lord,' shall enter the kingdom of heaven, but he who does the will of My Father in heaven. (Matthew 7: 21)

> He who has my commandments and keeps them, it is he who loves Me. (John 14: 21)

> 5. But in accordance with your hardness and your impenitent heart you are treasuring up for yourself wrath in the day of wrath and revelation of the righteous judgment of God, 6. who *"will render to each one according to his deeds."* (Romans 2: 5-6)

16. Do you not know that to whom you present yourselves slaves to obey, you are that one's slaves whom you obey, whether of sin *leading* to death, or of obedience *leading* to righteousness? 17. But God be thanked that *though* you were slaves of sin, yet you obeyed from the heart that form of doctrine to which you were delivered. 18. And having been set free from sin, you became slaves of righteousness. (Romans 6: 16-18)

But they have not all obeyed the gospel... (Romans 10: 16)

And having been perfected, He became the author of eternal salvation to all who obey Him. (Hebrews 5: 9)

But be doers of the word, and not hearers only, deceiving yourselves. (James 1: 22)

Since you have purified your souls in obeying the truth through the Spirit... (1 Peter 1: 22)

For the time *has come* for judgment to begin at the house of God; and if *it begins* with us first, what will *be* the end of those who do not obey the gospel of God? (1 Peter 4: 17)

3. Now by this we know that we know Him, if we keep His commandments. 4. He who says, "I know Him," and does not keep His commandments, is a liar and the truth is not in him. (1 John 2: 3-4)

Now he who keeps His commandments abides in Him, and He in him. (1 John 3: 24)

Many men struggle heavily with the idea that God has established conditions for receiving His grace. Such conditions, they say, tend to destroy the very idea of grace as a gift. If receiving grace relies upon any action performed by man – or in the case of baptism, an act to which man submits – then it can no longer be considered a gift. According to these men, if receiving grace is linked to a man meeting certain provisions that God has set forth, it suggests that God owes salvation to all who complete the task. Yet the grace that comes as a result of men keeping His commands is simply His fulfillment of a promise. It is not a matter of debt.

A striking example of how God joins faith with works to accomplish His will is provided in the story of Jericho. God told Joshua, *'I have given Jericho into your hands'* (Joshua 6: 2). Nothing the Israelites could do would earn them the city of Jericho. It was a gift God was giving them. Yet, while it was a gift in that it was *given*, their receiving of Jericho was conditional. The Israelites were required to march around the city six days in a row. On the seventh day the priests were to blow their trumpets and the people would shout, at which time the walls of the city would crumble (Joshua 6: 3-5). Of course, the marching and the trumpets and the shouting did not collapse the walls, nor did these actions in any way earn the Israelites a right to enter the city. Yet, their obedience was critical. Their possession of the city was contingent upon fulfillment of God's command. So it is with salvation. While it is a gift, in that it cannot be earned, it is still conditioned upon our faithfulness to the commands He has established.

If God expects nothing from man for redemption, as many maintain, what is it that separates those who are saved from those who are lost? If we say it is the fact that those who are saved are forgiven of their sins, this begs the question, exactly *why* are they forgiven? If it is through belief, repentance, confession, and the Sinner's Prayer, the saved have done something – performed some action or fulfilled some condition – in response to the gospel message *in order to be saved*.

Contrary to the popular view that salvation comes through belief/faith only, if we are completely honest in our approach to Scripture, we will recognize that the New Testament writers steadfastly teach that salvation is a matter of faithful obedience to the gospel message. This, rather than faith only, is unquestionably the prevailing theme of the Bible. Redemption is not a matter of meritorious works, but it is undeniably a matter of obedience, including submission to the command of baptism. If we deny this we find ourselves challenging the inspired instructions offered by Peter, Paul, James, and John as well as Jesus Himself. Those, then, who deny that baptism is essential in our response to the gospel message, have replaced the biblical teaching of salvation without works with a doctrine that teaches salvation without obedience.

God's Employment of Men in Administering Baptism

Baptism is administered to others by the hands of men; a fact that is often considered an indication of the purely physical nature of this rite, thus making it a human work. However, historically God has consistently turned to men in the administration of His commands. He worked through Moses and the prophets in His dealings with the children of Israel. Similarly, the sacrifices of the Old Testament were given to the priests so that they might be offered to God. It is God's tendency to work through men and we discover that this is especially true when it comes to baptism.

The various baptisms mentioned in Scripture bring to light a harmonious relationship between the value of the baptism being performed and man's active role in its execution. Noah did not bring the waters of the flood upon the earth; yet we cannot help but notice that the salvation of Noah and his family came through the work of his hands as he built the ark, a direct complement to God's work in sending the rain. While the purpose of the water was to destroy, the work Noah performed was the instrument God used to lift him and his family to safety. God certainly could have saved Noah without the ark, but He wanted Noah to take an active role in the saving of his family. In a similar fashion, He has decided to have baptism administered by the hands of men. He has chosen to have men participate in the saving of men

As the Israelites were *'baptized into Moses'* at the crossing of the Red Sea (1 Corinthians 10: 2), God worked through Moses to rescue them from their life of slavery. It was a baptism where God sought Moses' assistance in freeing the Israelites. Additionally, Jesus received water baptism at the hands of John the Baptist. According to Matthew's account of the event, God the Father chose the occasion of Jesus' baptism to offer His blessing upon the ministry of God the Son (Matthew 3: 16-17). John provided the physical component of immersion in water while God the Father supplied the spiritual effect as the Spirit descended and He voiced His approval.

Perhaps most significant, however, is the relationship between the crucifixion of Christ, which we can rightfully view as the most powerful baptism ever experienced, and the meaning of that baptism. This was a baptism administered by humans in that it was men who crucified Him. Men participated in the physical aspect of this baptism (the crucifixion) while God managed the spiritual side, as Jesus rose from the grave. Interestingly, the involvement of men seems to have given this baptism, through which eternal life was made possible, even greater meaning since God intended for this baptism to be personal. The fact is, we nailed our own sins to the cross (2 Corinthians 5: 21). When we as men are forgiven of our trespasses, not only are we no longer guilty of past sins, but we are also united with Him personally at that time (Romans 6: 5). No other baptism offered this kind of intimacy. Paul draws attention to the personal nature of Christian baptism in the sixth chapter of

Romans. While the flood and the Red Sea denote corporate baptism, as a number of people were rescued simultaneously, the significance of Christian baptism is that it is a personal matter between a believer and God as each one shares in the crucifixion of Christ.

*   *   *   *   *

In New Testament times, baptism was not considered an act of human achievement, but a spiritual experience that was common to all believers (Acts 2: 41; Romans 6: 1-4; 1 Corinthians 12: 13; Galatians 3: 27; Colossians 2: 11-12; Titus 3: 5; Hebrews 10: 22). Despite the many voices proclaiming it today, the apostles never taught that baptism could or should be considered a human work. When it is presented in the New Testament, water baptism is consistently portrayed as a matter of man's response to the gospel message. If men wish to teach that baptism is a human accomplishment, it seems the burden is on these men to provide us with Scripture to support this claim. Given the fact that no such Scripture can be found to support such a doctrine, we are obligated to accept the words of Jesus and the apostles concerning the effects of the rite of baptism as taught in Scripture – forgiveness of sins, the gift of the Holy Spirit, membership in the body, etc.

NOTES FOR CHAPTER 11

1. Many look to Martin Luther as a great advocate of salvation through faith only. While this is certainly a concept taught by Luther, his view of salvation through faith only, absent works of men, stands in stark contrast to the modern-day perspective regarding faith without works. Luther understood that the precepts of God, such as baptism in water, were not works of men, but works of God without which man could not attain salvation. Following are some of his remarks regarding baptism:

> [I] affirm that Baptism is no human trifle, but that it was established by God Himself. Moreover, He earnestly and solemnly commanded that we must be baptized or we shall not be saved. No one is to think that it is an optional matter like putting on a red coat. It is of greatest importance that we hold Baptism in high esteem as something splendid and glorious. The reason why we are striving and battling so strenuously for this view of Baptism is that the world nowadays is full of sects that loudly proclaim that Baptism is merely an external form and that external forms are useless.... Although Baptism is indeed performed by human hands, yet it is truly God's own action. Luther, Martin (1978), _Luther's Large Catechism_, (Saint Louis, MO: Concordia) pp. 98-99.

But our know-it-alls, the new spirit people, claim that faith alone saves and that human works and outward forms contribute nothing to this. We answer: It is of course true that nothing in us does it except faith, as we shall hear later. But these blind leaders of the blind refuse to see that faith must have something in which it believes, that is, something it clings to, something on which to plant its feet and into which to sink its roots. Thus faith clings to the water and believes Baptism to be something in which there is pure salvation and life, not through the water, as I have emphasized often enough, but because God's name is joined to it.... It follows from this that whoever rejects Baptism rejects God's word, faith, and the Christ who directs us to Baptism and binds us to it. Luther, Martin (1978), *Luther's Large Catechism*, (Saint Louis, MO: Concordia) pp. 101-102.

Prior to the time of Luther, perhaps the one man who stood out as an advocate of salvation through faith alone was Augustine of Hippo (354-430 AD). His remarks here reflect that very view:

All the blessings which God hath bestowed upon man are of his mere grace, bounty, or favour; his free, undeserved favour; favour altogether undeserved; man having no claim to the least of his mercies. It was free grace that "formed man of the dust of the ground, and breathed into him a living soul," and stamped on that soul the image of God, and "put all things under his feet." The same free grace continues to us, at this day, life, and breath, and all things. For there is nothing we are, or have, or do, which can deserve the least thing at God's hand. "All our works, Thou, O God, hast wrought in us." These, therefore, are so many more instances of free mercy: and whatever righteousness may be found in man, this is also the gift of God. Preached at St. Mary's, Oxford, before the University, on June 18, 1738.

Yet, as with Luther, Augustine's understanding of salvation through faith only did not suggest that the precepts of God were unnecessary, but that they were essential with respect to salvation.

"There are two REGENERATIONS...the one ACCORDING TO FAITH, which takes place in the present life BY MEANS OF BAPTISM; the other according to the flesh, which shall be accomplished...by means of the great and final judgment." Augustine, Book 20, Chapter 6 [commenting on the Revelation:].

2. The law to which Paul refers in his letter to the Ephesians may not be limited strictly to the law of Moses, but to law in general, as men are held accountable for those laws to which they are subject. Adherence to any law is ineffectual when it comes to righteousness and/or salvation; otherwise salvation could be *earned* without the blood of Christ. No matter how much an individual obeys the law, he will fall short. If, then, salvation relied upon man's obedience to law – any law – no one would be saved. Thus, salvation is available only through the blood of Christ.

3. G. R. Beasley-Murray, <u>Baptism in the New Testament</u>, William B. Eerdmans Publishing Company, 1994, p. 262.

4. Huldreigh Zwingli, "Of Baptism," in Zwingli and Bullinger, "Library of Christian Classics," Vol. 24, ed. And tr. G. W. Bromiley (Philadelphia Westminster Press, 1953), p. 153.

Chapter XII

Baptism Vs Special Circumstances

What If Baptism Is Not Possible?

Some men challenge the necessity of baptism by claiming that there may be circumstances when this kind of command would *seem* unfair. For instance, imagine that a soldier on the battlefield wishes to accept Jesus as Savior but, with no water or time available, has no opportunity for baptism. They reason that, if the soldier died on that battlefield, God would not be so unjust as to deny him/her eternal life for failure to submit to baptism when there was no opportunity for it at the time. The same question might also be asked concerning someone who, on a deathbed, wants to follow Jesus but is physically unable to submit to immersion in water.

A situation that involves a person who *cannot* be baptized does not really address the salvation or condemnation of the man or woman who simply denies God's call to baptism, which is the focus of this book. Nor does such a case offer a legitimate challenge to baptism as a condition of salvation. The possibility that God might have compassion for someone who *cannot* be baptized demonstrates nothing. It is simply an attempt to persuade us that if a convincing exception to the command for baptism can be argued, then we are somehow forced to admit that there is no such command.

Human laws are written with the intent that they should be applied evenly to all men who live under those laws. Still, we all recognize that, while speed limit laws are to be obeyed by everyone, an exception might apply under certain conditions, such as rushing someone to the hospital in a life or death situation. Similarly, the punishment for taking the life of another human being is severe, yet we understand that in the case of self-defense, once again, a life or death situation, the circumstances take precedence over the law. While we recognize these exceptions, the laws still apply to everyone who does not find himself/herself in such an extreme situation. If we as men, created in the image of God, can grasp this kind of reasoning, surely we can expect even greater wisdom from God. That does not mean that God makes these exceptions. We do not know exactly how God views these kinds of circumstances. However, the possibility that God might offer an exemption to baptism under exceptional conditions should not be construed as permission to ignore His command concerning baptism.

Ironically, there is an unintended consequence that results from the wartime and deathbed scenarios presented here. Given such extreme settings where baptism is not an option in catastrophic situations, the subtle implication is that the person involved *would be baptized* if at all possible. This does not disprove, but sustains the significance of baptism. While the point is to deny the necessity of baptism, the idea that God would make an exception for someone *desiring to obey* is a clandestine acknowledgment of baptism's importance. Therefore, if God would be willing to make an exception due to extraordinary circumstances, the command for baptism would still apply to all who have access to water sufficient for immersion. That having been said, we should take note that Paul, in his letter to the Romans, recognized the fact that some people may never have the opportunity to participate in the covenant that has been established by the blood of Christ.

> 11. For there is no partiality with God. 12. For as many as have sinned without law will also perish without law, and as many as have sinned in the law will be judged by the law 13. (for not the hearers of the law *are* just in the sight of God, but the doers of the law will be justified; 14. for when Gentiles, who do not have the law, by nature do the things in the law, these, although not having the law, are a law unto themselves, 15. who show the work of the law written in their hearts, their conscience also bearing witness, and between themselves *their* thoughts accusing or else excusing *them*) 16. in the day when God will judge the secrets of men by Jesus Christ, according to my gospel. (Romans 2: 11-16)

It is honestly difficult to know if the scenario of the soldier on the battlefield, or any similar situation, is addressed within the scope of this text. Whether someone who has previously rejected God at a time when he/she did have the ability to meet Him in baptism might, in the end, bypass that command with a sincere heart when baptism is not possible, is a decision that men cannot make. What we can say, however, is that Scripture offers no such exception to the call for baptism. Still, Paul delivers a clear message that God views differently those who hear and reject His precepts and those who never hear.

At best we can only acknowledge that situations like these are not mentioned in Scripture. Perhaps the reason for this omission is simply that God does not want us to agonize over the person whose circumstances might prevent him/her from being baptized. After all, in that kind of setting we can have no effect. Therefore, they are His concern alone. Our role is simply to teach the gospel message to those on whom we can have some saving influence.

The Day of Pentecost and the Gentile Conversion

Certain events in the Bible are often at the center of the debate over the water/Spirit relationship of baptism. The Day of Pentecost is one such case. On that day the Holy Spirit was poured out upon men (Acts 2: 1-4). Many men believe that this *must* be the baptism prophesied by John. This *must* be the baptism that saves. Yet, it is in Acts 2: 38 that the word *baptized*, as a command of God, is first linked to men receiving the Holy Spirit. Nor was this outpouring of the Spirit the baptism that Jesus commanded of His disciples (Matthew 28: 19) since His direction was for them to baptize others – men baptizing men.

The story of Cornelius and the other Gentiles who were with him in Ceasarea is also central in the discussion of water baptism (Acts 10: 1 – 11: 18). This incident, shoulder to shoulder with the experience of Pentecost, is considered key by those who deny the salvation value of water baptism. What is very telling, however, is the reason that these passages are at the heart of the discussion; it is because these are the only instances recorded in the Bible that show men receiving the Holy Spirit prior to water baptism.

It is true that these incidents are critical to the debate, but not in the manner most often noted. What makes these occasions significant is the unrivaled magnitude of the events. A mighty wind accompanied by tongues of fire cannot be considered a normal activity either before or after Pentecost in and around Jerusalem. Pentecost was a pivotal moment in time in that God's new covenant came into being. It was a moment greater than the day God established His covenant with Abraham or provided the Ten Commandments to the Israelites, since this covenant was established by the blood of Christ.

The suggestion that these episodes are the normal manner by which men in the first century received the Holy Spirit overlooks the significance of these events. Either inadvertently or intentionally, the biblical fact that no one else received the Spirit in this manner must not be ignored. For instance, on the Day of Pentecost, in the second chapter of Acts, we find no mention of anyone, save those in the house where the Spirit was poured out, experiencing the same phenomenon or receiving spiritual gifts (e.g., speaking in tongues). In the accounts of the Ethiopian eunuch (Acts 8: 26-39), Lydia (Acts 16: 13-15), and the Philippian jailer (Acts 16: 25-34), we do not find any such manifestation of the Spirit. Not even in the report of Saul's conversion (Acts 9: 1-19) is this kind of phenomenon recorded.

When we examine the conversion experiences of the Samaritans (Acts 8: 1-17) and the Ephesians (Acts 19: 1-7), we discover that the Holy Spirit did not *fall upon* them, and no spiritual gifts were witnessed, until an apostle had laid hands on them. Of course, upon their submission to baptism, given the principles of baptism that we discussed earlier, it is not unreasonable to expect that they would have been saved and received the gift (*indwelling*) of the Spirit prior to the touch of the apostles' hands.

Peter explained on the Day of Pentecost that the promises of forgiveness and the gift of the Spirit were for everyone who repented and submitted to baptism. The promise was even extended to *'all who are afar off'* (Acts 2: 39). This would include the Samaritans as well as anyone upon whom the apostles did not lay their hands. It was surely true of the conversion of Lydia and others where no supernatural gifts are mentioned. Based upon the information available to us, we can only conclude that the manifestation of the Spirit that was witnessed on these two occasions (Pentecost and Caesarea) was not the normal manner by which men would receive the Spirit, but the greatest of exceptions. Additionally, we cannot ignore the fact that these incidents involved apostles. Their role as agents for the distribution of miraculous works of the Spirit in the first century is significant to these events and must not be discounted.

Pointing to extraordinary events such as these and concluding that they are the manner by which all men are saved, when they clearly are not, is a questionable approach to developing scriptural doctrine. Furthermore, while many maintain that water baptism is a *sign* of salvation, these two occasions reveal that it was not water baptism, but the outpouring of the Spirit, along with speaking in tongues, that served as a sign to others that God was present. This is confirmed for us by Paul as he instructed the Christians at Corinth concerning gifts of the Spirit.

Therefore tongues are for a sign, not for those who believe but to unbelievers... (1 Corinthians 14: 22)

On the Day of Pentecost this served as a sign to those who had traveled to Jerusalem for the festivities. The members of the crowd were unbelievers until they heard the apostles speak in tongues. In Caesarea, the outpouring of the Spirit served as a sign for Peter and those who were with him so that they would recognize the handiwork of God and understand His plans for the Gentiles. Peter was unsure that Christianity was for Gentiles until God offered witness on their behalf by bestowing them with the Spirit and they, too, spoke in tongues.

It appears from Scripture that the events of Pentecost and the conversion of the Gentiles were moments of God's miraculous intervention, as discussed in the Preface of this book. God used the outpouring of the Holy Spirit as a sign in order to convey a message to those present at the time – lessons we are able to see in hindsight. Pentecost unveiled the Holy Spirit and the authority of the apostles while Caesarea affirmed God's plan for the Gentiles. The uniqueness of these incidents prohibits us from establishing any doctrine about the salvation of men. These episodes must be recognized for their unique place in history rather than reasoning that they somehow reflect common experience for all Christians.

From Saul to Paul

As Saul of Tarsus journeyed to Damascus in pursuit of Christ's followers, the Lord stopped him (Acts 9: 1-19). A bright light blinded Saul as the Lord introduced Himself and questioned him regarding his persecution of the church. Following the instructions given to him, Saul had those men who were with him lead him to Damascus where he would *'...be told what you must do'* (v. 6) – NIV. Three days of fasting ensued as Saul undoubtedly sought answers to some deep and soul-searching questions.

17. And Ananias went his way and entered the house, and laying his hands on him he said, "Brother Saul, the Lord Jesus, who appeared to you on the road as you came, has sent me that you may receive your sight and be filled with the Holy Spirit." 18. Immediately there fell from his eyes *something* like scales, and he received his sight at once; and he arose and was baptized. (Acts 9: 17-18)

12. Then a certain Ananias, a devout man according to the law, having a good testimony with all the Jews who dwell *there*, 13. came to me;

and he said to me, "Brother Saul, receive your sight." And at that same hour I looked up at him. 14. Then he said, "The God of your fathers has chosen you that you should know His will, and see the Just one, and hear the voice of His mouth. 15. For you will be His witness to all men of what you have seen and heard. 16. And now, why are you waiting? Arise and be baptized, and wash away your sins, calling on the name of the Lord." (Acts 22: 12-16)

God sent a reluctant Ananias to teach Saul what he needed to know. We are not told much about Ananias. For that reason, we do not know if he had received the spiritual gift of healing through the hands of the apostles or if the healing of Saul was a unique experience for him. Nonetheless, Ananias told Saul that God had sent him so that he (Saul) could regain his sight and receive the Holy Spirit. He then laid his hands on Saul whose sight was instantly restored. Saul was then immediately baptized as instructed by Ananias.

A number of Bible scholars believe and teach certain things about Saul's conversion that simply are not reflected in the text, suggesting, for instance, that Saul was saved on the Road to Damascus during his conversation with the Lord. As we consider what Scripture reveals about this meeting between Jesus and Saul, nothing in Luke's narrative indicates that Saul was saved at that time. It is true that he addressed Jesus as *Lord* during the encounter, but this cannot be interpreted to mean that Saul was saved. In fact, when he first addressed Him as *Lord*, Saul was simply seeking to learn the identity of this powerful being as he said, '*Who are You, Lord?'* (Acts 9: 5) This cannot be considered submission to Christ since he did not know to whom he was speaking. Once he learned the identity of his accuser, Saul asked, '*Lord, what do You want me to do?'* (Acts 9: 6) While there is a sense of submission in this question, the impression is that Saul knew he was facing God. The passage does not say that he was saved – only that he wished to know what was expected of him. Realizing that he had been living a life that conflicted with God's will, Saul spent three days fasting in the city of Damascus. Compared to others, such as Cornelius and the eunuch, who celebrated their salvation, we have no reason to infer that Saul was saved during his first meeting with the Lord.

As Paul (Saul) told the Israelites in Jerusalem of his Damascus experience (Acts 22: 6-17), we learn that it was after he had received his sight that Ananias proceeded to explain to him the message of the gospel and what God expected from him. Since he had neither heard the gospel message nor received forgiveness of sins until he met with Ananias in Damascus, we have no reason to believe that Saul was saved on the Road to Damascus.

The claim is also made that Saul received the Holy Spirit at the same time that he regained his sight as Ananias laid hands on him. However, in an honest review of the passage we find that this teaching is also absent from the text. We are not told that Saul received the Spirit when Ananias laid hands on him. We are told only that he regained his sight at that time. The narrative gives us no reason to believe that he received the Holy Spirit at the same time.

When men presume that Saul received the Holy Spirit at the moment he received his sight, they are essentially discarding the text of the passage. Ananias approached Saul with a twofold mission. His first task was to help Saul recover his sight. The second reason for Ananias' visit was for Saul to be filled with the Holy Spirit. The first portion of this mission was fulfilled as Ananias laid his hands on Saul and his sight was restored. Having regained his sight, Ananias told Saul that he should be baptized. We understand from Acts 2: 38 that the Spirit was to be received by those who were baptized. We have every reason to believe that this same principle would apply equally to Saul. Therefore, we can reason that he would have received the Spirit at the time of his baptism in keeping with scriptural instruction. This would have fulfilled Ananias' dual mission.

Finally, the claim by many that Saul's sins were washed away by *calling on the name of the Lord*, independent from his immersion in water, is a very feeble interpretation of the text. Since we know from other passages that sins are washed away at the time of baptism (Acts 2: 38), the view that it was some kind of *calling*, without submission to *baptism*, that washed away his sins would conflict with the association that has already been provided in Scripture between baptism and forgiveness. Ananias' point to Saul about *washing* his sins away allies much more cleanly with his instructions concerning the waters of baptism than with a *calling* that many insist is Paul's verbal plea to God for forgiveness. While confessing Jesus as Lord is considered critical to salvation (Romans 10: 10), in itself it is not portrayed as the moment of forgiveness in any passage of Scripture. However, invoking the Lord's name in baptism as a matter of calling on Him, to which Ananias' words clearly point, simply connects the *calling* to the *baptism* in which Saul's sins would be forgiven. Ananias was identifying baptism as the very manner by which Saul should call on the name of the Lord.

Once again, the incident with Saul on the Road to Damascus was a matter of divine revelation that was designed specifically to convert him into an apostle to the Gentiles. Scripture offers this as the very reason for God's intervention (Acts 22: 14-15). We cannot establish a doctrine of salvation without baptism from this episode since Scripture does not say that Saul was saved prior to baptism. In fact, we have a wealth of evidence that this was not the case. However, the Damascus experience does provide us with a better understanding of the growth and dynamics of the early church as Paul was sent to minister to the Gentiles. Instances of miraculous intervention such as this are simply not intended to provide us with doctrinal instruction. God's encounter with Saul was unique since he was to take on a special role in the early church.

The Thief on the Cross

> 39. Then one of the criminals who were hanged blasphemed Him, saying, "If You are the Christ, save Yourself and us." 40. But the other, answering, rebuked him, saying, "Do you not even fear God, seeing you are under the same condemnation? 41. And we indeed justly, for we receive the due reward of our deeds; but this Man has done nothing wrong." 42. Then he said to Jesus, "Lord, remember me when You come into Your kingdom." 43. And Jesus said to him, "Assuredly, I say to you, today you will be with Me in Paradise." (Luke 23: 39-43)

Most discussions about the redemptive value of baptism seem to eventually drift to the topic of the thief on the cross. Often, the cry is, *I want to be saved like the thief on the cross!* Yet those who want to be saved *like the thief* fail to realize that this could only be accomplished by reversing time by roughly two thousand years. It then involves their painstaking death in a manner that was reserved for the lowest form of character in society (Galatians 3: 13). Then again, maybe the idea is not to be saved *exactly* like the thief. It could be that someone wishing to be saved like the thief simply wishes to live a life of sin and deceit and, at the moment prior to death, have the good fortune of being in the right place at the right time to be forgiven and attain salvation.

Ultimately, when a person says they want to be saved *like the thief,* what they are really saying is that they want to be saved specifically without water baptism. Relying on the example of the thief, who was apparently saved without baptism (and who clearly had no opportunity for it at the time), the belief is that anyone may be saved without submitting to water baptism. The fact that the thief lived under the law of the old covenant rather than the new covenant of grace is considered meaningless to the person who either does not understand or, worse yet, does not care.

It is a bit embarrassing when, in an attempt to defend the necessity of baptism, someone suggests that this thief *may have been* baptized by either John the Baptist or one of Jesus' disciples. While it is certainly possible, since he did recognize who Jesus was, it is highly unlikely. Although we know very little about this man, we do know that he was a thief. His guilt is never in question. He told the other thief who was opposite him that their punishment was justified – a confession as clear as any that was ever made. The likelihood that the thief had been baptized diminishes when we realize that, in his appeal to Jesus, the thief never suggested that he had been baptized. He did not cite baptism as a reason for Jesus to remember him. Still, it was not merely the good fortune of being nailed next to Christ that brought salvation to this man. Two thieves were present but only one was saved. It was his willingness to accept Jesus as the Son of God and his request to be remembered in Jesus' coming kingdom that saved him. Given his humble words to Jesus, we have every reason to believe that the man was repentant, which Jesus obviously recognized.

Since it is reasonable to conclude that baptism was not a factor for the thief on the cross, why should we believe baptism is essential for us today? This is the case presented by those who turn to the thief as an example of salvation without baptism. What we must do, then, is consider how the details of the new covenant affect us in a manner that is very different from the thief.

In his message to the Romans, Paul expressed his deepest hope that those Israelites who still attempted to live under the law would come to a better understanding of grace (Romans 10: 1-13). In his teaching he explained to them that confession of Jesus as Lord and belief in the resurrection of Christ are vital to salvation both for the Israelites and for the Romans. Since confession of Jesus as Lord is essential, the person who refuses to make that confession should not expect to spend eternity with Him. Similarly, since the resurrection of Jesus is the very thing by which death was conquered and eternal life was offered, a man's belief in that resurrection is central to his salvation.

Those who claim that the thief's salvation – without baptism – is a legitimate model for salvation in the church age have apparently failed to notice that the thief did not, and in fact could not, believe in the resurrection. Christ had not yet died when He told him, *'Assuredly, I say to you, today you will be with Me in Paradise.'* Therefore, belief in the resurrection, while vital for *our* salvation, did not apply to the thief. This is because, unlike the thief, we live in God's covenant of grace.

Faith in the resurrection as a matter of salvation is a glaring example of the difference between our circumstances and the thief's situation. Belief in Jesus' resurrection lies at the very core of man's opportunity for eternal life in the church age. This was not true for the thief. Therefore, we cannot look to the example of the thief to challenge the role of baptism, since the circumstances surrounding that incident are not relevant to salvation in the church age. If belief in the resurrection played no part in our salvation, we might consider the thief to be an example of salvation today. However, since belief in the resurrection cannot be dismissed in the church age, the manner in which the thief was saved has no bearing on the salvation of modern men.

Who would accept that anyone could be saved without the Holy Spirit? Yet, if we are to accept that the thief is an example for us, we must receive our salvation without the involvement of the Holy Spirit. Regardless what a man or woman might believe about baptism with the Holy Spirit, very few would ever consider discounting the role of the Spirit within God's kingdom. In Jesus' own words we find that, unless a person experiences spiritual birth, he/she cannot enter the kingdom (John 3: 5). The apostle John even portrays the Spirit as a witness, *'that God has given us eternal life, and this life is in His Son.'* (1 John 5: 11). While some men may claim that the thief did, somehow, receive the Holy Spirit prior to his death, Scripture does not support this claim, nor is it implied in the text. In fact, we learn from Scripture that the Holy Spirit would not be given until after Jesus had ascended to heaven (John 7: 39).

Those who insist on using the thief as an example of salvation in the church age are apparently unconcerned with this inconsistency. Yet, just as we must believe in the resurrection if we are to be saved, we must also experience a spiritual birth before entering the kingdom. This birth involves the work of the Holy Spirit at the time of conversion (John 3: 5; 1 Corinthians 12: 13). One who fails to experience spiritual birth will not see the kingdom. He will not be saved. The only means we have available to us today for entering the kingdom of God entails the work of the Holy Spirit. Since spiritual birth is essential, a birth that was unknown to the thief, his salvation cannot be viewed as an example of salvation in the church age.

In his epistles Paul spends a great deal of time teaching disciples about the body of Christ, which is the church. He refers to the body of Christ as one of the unique unifying elements of Christianity (Ephesians 4: 4). Indeed, each one who is saved is considered a member of the body of Christ (1 Corinthians 12: 13). For those who are saved, membership in that body is not optional, but essential and automatic. According to Paul, it is the members of that body who are heirs to the kingdom (Ephesians 3: 6). That being the case, who would wish to escape membership? Yet, the thief on the cross, whom so many cite as an example of salvation, was not a part of the body of Christ. He could not have been a member of the body since it was not established until the Day of Pentecost, weeks after his death.

While many may consider this disparity insignificant, it is fair to say that God does not. Once again, if the thief is a useful example of salvation for the church age, we have no need to be members of the body. If, however, only those who are members of that body will inherit the kingdom of God, membership in that body must be important with respect to salvation. In that case, the manner in which the thief was saved can have no bearing on the manner in which men are saved today.

There are stark differences between our situation today and the circumstances surrounding the thief's salvation. We live in a different age than the thief. Additionally, the thief's situation was exceptional in that he lived while Jesus roamed the earth. Jesus forgave several individuals while He was on earth, including a paralytic (Matthew 9:2) and the woman who washed His feet (Luke 7: 47-48). He declared, and even demonstrated, the fact that He had the authority to forgive sins *while He was on earth* when He was questioned by the Pharisees (Mark 2: 5-11). However, these are not models for salvation in the church age. The constant effort by many to portray them as examples of how men are saved challenges the very heart of the gospel message that is presented in Scripture.

While Jesus' disciples, as well as John the Baptist, performed water baptism prior to the death of Christ, that baptism must be placed in proper perspective. Certainly it was considered a baptism for the forgiveness of sins (Mark 1: 4; Luke 3: 3), but it was limited in scope since its symbolic nature was yet to be realized. John's baptism was performed in anticipation of Christian baptism in the same manner that his ministry was intended to prepare the way for Christ. The baptism of John was never identified as essential for salvation.

Baptism was not introduced as an element of salvation until after Jesus' resurrection (Mark 16: 16, Acts 2: 38, 1 Peter 3: 21) and well after the death of the thief. Pointing to the thief on the cross to support a doctrine of salvation without baptism is similar to offering Moses, Elijah, or Abraham as suitable examples. It is true that, in the end, it is the blood of Christ that saves even these great men of God. However, we have no reason to look to the thief on the cross as a legitimate example of salvation in the church age.

Chapter XIII
A Matter of Choice

The Nature of God

God is gracious – a point upon which all believers will surely agree. Those who believe that the Bible is the true Word of God will also grant that God created man in His image (Genesis 1: 26) and that He loves all men (John 3: 16). When God formed man He instilled within us the ability to make choices regarding our own actions (Judges 5: 8; Proverbs 1: 29; 1 Peter 5: 2); that is to say, God gave us free will. It was important that men have the ability to make free will choices. It was God's plan to have a true relationship with His creation. He wanted man's love; not a love dictated by God, but a love that was chosen by men. Without free will it would not be possible for men to make such a choice.

God is holy (1 Peter 1: 16). In fact, we understand from Scripture that it is His nature to be holy (2 Peter 1: 4). The holiness of God that is revealed in Scripture provides us with the understanding that God is pure, undefiled, virtuous, and divine. He is a God who not only has never done wrong but, because of His nature, He cannot do wrong (Titus 1: 2; James 1: 13). God is also completely righteous (Exodus 9: 27). Righteousness involves much more than an understanding of right and wrong. The idea of righteousness implies fairness or justice. Righteousness not only knows the difference between right and wrong, but it recognizes that good must be rewarded and evil must be punished. The righteous nature of God reveals that He is always fair and that His judgments are completely just.

Parents tend to establish rules for their children based on their understanding of right and wrong and what they believe is in the best interest of the child. In like manner, God has established guidelines that are intended to assist us in our walk with Him. God has a desire to commune with men. However, in our sinful state communion with God is not possible since God is holy. For this reason He has provided us with guidelines – so that we may be a holy people presentable to Him.

The Choice of Adam and Eve

We witness man's resistance to God's guidance near the very outset of the relationship. Adam and Eve were the first to test the boundaries God had set in place for mankind. Since most are undoubtedly familiar with the account of Adam and Eve, we will simply note that God had provided these two with one simple instruction – they were to avoid the *tree of knowledge of good and evil*. They could not eat of its fruit. In fact, they were not supposed to touch that particular tree. While this command does not appear to be overly oppressive, since they apparently had plenty of food, for some reason they simply could not resist the temptation. The lesson from Adam and Eve's sin reveals not only the weakness of man, but the deceptive nature of Satan. He convincingly claimed that God was lying to them when He forewarned them:

> You shall not eat it, nor shall you touch it, lest you die. (Genesis 3: 3)

Satan, in the form of a crafty serpent, persuaded the woman that God's way was not the only way and not necessarily the best way. He told Eve:

> You will not surely die. (Genesis 3: 4)

From that point on man became easily fooled by Satan as he has constantly challenged God's instructions. This kind of rebellion against God has led us on a path where many men, while claiming a life of obedience, will freely resist God's directions simply because they don't like them.

The Fiery Serpent

Scripture offers a number of examples where people were faced with choices. While men were always free to choose what path they would take, each decision involved either a reward or a consequence. So it is with the gospel message. While men and women are free to choose whether they will obey the commands of God with respect to the gospel message, rewards and consequences are fully dependent upon the choices we make.

In a rebellious manner, the children of Israel cried out against the God of Abraham. God, in turn, sent serpents among them as punishment. As they began to repent of their sin God made available to them a means to survive the poison of the serpents.

> Then the Lord said to Moses, "Make a fiery serpent, and set it on a pole; and it shall be that everyone who is bitten, when he looks at it, shall live." (Numbers 21: 8)

218

While each one could decline the offer of life by refusing to look at the serpent, the foolishness of that decision should be obvious. Why would anyone refuse to do something so simple knowing that the reward of obedience was life and the consequence of refusal was death? Giving up an opportunity for life by failing to obey such a simple command seems senseless.

David's Choice

God made it clear that no one but the Priests were allowed to touch the Ark of the Covenant. In order to help the Israelites obey this command He gave them instructions as to how the Ark should be carried – the Ark was to be carried on poles (Exodus 25: 13-15). However, King David and his captains and other leaders believed they knew best and decided to build a new cart to carry the Ark from a place called Kirjath Jearim back to Judah where David believed it should be. David was undoubtedly very sincere in his desire to please God with the new cart. Two men, Uzza and Ahio, drove the cart that carried the Ark.

> 9. And when they came to Chidon's threshing floor, Uzza put out his hand to hold the ark, for the oxen stumbled. 10. Then the anger of the Lord was aroused against Uzza, and He struck him because he put his hand to the ark; and he died there before God. (1 Chronicles 13: 9-10)

Uzza earnestly attempted to prevent the Ark from falling to the ground. Had David followed God's instructions, Uzza would not have died because an ox happened to stumble. As a result of David's choice to disobey God, Uzza, an innocent, died even in his sincere effort to protect the ark. His action, no matter how sincere, was contrary to God's command. God became angry with Uzza, and he died in his sincerity.

Naaman, Moses, and the Blind Man

Naaman was a commander in the army of Syria who happened to develop leprosy. Through the advice of his wife's maidservant he sought out Elisha, the prophet, hoping to be cured. Elisha told Naaman to go and wash (dip or bathe) in the Jordan River seven times. Naaman was not thrilled about the prospect of bathing in such a filthy body of water and would have preferred either the Abanah or the Pharpar. He now faced a decision whether he would heed God's instructions (given through the prophet). Naaman eventually yielded and washed in the Jordan. When he came up from the water the seventh time he was cleansed of his leprosy (2 Kings 5: 1-14).

Few men would believe that Naaman would have been healed of his leprosy if he had rejected Elisha's instructions. If he had gone to another river (such as the Abanah or Pharpar) and dipped himself seven times, we have no reason to believe he would have been healed. Had he gone to the Jordan and dipped himself three...four...five...even six times, Naaman would have remained a leper. Had Naaman failed to follow Elisha's directions we would not expect him to be healed. The *only* course of action for Naaman to be healed was for him to, '*Go, wash yourself in the Jordan seven times...*' (v. 10).

* * * * *

Moses understood God's command. He was to speak to the rock in the Wilderness of Zin and water for the Israelites would come forth (Numbers 20: 7-12). While the command was not a difficult one, Moses saw fit to defy God. As a result, he was not allowed to enter into the Promised Land.

* * * * *

At a certain time during His ministry Jesus came upon a man blind from birth. Jesus formed some mud with a mixture of saliva and dirt and placed it on the man's eyes. He then told the man to go and wash his eyes in the Pool of Siloam (John 9: 1-7). Who would believe, if this man had said to himself, *Jesus already touched me; therefore I need not to go to the pool of Siloam,* his blindness would have been healed? Of course, no one would believe that. Nor did he seem to question Jesus' directions. His response was simple obedience.

The Nature of God's Instructions

As we consider the many examples in Scripture where men made choices about whether or not they would obey God, we find that the nature of the instruction given was never in question. Gideon knew what God expected of him. He realized that he was to lead the Israelites in battle against the Midianites and defeat them. He laid out a fleece, not as a manner of determining what

God wanted him to do, but to assure himself that it was actually God who was calling him (Judges 6: 36-40). Noah did not question God's instructions for building an ark, but followed them precisely without hesitation (Genesis 6: 22). Similarly, those to whom Jesus gave direction in the Great Commission followed His instructions. They went out and made disciples through teaching and baptism (Matthew 28: 18-20).

God has made a practice of making His instructions clear and easy to understand. It is not, nor has it ever been, the nature of the instruction that is in doubt. In simple words God has made His intentions known. Those who heard these words of the Great Commission understood what was expected of them. Throughout the book of Acts, as the word spread and the church, the body of Christ, was established, it was understood that in baptism sins were forgiven, the Holy Spirit was received, and people were added to the body of Christ.

We should give some deeper consideration to the nature of the remarks in the Great Commission. The recorded words spoken by Jesus after His resurrection are extremely limited in number. While He undoubtedly offered the disciples a great deal of teaching prior to His ascension, only a handful of comments are offered up in Scripture. Since so few words are actually recorded it is safe to assume that the words that are documented must carry considerable weight. A review of the Great Commission reveals the timelessness of the message.

'All authority has been given to Me in heaven and on earth.' Jesus' authority was not temporary. He was/is God. For all time He holds within Himself full authority in heaven and on earth. *'Go...and make disciples of all nations.'* Surely no one would doubt that this call to *make disciples* is just as important today as it was on the day the words were spoken. He then stated, '...t*eaching them to observe all things that I have commanded you.'* This is a challenge to all men to teach other men to live lives that honor God. *'And lo, I am with you always, even to the end of the age.'* This one speaks for itself.

The words Jesus spoke at this time make it very clear that the message and commands of the Great Commission were intended to span the entire church age. However, in a conversation filled with teaching that is obviously meant to continue *to the end of the age*, many still refuse to acknowledge that *'baptizing them in the name of the Father and of the Son and of the Holy Spirit'* is an enduring command. Yet timelessness is clearly Jesus' intent – a fact that those who stood before Him surely recognized.

It is important to understand that there is a difference between the *will* of God and the *instructions* (commands) of God. God's *will* is about His purpose or desire. For instance, it is God's *will* that man should be faithful to Him as a holy being. We receive *instructions* from God so that we will know *how* to accomplish His will. Still, God does not force us to do His will or to follow His instructions. Each one has the freedom to choose whether he/she will follow the path God has chosen for us to become a holy people. The biblical roadmap leads the way. We find countless examples in Scripture where men were given the opportunity to choose whether or not to accept God's instructions. Like them, we have been offered a similar opportunity. Also like them, we will undoubtedly reap the rewards or suffer the consequences of the decisions we make.

Having received biblical instruction concerning baptism throughout the New Testament from men of God, many simply decline to accept it. Perhaps it is because, unlike Naaman or the blind man, the rewards and consequences are not realized instantaneously. Yet, while they are unwilling to believe that these two men would have been healed without obeying the instructions given, many claim exemption for themselves regarding God's precept of baptism.

*　*　*　*　*

One major problem we face in a discussion about baptism is that some men attempt to place the whole of salvation on obedience to baptism. Often the question is posed, *Does baptism save?* The more appropriate question that should be asked is, *'Can a person be saved without baptism?'* Certainly a man cannot be saved by faith alone. James made this clear when he explained that faith without action is useless (James 2: 20). Therefore, no one can attain salvation through faith alone. Yet, can anyone be saved without faith? Of course, the answer is an unwavering "No!"

This same teaching can be applied to confession and repentance. Neither repentance nor confession can, in itself, bring about salvation. Still, no one can be saved without them. The question regarding baptism is just as relevant. Can a man be saved without baptism? God has made it clear in Scripture that baptism is a vital component of His plan of salvation – a component that we must not ignore. Each one has a choice to make with respect to baptism. However, the choice we face is not whether baptism is God's instruction to man. The choice we face is whether or not we, like Naaman and the blind man, will follow directions clearly given.

Chapter XIV
What Is Baptism with the Holy Spirit?

Some of the controversy surrounding baptism can be traced to the way men view the roles of various baptisms that appear in Scripture. Of concern are the questions that have been raised about the respective functions of *water baptism* and what both Jesus and John the Baptist referred to as *baptism with the Holy Spirit.*

References to baptism with the Holy Spirit are very limited in Scripture. While the scarcity of the phrase is part of the issue, the greater challenge for us is the fact that God's Word does not tell us, in so many words, the precise meaning of this expression. For that reason, if we are to have a beneficial discussion it is best to approach the topic without pre-conceived ideas as to what the phrase means. We know that regeneration is linked to the work of the Holy Spirit in certain passages such as Romans 15: 16, 1 Corinthians 6: 11, and Titus 3: 5. Whether or not this represents *baptism* with the Spirit is something upon which many cannot agree.

The truth is, most men are so intent on their own belief about the meaning of baptism with the Holy Spirit that nothing will change their minds. Yet it is possible that we as men have approached the subject of baptism with the Holy Spirit without really taking into consideration all that the Bible has to offer on the subject. As we consider those occasions in Scripture where the term *baptism with the Spirit* is used, there are things that challenge some of the more commonly held views on the subject.

Four passages where this phrase is spoken (Matthew 3: 11; Mark 1: 8; Luke 3: 16; John 1: 33) should be seen as one occurrence since they simply address the same incident four different times. Each of the gospel writers wrote concerning John the Baptist's prophecy about baptism with the Spirit. The next occasion where it is used finds Jesus, after the resurrection and prior to His ascension, restating John's prophesy that is found in the four passages mentioned above.

5. for John truly baptized with water, but you shall be baptized with the Holy Spirit not many days from now. (Acts 1: 5)

Later, in Caesarea, Peter used the same words when he witnessed the Holy Spirit *falling upon* the Gentiles (Acts 11: 16), apparently linking this event to Jesus' prophecy prior to Pentecost (Acts 1: 5). In his first letter to the Corinthians Paul reminded them that they had been '*washed...sanctified...justified...by the Spirit...*' (1 Corinthians 6: 11). He also wrote that we, as the body of Christ, can find unity in the fact that '*by one Spirit we were all baptized into one body*' (1 Corinthians 12: 13). The challenges that these passages present are numerous given the limited views of men concerning the meaning of *baptism with the Holy Spirit*. We will address these difficulties after we have taken a closer look at the various stands men have taken regarding the meaning of this phrase.

Power Received – The Day of Pentecost
One prominent belief about the meaning of baptism with the Holy Spirit is that it speaks of a mysterious manifestation of the Spirit by which God gives miraculous spiritual gifts, such as the ability to speak in unknown tongues or to prophesy. Some also teach that this is the time of salvation. Others hold a similar view, believing that this distinctive work of the Spirit represents a second blessing – a supernatural whelming of the Spirit, including speaking in tongues, that often occurs *after* a man has been saved. Those who hold this view claim that the event portrayed in the following passage is the very definition of baptism with the Holy Spirit about which both John the Baptist (Matthew 3: 11) and Jesus (Acts 1: 5) prophesied:

> 1. When the Day of Pentecost had fully come, they were all with one accord in one place. 2. And suddenly there came a sound from heaven, as of a rushing mighty wind, and it filled the whole house where they were sitting. 3. Then there appeared to them divided tongues, as of fire, and *one* sat upon each of them. 4. And they were all filled with the Holy Spirit and began to speak with other tongues, as the Spirit gave them utterance. (Acts 2: 1-4)

The notion that baptism with the Holy Spirit is a spiritual event initiated directly by God makes sense given the remarks made by John the Baptist (Matthew 3: 11; Luke 3: 16) where he seemed to contrast water and Spirit baptism. The word *baptism* suggests an immersion – in this case it would be an immersion in or with the Spirit. The portrayal of the Spirit being *poured out* on those present on the Day of Pentecost easily harmonizes with the idea of immersion. Note that the *house was filled*. Just as the earth was completely submerged in the flood, so the Spirit was poured out on that day. In a house that was filled with the Spirit, these men were fully immersed.

A miraculous event occurred on the Day of Pentecost as the apostles were overwhelmed by, and filled with, the Holy Spirit and began to speak in other languages. They then proceeded to preach to the crowds gathered in Jerusalem. The crowd probably included many of the same Jews who were present at the time of Jesus' crucifixion. Perhaps some had even seen the risen Christ. This was almost certainly true of the one hundred twenty disciples mentioned in the first chapter of Acts. Even those who were not present for the crucifixion were probably familiar with the incident as friends and family shared the details of Jesus' death. They understood fully the events surrounding the message delivered by the apostles. Realizing they had crucified the Messiah, the people asked, *'Men and brethren, what shall we do?'* (Acts 2: 37). Given the circumstances, it is completely understandable why the message impacted them and three thousand responded.

As we consider the occasion of the Day of Pentecost, it is easy to see that the event described by Luke in Acts 2: 1-4 was the *initial* outpouring of the Spirit upon mankind for the church age, and this through the apostles. The fact that the apostles received power on that day is actually quite interesting when you consider the fact that Jesus had already granted them the ability to drive out demons and heal the sick (Matthew 10: 1). If they could already do these things, what power did they receive at Pentecost?

Evidently, on the Day of Pentecost the apostles realized an expansion of the powers already given. The *authority* they had received earlier in Jesus' ministry was rather limited in nature. However, once Pentecost arrived and the power of the Holy Spirit was unleashed, we discover that the apostles performed works in ways not possible prior to that day. They spoke in foreign tongues they had never studied (Acts 2: 1-13), performed miracles well beyond casting out demons and healing the sick (Acts 2: 43), and they were now able to distribute spiritual gifts to other believers by laying hands on them (Acts 8: 17-18; Romans 1: 11).

The Day of Pentecost – A Proper Biblical Perspective

Much confusion exists among men today concerning the Day of Pentecost. Since there is so much misunderstanding, it is vital that we consider, from a biblical perspective, the activities of the day, including the outpouring of the Holy Spirit that was experienced at that time (Acts 2: 1-4). A better understanding of the first two chapters of the book of Acts is crucial since they are the source of considerable doctrinal differences among men. For instance, before He ascended to heaven Jesus promised His listeners that they would receive power as the Spirit came upon them (Acts 1: 8). Some men maintain that this promise of *power* was meant for all men and women who accept Jesus as Savior. There is also widespread acceptance that, as the Holy Spirit first fell upon men on the Day of Pentecost and they were filled with the Spirit (Acts 2: 1-4), the experience involved more than the twelve apostles. Yet we find that an honest reading of the text exposes some real weaknesses in this argument.

It is evident from Scripture that when Jesus prophesied about the coming of the Holy Spirit and the power these men would receive, He was speaking specifically with the apostles. We know this from the details of the passage. First of all, Luke expressly references the apostles in the narrative (Acts 1: 1-11). Secondly, when two angels appeared to the men after Jesus had ascended, they addressed them as, *'Men of Galilee'* (Acts 1: 11), a pointed reference to the apostles who were chosen while Jesus was in Galilee (Matthew 4: 18-21; 9: 9 – 10: 4). As these men returned to Jerusalem from the Mt. of Olives, Luke provides us with their exact identity.

> 12. Then they returned to Jerusalem from the mount called Olivet, which is near Jerusalem, a Sabbath day's journey. 13. And when they had entered, they went up into the upper room where they were staying: Peter, James, John, and Andrew; Philip and Thomas; Bartholomew and Matthew; James *the son* of Alphaeus and Simon the Zealot; and Judas *the son* of James. (Acts 1: 12-13)

Later, in the same chapter, we are told of a gathering where Peter addressed the entire body of believers in Jerusalem, a group numbering roughly one hundred twenty (Acts 1: 15). During that assembly Matthias was chosen to replace Judas as an apostle. We learn that, *'he was numbered with the eleven apostles'* (Acts 1: 26).

Finally, on the Day of Pentecost, we discover that *'they were all with one accord in one place... '* (Acts 2: 1).

Since the apostles had met with the entire body of disciples earlier in chapter one, a large number of people believe that the word *all* in this verse (Acts 2: 1) represents the one hundred twenty believers mentioned in the previous chapter. These same men claim that all of the one hundred twenty disciples received the outpouring of the Spirit on that day (Acts 2: 1-4). Yet the last group mentioned prior to the word *they* is found in the previous verse (Acts 1: 26), which is not a reference to the one hundred twenty, but to the twelve apostles as Matthias was added to their number. This is more easily realized when we ignore the chapter break that has been inserted between these verses. Of course, while the mention of the apostles in the previous verse is a strong argument, in itself it is not conclusive. However, the subsequent verses provide rather impressive evidence that it was only the apostles who were gathered together on the Day of Pentecost as the Spirit came upon them (Acts 2: 1-4).

First of all, the crowd in Jerusalem recognized that all those who were speaking in tongues were from Galilee (Acts 2: 7). This was true of the apostles (we can assume that Matthias was from Galilee) as well as certain other believers, including Jesus' family and Mary Magdalene. However, in order for us to conclude that each of the one hundred twenty disciples received this same gift we must not only assume that every one of them came from Galilee, but that the crowd would actually be able to recognize this fact with relative ease. This is not only highly unlikely, but is essentially unrealistic given the diversity of Jesus' early followers. While many of His disciples were from Galilee, many were not. Mary, Martha, and Lazarus came from Bethany, a short distance from Jerusalem, and were very likely part of this family of believers. Barnabas was from the Island of Cyprus while Zaccheus and Bartimaeus both came from Jericho on the eastern border of Judea. Also, let us not forget Joseph, the disciple from Arimathaea who asked Pilate for Christ's body so that he might give Him a proper burial (Matthew 27: 57).

The most convincing piece of evidence, however, is the fact that John Mark, who was the author of the gospel of Mark and a cousin to Barnabas (Colossians 4: 10), along with his mother Mary, were from Jerusalem. They were not Galileans, yet they were among Jesus' earliest disciples. Scholars agree that they were among these followers in Jerusalem after Jesus' death and resurrection. Certain incidents in the life of Christ that are mentioned in Mark's gospel indicate that he was an eyewitness to the events. Furthermore, a great many scholars assume that the upper room where the disciples prayed together (Acts 1: 13) was located at Mary's home, believing this to be the same room where Jesus shared the Last Supper with the apostles the night before His death (Mark 14: 15). The early church met there at least occasionally (Acts 12: 12) and probably regularly.

If the house where Jesus shared the Lord's Supper was not Mary's house, it was undoubtedly the home of another Judean disciple – perhaps Joseph of Arimathaea or someone else – since we know from Scripture that this person was unknown to the apostles prior to Passover (Matthew 26: 17-18; Mark 14: 12-16). Therefore, we can easily determine that not all of the one hundred twenty disciples were Galileans which means that not all of the one hundred twenty disciples received the outpouring of the Holy Spirit and spoke in tongues (Acts 2: 1-7).

Secondly, Luke specifically identifies those men who were speaking in tongues as the apostles as Peter defended them against the accusation of drunkenness

12. So they were all amazed and perplexed, saying to one another, "Whatever could this mean?" 13 Others mocking said, "They are full of new wine." 14. But Peter, standing up with the eleven, raised his voice and said to them, "Men of Judea and all who dwell in Jerusalem, let this be known to you, and heed my words. 15. For these are not drunk, as you suppose, since it is *only* the third hour of the day. (Acts 2: 12-15).

Another point that should not be overlooked is that, when the crowd responded to the gospel message that was spoken, they did not address the one hundred twenty disciples, but those doing the preaching, who were the apostles (Acts 2: 37). Since all those who were gathered together received the gift of tongues (Acts 2: 4), based upon the compelling evidence available to us in Scripture, it is clear that only the apostles *'... were all with one accord in one place..., '* (Acts 2: 1). In a fair-minded reading of the text, we can come to no other conclusion.

Some will still insist that the narrative could be interpreted to allow for the outpouring of the Spirit on all of the one hundred twenty disciples. However, this is possible only if we are willing to ignore the details of the text. It is by no means an objective view; nor is this position in keeping with Jesus' promise of the power (*dunamis - suggesting something beyond normal human capabilities*) they would receive when the Holy Spirit came upon them (Acts 1: 8). These men were given powers well beyond the miraculous spiritual gifts (*charisma*) experienced by others later in the book of Acts. The gift of tongues was merely one example of the power received by these men on that day. In order to conclude from Luke's account that all of the disciples were involved, we must somehow accept that the Holy Spirit bestowed the gift of tongues on *all* the disciples while granting greater powers only to the apostles (Acts 2: 43). That is a scenario that cannot be inferred from the text.

Despite compelling biblical evidence to the contrary, many continue to insist that the outpouring of the Spirit on the Day of Pentecost was received by all of the one hundred twenty disciples. Many men maintain that, on that day, each of these disciples received the ability to speak in tongues in the same manner, and at the same time as the apostles. Of course, some may be wondering what difference it makes who received the Spirit miraculously on the Day of Pentecost. Does it really matter if it was the one hundred twenty disciples or only the apostles?

A proper understanding of the events of the Day of Pentecost is critical. The claim that all of the disciples received the outpouring of the Spirit has resulted in a somewhat distorted view of these events and, consequently, a skewed perspective of the apostles' role in the early church. The position of the apostles was unique within the kingdom. They were the instrument through whom the Holy Spirit was introduced to mankind. The Spirit came *to* other men *through* the apostles, both in a general sense and even more specifically in relation to the spiritual gifts that were experienced in the first century church. Insisting that each of the one hundred twenty disciples received the Spirit in the same manner as the apostles, despite overwhelming biblical evidence, undermines the nature of the apostles' role in the church.

The example of Pentecost, as men disregard the details of the text in favor of personal views, demonstrates the ease with which men tend to discount biblical teaching, no matter how straightforward it may be, when it does not support their own beliefs. If men are willing to ignore basic information such as this with such ease, how much would they be willing to forsake biblical teaching on issues of even greater significance if they so choose?

If we wish to come away with a proper perspective of the Day of Pentecost, and as a matter of respect for the Word of God, we must recognize the exceptional status that was bestowed upon the apostles on that day. Hopefully, pointing out this example where the teaching of men is visibly inconsistent with Scripture will challenge others to reconsider many of the lessons they have learned generally about what Scripture actually says.

Baptism with the Holy Spirit – The Gentiles

The prophecy of John the Baptist concerning baptism with the Holy Spirit (Matthew 3: 11), which Jesus later echoed (Acts 1: 5), was now fulfilled. The Day of Pentecost had come and, according to the view discussed early in this chapter, baptism with the Holy Spirit had been experienced. That, however, is not the end of it. The miracle described here is mentioned one other time in Scripture. A few years later Peter was summoned to Caesarea to the house of Cornelius, a Gentile. It was there that he, and those with him, witnessed a similar outpouring of the Holy Spirit on those in Cornelius' house (Acts 10: 44-46). In the eleventh chapter of Acts, Peter, while he was recalling the incident for the Jews in Jerusalem, explained how these Gentiles had received the Holy Spirit in a manner similar to what the apostles had experienced on the Day of Pentecost (Acts 11: 15-16).

Pentecost and Caesarea: One View – Two Perspectives

Among those who believe that the outpouring of the Spirit at Pentecost represents baptism with the Holy Spirit, there are two very different opinions. Some maintain that this supernatural manifestation of the Spirit was common among Christians in the first century and may be received today in the same manner that it was experienced on the Day of Pentecost. There are, of course, some biblical issues when it comes to defending this belief.

The first problem with this point of view is that receiving the Spirit in this manner was actually very rare in the first century. Scripture records only two incidents when this occurred. If this manifestation of the Holy Spirit was commonplace, as some would have us believe, Peter would have seen it among the Jewish Christians of his day. However, when Peter witnessed the outpouring of the Spirit upon the Gentiles in Caesarea, he was reminded of Jesus' prophecy and how they had received the Holy Spirit *'at the beginning'* (Acts 11: 15-16). The very fact that Peter considered the incident in Ceasarea an *anomaly* should erase any notion that episodes such as this were routine in the early Christian community.

It is very telling that, beyond these two incidents, Scripture makes no mention of the Spirit falling on anyone without the touch of an apostle's hand. Some men turn to 1 Corinthians 12: 13 and suggest that Paul is discussing this phenomenon, but the verse simply does not allow for that interpretation. According to Paul's words in that passage, *'we are all baptized by one Spirit.'* He was speaking of a baptism common to all Christians. However, when Peter was with the Gentiles, he pointed out the fact that he had only witnessed this phenomenon once before. It is evident from Peter's response that this was something most rare as opposed to the common baptismal experience discussed by Paul.

*   *   *   *   *

There is an alternate stand taken by many who accept that Pentecost and Caesarea do, indeed, illustrate true baptism with the Spirit. Some men insist that these two episodes represent *complete and final* fulfillment of all prophecies regarding this kind of baptism in the church age. They believe that these prophecies were totally and completely fulfilled, never to repeat, once the Gentiles had experienced baptism with the Spirit. Once again, however, some serious challenges plague this position.

Paul, in his first letter to the Corinthians, indicated that baptism *by*, or *with*, the Spirit is something that was known to all Christians (1 Corinthians 12: 13). More than this, baptism with the Spirit must be experienced by all Christians if, as Paul claims, it is intended to be a unifying element within the body of Christ. Therefore, we cannot limit baptism with (or by) the Spirit to these two occasions.

We also face a challenge from the prophecy offered by John the Baptist (Matthew 3: 11). Since Jesus' statement regarding power received on the Day of Pentecost was directed at the apostles (Acts 1: 8), we *could* argue that His prophecy regarding baptism with the Spirit at that time (Acts 1: 5) was given with the same focus – to the apostles. However, this is not true of John's prophecy. When John the Baptist uttered his prophecy about baptism with the Spirit he did not focus on any specific group of people. Additionally, John spoke these words before Jesus selected those men who would later become apostles. Actually, he spoke these words prior to Jesus' own baptism. Consequently, in an honest reading of the text we can only conclude that when John said, *'He will baptize you with the Holy Spirit and with fire'* it was a prophecy targeting, at the very least, all Jewish believers. Therefore, while it would be foolish to deny that Pentecost and Caesarea represent at least one form of baptism with the Spirit, it would be narrow-minded to confine our view of this baptism to these two incidents or to this kind of experience. Baptism with the Spirit must carry with it an even greater significance.

Gifts of the Spirit

Many men believe that the miraculous gifts (e.g., speaking in tongues, prophecy, etc.) that were present among first century Christians were a result of *baptism with the Spirit* as it was experienced in Jerusalem on the Day of Pentecost and later at the house of Cornelius. This view comes from a misunderstanding of the gifts of the Spirit that were distributed to these early Christians.

The means by which spiritual gifts were received by men in the first century was through the touch of an apostle's hands. Several passages of Scripture confirm that, with the exceptions of Pentecost and Caesarea, where Cornelius lived, an apostle's touch was necessary to bestow these extraordinary gifts (Acts 8: 14-17; 19: 6; Romans 1: 11-12; 2 Timothy 1: 6). While it was certainly the Spirit who distributed the gifts (1 Corinthians 12: 11), when the method of distribution is discussed it is always through the hands of the apostles. Pentecost and Caesarea were unusual in that the Holy Spirit was received without an apostle's touch. Yet, even on those two occasions at least one apostle was present.

The fact that spiritual gifts were distributed through the apostles is one of the significant issues surrounding the identity of those who received the outpouring of the Spirit on the Day of Pentecost. The ability to distribute these gifts was evident among the apostles after they received the outpouring of the Holy Spirit (Acts 2: 1-4). This method of the distribution of spiritual gifts in the first century helps us better understand the relationship of the apostles to the work of the Spirit in the early church. The Holy Spirit worked specifically through the apostles. When Philip, who was not an apostle, was in Samaria he did not distribute spiritual gifts. He could not. Peter and John traveled to Samaria and distributed these gifts (Acts 8: 12-15) to the converts there. The ability to distribute these gifts was exclusive to the apostles and indicative of their special role in the church.

The Moving of the Spirit – Acts 4: 29-31

Some may wonder about the fourth chapter of the book of Acts. Could this not be an example of baptism with the Holy Spirit? In this instance Peter and John were taken before the chief priests and elders, accused of teaching about Jesus after they had healed the lame man at the temple. When they returned to their own and explained what had taken place, everyone began praising God and praying. As they continued, the place where they were gathered shook as in an earthquake and they were all filled with the Spirit (Acts 4: 29-31).

The information is a bit sketchy in that no details are offered regarding those with whom Peter and John were meeting at the time. While it may have been only the apostles, it is also certainly possible, and perhaps likely, that more than the apostles were present. Still, we can easily determine that this is not the same outpouring of the Holy Spirit mentioned in Acts 2: 1-4. First of all, the Holy Spirit did not *fall upon* them as He had on the Day of Pentecost. Secondly, no miraculous gifts of the Spirit were evidenced at this time. More importantly, however, at the house of Cornelius, Peter seems to only recall the Day of Pentecost as a comparable event.

It is possible that God did, at this time, send a refreshing of the Holy Spirit upon those present. Another possibility is that the shaking of the house stirred the Holy Spirit who already dwelt in those who were there, causing them to speak the word of God boldly.

Water and Holy Spirit Baptism Together

The other prominent view with respect to baptism with the Holy Spirit is that this takes place at the time of water baptism. The understanding from Scripture is that baptism with the Holy Spirit does not point to the Spirit *falling on* men and bestowing miraculous gifts, as was reported on the Day of Pentecost and later at the house of Cornelius. The belief is that the prophecies regarding baptism with the Holy Spirit (Matthew 3: 11; Acts 1: 6) are fulfilled when a person is baptized in water. According to this view, it is at that time that he/she receives the promised gift (filling/saturation) of the Holy Spirit. Scripture reveals that this, too, first occurred on the Day of Pentecost (Acts 2: 38).

Those who believe that baptism with the Holy Spirit occurs upon one's immersion in water have determined that there is one baptism, as taught by Paul (Ephesians 4: 5), but that the nature of that baptism is twofold. It is a baptism that has the capacity to join the physical world of man with the spiritual world in which God dwells. Thus, when Paul explained that we are unified by baptism (1 Corinthians 12: 13), he recognized that the work of the Spirit that unites us in the body of Christ occurs during water baptism. Peter instructed the crowd on the Day of Pentecost about the *'gift of the Holy Spirit'*. Not only did Peter teach that, at the time of baptism, each one would receive the gift of the Holy Spirit, but he also explained that this gift was promised to all obedient believers (Acts 2: 39).

Several Bible passages speak of a connection between the Holy Spirit and the act of water baptism. Paul confirmed this when he arrived at Ephesus and met with several men who had previously received the baptism of John.

> 1. And it happened, while Apollos was at Corinth, that Paul, having passed through the upper regions, came to Ephesus. And finding some disciples 2. he said to them, "Did you receive the Holy Spirit when you believed?" So they said to him, "We have not so much as heard whether there is a Holy Spirit." 3. And he said to them, "Into what then were you baptized?" So they said, "Into John's baptism." 4. Then Paul said, "John indeed baptized with a baptism of repentance, saying to the people that they should believe on Him who would come after him, that is, on Christ Jesus." 5. When they heard *this*, they were baptized in the name of the Lord Jesus. (Acts 19: 1-5)

When Paul learned that these disciples had not *heard* of the Holy Spirit he immediately concluded that they had not been baptized in the name of Jesus. His question to them in verse three makes clear the point Paul was making. He recognized that, if they had been baptized in the name of Jesus, they *would have known* the Holy Spirit. Similarly, Jesus taught Nicodemus that being born again involves a birth of both water and Spirit (John 3: 3-5). Jesus' words reveal a direct link between the Holy Spirit and water as a person is reborn, a connection that was later confirmed by Paul in his letter to Titus (Titus 3: 4-7).

Paul once again binds together water and the Spirit as he instructs the Corinthians concerning sanctification and justification (1 Corinthians 6: 9-11). Pointing to the many evils by which men are often consumed, he explained to the Corinthians that the *Holy Spirit* had separated them from such corruption as they were *washed* in baptism. The statement ties their cleansing to the moment of baptism. These works of the Spirit, done in the name of Jesus, are essentially accomplished simultaneously in baptism. The Corinthians were sanctified (consecrated) and justified (rendered innocent or free from sin) as they were washed (baptized). The washing to which Paul refers is unquestionably water baptism, to which the original Greek attests.

The word translated *washed* is απολουω (*apolouo*), which is derived from two other Greek words. The first of these words is απο (*apo*) meaning: *separation or departure.*[1] The second is λουω (*louo*), which means, *to bathe (the whole person).*[2] The New Strong's Exhaustive Concordance of the Bible, in its explanation of the word's meaning, draws a clear distinction between this word and νιπτω (*nipto*), which suggests only a partial washing, such as the hands and/or feet. Thus Paul is pointing to a literal washing rather than a figurative use of the word. In this passage (1 Corinthians 6: 9-11) he describes a separation from the list of unrighteous acts by the Corinthians. That separation from sins (justification and sanctification) is achieved in Jesus' name, by the Holy Spirit, through faith, in the washing of the entire person – in water.

Baptism of the Three Thousand

Many men believe that Holy Spirit baptism was meant to replace water baptism. After all, John said he baptized with water but that Jesus would baptize with the Holy Spirit. This certainly *sounds* like replacement. However, the Holy Spirit did not discard water baptism when He came into the world, but joined Himself intimately to the rite of immersion. That is what happened on the Day of Pentecost. The Holy Spirit did not replace water baptism; He enhanced it.

If the baptism commanded by Peter on the Day of Pentecost was the same *baptism with the Spirit* that the apostles had received (Acts 2: 1-4), no water baptism would have been necessary *after* the Day of Pentecost. After all, why baptize each one with water when Jesus could simply baptize them with the Spirit as He had done with the apostles? Pentecost was an opportune time to completely abandon the water baptism of John and Jesus that was administered prior to His death and replace it with baptism in the Spirit.

While many reject the notion, there is every reason to believe that the baptism received by the three thousand on the Day of Pentecost was baptism in water and no reason to believe that it was anything else. First of all, as previously stated, no mention is made of any others on that day receiving miraculous gifts, such as speaking in tongues. Secondly, at no time in Scripture do the apostles ever *teach* anyone to be baptized with the Holy Spirit. Receiving the Spirit is a promise to be fulfilled rather than a response by men. However, the Bible is filled with narratives where the apostles both taught and administered water baptism *after* the Day of Pentecost. Finally, the two times Scripture does record the Holy Spirit being *poured out* in this extraordinary manner, it is not initiated by the apostles, but by God Himself.

The belief that Christian baptism in water in the name of Jesus might have been abandoned on this day is especially unfounded since, until that time, no one had been baptized in this manner. Christian baptism *first occurred* on the Day of Pentecost. It is a bit awkward to suggest that the apostles abandoned this rite before it was ever administered. Many had received the baptism of John. That, however, was not baptism in the name of Jesus that was commanded by Jesus and taught by the apostles.

Peter and the other apostles on the Day of Pentecost were faithfully following the instructions they had received from Jesus in the Great Commission when He had charged them to '*go...make disciples...baptizing...teaching*' (Matthew 28: 19-20). Receiving the Holy Spirit was then promised as a result of repentance and baptism (Acts 2: 38). Christian baptism was established on the Day of Pentecost. Water baptism was not abolished; it was enriched as the Holy Spirit now joined Himself to this celebration of faith.

Baptism *in* the Spirit, *with* the Spirit, or *by* the Spirit?

These limited views make it very difficult for us to easily identify the exact nature of *baptism with the Spirit*. Yet there is one more point to be made. We must determine if we are baptized *by the Spirit*, *with the Spirit*, or *in the Spirit*. For instance, John the Baptist prophesied that men would be baptized *in the Spirit*

(Matthew 3: 11). However, Paul told the Corinthians that we are all baptized *'by one Spirit into one body'* (1 Corinthians 12: 13). In this case is the Spirit the *administrator* of baptism or is He the one *into whom we are baptized?* Still other passages where the Greek phrase, '$εν$ $ενι$ $πνευματι$,' appears it is translated *'with the Spirit.'* Quite often the same verse is translated differently in various versions of the Bible. How, then, can we reconcile these thoughts if we are to be true to the meaning of *baptizo* as immersion? All of this can be very confusing.

Most scholars agree that proper translation of this phrase in a particular setting relies heavily on the surrounding text. John the Baptist distinguished baptism *in* (NIV) or *with* (NASB) water from baptism *in* (NIV) or *with* (NASB) the Holy Spirit when he prophesied about the baptism that Jesus would provide. Generally, most translators agree that the words *by*, *in*, or *with*, could easily be used interchangeably in each of those passages where *baptism with the Spirit* is mentioned. It seems the most consistent and most widely used translation is *'with the Spirit.'* This certainly offers us flexibility in determining the role of the Spirit and allows men to decide for themselves what they want to believe. However, that seems to be the easy way out and this is a much too important issue to simply take the easy way out.

It is certainly easy to understand how the *pouring out* of the Spirit on the Day of Pentecost and later in Caesarea could be viewed as baptism *'in the Spirit.'* Those involved were miraculously enveloped and overwhelmed by the Spirit in a mighty way. Surely they experienced immersion in every sense of the word. Yet if, as Paul said, we are baptized by the Spirit on Christ's behalf (1 Corinthians 12: 13), how does this fit with the prophecy of John the Baptist (Matthew 3: 11)?

It is difficult for us, given our human limitations, to fully grasp the function of the Holy Spirit in water baptism. We find in Scripture that baptism is the time when the Holy Spirit indwells the new Christian (Acts 2: 38) and that the Holy Spirit plays a significant role in our lives from that moment. Given these facts, perhaps we should consider the possibility that *baptism with the Spirit* does not simply point to a specific spiritual event like Pentecost or water baptism, but characterizes a life that is *fully immersed in the Spirit.* Rather than pointing to a one-time spiritual *experience*, it seems more reasonable that baptism with the Spirit is meant to portray our *continued* immersion in the Holy Spirit.

When John the Baptist mentioned that Jesus would baptize men *'with the Spirit'* (Matthew 3: 11), we automatically assume that he is contrasting the *events* of baptism in water and baptism in the Spirit. However, it may be that John is not distinguishing between specific incidents, but between an event (water baptism) and a way of life (Spirit baptism). This would explain why he considered baptism with (or in) the Spirit infinitely superior to the purification ceremony of water baptism.

As Jesus restated the prophecy of John the Baptist concerning water and Spirit baptism, rather than speaking of a specific incident, it is possible, perhaps even likely, that He was talking about the manner in which their lives would be immersed in the Spirit, an immersion that would *begin* on the Day of Pentecost (Acts 1: 5). As Peter witnessed the outpouring of the Spirit on the Gentiles we look to the gift of tongues they received and automatically conclude that his reference to baptism with the Holy Spirit is specific to that moment. Yet it is possible that he was contemplating not only that episode, but the fact that a life immersed in the Spirit was also available to the Gentiles.

The picture of the early Christians that is offered up in the New Testament reveals people who seemed to *walk in the Spirit* (Galatians 5: 25). These were not people who simply received a momentary baptism with the Spirit, but people who were continually immersed in the Spirit and were being renewed on a daily basis (2 Corinthians 4: 16). This fits nicely with Paul's remark to the Corinthians concerning unity in the body as they were immersed with one Spirit into that body. That spiritual immersion continued as they walked and lived in the body of Christ. Limiting baptism with the Spirit to an event seems to diminish the significance both Christ and the apostles intended. The Christian, according to Scripture, is to be immersed in the Spirit each and every day. Surely this is the true nature of baptism with the Spirit.

What we are seeking, then, is not necessarily the time of baptism with the Spirit, since we cannot legitimately limit it to a specific moment. Baptism with the Spirit, like faith, is a journey – a way of life. Immersion in the Spirit is the seal that continues with us in our daily walk (Ephesians 1: 13). The question to which we seek an answer, then, is this: *At what time does baptism with the Spirit begin?*

Instruction Vs Narrative Concerning Baptism

The belief that baptism with the Holy Spirit occurs, or begins, independent from water baptism, is founded upon some individual incidents in the book of Acts where people experienced a miraculous manifestation of the Spirit rather than the baptismal instruction that is offered throughout God's Word. One major flaw in this approach is that the passages that are used to develop this belief are not instructional passages. Instead, they are narrative passages recounting events involving the apostles and the first century Christians. Instruction concerning baptism on the day of Pentecost is not found in the incident where the Holy Spirit was poured out upon the apostles (Acts 2: 1-4), but in Peter's sermon to the crowd (Acts 2: 38). It is unwise to attempt to draw doctrinal conclusions from *episodes* in Scripture unless corroborating support can be found in passages where the words are intended to teach, especially when the event smacks of divine intervention. We have no legitimate reason to form any beliefs about baptism from those occasions when the Holy Spirit manifested Himself in such an extraordinary fashion since we are offered no instruction concerning this phenomenon.

A number of historical events are related to us throughout Scripture upon which no doctrine has been formed. We find in the book of Luke, when Jesus met with Zaccheus, that the man vowed to offer half of all he owned to the poor. In response Jesus told him, *'Today salvation has come to this house...'* (Luke 19: 9). Can we, based on this episode, develop a doctrine that salvation comes by giving away half of all that we own? Of course we cannot. That would be absurd. The account simply details an event that occurred, providing information on the life of Christ and His followers. Certainly we must give generously as we are *taught* in Scripture (2 Corinthians 9: 6), but a doctrine of salvation in exchange for half of one's wealth would be foolish.

As Paul traveled on the Road to Damascus, God blinded him with a bright light from heaven. Yet who has developed a doctrine claiming that physical blindness is necessary for salvation? No such doctrine has been established. The reason is that this was a moment of divine revelation intended to call Paul to be an apostle to the Gentiles. It says nothing about the manner in which men are saved.

Those who believe that baptism with the Holy Spirit occurs at a time other than water baptism view the outpouring of the Spirit on the Day of Pentecost as instruction concerning baptism with the Holy Spirit. This event, however, should not be considered instructional since it cannot be reconciled with the events at the house of Cornelius (Acts 10: 44) where no tongues of fire were present. The occasion of Pentecost is also unlike other instances such as Samaria (Acts 8: 14-16) or Ephesus (Acts 19: 6) where the Spirit fell upon no one without the touch of the apostles' hands.

The fact is, when individuals and groups received *instruction* concerning baptism in the New Testament, the subject was consistently baptism in water. Jesus, looking ahead to the establishment of the church, commanded His disciples to baptize in water (Matthew 28: 19-20). Peter taught that water baptism was the manner in which a person was saved (1 Peter 3: 21). Paul addressed the significance of water baptism in his letters to the various churches (Romans 6: 1-10; 1 Corinthians 1: 12-17; 12: 13; Galatians 3: 27; Ephesians 4: 5; Colossians 2: 12). These instructional words found throughout Scripture provide tremendous consistency and insight with respect to the role of baptism in the church.

What Is the Biblical Answer Concerning Spirit Baptism?

When does baptism with the Holy Spirit begin? Biblical support falls in favor of baptism with the Spirit that begins at the time of water baptism. This is the kind of baptism with the Spirit that is taught by Peter, Paul, and Luke in their inspired writings (Acts 2: 38; 19: 1-5; Romans 6: 3-4; 1 Corinthians 6: 11; 12: 13; Colossians 2: 11-12; Titus 3: 5; Hebrews 10: 22; 1 Peter 3: 21). The Holy Spirit entered the world of man and integrated Himself into water baptism on the Day of Pentecost. If God intended for men to receive the Holy Spirit at a time other than water baptism, no reasonable explanation can be given for the Holy Spirit to be associated *with* water baptism. Additionally, the Bible never suggests that God, through the apostles, ever modified this relationship between the Holy Spirit and immersion in water.

It is also reasonable to conclude that the outpouring of the Spirit that was experienced on the Day of Pentecost was a form of baptism with the Spirit. Given Jesus' prophecy as He spoke with the apostles (Acts 1: 5) and Peter's reference to that prophecy at the house of Cornelius, we would be foolish to deny it. Additionally, since Peter considered this to be baptism with the Holy Spirit (Acts 11: 15-16), and if we are to be true to Scripture, then we must also accept that the incident in Caesarea at the house of Cornelius was also a form of baptism with the Spirit.

However, the outpouring of the Holy Spirit that was experienced on these two occasions should not be viewed as the manner by which *all* believers received the Holy Spirit into their lives. On the contrary, if Peter saw the episode with Cornelius as some kind of rare phenomenon, so, too, should we. Scripture offers considerable instruction that identifies water baptism as the time the Holy Spirit insinuated Himself into each one's life.

Paul indicates that *all* Christians are *baptized by one Spirit into one body* (1 Corinthians 12: 13). The *one baptism* that was common to all Christians was not the outpouring of the Spirit that was experienced by a few on two separate occasions, but water baptism in which the gift (indwelling) of the Spirit was promised (Acts 2: 38; Titus 3: 5-6). In each case, the outpouring of the Holy Spirit that was experienced by the few seems to have served its divinely intended purpose fully at the time it occurred. On the day of Pentecost the apostles were endowed with powers and the gift of tongues in order to teach and persuade men that Jesus was truly the Messiah. Peter and his associates were convinced by this outpouring of the Spirit upon the Gentiles at the house of Cornelius that the gospel message was no longer limited to those of Jewish descent. These uncommon manifestations of the Spirit were not intended to teach us about the manner in which baptism with the Spirit would be experienced. These incidents should be recognized for their uniqueness. They were exceptional events for extraordinary times and should be viewed with that in mind. According to Scripture, immersion in the Spirit that is intended for the church age begins with our immersion in water.

NOTES FOR CHAPTER 14

1. James Strong, LL.D., S.T.D., The New Strong's Exhaustive Concordance of the Bible, Greek Dictionary of the New Testament, p. 14, 1990, Thomas Nelson Publishers.

2. James Strong, LL.D., S.T.D., The New Strong's Exhaustive Concordance of the Bible, Greek Dictionary of the New Testament, p. 45, 1990, Thomas Nelson Publishers.

Chapter XV

In Whose Name Must I Be Baptized?

Jesus commanded the apostles to baptize *'in the name of the Father and of the Son and of the Holy Spirit'* (Matthew 28: 19). It is a command with which we are all very familiar. It seems odd, then, that through the balance of the New Testament, including the Day of Pentecost shortly after Jesus offered this Great Commission, the apostles *seem* to baptize simply in the name of Jesus (Acts 2: 38; 10: 47-48; 19: 5).

The examples in the passages mentioned above are typical of New Testament baptism. At no time in the New Testament do we find an occasion where someone is actually baptized in the name of the Father, Son, and Holy Spirit. This appears to be a potential inconsistency between the words of Jesus and the actions of the apostles. The possible explanations are limited. It could be that the apostles misunderstood the words uttered by Jesus; or perhaps they fell into disobedience by failing to follow Jesus' instructions properly.

If this apparent inconsistency represented disobedience on the part of the apostles, no doubt it would have been highlighted within the pages of Scripture. A wayward apostle was not to be taken lightly. Such was the case when Peter used rather poor judgment in one particular instance (Galatians 2: 11-13). Paul rebuked Peter and others for wrongfully distancing themselves from the uncircumcised Gentiles. Peter's error was displayed for all to see. Rather than covering up the incident, God took the opportunity to provide a lesson for us all. Therefore, if the seeming discrepancy on the part of the apostles to baptize in the name of Jesus is not described as an error or disobedience, another explanation must be found. That leaves us with only two possibilities.

The first possibility is that the apostles never baptized in the name of the Father, Son, and Holy Spirit, but in the name of Jesus alone. The authority of Jesus is truly genuine and irrefutable. He holds within His being *all the authority of heaven and earth* (Matthew 28: 18). In order to accept that He is a Savior who has the ability to take away sins we must acknowledge that all authority is His. If He did not have the authority He claimed He must be considered a fraud, at which point everything He ever said could be called into question. He would be a sinner (a liar) and as such would lack the standing to take away sins. Thus, one option that must be given serious consideration is whether or not God regards baptism *in the name of Jesus* equivalent with baptism *in the name of the Father, Son, and Holy Spirit.*

A number of New Testament passages speak of the oneness of the Father and Son (John 8: 19; 14: 6-9; Acts 4: 12). That is pretty much the theme of the entire fourteenth chapter of the Gospel of John. Many other passages also reveal the unity between Jesus and the Holy Spirit (Luke 4: 18; John 4: 24; 2 Corinthians 3: 17). Upon close examination, it seems evident that the idea of the Father and the Son and the Holy Spirit cannot be easily separated into three individual entities.

> And Jesus came and spoke to them, saying, "All authority has been given to Me in heaven and on earth." (Matthew 28: 18)

> ...yet for us *there is* one God, the Father, of whom *are* all things, and we for Him; and one Lord Jesus Christ, through whom *are* all things, and through whom we *live.* (1 Corinthians 8: 6)

> For in Him (Christ) dwells all the fullness of the Godhead bodily. (Colossians 2: 9)

> 9. Therefore God also has highly exalted Him and given Him the name which is above every name, 10. that at the name of Jesus every knee should bow, of those in heaven, and of those on earth, and of those under the earth, 11. and *that* every tongue should confess that Jesus Christ *is* Lord, to the glory of God the Father. (Philippians 2: 9-11)

We truly honor and worship God the Father only when we honor and worship the Son. The name of Jesus is to be placed above all other names. God the Father awaits us as we come to Him *in the name of Jesus.* Thus, there seems to be little difficulty in recognizing that the name of Jesus carries with it sufficient authority that we might be baptized in that name. A more in-depth look at the passage in Matthew that mentions the Father, Son, and Holy Spirit, offers even more insight that could help explain this apparent disparity.

> 19. Go therefore and make disciples of all nations, baptizing them in the name of the Father and of the Son and of the Holy Spirit, 20. teaching them to observe all things I have commanded you; and lo, I

am with you always, *even* to the end of the age. Amen.
(Matthew 28: 19-20)

An interesting point from this passage is the manner in which the Father, Son, and Holy Spirit are addressed. The disciples are instructed to baptize in the *name* of the Father and of the Son and of the Holy Spirit. They are not told to baptize in the *names* of the Father and of the Son and of the Holy Spirit. The word *name* is singular, not plural. Father, Son, and Holy Spirit are not names held by three distinct entities, but rather, they are three titles or positions attributed to the Godhead (Acts 17: 29; Romans 1: 20; Colossians 2: 9). The apostles were not to baptize into three names, but in the three as one. That one was Jesus. If it is true that the apostles baptized only in the name of Jesus, this scenario provides sufficient explanation for their actions.

*   *   *   *   *

The second possible solution to the question of *in whose name* we should be baptized is this: the apostles did, in fact, baptize *'in the name of the Father and of the Son and of the Holy Spirit.'* While some may deny it vigorously, this possibility deserves serious consideration.

Mere days after Jesus issued the Great Commission the Holy Spirit was poured out on the Day of Pentecost. On that day, Peter told the crowd that they must be baptized *in the name of Jesus*. Shall we attribute this departure to poor memory on the part of the apostles? Did they simply fail to understand the command given to them by Christ, or was it possibly an act of defiance since Jesus had left them? How about *none of the above*?

Baptism was not really new to the Jews in Jerusalem. Even prior to the time of John the Baptist they had observed the practice of proselyte baptism for Gentiles who wished to convert to Judaism. When John the Baptist came baptizing with water, the Bible makes no mention of people asking him to explain the meaning of baptism. They recognized that it was the zenith of a life-changing decision.

When Peter directed the Jews on the Day of Pentecost to be baptized in the name of Jesus, it makes sense that his intent was to distinguish Christian baptism from any other baptism they may have witnessed in the past (e.g., the baptism performed by John).

This does not mean that they would not be baptized in the name of the Father and of the Son and of the Holy Spirit, but that Peter was presenting this baptism to them through (by the authority of) Jesus Christ about whom he had just finished speaking.

This explanation is made even more probable when we consider Paul's meeting with the men in Ephesus (Acts 19: 1b-3). When Paul realized these men had not heard of the Holy Spirit, he assumed they had not been baptized in the name of Jesus. He naturally responded by asking them exactly what baptism they had received (Acts 19: 3). In this instance Paul is clearly using the name of Jesus to contrast the baptism of John and Christian baptism. Paul's point is that, had they been baptized in the name of Jesus, they would have known of the Holy Spirit since the name of the Father and the Son and the Holy Spirit would have been invoked at the time of their immersion.[1] Later, during his appeal for unity in his letter to the Corinthians, Paul once again mentions the direct relationship between the Holy Spirit and immersion in water (1 Corinthians 6: 11; 12: 13).

The possibility that the apostles baptized in the name of the Father, Son, and Holy Spirit is certainly supported by other writers in the first and second centuries. Justin Martyr, a man from the second century recognized as one of the Ante-Nicene Fathers, wrote about the baptism that was practiced at that time.

> For, in the name of God, the Father and Lord of the universe, and of our Saviour Jesus Christ, and of the Holy Spirit, they then receive the washing with water.[2]

Perhaps the dilemma of *whose name* should be invoked in baptism comes from the fact that many view this in terms of a precise *formula* of words that must, in keeping with some biblical edict, be uttered at the time one is immersed. This does not seem to be the intent of Scripture. While Jesus does speak of baptism *'in the name of the Father and of the Son and of the Holy Spirit,'* and the apostles teach baptism *in Jesus' name,* the two do not necessarily conflict. Emphasis on Jesus as the Son of God and Savior of the world is the matter of significance when it comes to baptism. Of prime importance in the gospel message is *recognition* that our salvation comes through Jesus and it is at the time of baptism that His blood is applied to our sins (Colossians 2: 11;

Hebrews 10: 19-22), washing them into nothingness. That is the essence of these two statements.

When Jesus told the disciples to baptize *'in the name of the Father and of the Son and of the Holy Spirit'* He prefaced the statement with a remark concerning His own authority. He was presenting them instructions that were to be carried out in His name, or by His authority. Thus baptism *in Jesus' name* was never intended to identify the precise verbiage that is to be spoken during baptism; rather it was the manner in which the apostles regarded Jesus' authority to command baptism of those who would follow Him. We find the apostles performing various other acts in the New Testament *in Jesus' name*. Most often it involved physical healing or casting out demons (Acts 3: 6; 4: 10, 30; 16: 18). They also preached the *name of Jesus* (Acts 11: 20). These were not about a formula of words, but pointed specifically to the source of authority by which these things were accomplished. Everything the apostles did from Pentecost forward was founded upon that authority, including baptism. Since Jesus ordained baptism in His name or by His own authority, perhaps we should baptize invoking the *name* specifically commanded by Him (Matthew 28: 19).

What, then, is the answer? Should men be baptized *in the name of Jesus* or *in the name of the Father and of the Son and of the Holy Spirit*? Certainly we can argue that the name of Jesus carries with it the power to save us from our sins. Yet, Jesus specifically commanded that we should baptize in the latter. There also appears to be reasonable evidence, implicitly stated, that the apostles did indeed baptize in the name of the Father and of the Son and of the Holy Spirit in the first century. Paul clearly associated the recognition of the presence of the Holy Spirit with the rite of Christian baptism. When the Ephesians explained that they had not even, *'...heard whether there is a Holy Spirit'* (Acts 19: 2), Paul assumed they had not received Christian baptism. His statement offers a direct link between the recognition of the Holy Spirit and water baptism. Given this kind of testimony, as well as the witness of others from the early church, baptism in the name of the Father, Son, and Holy Spirit, is what also makes the most sense for us today.

NOTES FOR CHAPTER 15

1. The suggestion that Paul's comment, "Into what then were you baptized?" denotes baptism in the name of the Father, Son, and Holy Spirit, is noted in the _New Advent Catholic Encyclopedia, Baptism, VI, Matter and Form of the Sacrament_.

2. The First Apology of Justin Martyr, Chapter LXI.-Christian Baptism.

Chapter XVI
Paedobaptism: Scriptural?

While the subject of baptism often stirs conflict among believers on a variety of levels, perhaps no point is more controversial than that of paedobaptism (infant baptism). It is a ritual that is performed by many and, accordingly, deserves serious consideration. Interestingly, the practice of infant baptism originates from two unrelated points of view. Some see baptism as the time when sins are forgiven, a principle that is solidly founded in Scripture. This naturally raises a question about why sinless beings such as infants would need sins removed from their lives. The belief that a newborn needs forgiveness is based upon the principle of original sin, the assumption that each one who enters this world carries inherently the guilt of sin. If then, children are born guilty of sin, and baptism is the manner in which sin is removed, baptism of children is reasonable.

There are those, however, who embrace the doctrine of infant baptism yet do not believe that sins are erased at the time of baptism. Instead, they regard the rite of baptism as the mechanism that admits the child into the body of believers. Each of these viewpoints (forgiveness or membership into the body) relies heavily on what is seen as a link between water baptism in the new covenant and Jewish circumcision in the first covenant.

Original Sin

The numerous arguments offered in support of, or opposition to, infant baptism must be able to withstand biblical scrutiny if they are to be believed. A doctrine or creed that is not supported by Scripture and does not harmonize with the fullness of God's Word must be deemed unreliable and dismissed accordingly. The Catholic Encyclopedia offers a lengthy discussion on the topic of original sin. This is only natural since it is a basic teaching of the Roman Catholic Church.

> Original sin may be taken to mean: (1) the sin that Adam committed; (2) a consequence of this first sin, the hereditary stain with which we are born on account of our origin or descent from Adam.

> From the earliest times the latter sense of the word was more common, as may be seen by St. Augustine's statement: "the deliberate sin of the

first man is the cause of original sin" (De nupt. et concup., II, xxvi, 43).
It is the hereditary stain that is dealt with here. As to the sin of Adam
we have not to examine the circumstances in which it was committed
nor make the exegesis of the third chapter of Genesis.[1]

It is difficult to draw from the pages of Scripture a doctrine that
recognizes the *guilt* of original sin, despite the many voices
making the claim. The truth is, the phrase *original sin* does not
appear in the Bible. Therefore, in order for us to draw any
conclusions concerning the subject, we must determine whether or
not the doctrine of original sin blends with the overall message that
is provided in God's Word.

12. Therefore, just as through one man sin entered the world, and death
through sin, and thus death spread to all men, because all sinned — 13.
(For until the law sin was in the world, but sin is not imputed when
there is no law. 14. Nevertheless death reigned from Adam to Moses,
even over those who had not sinned according to the likeness of the
transgression of Adam, who is a type of Him who was to come. 15. But
the free gift is not like the offense. For if by the one man's offense
many died, much more the grace of God and the gift by the grace of the
one Man, Jesus Christ, abounded to many. 16. And the gift is not like
that which came through the one who sinned. For the judgment which
came from one offense resulted in condemnation, but the free gift
which came from many offenses resulted in justification. 17. For if by
one man's offense death reigned through the one, much more those
who receive abundance of grace and the gift of righteousness will reign
in life through the one, Jesus Christ). 18. Therefore, as through one
man's offense judgment came to all men, resulting in condemnation,
even so through one man's righteous act the free gift came to all men,
resulting in justification of life. 19. For as by one man's disobedience
many were made sinners, so also by one man's obedience many will be
made righteous. (Romans 5: 12-19)

This is certainly a challenging passage. Yet it is easier to
understand when we recognize the fact that the proposition of
verse twelve is answered in verses eighteen and nineteen, while
everything in between is simply meant to provide further insight
into the problems caused by Adam's sin and the solution brought
about by Christ's sacrifice.

Death entered into the world through Adam and consequently
spread to all of mankind (Romans 5: 12-13). As we think about the
consequences of Adam's sin, certain things must be taken into
consideration if we are to understand what Paul is saying in this
passage. The first is that it is death, rather than sin, that ultimately

spread from Adam to all men. Death crept into the world through Adam's sin and ultimately extended to men everywhere. Death is a consequence of Adam's sin. Yet, according to Paul's words, the death of any individual, such as an infant, is not necessarily due to his/her own *guilt*. He mentions that some will die without having sinned as Adam sinned (v. 14). What is so peculiar about Adam's sin – the sin that brought death upon mankind? Paul noted that, unlike Eve's sin, where she was deceived by Satan, Adam's sin was *deliberate* (1 Timothy 2: 14). Similarly, Paul identifies Adam's sin in the Romans passage as *disobedience* (v. 19). Adam sinned intentionally. As a result, Adam and his descendants are subject to death. That explains how it can be that a man might die without having sinned *as Adam sinned.*

Paul noted that, *'sin is not imputed when there is no law.'* Exactly what law, then, would apply to an infant? Awareness of right or wrong does not exist at that stage of life. An infant is even incapable of evil thoughts. Paul addresses this point just prior to his claim that all have sinned in Romans 3: 23.

> 20. Therefore by the deeds of the law no flesh will be justified in His sight, for by the law is the knowledge of sin. 21. But now the righteousness of God apart from the law is revealed, being witnessed by the Law and the Prophets, 22. Even the righteousness of God through faith in Jesus Christ, to all and on all who believe. For there is no difference; 23. for all have sinned and fall short of the glory of God. (Romans 3: 20-23)

Without law there is no knowledge of sin (Romans 3: 20). For the infant there is no law, nor is there any knowledge of sin. When Paul stated that all have sinned, he was specifically talking about the availability of God's righteousness *'through faith...to all and on all who believe.'* He is not discussing the innocent newborn, but those who have the ability to make life decisions.

> For I, the Lord your God, am a jealous God, visiting the iniquity of the fathers upon the children to the third and fourth generations of those who hate Me... (Exodus 20: 5)

> The Lord is longsuffering and abundant in mercy, forgiving iniquity and transgression; but He by no means clears the guilty, visiting the iniquity of the fathers on the children to the third and fourth generation. (Numbers 14: 18)

While God may punish children for a father's sin, the guilt of that sin still belongs to the father, and not the children. In fact, when you think about it, what more effective discipline exists to penalize the guilty than by punishing his descendants for his sin? Such was the case with King David. The child he fathered with Bathsheba died, not because of anything the child had done, but as a direct result of David's sin (2 Samuel 12: 14). The prophet Ezekiel, who lived during the Babylonian exile, addressed the biblical principle that we as men are not held responsible, as a matter of eternal judgment, for the sins of others.

> The soul who sins shall die. The son shall not bear the guilt of the father, nor the father bear the guilt of the son. The righteousness of the righteous shall be upon himself, and the wickedness of the wicked shall be upon himself. (Ezekiel 18: 20)

There is, of course, David's claim that he was conceived in sin (Psalm 51: 5). David is not saying that the manner of conception is evil. Additionally, we have no reason to believe that David was born out of wedlock as a matter of sin. Still, he does say that he was conceived in sin. Of all biblical passages that address the sins of man, the language here could be interpreted to mean *original sin*, but only if we choose to ignore the context of the words. We must take into account the poetic character of the Psalms where hyperbole and metaphor are the rule rather than the exception.

David's sorrow appears to be twofold. First, he seems to be suggesting that he can remember no time when sin was absent from his life. He is grief-stricken over his separation from God because of sin. Yet the sins about which David is distraught (v. 5) are sins he consciously committed against God (v. 4) rather than the sins of others (such as Adam). Secondly, and perhaps even more relevant, David recognizes that men are prone to sin. That is to say, men are inclined to sin when temptation presents itself.

Nothing connected with David's conception or birth would be considered evil or sinful even in the eyes of God. As David considered his own sinful nature, he repented to God for the sinful *choices* he had made. The passage apparently denotes David's regret specifically over his fornication with Bathsheba and the murder of her husband Uriah – sins that have nothing to do with David's infancy.

When Noah exited the ark, God promised to *'never again curse the ground for man's sake, although the imagination of man's heart is evil from his youth...* ' (Genesis 8: 21). This passage speaks of man's evil heart *beginning with his adolescence* (מנצריו), or pre-adulthood, not in conception or infancy.

If, as many claim, all men are conceived in a sinful state, this would have been equally true of Jesus. After all, He was a descendant of Adam. However, the passage from Ezekiel plainly denies the claim that the guilt of sin passes from generation to generation. Consequently, God views each one who enters this world through childbirth as an innocent being.

It appears that these passages (Romans 3: 20; Ezekiel 18: 20) provide us with a qualification of Romans 3: 23. As we consider Paul's comment that *all have sinned,* which he echoes in Romans 5: 12, it is reasonable to conclude, given the support from other passages, that all men who have the *opportunity* for sin have, at least once, fallen short. His remarks lie within the context of those who have the capacity for faith (Romans 3: 26). For that reason Paul could boldly proclaim that, among those who have the opportunity, *'all have sinned.'* (Romans 3: 23). Ezekiel, however, indicates that God considers each one to be perfect from the moment of conception until his/her first sin.

*   *   *   *   *

While the idea of original sin conflicts with instruction found in God's Word, it would be foolish to suggest that Adam's sin has had no effect. Even though we are not *guilty* of Adam's sin in the strictest sense of guilt, it seems clear from Paul's words (Romans 5: 12-18) that there is an *effect* on all men that originates from that sin whereby *'many were made sinners'* (v. 19). This seems to be the trait that has carried to all men as a result of Adam's sin. His disobedience has left a mark on the face of mankind, although the nature of that mark is not entirely clear. We are not given an explanation of exactly how Adam's sin affects us, but we are told that we do not bear the guilt of that sin. Consequently, God has not placed upon our shoulders the obligation to remove that blemish.

It is important to note that, while Paul acknowledges the effect of Adam's sin on other men, he immediately distinguishes between the impact of that sin upon mankind and its effect upon Adam himself. Adam's sin was a sin of choice. He was disobedient. In whatever manner his sin has touched other men the effect on them is different than that realized by Adam. He alone is responsible for his sin while others are responsible for sins they have committed (Ezekiel 18: 20).

With these things in mind, we need to decide whether baptism is appropriate for infants *even if* we bear in any way the burden of Adam's sin. While we learn from Paul that, as a result of Adam's disobedience, *'many were made sinners'* (Romans 5: 19), we find that Christ's obedience compensates for that effect. Paul indicates that the obedience of Christ on the cross has an offsetting impact on those who may be affected by Adam's sin. We also learn that Jesus' obedience is not equal to, but far superior to, Adam's disobedience. Paul says it is *'much more'* (v. 15). Addressing the obedience and disobedience of Jesus and Adam respectively, Paul repeats himself a number of times in order to make his point clear (Romans 5: 12-19). Death came through Adam while life comes through Christ (v. 17). Condemnation came through Adam while forgiveness comes to us through Jesus (v. 16). Our sinful nature came through Adam while righteousness comes through the Lord (v. 19).

We also learn from Paul that Jesus' obedience counteracts Adam's disobedience in a similar manner. That is to say, if Adam's sin is *automatically* assigned to men in some fashion, it seems that Christ's sacrifice, providing the opposite and even more forceful effect, is also intended to *automatically* apply in overcoming that sin. That is what Paul meant when he said, *'as by one man's offense...so through one man's righteous act'* (v. 18). Again we find, *'as by one man's disobedience...so also by one man's obedience'* (v. 19). Whatever is true of Adam's offense, the exact opposite is true of Christ's righteous act. This would explain a great deal about God's view of the innocence of infants and children.

In that same vein, when sin becomes a matter of choice, as it was with Adam, the man who gives in to temptation is held accountable for the sin committed. In that case, it stands to reason that seeking forgiveness must also be by choice – via repentance and baptism (Acts 2: 38, 1 Peter 3: 21).

The apostles have taught us in the New Testament that baptism serves a specific purpose in that it is the moment of forgiveness of sins. Yet baptism is *consistently* joined with belief and repentance when it comes to seeking forgiveness. Baptism, combined with repentance, is relational in that repentance gives forgiveness a sense of *meaning* for those who submit to the Lord in baptism.

When sin becomes personal as we choose to sin, baptism is designed to forgive sins committed *'in the likeness of the transgression of Adam'* (Romans 5: 14). That is the precise focus of the baptism of the New Testament.

New Testament Omission of Infant Baptism

The New Testament never mentions the baptism of infants and this silence in Scripture must be considered a key factor in any discussion of the subject. We find no biblical support for infant baptism either through *direct command* or *necessary inference.* In fact, if we honestly examine passages that are used to defend this practice, it is difficult to see how the subject could ever arise. Matthew recorded what Jesus had to say about children. Jesus not only clearly recognized their innocence, but this was the very focus of His remarks.

> 1. At that time the disciples came to Jesus, saying, "Who then is the greatest in the kingdom of heaven?" 2. Then Jesus called a little child to Him, set him in the midst of them, 3. and said, "Assuredly, I say to you, unless you are converted and become as little children, you will by no means enter the kingdom of heaven." (Matthew 18: 1-3)

> But Jesus said, "Let the little children come unto Me, and do not forbid them; for of such is the kingdom of heaven." (Matthew 19: 14)

Rather than suggesting that children should be held accountable for sins they had not committed, Jesus taught His disciples that we, as adults, must become *like* them in order to enter the kingdom of heaven. Children are the epitome of innocence. He did not call for them to be baptized, although we know that Jesus' disciples had already been performing baptisms (John 3: 22; 4: 1-2). Instead of commanding baptism, Jesus claimed that children are an example of what we are to become when we are converted.

The Candidate for Baptism

While passages illustrating infant baptism cannot be found in Scripture we can, with relative ease, locate a number of passages that appear to challenge the practice. Although these verses do not speak specifically about infants, they certainly provide insight into who might be considered an acceptable candidate for baptism.

And he (John) went into all the region around Jordan, preaching a baptism of repentance for the remission of sins. (Luke 3: 3)

I indeed baptize you with water unto repentance. (Matthew 3: 11)

Then Peter said to them, "Repent and let every one of you be baptized in the name of Jesus Christ, for the remission of sins..." (Acts 2: 38)

The baptism of Scripture was *for* forgiveness. Accompanying baptism, each one was to repent of the sins he/she had committed. Jesus' remarks[2] suggest that children would not be held accountable for sins until they matured to a point when they could understand the concept of sin. Jesus viewed small children as completely innocent beings. They are innocent precisely because they have no understanding of sin. How can a small child or infant repent of sins of which he has no understanding? This is a primary reason the biblical authors failed to address infant baptism.

As we explore Scripture, a pattern develops with respect to baptism. In every case, those who were baptized made a clear decision in favor of baptism based upon the teaching they had received. Philip told the Ethiopian eunuch that he could be baptized *if he believed.* Those on the Day of Pentecost (Acts 2: 41) *'gladly received his word'* prior to baptism. Jesus stated that prior to baptism one must believe the gospel message. (Mark 16: 16)

Explaining how an infant could *gladly receive* the word or *believe* in Jesus when the child lacks the ability to understand the teaching presents an especially difficult problem for those who wish to teach infant baptism. Combined with the fact that Jesus acknowledges a purity of heart with respect to children, it is difficult to establish the doctrine of infant baptism from the Bible.

In quoting Jesus' words concerning baptism, it has been suggested that Mark might not be placing belief *prior* to baptism (Mark 16: 16) in a chronological sense, but that his intent was to simply place an emphasis upon belief. In that case, the infant who is baptized and later believes would satisfy this obligation. The weakness of this view can be found in the fact that, throughout the whole of Scripture, belief is presented as the initial step an individual must take toward salvation (Acts 8: 36-37; 16: 31-33; Romans 10: 10). The idea that one might repent or confess prior to belief is, of course, unimaginable. Additionally, Scripture places the responsibility for repentance and confession squarely upon each believer as a matter of decision (Acts 2: 38; Romans 10: 9). A parent cannot repent or confess Jesus as Savior on behalf of an infant since the Bible portrays these as subject to the decision-making of the person involved. So it is with baptism. God's Word portrays baptism as a matter of personal conviction – a matter of choice (Acts 18: 8; Galatians 3: 27).

What Is a Household?

The use of the word *household* in certain narratives within the book of Acts (Acts 16: 14-15, 30-33; 18: 8) has become central to the defense of infant baptism. Those men who practice infant baptism believe that this *could* indicate that a decision *may* have been made by the head of the house to have each one in the house receive baptism; and that this *may* have even included infants. The story of Lydia is a prime example of this. We are told by Luke that her entire household was baptized (Acts 16: 15). From this comment some men have *concluded* that small children who were not old enough to understand and make an informed decision participated in this baptism. The truth is we cannot make that determination from the words of the text. We have no reason to draw this kind of conclusion from the passage, particularly since it seems contrary to the instructions provided by the apostles. Since we cannot conclude that infants were ever baptized in the New Testament, it is a stretch to teach that they *must* be baptized. In the words of Alexander Campbell, *'Positive ordinances demand positive proof...'*[3]

In the account of the Philippian jailer (Acts 16: 30-33) *'...they spoke the word of the Lord to him and to all who were in his house.'* Since the word was spoken *'to all who were in his house'* it is reasonable that they all must have had the ability to hear and understand the word being spoken. They, therefore, would also have the ability to respond individually to the message being taught. It is simply impossible to *conclude* from this incident that infants were baptized.

As Crispus listened to the gospel message from Paul, he *'believed on the Lord with all his household.'* We are not told that Crispus alone believed or that he believed on behalf of others, but that he believed *'with all his household'*. Those who were *baptized* were those who *believed*. The fact that Crispus was a ruler of the synagogue indicates that he was probably not a young man with small children. A position of such prominence was reserved for men who had proven themselves over time.

Quite often the mention of *household* in Scripture is not even a reference to immediate family, but to others (servants, etc.) who dwell there, as was the case with Cornelius when he called his *'household servants'* ($\tau\omega\nu$ $oικετων$) (Acts 10: 7). This is the more reasonable conclusion as we consider the household of Crispus. It may also be the case with Lydia. Still, that does not mean infants can be ruled out since a household can also include infants. Instead, it is the statement regarding the belief of those who were baptized that is most convincing.

While we cannot determine the absence or presence of infants in these households, we can absolutely state that infants are not mentioned. That means that either (1) no children who were too young to understand the gospel message were present at the time or (2) they were not given consideration in the text because they were not viable candidates for belief and baptism or (3) they were, indeed, baptized without being mentioned. Therefore, we must depend on the greater landscape of Scripture if we are to sort this out.

Those who teach the doctrine of infant baptism often insist that, in those instances where many were gathered, such as Pentecost, children (infants) must not only have been present, but they also must have been baptized. The belief is that it is practically impossible to have such a gathering with no children present. Yet, when we do encounter a crowd where the gospel is preached and, arguably, infants *must have been* present (due to the large crowds), baptism was limited to men and women. For instance, as Philip preached in Samaria, he preached to crowds of people.

> 5. Then Philip went down to the city of Samaria and preached Christ to them. 6. And the multitudes with one accord heeded the things spoken by Philip, hearing and seeing the miracles which he did...12. But when they believed Philip as he preached the things concerning the kingdom of God and the name of Jesus Christ, both men and women were baptized. (Acts 8: 5-6, 12)

As Philip spoke to *multitudes* in Samaria, where the likelihood of the presence of small children and infants was strong, it was still men and women who were baptized. Here we find no hint that infants were baptized. It is a considerable leap to assume that infants were baptized simply because they may have been present on certain occasions (e.g., the jailer, Lydia, or Crispus). Similarly, when Paul preached in Corinth, it was those who *heard* and *believed* who were baptized (Acts 18: 8). We would be wise to follow this consistent biblical pattern today concerning the relationship between belief and baptism.

Baptism and Circumcision

In the third chapter of this book, we discussed the belief that baptism in the new covenant was meant to replace circumcision from the first covenant. This belief lies at the heart of the doctrine of infant baptism. Therefore, a more in-depth examination of this relationship is necessary if we are to determine exactly what Scripture says about the nature of baptism and circumcision.

On the eighth day after a male Israelite was born he would be circumcised according to the law (Genesis 17: 12). Many believe that since circumcision might be considered, in essence, initiation into the old covenant, the ceremony that initiates into the new covenant must have replaced it. That initiation ceremony is viewed as baptism. This is the basic premise for the practice of infant baptism. Just as Israelite male infants were acknowledged in the old covenant through circumcision, the child of today is *recognized* as a faithful member of the new covenant through baptism. However, as Mont W. Smith explains, there is clear difference between a covenant sign, such as circumcision, and the oath taken by a participant in a covenant as a matter of conviction.

> There is a difference between the oath or pledge of a covenant and the "sign" of a covenant. The Hebrew for oath was *alah*. It was also used for "the curse of covenant," because an oath was both a commitment and a self-curse. The sign of a covenant was *'ot*. The oath was walking between the halves of the slain animals, touching "the blood of the covenant." A sign was a visible representation or memorial to that ceremony. It may have been a pile of rocks (Gen. 31:44f), or a rainbow (Gen. 9:13), or others. The oath swearing of God and Abraham was passing between the halves (Gen. 15:17, 18). The sign of the covenant that night was circumcision (17:11). The sign of the Mosaic covenant was the Sabbath (Exod. 31-13). The sign of the Christian covenant was possessing the holy Spirit or living the kind of life Jesus did (Eph. 1: 13).[4]

In the Old Testament, circumcision was performed on each male infant born into the Israelite lineage. God established the rite of circumcision as a sign of the covenant He formed with Abraham saying, '*...and it shall be a sign of the covenant between Me and* *you'* (Genesis 17: 11). Circumcision was intended to be a constant memorial, or reminder, of their covenant. However, while circumcision was a sign of the Abrahamic covenant, membership in that covenant was recognized as a birthright (Genesis 17: 1-8). In like manner, just as membership in the first covenant came through childbirth, in the New Testament we are told that participation in the kingdom of heaven comes through a second birth (John 3: 3; Galatians 4: 21-31; 1 Peter 1: 23; Titus 3: 5). What we must determine is whether baptism is a covenant sign in the likeness of circumcision, or the oath (*alah*) through which we are reborn, thus establishing us in the new covenant.

In the Old Testament, not every covenant was given a sign (e.g., the Davidic covenant) and not every sign was a covenant sign. While we read of many *signs* in God's Word, the truth is that a covenant sign was/is very rare. We read of many signs that God used to reveal His handiwork (1 Kings 13: 2-3; 2 Kings 19: 29-31; Isaiah 66: 19; Ezekiel 4: 3). However, these were not covenant signs. For instance, Jonah's adventure, as he spent three days in the belly of a fish, was a sign of Jesus' burial (Matthew 12: 39), yet it was not a covenant sign. In the New Testament, the baby Jesus *'...wrapped in swaddling cloths, lying in a manger'* (Luke 2: 12) was a sign for the shepherds, but it was not a covenant sign.

In order for an event or object to be regarded as a covenant sign it must exhibit certain characteristics. First of all, the item or event must be *proclaimed* to be a covenant sign. Arnold G. Fruchtenbaum, an expert in the Old Testament and Hebrew culture, remarks *"what is a sign of a covenant is what God calls a sign of a covenant and therefore, I would agree that 'a sign must be formally declared'".*[5] Furthermore, as we consider the history of these signs in Scripture, we discover one more common trait. A consistent feature of a covenant sign, such as the Sabbath Day (Exodus 31: 13-17), is that it *persists* throughout the life of the covenant, either perpetually or repeatedly, as a reminder of promises that have been made. Since the purpose of a *covenant* sign is remembrance, its continuation is vital.

When a man and woman marry they exchange rings as a *sign or seal* of the covenant they have made. The continued presence of those rings serves as a daily reminder of promises made. When God established His covenant with Noah, He stated, *'I set My rainbow in the cloud.'* The rainbow was/is the sign of that covenant. Each time a rainbow appears it serves as a reminder not only to men, but also to God, that He promised to never again destroy the entire earth with a flood (Genesis 9: 11-17). Finally, God's covenant sign with Abraham was the sign of circumcision, which a man would carry with him permanently in full recognition that his inheritance, including the promise of the coming Messiah, was through Abraham's seed. No *covenant* sign in the Bible fails to meet both conditions of declaration and continuation.

When it comes to linking baptism to the first covenant, Scripture indicates that it should be most closely associated with a child's birth into that covenant, a point made in Chapter II. This is true for a couple of very important reasons. The first is the fact that, as we study the teaching of Jesus and the apostles, they never suggest that baptism is a *sign* much less proclaim it to be a sign. Remember that a qualification for a covenant sign is that its status as a sign must be specifically declared. It is certainly symbolic of the death, burial, and resurrection of Jesus (Romans 6: 1-4; Colossians 2: 11-12), but the ceremony of baptism lacks the characteristics of a covenant sign. The presence of symbolism does not automatically confer the status of *covenant sign* to an object or event. A covenant sign is meant as a continuing reminder of the promises and responsibilities of the members of that covenant.

Secondly, baptism in the new covenant, like childbirth before it, is recognized in Scripture, not as a sign, but as the passageway through which one becomes a participant in the covenant. Just as men are physically born only once, so they are born once spiritually. Thus, baptism is no more a sign in the new covenant than a child's birth was a sign in the first covenant.

The relationship between baptism in the new covenant and childbirth into the old covenant becomes even more obvious when we review God's covenant with Noah. Peter called the waters of baptism an *antitype* to the waters of the flood (1 Peter 3: 21). Yet it was the rainbow not the water that served as the *sign* of the covenant between God and Noah just as circumcision was the sign between God and Abraham. The water, on the other hand, represented an immersion (baptism) of the entire earth, resulting in regeneration and renewal of the world God had created. If God intended for us to treat baptism as a covenant sign, as many people maintain, Peter would have likened baptism not to the *waters* of the flood, but to the rainbow, which was/is the sign of that covenant.

One question consistently remains unanswered by those who teach the circumcision/baptism connection, and it is a question that begins with the baptism performed by John the Baptist. John's baptism, which offered forgiveness of sins, was performed on none other than the Israelites. If baptism was intended to replace circumcision, it seems circumcision would have been abolished at that time. However, circumcision was not eliminated during the period of time that John baptized. Those who were baptized also practiced circumcision faithfully. Even upon the institution of Christian baptism on the Day of Pentecost, no thought was given to the rite of circumcision. The Israelites, including those who were converted Gentiles, practiced circumcision without even considering that it may have been replaced. Not until several years later, as Gentiles entered the church, did the topic of circumcision arise within the new covenant.

In Antioch, a question was raised about circumcision, a storyline that can be found in the fifteenth chapter of Acts. At that time some Jews believed and taught that circumcision was essential for both Jews and Gentiles within the new covenant. This fact alone reveals that they did not regard baptism as a replacement for circumcision. As the quarrel came before the apostles and elders in Jerusalem it was determined that, in fact, circumcision was not necessary for the Gentiles in the church age.

It is highly significant in this episode that the subject of baptism never surfaces. In a setting where the entire focus is the requirement of circumcision in the new covenant, if baptism should be considered its replacement, it is not possible that the apostles and elders would be silent on the matter. If baptism was intended as a replacement for circumcision, and the apostles were aware of this, they would have said so at this time since it was the responsibility of the apostles to teach the full truth of God. Their staggering silence concerning any connection between the two at the time of the Jerusalem Council wholly repudiates the claim.

When the matter of circumcision came before the church leaders, instead of teaching baptism as the new circumcision, they *came together to consider this matter'* (Acts 15: 6). Thus they weighed the necessity of circumcision even in the presence of baptism. The bigger issue, of course, involved the commandments of the Mosaic Law and their relationship to the covenant of grace. Yet, in their answer we find not even the slightest hint of a relationship between baptism and circumcision. Baptism was simply not a factor in the decision to dismiss circumcision for Gentiles. Furthermore, Christian Jews continued to practice circumcision faithfully after the Jerusalem Council even as they submitted to Christ in baptism. Thus the early church consisted of both circumcised and uncircumcised Christians. It is evident, then, that a link between baptism and the circumcision of Israelite infants was never considered in the first century church.

What *is* clear from Scripture is that the role of baptism in the covenant of grace differs significantly from the role of circumcision in the old covenant. Indeed, we have already seen that the precedent for baptism lies, not in circumcision, but in the various washings of the old covenant as well as God's use of water for the creation (birth and rebirth) of life.

Circumcision and the Death of Christ

If we seek an association between circumcision in the old covenant and a parallel in the new covenant, the most reasonable connection can be found in the death of Christ. This is not to suggest that Jesus' death should be considered some kind of sign of the covenant, but circumcision is certainly represented within this setting. Paul states, *'In Him you were also circumcised with the circumcision made without hands, by putting off the body of the sins of the flesh, by the circumcision of Christ'* (Colossians 2:11). Paul does not state that this is the circumcision of baptism, but the circumcision of Christ, as our sins are removed by means of His death. Once again we turn to Mont W. Smith for clarification on this point:

> A passage in Colossians used the words circumcision, sinful nature, the circumcision of Christ, and baptism as burial together in a discussion. Paul did not equate circumcision with baptism. He did not use them in parallel. The "circumcision not done with hands," that is, "the circumcision of Christ," was His death. He was cut off. His entire body on the cross was "circumcised." The Christian joined Christ at baptism when he participated in that death and resurrection.[6]

In this case, like childbirth and circumcision in the first covenant, Paul's remark concerning circumcision and the ceremony of baptism are in such close proximity that many fail to recognize the message the apostle intended to convey. The *'circumcision made without hands'* is the removal of our sins that is promised at the time of baptism (Acts 2: 38) based upon the death of Christ, which is linked to circumcision. The decision to be baptized is ours to make. The circumcision (cutting off or removal) of our sins is the work of God that occurs as we submit in the waters of baptism, making us holy in His eyes.

Infant Baptism and the Day of Pentecost

Often those who attempt to make the case for infant baptism turn to the Day of Pentecost, and some of Peter's remarks there, in defense of that view. The following statement is considered very significant when it comes to the role of the children of Christian parents within the new covenant:

> For the promise is unto you, and to your children, and to all who are afar off, as many as the Lord our God will call. (Acts 2:39)

The first thing we must recognize from this verse is that those to whom Peter was speaking were not yet Christians. Since paedobaptism is understood to be for children of parents who are already established within God's covenant, this passage must not apply since Peter was not speaking of the children of Christian parents. In the following verses we learn that only *'those who gladly received his words were baptized; and that day about three thousand souls were added to them'* (Acts 2: 41). Those to whom Peter spoke these words did not all accept Christ. He also mentioned *'all who are afar off,'* men and women who had yet to hear the gospel and even those who were yet to be born. These are timeless words spoken by Peter, and they must apply equally to *'you, and to your children, and to all who are afar off.'*

The word *'children'* in this instance is not aimed at the immediate children of those present in the crowd. Peter has in view generations, not infants and adolescents. This is made clear as we realize that the promise is also to *'all who are afar off.'* For all time the call is from God to all those who are able to respond to the message Peter had just delivered, and are able to do so in the manner in which Peter calls upon them to respond; that is, *repent and be baptized.*

The Unnecessary Inference of Infant Baptism

God views marriage as a covenant and, therefore, does not take it lightly. Paul recognized that some, having accepted Jesus as Savior, might find themselves married to someone who was an unbeliever (1 Corinthians 7: 12-19). This was undoubtedly a common situation in the early church as men and women learned the message of the gospel and some believed while others did not. In fact, it is not that uncommon in our own day and age. However, even though one spouse accepted Christ as Savior while the other did not, it was not God's desire that the marriage would fall apart. While the choice between God and spouse must clearly result in a choice for God, Paul suggested that if that choice was not necessary, the marriage might endure.

In what Paul describes as his own words, he explains that those who believe have a sanctifying effect upon the unbelieving spouse. That does not mean that the spouse who is an unbeliever is saved. It appears, however, that simply having such an intimate relationship with one of God's children, and loving that person, provides a blessing to the unbelieving spouse.

Of special interest in this passage is Paul's view of the children. They are holy (v. 14). While this may be a reference to the holiness of the child with respect to the relationship of the parents, since it is a loving relationship within the covenant of marriage, in a passage that focuses on the child of a believer, it is significant that we find no mention of baptism.

Infant baptism is an excellent example of doctrine that has been built upon a foundation of scriptural silence. While the old covenant assigns infant circumcision its rightful place within the framework of that covenant, no such teaching regarding baptism can be found within the pages of the covenant of grace, which is the New Testament. Passages that are used to defend this practice seem to be considered legitimate by many despite the fact that infant baptism is never mentioned. In order to reach a conclusion in favor of infant baptism based upon these writings, certain assumptions must be read into the text - assumptions that cannot be supported when the balance of Scripture is taken into consideration.

Infant baptism is not taught in Scripture. Instead, it is a doctrine that has been developed from unspoken inferences that are drawn from certain passages. The problem with establishing the necessity of infant baptism lies in the fact that we can find no passage where infant baptism even occurred, much less where it was ordained or commanded as part of the gospel message. Yet there are numerous passages of Scripture that clearly indicate the unreasonableness of this teaching (Mark 16: 16; Acts 2: 38; 8: 37;

16: 31). The Catholic Encyclopedia does not offer much Scripture on the subject (only Romans 5: 12 and 1 Corinthians 12: 12). Most support is drawn from writers beginning in the late second century or later when the doctrine of infant baptism was just beginning to develop. The same is true of all pro-infant baptism literature. Even John Calvin, an eager supporter of infant baptism, did not offer his defense of the rite based upon scriptural example. His approach to the subject was founded on a personal view that, *'...whatever belongs to circumcision, except the difference of the visible ceremony, belongs also to baptism.'*[7]

Paedobaptism and Immersion

As we consider the history of the baptism of infants, we often find men insisting that this was a practice handed down by the apostles. Yet it is plain to see that the baptism of Scripture was by immersion in water. This is a truth that is acknowledged even by those who promote infant baptism. John Calvin recognized the baptism of the New Testament as immersion in water, stating, *"The word baptize signifies to immerse, and the rite of immersion was practiced by the ancient church."*[8] So, too, John Wesley and Martin Luther both agreed that immersion was the baptism of Scripture. In keeping with their understanding that immersion was the baptism of the first century, these men realized that it was *highly* unlikely that paedobaptism was a practice of the apostles. In fact, Luther even went as far as to concede that proof of infant baptism by the apostles was clearly lacking in Scripture as he remarked:

> "It can not be proved by the sacred Scriptures that infant baptism was instituted by Christ, or began by the first Christians after the apostles."[9]

If we are to maintain that infant baptism was a practice of the early church, we must be able to reconcile this with the immersion that was practiced at that time. Did Jesus and the apostles immerse infants as a matter of baptism? Scripture offers no evidence that this ever occurred or that it was commanded. The practice of immersion in the early church, combined with the qualifications of a baptismal candidate that are presented in God's Word (e.g., belief, repentance, etc.), simply prohibit the establishment of the doctrine of infant baptism from the apostles' writings.

Forgiveness through Baptism Alone

Those who endorse infant baptism have mistakenly ascribed to this rite a characteristic that Scripture does not. Man is not able to receive forgiveness of sins through baptism alone any more than through faith alone. When forgiveness of sins is attributed to baptism, it is consistently portrayed in conjunction with the other precepts God has established, such as belief and repentance. In fact, repentance is shown in Scripture to be at least as important for forgiveness as is the rite of baptism (Acts 3: 19; 13: 24; 17: 30). Peter taught forgiveness, not for those who were merely *baptized*, but for those who *repented and were baptized* (Acts 2: 38). Jesus did not declare that those who were *baptized*, but that those who *believed and were baptized*, would be saved (Mark 16: 16). Scripture does not place the whole of forgiveness upon submission to baptism.

No convincing debate in favor of infant baptism is found in the New Testament. The general theme of baptism in Scripture, which involves belief, repentance, and the human decision-making process, provides impressive evidence that New Testament baptism was never intended to be performed on infants. A relevant question, however, is whether or not infant baptism does any harm.[10] Even if infant baptism provides no forgiveness, since the newborn has not sinned, what damage can it do? Perhaps it is better to proactively baptize the infant rather than take the risk that he/she might die and not go to heaven. It is a legitimate point that should be given consideration.

Infants are not immersed – the one mode of baptism taught and practiced in the Bible. Yet the child who is sprinkled as an infant may be raised with the understanding that he/she has been scripturally baptized and, therefore, has no need for the one true baptism of repentance and forgiveness. The Bible teaches repentance and baptism (immersion) as the mechanism in which we receive forgiveness of sins and the indwelling of the Holy Spirit. While this presumably occurs at a time of confirmation later in the child's life, this is not how these matters are portrayed in Scripture, nor is the teaching of confirmation found there. In God's Word, repentance is accompanied by baptism. Could infant baptism be harmful? There is no doubt about the possible implications.

In short, infant baptism cannot be supported in an honest search of the Scriptures. Why some practice this rite when no appreciable encouragement can be found in God's Word is puzzling. It is distressing that such a practice could cost the souls of many who might have been saved.

NOTES FOR CHAPTER 16

1. New Advent, Catholic Bible, Original Sin.

2. Campbell, in a <u>REVIEW OF BISHOP KENRICK'S TREATISE</u>, regarding infant baptism, states the following in answer to Kenrick's argument. First is stated the argument in favor of infant baptism, and then Campbell's response:

> *Bible Argument, No. I.*--"Who," says the bishop, "would venture to deny that they can be saved of whom Christ has said, 'Suffer the little children to come to me, and forbid them not, for of such is the kingdom of God!'"
>
> To this argument I have four objections:-- [315]
>
> 1. It changes the subject of discussion. It is *baptism,* and not salvation, for which the bishop pleads; and now he talks of salvation, and asks, "Who can deny that infants can be *saved.*"
>
> 2. These children were brought to the Messiah, neither for baptism nor for salvation, but for his blessing.
>
> 3. They were brought to Jesus *before* Christian baptism was ordained; and, therefore, their case can have no logical nor scriptural connection with baptism.
>
> 4. Jesus does not say that the kingdom of God is composed of *little children;* but of such as are, in some respects, *like them.* The English Hexapla, in all its versions, even including the Rheims, has "of such," and not *of them.* The late Polyglot, containing eight languages, which I have just examined, also favours this version. The French version expresses the full sense of them all. It reads in Matt. xix. 13; Mark x. 14; Luke xv2i.15, *Qui lour ressemblent.* The kingdom of God is of those who *resemble* them. There is not, then, a single version of the New Testament, in either Bagster's Hexapla, or in Bagster's recent splendid Polyglot Bible, containing the Greek, Hebrew, Latin, English, French, German, Italian, and Spanish approved versions, that justifies the bishop's gloss. Alexander, Campbell, <u>Christian Baptism, with Its Antecedents and Consequents</u> B O O K S I X T H. CHAPTER I. (1851).

3. Campbell's continued <u>REVIEW OF BISHOP KENRICK'S TREATISE</u> addresses the issue regarding the conversion of households. First the claim and then the rebuttal:

> "We are challenged to show that the Apostles baptized infants. Had we a detailed enumeration of their ministerial acts, the challenge would be reasonable; but the book styled their Acts contains only some of the chief facts which marked the origin and proved the divine authority of the Christian church. Yet even there it is said that Lydia 'was baptized and her household,' and the jailer 'was baptized and presently all his family;' and St. Paul testifies that he 'baptized also the household of Stephanas.' It cannot indeed be proved that infants were in these families; but the presumption is that there were, and

the general expressions naturally lead us to consider the baptism of all the children as following the conversion of the parent." [319]

Our resolute champion for the infant rite, in his self-respect and candour, is, it appears, in the end of his enumeration of households baptized, constrained to give up his own argument deduced from them, and to acknowledge that an infant cannot be found in any one of them. So these, too, are abandoned, and his dernier resort is to tradition--ecclesiastic tradition. He, of course, desires to find in the first century or second century some case that would favour the idea. Beginning with Justin Martyr, who flourished about the middle of it, and then proceeding to Irenæus, who flourished at the end of it, he cannot find a clear allusion to it, much less a positive proof of it; for infant baptism is not so much as named in any fragment of ancient tradition during the first and second centuries. No living man can find any allusion to it, or account of it, till in the third century, and even then there is little certain and less indicative that it had obtained in the Christian church so called.

Positive ordinances demand positive proof as certain as divine ordinances require the proof of divine authority. But neither he nor any other man can, from the oracles of God, or from ecclesiastical history, produce any direct, positive proof, human or divine, for infant baptism during the first two hundred years of the Christian age. Alexander, Campbell,Christian Baptism, with Its Antecedents and Consequents BOOKSIXTH CHAPTER I. (1851)

4. Smith, Mont W, "What the Bible Says About Covenant", page 309-310, College Press, 1981.

5. This quote was received in a personal e-mail from Mr. Frutchenbaum to the author of this book.

6. Smith, Mont W, "What the Bible Says About Covenant", page 310, College Press, 1981.

7. Calvin, John, Institutes of Christian Religion, Book 4, Chapter 16.

8. Brants, T.W., The Gospel Plan of Salvation p 223, Nashville: Gospel Advocate, reprint, 1977.

9. Brants, T.W., The Gospel Plan of Salvation p 315, Nashville: Gospel Advocate, reprint, 1977.

10. Campbell takes a somewhat more assertive approach in opposing infant baptism, referring to it as The Evil of Infant Baptism. His point, first and foremost, is that God seeks what Campbell calls will-worship.

HAVING been able to find *no good* in infant baptism, nor in infant sprinkling, (for I must always consider them as distinct things,) I now proceed to inquire, Is there any *evil* in it? In answering this question, I desire to be guided by three things only--Scripture, reason, and fact: neither by passion nor by prejudice; nor, I trust, will the fear of the frown of any mortal ever deter me from declaring the truth on this, or any other topic on which I am fairly called to express my sentiments. I answer the question now proposed, with the utmost coolness and deliberation; and feel no hesitation in declaring that infant sprinkling is a *manifold evil.* This I shall instance in a few respects:--

1st. It is "*will-worship.*" By the term *will-worship,* I understand worship founded upon the *will* of man, and not on the *will* of God. "In vain do they worship me," saith Christ, "teaching for doctrines the commandments of men." The preceding pages show that the rite of infant sprinkling is as much a tradition of men as the *scrutiny,* the *exsufflation* by which devils are expelled, the *insufflation* by which the Spirit of God is communicated, the *consecration* of the wafer, the *chrismal unction,* the *lighted taper,* and the *milk* and *honey,* which are but seven of the twenty-two appendages to infant sprinkling, made by the church of Rome. Now, as all will-worship is a disparagement of the worship appointed of God, it is, consequently, a reflection upon his wisdom, and obnoxious to his displeasure. It is as contrary to his revealed will as the presenting of "strange fire" upon his altar was in the days of Nadab and Abihu. And, indeed, every religious practice which is not founded upon an explicit revelation of the will of Heaven, is will-worship. The [405] language of it is this, "Thou shouldst have appointed this, and we are supplying a defect in thy wisdom or goodness." Such is the spirit of every innovation in divine worship. Alexander, Campbell, <u>Christian Baptism, with Its Antecedents and Consequents</u> BOOKSIXTH CHAPTER V2I. (1851).

Chapter XVII
Baptism and Biblical Harmony

Man is saved by grace through faith in Jesus (Ephesians 2: 8). That is a lesson that echoes throughout the pages of Scripture. Since the idea of salvation through faith is available to us only by the grace of God, many have difficulty understanding how the physical elements of baptism could be included in a plan of salvation that appears spiritual in its nature. The resulting struggle brings many to a point of decision concerning baptism and how it does or does not affect our relationship with God. This has led a number of believers to reason that, if man is saved by grace through faith, baptism can have no direct role in God's plan of salvation.

Of course, the greatest problem facing anyone who denies the redemptive role of baptism is found in the many passages of Scripture where baptism is recognized as a condition of salvation (Mark 16: 16; Acts 2: 38; 22: 16; Romans 6: 1-4; 1 Peter 3: 21). It is impossible to find unity between a literal reading of these passages and a view of salvation that excludes baptism. Consequently, men have come to assume that these passages simply do not mean what they say, having determined that this would contradict the gospel message of salvation by grace through faith that is presented in the Bible. Rather than seeking a natural harmony within Scripture concerning baptism and the message of salvation, men have begun redefining any passage that presents baptism as a matter of salvation. This is like trying to place a square peg in a round hole. The truth of the matter is that passages linking baptism to salvation fully harmonize with the message of grace through faith when we accept the meaning that is understood if we simply read the text the way it is written.

Baptism in Harmony with Grace

The grace of God that is illustrated in the Bible is the only grace most people know. This is, of course, understandable. After all, the idea of grace originated from God. Yet, grace is not always associated directly with salvation or eternal life. Created in His image, men are able to show grace toward one another. The difference for men is that we are unable to grant eternal life or cleanse a man from his sins. Still, grace can be present among men without the result of salvation or any relationship to things spiritual. The grace of one man toward another, which is a reflection of the grace of God, is related directly to one's unselfish giving and/or sacrifice for the good of another.

Grace is essentially about giving; a truth that few would ever care to challenge. However, grace exceeds the idea of simply giving a gift or sacrificing for the good of another. Many men offer gifts (birthday, anniversary, etc.) or willingly sacrifice for others daily without offering grace to that person. That is because simply giving a gift or offering a sacrifice does not automatically qualify as an act of grace. For instance, the Old Testament Israelites, in sacrificing to God, were certainly not offering Him grace. Often gifts are given where grace is absent.

It is important to recognize that the true nature of a gift – any gift – is that it is unearned. Whether grace is present or absent does not change this simple truth. Indeed, once something is earned by any means it is no longer a gift, but a wage. A *gift* must be offered freely and not as a matter of obligation.

What is it that separates mere gifting from what may be considered a gift of grace? Grace is present when a gift (often in the form of good will or kindness) is not only freely given, but when it is offered to someone who is *least deserving* of that gift. The less deserving a man is, the greater the gift of grace becomes (Luke 7: 41-43). In fact, grace is maximized when the person receiving the gift (or act of kindness) actually *deserves* exactly the opposite of what he/she receives. It is showing compassion and mercy when revenge is warranted. Because of this, grace must be considered rather mysterious. Offering something precious to someone who is least deserving of the gift makes no sense to the human mind. Yet this is what God has done. Grace finds no greater example than the grace of God that is revealed in Scripture. What could be a more charitable act of grace than offering life to those who have earned death? (Romans 6: 23)

The concept of grace suggests that, when the gift is given, there is some risk to the giver. This is partly due to the fact that, where grace is concerned, the gift given often involves the giver's participation on a personal level. If we give to someone a gift that holds little meaning for us, while the recipient may appreciate the gesture, what occurs with that gift once it has been given will likely be of little concern to the giver. However, it is when we give something that is precious to us, and that is perhaps a part of us, that we seek assurance that the gift given will be cared for just as we would care for it. The more personal and precious the gift is, the greater will be the concern over its care once it has been given. Indeed, when the gift is given in grace, the concern over the care of the gift tends to increase. Giving to someone something very special when that person has shown little regard in the past for things precious is certainly cause for concern.

Men have an incredible opportunity to have a relationship with God for which we are most undeserving. That opportunity, which is the essence of grace, is founded upon the very personal sacrifice of God's only Son whose life was given on our behalf. It simply cannot get more personal than that. Yet, with this gift there is risk involved even for God since the sacrifice could be for naught. It is possible that no one would be willing to accept this gift of grace. Therefore, when someone does accept what God has offered – that which is so personal – the heavens rejoice over the one who has been reconciled to God (Luke 15: 7) because the angels realize the price God has paid.

The relationship on earth that most closely resembles the bond between Christ and His church is that of a marriage. The marriage relationship offers an earthly example that provides a likeness of the spiritual relationship that God has always intended to have with His people. At various times in the Bible the covenant between Christ and the church is compared to marriage (John 3: 29; Ephesians 5: 25), which could be considered the most precious of relationships among men.

A wedding ring is symbolic of many elements of the relationship between a man and woman in the covenant of marriage. Giving a ring not only represents a person's love for someone, but it establishes a life-long commitment to the one from whom the ring is received. That commitment involves much more than a mere promise to wear the ring as a reflection of that love. Acceptance of the ring seals the promise to respect and honor the life of the giver. The ring represents the life of the giver who is, in essence, offering his/her life to its recipient as a free gift. How much more precious can any gift be than the gift of one's life?

When a person accepts a wedding ring, it places upon the shoulders of the prospective husband/wife the responsibility to care for the life given (represented by the ring) in a manner that recognizes the extraordinary nature of the gift. In marriage, it is both the privilege and responsibility of the husband to treat his wife in a manner that offers her greater happiness than she would have known without him. Similarly, it is the wife's opportunity, as well as her responsibility, to bring a joy into her husband's life that he would not have known without her.

As a man and woman exchange vows and rings in the wedding ceremony, it is the privilege of those in attendance to witness a most remarkable event. It is an event that, according to Scripture, may be considered somewhat spiritual, especially since it takes place in a manner invisible to the naked eye. As vows are exchanged and commitments are made, Scripture tells us that *'they shall become one flesh.'* (Genesis 2: 24) The man and woman, then, are united in marriage with a bond that truly transcends man's physical nature. No doubt this was God's design from the beginning.

Each couple tends to design the marriage ceremony to their personal specifications. Still, there are certain elements of the ceremony that most consider significant, and these are included in nearly every wedding ceremony in some form. There are, of course, the vows and the ring exchange. Many will include a unity candle that symbolizes the fact that these are no longer two separate beings, but a family of two. The kiss, then, is the seal that completes the transformation of the two into one.

Beyond these standard elements of a wedding, the bride and groom will individualize the ceremony by including items of a personal nature that are intended to attach special meaning to the day. Perhaps they will introduce a video of the history of their relationship or a song that carries with it a very special meaning. Regardless of the details of the day, there can be no doubt that the wedding ceremony is intended to represent things significant to the bride and groom.

The fact that rings and life-long commitments are offered within the setting of the wedding ceremony in no way lessens the sanctity of either the gift or the commitment. On the contrary, the ceremony is the very manner in which these are given a place of special honor. Men view the wedding as a thing of joy and an opportunity to recognize that something remarkable occurs at that time. The wedding ceremony is the time when everyone understands that the union between the bride and groom is made complete. In recognition of that fact the bride then takes the name of the groom as her own, taking on his likeness. His name is not hers prior to the ceremony. However, the change that occurs during the service gives her the right to identify with him, and he with her.

The wedding ceremony effectively raises the stakes for those who have decided to engage in the commitment of marriage. Submitting to one another in wedlock compels the participants to seriously consider the nature of that commitment as well as the consequences of breaking the vows that are spoken at that time.

God has chosen a ceremony as the time when He will give the gift of life through His only begotten Son to those who are willing to receive it. That fact does not in any way detract from the value of the gift any more than the wedding ceremony diminishes the gift of the bride to the groom or vice versa. On the contrary, it is a person's willing participation in this ceremony that accords the gift the highest of honors.

It is important to realize that, within the framework of the ceremony of baptism, the gifts given and received are not completely one-sided. It is not simply a matter of God bestowing upon us the gift of eternal life while He receives nothing in return. What God seeks is reconciliation with mankind. That reconciliation is not possible as long as sin separates us from God. We understand from Scripture that it is at the time of baptism that sins are removed (Acts 2: 38; Colossians 2: 11) as a barrier between God and man. This, as well as the offering of the individual's life as a living sacrifice to God (Matthew 10: 39; Romans 12: 1), are what He receives in return.

Just as the wedding couple designs their ceremony to include those things they consider most significant and most personal, so God has designed the ceremony of baptism. We know His aim in baptism is to reflect the imagery of the death, burial, and resurrection of Christ. This is understandable given the significance of the gift. For Him it is personal, representing the unequaled nature of the sacrifice He has made. Paul wrote about the personal aspect of this ceremony from God's perspective as he explained to the Romans:

3. Or do you not know that as many of us as were baptized into Christ Jesus were baptized into His death? 4. Therefore we were buried with Him through baptism into death, that just as Christ was raised from the dead by the glory of the Father, even so we should walk in newness of life. 5. For if we have been united together in the likeness of His death, certainly we also shall be *in the likeness of His* resurrection, 6. Knowing this, that our old man was crucified with *Him*, that the body

of sin might be done away with, that we should no longer be slaves of sin. (Romans 6: 3-6)

The ceremony of baptism has been designed in a manner that makes participation very personal, both for the convert and for the Father. It reflects those elements that God deems most important as we are buried in water where, according to Paul, our unity with Christ occurs. As that unity takes place and we rise from the water, just as the bride takes on the likeness of the groom by accepting his name as her own, so the new Christian takes the identity of Christ, walking *'in newness of life.'* His name is not ours prior to baptism. However, the change that occurs during the ceremony gives us the right to identify with Him according to His promise (Acts 2: 38).

It is certainly unfair to view baptism as something that men have added to Christ's sacrifice, thereby diluting the meaning and power of the blood. On the contrary, Baker's Dictionary of Theology states:

> ...the action itself is divinely ordained as a means of grace, i.e., a means to present Christ and therefore to fulfil the attesting work of the Spirit. It does not do this by the mere performance of the prescribed rite; it does it in and through its meaning.[1]

If this ceremony of baptism is, by God's own design, *divinely ordained* as the time when we are united with Christ, we must learn to accept that fact. Baptism must be recognized as the time when we are both united with Christ and reconciled to the Father. Receiving God's gift of grace in a ceremony designed by Him specifically for that purpose cannot devalue the gift that is received. On the contrary, the ceremony is the very manner in which Jesus' sacrifice is most genuinely honored. Baptism is mentioned more than one hundred times in the New Testament. This fact undoubtedly reflects the significance of the baptismal water from God's perspective. It is understandable, then, why Jesus would proclaim to His disciples:

> He who believes and is baptized will be saved...(Mark 16: 16)

Baptism in Harmony with Faith

While we are saved *by* grace, which is the means of salvation, we are also saved *through* faith, the pathway to salvation (Ephesians 2: 8). However, the biblical teaching of salvation through faith seems to present an additional dilemma for many people. While Paul's statement concerning salvation *'by grace through faith'* is very direct, several other passages of Scripture present teaching about a number of conditions men must meet in order to receive salvation. Many believe that accepting these passages at face value would destroy the very fabric of *grace through faith* that Paul presents. Therefore, the unfortunate reaction of some men is to amend biblical teaching about faith so that it might fit their own belief system.

The prominent teaching within evangelical circles is not that salvation comes by grace through faith, as Paul states so clearly; rather the claim is made that salvation comes by grace through faith *only*. The doctrine of salvation through faith only ultimately identifies saving faith as simply intellectual and emotional acceptance of, and trust in, the deity of Christ as well as His crucifixion for our sins and His resurrection to conquer death. The claim is that one is saved when he/she initially recognizes and accepts the fact that Jesus is the Son of God. This, however, is not the way the apostles portray faith in Scripture. It is best that we allow Scripture to define for us the true nature of faith through which eternal life is ultimately granted.

In his proclamation that men are saved by grace through faith (Ephesians 2: 8) Paul does not define saving faith for us. He certainly tells us what it is not (works), but falls short of explaining exactly what it is that constitutes saving faith. He does not state that it is purely mental acknowledgement of Jesus as Lord, but he also does not say that it may be more than this. Therefore, based solely upon Paul's words to the Ephesians, we could determine that the faith that offers eternal life is, indeed, belief only. However, we cannot necessarily learn what faith *is* from a passage that simply tells us what it *is not*. If we are to be honest students of the Word, it is important that we take the time to discover whether or not, within the pages of Scripture, saving faith is defined. Indeed, Paul has provided additional insight in certain other epistles concerning the make-up of redemptive faith.

Paul differentiates between works and faith when it comes to salvation (Ephesians 2: 8). Yet, we discover that God's Word associates faith with human activity more often than with salvation, although it is true that these two elements (faith and works) are essentially inseparable (James 2: 20). In fact, despite modern claims, at no point does the New Testament identify the time of initial faith as the time of initial salvation. That is because faith is not simply about our first moment of belief in Jesus. Instead, faith speaks to our participation in life as our deeds reflect our commitment to God (Romans 1: 17). It is those things that we *do*, through faith, that ultimately bring about salvation. The image of faith that we find in Scripture is really a picture of faithfulness.

In the book of Romans, a book consisting of sixteen chapters, the word faith ($\pi\iota\sigma\tau\iota\varsigma$) appears thirty-eight times. We can rightfully conclude, then, that faith is the central issue Paul addresses in his words to the Romans. Using an approach comparable to his letter to the Ephesians, Paul establishes in Romans a theme of grace through faith, stating again that grace does not come by works (Romans 3: 20-31). Those who view the first few chapters of this letter as Paul's full declaration of the gospel attempt to isolate chapters one through five from the balance of the letter, a proposition that defeats Paul's purpose. The first verses of the sixth chapter are directly related to the last verses of chapter five offering an uninterrupted flow of Paul's instructions concerning the difference between justification by the law or by grace. It is a theme that envelops the entire epistle.

In this letter we learn that Paul was sent to teach all nations to be obedient to the gospel message (Romans 1: 5; 15: 18-20). Much of Paul's teaching in chapters six through sixteen of the book of Romans focuses on illustrating the faith that he has discussed in the first few chapters – the faith by which men are saved. Despite his emphasis on the difference between faith and works as a means to salvation, we find that Paul deliberately teaches the *necessity* of obedience as a matter of salvation (Romans 2: 8; 6: 16-18). Some form of the word *obey* (obedience, etc.) appears in Romans no less than thirteen times. Therefore, we cannot honestly say that *obedience* to the gospel is in any way equivalent to the *works* of Ephesians 2: 8. Since Paul specifically distinguishes between obedient faith and works of merit, we must openly reject the claim that faith *not of works* somehow equates to faith *not of obedience*.

As Paul considers the nature of saving faith, he never discusses the initial moment of faith – that is to say, he does not identify faith as something that occurs at a specific moment in time. Instead, he views faith in terms of activity. Paul begins his discussion of the nature of saving faith by pointing to our obedience in the waters of baptism (Romans 6: 1-23). This is most appropriate since the spiritual activity that occurs at the time of baptism, according to Paul, relies upon our faith (Colossians 2: 11-12). In the eighth chapter of the book of Romans, Paul identifies faith in terms of our walk with God. Because the Holy Spirit dwells in us through faith, we *do not walk according to the flesh, but according to the Spirit'* (Romans 8: 1).

In the tenth chapter of Romans, Paul explains how we come to faith. We learn that faith comes by hearing the gospel message (Romans 10: 17). Once again faith is defined in terms of our response to that message, as a matter of salvation, as we believe the gospel and confess Jesus as Lord (Romans 10: 9-10). The general theme of the eleventh chapter of Romans focuses on obedient faith as the means by which we are grafted as branches to the tree of eternal life, while the twelfth chapter recognizes that not all men have an equal portion of faith. In the fourteenth chapter the apostle completes this thought, urging the Romans to always consider the influence of their actions upon those who may be weaker in the faith. Paul closes his letter to the Romans, encouraging his readers to remain obedient to the commands of God and faithful to the gospel message through which their relationship with God was established (Romans 16: 25-26).

Scriptural instruction about obedience to the gospel message is hardly limited to the book of Romans. It is a central theme from Acts through Revelation. Luke wrote of priests who, in their acceptance of Jesus, were *'obedient to the faith'* (Acts 6: 7). Paul told the Thessalonians that God would punish eternally *'those who do not obey the gospel'* (2 Thessalonians 1: 8). Peter challenged the salvation of *'those who do not obey the gospel'* (1 Peter 4: 17).

Paul told the Philippian jailer to, *'Believe on the Lord Jesus Christ, and you will be saved... '* (Acts 16: 31). This statement is as beautiful as it is true. Believing on Jesus is absolutely central in our path to salvation. The belief ($\pi\iota\sigma\tau\epsilon\upsilon\sigma o\nu$) of which Paul spoke in teaching the Philippian jailer (Acts 16: 31) may be considered closely associated with the faith ($\pi\iota\sigma\tau\epsilon\omega\varsigma$) of Ephesians 2: 8. In the Greek, while the word *'believe'* ($\pi\iota\sigma\tau\epsilon\upsilon\omega$) is similar to *faith* ($\pi\iota\sigma\tau\iota\varsigma$), the difference between them must be recognized. Belief, as Paul taught the jailer, suggests the placing of one's trust in Jesus. The faith through which salvation is received is belief carried to its logical conclusion of *faithfulness*. It is obedient belief. This distinction is well demonstrated in the story of the rulers who actually believed on Jesus but failed to follow through with their conviction.

> Nevertheless even among the rulers many believed (επιστευσαν) in Him, but because of the Pharisees they did not confess Him, lest they should be put out of the synagogue. (John 12: 42)

Here the apostle John uses a form of the same word that Paul used when he told the jailer he must *believe* to be saved. According to John these men did believe. Yet, despite their belief, these rulers did not carry that belief through to the conclusion of faithfulness since *'they did not confess Him.'* Their priorities were such that maintaining a position in the synagogue was most important to them. We can biblically conclude that without a willingness to confess Jesus as Savior, men cannot be saved (Romans 10: 9). We can also determine that there is a difference between trusting that Jesus is the Son of God (belief) and the level of faithfulness necessary to receive salvation.

Based upon this episode we can determine that, had the Philippian jailer believed on Jesus, as did the rulers at the synagogue, but never carried that belief forward to the point of the faithfulness of Ephesians 2: 8, he would not have received salvation. Paul certainly recognized that fact and would have fully explained to the jailer that faithfulness was essential in answer to his question, *'Sirs, what must I do to be saved?'* (Acts 16: 32). Had Paul taught the man to merely believe *(πιστευω)* in Jesus he would have remained in the same condemned state of the believing rulers in the synagogue.

In the New Testament, we find that the benefits received as a result of obedient faith are also recognized as benefits of the combination of belief, repentance, confession, and baptism – these four representing obedience to the gospel message (1 Peter 4: 17).[2] So exact are these characteristics and benefits that the sum of these four might be considered interchangeable with the *saving faith* that is taught by the apostles. We receive forgiveness of our sins through baptism (Acts 2: 38; Romans 6: 6; 1 Corinthians 6: 11), repentance (Acts 3: 19), and faith (Galatians 2: 16). Sanctification is attained through the work of the Spirit and by our obedience (1 Peter 1: 2), by our belief in the truth (2 Thessalonians 2: 13), and by baptism (1 Corinthians 6: 11). Rebirth/renewal comes by baptism (John 3: 5; Romans 6: 5; Titus 3: 5) through faith in the work of the Holy Spirit (John 3: 5; Colossians 2: 11; Titus 3: 5). Just as we are united with Christ in faith (Ephesians 3: 17), we are also united with Him in baptism (Romans 6: 5). Receiving the Holy Spirit is a matter of faith (Galatians 3: 2), baptism (Acts 2: 38), and obedience (Acts 5: 32). Salvation is attained by faith (Ephesians 2: 8), obedience (Hebrews 5: 9), baptism (1 Peter 3: 21), repentance of our sins (2 Corinthians 7: 10), and confession of Jesus as Lord (Romans 10: 9). Adoption by the Father comes both through baptism and by faith (Galatians 3: 26-27).

The story of the salvation of Noah and his family parallels God's plan of salvation for the church on a number of levels, some of which are discussed in this book. One such similarity can be found in the grace/faith combination by which Noah was saved. God looked upon a world where, *'the wickedness of man was great ...every intent of the thoughts of his heart was only evil continually.'* (Genesis 6: 5) However, God looked down upon Noah and offered grace to Him (Genesis 6: 8). The fact that Scripture describes Noah as a just man should not be taken to mean that he was deserving of grace since Noah was certainly not sinless (Romans 3: 23). Yet he did stand out from all others and for this God offered him the opportunity to escape His wrath.

Unlike everyone else in his day, Noah actually had faith in God (Hebrews 11: 7). Yet it is the nature of that faith that is most notable. Noah spent decades building an ark to prepare for a flood. There is no indication that Noah ever complained about building the ark, insisting that God could save him and his family without it if He wished. He simply obeyed the clear command of God.

What is important is that Noah's faith was a faith that built an ark. Had Noah's faith fallen short of obedience to God's command to build the ark he, along with his family, would have perished despite the depth of Noah's faith or God's grace. Neither grace nor faith would have saved Noah without his obedience. He was not saved by mere intellectual/emotional faith, but by faithfulness. God's grace offered Noah an opportunity to be saved *if he built an ark*. Noah was saved by grace, but not by grace *alone*. Nor was he saved by faith *alone*. Instead, he was saved through faithfulness. The grace of God made contact with the faith of Noah as he obediently built the ark.

Men often challenge the teaching that one's salvation is dependent upon obedience to God's commands. Some men who oppose this teaching claim that, if obedience to any command is mandatory, it means that we must necessarily obey *all* of His commands, and that anything short of this would leave a man condemned. Insisting that the idea of grace relieves us of the obligation to obedience, they maintain that we cannot distinguish between commands where obedience is required and those that are simply intended to help us honor God.

What shall we say, then, about belief and repentance, both of which God *requires* from those who seek salvation? Since they are specific commands we obey in seeking redemption can we, in like manner, conclude that if these commands are essential all commands must be obeyed? The truth is not all Godly commands are required in the initial course of redemption.

Peter commands his readers to *be holy* (1 Peter 1: 16). However, without the grace of God at the time of our salvation we are incapable of holiness. We can only be partakers of God's holiness (Hebrews 12: 10). Yet at no time did the apostles teach holiness as a prerequisite to salvation. Holiness is bestowed upon us as we clothe ourselves with Christ (Galatians 3: 27) and receive the Holy Spirit (Acts 2: 38). Those to whom Peter wrote with the command to *be holy* were already Christians. His plea was for them to honor Jesus by living holy lives.

Jesus commanded that we *'...love one another; as I have loved you.'* (John 13: 34) Yet who on earth has the capacity for this kind of love? Nor is this depth of love demanded as a requirement for the salvation that is revealed in Scripture. Holiness and Christ-like love are ideals toward which we are commanded to strive. They are not treated in the Bible as precepts for one's salvation.

Those commands presented in Scripture as essential for our initial salvation (belief, repentance, confession, and baptism) are commands which we can easily obey. They do not involve building an ark. The truth is we have the *capacity* to believe that Jesus is the Messiah. We are *capable* of repenting of our sins and confessing Jesus as Savior. We also have the *ability* to be baptized for the remission of sins. That is what God has asked of us *in order to be saved*. He has not placed on our shoulders a hopeless task by asking us to do things we cannot do. In fact, given the utter simplicity of the commands, we have no excuse for refusing to obey the gospel.

Peter, in his first epistle, pointed to baptism as a matter of salvation (1 Peter 3: 21). Even more than this, he identifies baptism as that which saves. Yet Paul tells us that we are *'saved by grace through faith'* (Ephesians 2: 8-9). What approach can we then use to balance the teachings of two men whose work is inspired by God? There are a couple of options open to us. One approach would be to determine that in one of these two cases the writer did not mean exactly what he said. We could decide that Peter did not intend to identify baptism as a matter of salvation *or* that Paul did not mean that we are saved by faith. However, we would then face the challenge of determining which of the apostles wrote in error. That would be difficult since the words and teaching of each are direct and are supported in other apostolic writings.

Our second option is to treat the meaning of these two teachings from Peter and Paul as harmonious and complementary. In other words, let us discover how *both* statements, as they are written, might be true rather than meddling with the meaning of one so that it agrees, however awkwardly, with the other. This would inevitably lead us to a search through Scripture to better understand how these two elements, faith and baptism, are linked together within God's plan.

For the Christian, faith and baptism are designed to complement each other. Together they represent faithfulness. Baptism is always presented as a response of faith to the gospel message (Acts 16: 15; Romans 6: 3-4; Galatians 3: 26-27; Colossians 2: 12). If baptism is an act of faith, Scripture harmonizes fully as Peter proclaimed that we must *'be baptized...for the remission of sins'* (Acts 2: 38). As it was with Noah in building the ark, this is the time when the grace of God makes contact with the faith of man (Colossians 2: 12). Since we have already considered the parallel characteristics and benefits of faith and baptism, it would be pointless to restate them. It is sufficient to say that when men pit baptism against Paul's words that teach salvation by grace through faith, passages like these (Mark 16: 16; Acts 2: 38; Colossians 2: 12; 1 Peter 3: 21, etc.) *cannot* be satisfactorily reconciled. It is *only* when we view baptism as an act of obedient faith in God's divine plan that we find harmony in passages concerning faith and baptism.

NOTES FOR CHAPTER 17

1. Harrison, Everett F., Editor, Baker's Dictionary of Theology, p. 84-85, Baker Book House, 1960.

2. In his work, **Baptism in the New Testament**, G. R. Beasley-Murray has solidly examined the scriptural link between the benefits of faith and baptism, as have other authors. However, in God's plan of salvation the obedience of repentance and confession cannot be divorced from faith or baptism. That is not to say this was his intent since it surely was not, but these are no less relevant when it comes to saving faith. If we are to associate faith with baptism we must also recognize its association with repentance and confession in obedience to the gospel message.

Chapter XVIII
Baptism and Doctrinal Purity

Doctrinal Significance

Modern men tend to downplay the idea of doctrine as it is presented in Scripture. Doctrine is often considered to be a hindrance that should be avoided when determining what beliefs are acceptable. Multitudes have come to conclude that what we believe doctrinally is relatively unimportant, reasoning that essentially any belief in God/Jesus is sufficient. Exactly what is doctrine? Doctrine is teaching. Jesus' doctrine is the set of teachings He gave us in His own words and through the writings of the apostles. If a doctrine, or teaching, is not supported by God's Word – especially when it conflicts with God's Word – it should not be considered the doctrine of Christ.

Not all doctrine involves direct commands from God. We find that much doctrine in the pages of Scripture appears in the form of advice or guidance about how to live a holy life. Furthermore, we are told in the Bible that not every decision we face carries with it eternal consequences. At times we will face choices that will not necessarily interfere directly with our fellowship with God (Romans 14: 6-14). Paul and Barnabas were very close in their relationship. Nonetheless, the two were not always of one mind. Facing a decision regarding who would travel with them on a missionary journey, they parted ways and traveled separately due to a disagreement over one young man (Acts 15: 36-40).

Just as the choice of companionship on a journey need not directly affect our relationship with God, many other choices do not necessarily have eternal consequences. Doctrinal commands are not the *determining* factor when seeking to choose a spouse or career, the number of children one desires, or in what town a person will live. Still, Scripture provides guidelines (*doctrine in the form of sage advice*) to assist God's children in making decisions such as these, and it is always wise to seek guidance through prayer. Choosing an honorable profession is basic to Christian living, but countless moral and ethical careers are available for our choosing. When selecting a life partner we may wish to consider the wisdom of being joined with someone who shares our beliefs (2 Corinthians 6: 14). Yet we still have the freedom to make these kinds of choices. This is a freedom that is evident throughout God's Word. Likewise, in Paul's letter to the Christians at Thessalonica, he advised them regarding a Christian way of life rather than offering doctrinal commands.

> 15. See that no one renders evil for evil to anyone, but always pursue good both for yourselves and for all. 16. Rejoice always, 17. pray without ceasing. (1 Thessalonians 5: 15-17)

Since many decisions we face are not addressed through doctrinal commands, why would the author of the book of Hebrews caution his readers to beware of strange doctrines (Hebrews 13: 9)? Why would the apostles place such a strong emphasis on *adherence* to true doctrine (2 Timothy 4: 3-4)?

New Testament passages like those listed above indicate that abiding in Christian doctrine, as it is spelled out in Scripture, is vital. The apostles provide fair warning that certain teachings are completely unacceptable to God. Jesus has specific expectations of His followers. While some doctrine comes in the form of wise instruction regarding living a holy life, Jesus and the apostles regarded as critical certain elements of biblical doctrine.

Since certain biblical teachings *must* be followed, men must learn to distinguish between those decisions involving freedom of choice and those that simply demand obedience. Honest and thorough biblical study is crucial if we hope to understand the difference. In Scripture we learn the doctrine of Christ, those teachings that provide a foundation for His kingdom here on earth. These are the teachings that men who truly seek Christ must not ignore. For instance, salvation is available through Jesus alone. Worshipping other gods is forbidden (John 14: 6; Acts 4: 12). This is a doctrine that is not optional. It is a requirement.

Distinguishing between those elements of biblical doctrine that are meant to simply guide us and those that have eternal consequences can prove rather challenging. False teachers often present a very convincing case that a belief is scriptural when, upon close examination, it may not be. Thus, in the same book where Paul warns Timothy of false doctrines, he encourages Him to:

> Be diligent to present yourself approved to God, a worker who does not need to be ashamed, rightly dividing the word of truth. (2 Timothy 2: 15)

Like Timothy, all men are to be diligent in their study of the Bible in order to attain a true understanding of God's Word. Honest, devoted study is the vaccine that can prevent the *itching ears* (2 Timothy 4: 3) that are so willingly responsive to false teachers. God's Word holds within its pages all doctrinal authority. The only means we have available to fully grasp biblical doctrine and defend against those beliefs that lead astray is faithful and honest study as the Holy Spirit guides us to an even greater understanding.

The word doctrine(s) appears roughly fifty times in the New Testament. Jesus even termed His own teaching as doctrine.

> 16. Jesus answered them and said, "My doctrine is not Mine, but His who sent Me. 17. If anyone wills to do His will, he shall know concerning the doctrine, whether it is from God or whether I speak on My own authority." (John 7: 16-17)

He also noted that there existed doctrine (teaching) His disciples must be sure to avoid. He told them:

> 11. ...but beware of the leaven of the Pharisees and Sadducees. 12. Then they understood that He did not tell them to beware of the leaven of bread, but of the doctrine of the Pharisees and Sadducees. (Matthew 16: 11b-12)

The Pharisees were descendants of Abraham and worshipped the same God as the disciples. Yet, just as Cain's offering was unacceptable to God in days of old, so the doctrine of the Pharisees was not acceptable to God. They did not live in His way or keep the commands as God intended.

The apostles were very aware of false doctrines and continuously warned Christ's followers to beware of those who might teach anything contrary to what was taught by both Jesus and the apostles:

> ...that we should no longer be children, tossed to and fro and carried about by every wind of doctrine, by the trickery of men, in the cunning craftiness of the deceitful plotting... (Ephesians 4: 14)

> As I urged you when I went into Macedonia -- remain in Ephesus that you may charge some that they teach no other doctrine. (1 Timothy 1: 3)

> Do not be carried about with various and strange doctrines. (Hebrews 13: 9)

Biblically sound teachings are very important to the fitness of the body of Christ. While it is true that men are given freedom in Christ, spiritual freedom does not outweigh doctrinal purity. We do not have the spiritual freedom to simply believe what we wish to believe and still expect to receive eternal life. Once a teaching conflicts with the Bible, false doctrine results.

If there are doctrines that are false it stands to reason, and we are told in Scripture, that there is a doctrine that is true. That is the doctrine of Christ. The apostles charged the people to continue in the doctrine of Christ and offered greatly encouraging words to those who held fast:

> If you instruct the brethren in these things, you will be a good minister of Jesus Christ, nourished in the words of faith and of the good doctrine which you have carefully followed. (1 Timothy 4: 6)

The importance that was placed by both Jesus and the apostles upon following the teachings, or doctrine, they provided is very clear. Indeed, Timothy was commended by Paul for applying the *'good doctrine'* that he had *'carefully followed.'* Should we not follow the doctrine of Christ just as *carefully* as Timothy?

The Doctrine of Baptism

Among men there is a popular view that since God is such a gracious God He would never *really* send anyone to the eternal flames of hell. If what we believe is really not important as long as we are sincere, this teaching could be considered as legitimate as anything we might learn from Scripture. And yet, we know that it is unacceptable since it stands in direct contrast to biblical principles.

Repentance and belief in Jesus are essential in one's pursuit of eternal life (Acts 3: 19; 4: 12), a fact very few would ever dispute. Among those who profess Christ, essentially no one would consider belief in any deity other than Jesus a belief that could lead to salvation. Yet men tend to single out baptism, insisting that it is unrelated to salvation despite the words of the apostles.

There is an important difference between gospel and doctrine. The gospel is the message that reveals Jesus and leads men to accept Him as Savior. The honest presentation of the gospel message is a significant element of scriptural doctrine. The apostles taught that, as Jesus' disciples, we must abide in correct biblical doctrine (2 Timothy 4: 3; 2 John 9) and Peter demonstrated that a critical element of scriptural doctrine is faithful obedience to the gospel (1 Peter 4: 17). Baptism is, within the pages of Scripture, presented as a vital ingredient in our obedience to the gospel message.

Scripture is filled with testimony concerning the effects of baptism. Beginning with the ministry of John the Baptist and on through the epistles, this rite is identified as the point of forgiveness of sins (Acts 2: 38; 22: 16; Colossians 2: 11-13). It is also called the moment of regeneration or rebirth (John 3: 5; Romans 6: 4; Titus 3: 5). It is at the moment of baptism that we are freed from our slavery to sin (Romans 6: 17-18). Jesus commanded baptism as a matter of becoming a disciple (Matthew 28: 19) and attaining salvation (Mark 16: 16), a teaching that is confirmed by the apostle Peter (1 Peter 3: 21). Paul saw baptism as the moment we clothe ourselves with Christ (Galatians 3: 27). Both Paul and Luke viewed baptism as the point of entry into the body of Christ (Acts 2: 42; 1 Corinthians 12: 13). We also learn from the apostle Paul that baptism is the time of cleansing (Ephesians 5: 26), justification, and sanctification (1 Corinthians 6: 11).

Immersion in water represents the death, burial, and resurrection of Christ. Through our willing participation in baptism we are united with Christ in His sacrifice (Romans 6: 4-5). Just as the flood destroyed evil, offering a fresh start for mankind, baptism is a time of renewal. Peter recognized baptism as the means to salvation *through the resurrection of Christ* (1 Peter 3: 21) as Jesus' sacrifice is applied to our lives. This is the doctrine of baptism.

Men are commanded by both Jesus and the apostles to be baptized. Additionally, we are provided sufficient evidence that the baptism established in the Bible was baptism by immersion in water for the forgiveness of sins. It makes sense, then, that any other doctrine concerning baptism would conflict with the doctrine of Christ that is established in God's Word.

The comment has often been made that the teaching of any strict doctrine, such as baptism, effectively places limits upon God in His relationship with man. If, however, these teachings represent restrictions on God, they are limitations He has placed upon Himself. Each time God has established a covenant with men, He has limited Himself to the provisions of that covenant. God's covenant with Abraham restricted the *seed* through which Jesus would come to earth (Genesis 18: 18). The covenant with Noah assured that God would never again destroy all life with a flood (Genesis 9: 11-13). Such covenants placed boundaries and requirements not only on the deeds of men, but on God's actions as well. These limitations, however, were not set by the hands and minds of men, but by God. So it is with baptism. If God has chosen to establish conditions for us in our relationship with Him, even if those conditions seem to limit what He will or will not do, history reveals a God with the resolve to abide by His own decision.

Is it possible that someone in the church age might be saved without the benefit of immersion for forgiveness of his sins? We cannot know the answer to that question with any certainty since we have no clear vision beyond the moment of death. What we can demonstrate, however, is that within the New Testament, baptism is identified as a matter of salvation. While it will always be a matter of debate, Jesus' words to Nicodemus indicate that those who choose to bypass immersion in water will not enter heaven (John 3: 5).

The manner by which men receive justification and salvation, according to God's Word, involves man's submission in baptism for forgiveness of sins as a matter of spiritual birth (Mark 16: 16; John 3: 5; Acts 2: 38; Romans 6: 3-6; Colossians 2: 11-2). God has sanctioned no other teaching. Therefore, if someone in this age sees heaven without baptism, this could occur only by God's choice for reasons that He deems acceptable, as an exception to biblical doctrine. No man has the authority to teach exemption from the command since God has not given men license to dismiss baptism. Unfortunately, many simply refuse to accept immersion as a part of God's plan of salvation. This has lead to the belief that God *will* redeem that person who is not immersed despite scriptural instruction. Based upon this rationale, many have developed, and boldly teach, a gospel message that deliberately disregards the biblical role for baptism.

Doctrinal Purity Vs Sincerity of Heart
The argument is often raised that the eternal life of someone who earnestly seeks God could not possibly hinge upon obedience to a specific command, such as baptism, especially if that person

simply misunderstands what is expected of him. Surely sincerity of heart is the thing God desires rather than ritualistic compliance.

A book that attempted to address this issue appeared on the shelves of bookstores a few years ago. John Mark Hicks and Greg Taylor published their book <u>Down in the River to Pray</u>, a work that actually respects the significance that Scripture places upon baptism. There is no question that this book offers valuable insights into the apostles' teaching about baptism. It is a must read for any and all who care to have a better understanding of the value that the biblical authors have placed upon water baptism.

While the book contributes much to the discussion of baptism, especially in contrasting baptism and works, the authors have taken an interesting stand when considering the necessity of baptism. In essence, they have developed a view that recognizes the salvation status of those whom they have labeled *'transformed unimmersed believers.* [1] They have based their proposition on an Old Testament incident involving Hezekiah's observance of the Passover, suggesting that God might overlook disobedience in response to a man's honest desire to please Him.

Hezekiah, a Godly man who also happened to be king of Israel, wished to reinstate the Passover Feast that the Israelites had ignored for so long (2 Chronicles 30: 1-36). Unfortunately, the Israelites were unable to celebrate the feast at the time God had established for the Passover (v. 3). While God had allowed for an alternate time for the festival (Numbers 9: 11), it is difficult to say whether or not that exception might apply here. Yet, the timing of the celebration was not the only issue that the Israelites faced in honoring God with their commemoration, since some of those who came to participate were ceremonially unclean. This, too, was prohibited by law.

Recognizing the fact that they were not acting according to God's instructions concerning the Passover, Hezekiah asked for God's blessing upon the celebration even though they were not observing it in the exact manner, or at the specific time, God had commanded (v. 18). God, who has a passion for His people and a desire to commune with them, heard this prayer and accepted their worship despite the fact that they had not kept the *letter* of the law (v. 19). Hicks and Taylor have argued that this episode might explain how God may respond to disobedience with respect to baptism. They have compared the sincere un-immersed believer to these Israelites who, while they did not obey the commands of God precisely, worshiped Him honestly and sought His blessing. Even among those who embrace the biblical model of baptism as the moment of forgiveness and salvation, this proposal has certainly made an impact.

As appealing as this proposal may be, it seems to be a considerable leap to compare the prayer offered by Hezekiah, and answered by God, with the situation we face concerning baptism in modern times. In order to legitimately compare this event with man's present treatment of baptism, it would have been necessary for Hezekiah, and those who celebrated with him, to question whether God had actually established a specific time, or any rules about ceremonial cleanliness, in relation to the Passover. Then, progressing in a manner of their own choosing, by either neglecting the Passover completely or by ignoring God's established rules, they would need to assume that God would honor their decision, all the while insisting that they had not disobeyed any of His commands.

This may seem to be an insensitive commentary on the modern view of baptism, but it is not offered with malice or hardness of heart. Rather, it is given out of an honest concern for the souls of men. The modern man has not earnestly sought exemption from baptism, or its meaning, on the grounds that he has been prohibited from participating. Instead, he has chosen to exempt himself. The common view is that God never established baptism for the purposes taught in Scripture (Acts 2: 38; 1 Peter 3: 21). Thus, men have developed a view of the baptism that denies what is taught in God's Word, insisting that God must honor their belief.

The Jews in Jerusalem did not assume that God would respect their decision concerning celebration of the Passover Feast. Instead, Hezekiah humbly approached God and prayed that He would accept their worship *despite the inappropriateness of their actions*. Present-day dismissal of God's call to baptism as a condition of salvation is hardly the same as Hezekiah's prayer for God to make an exception. However, it does seem to offer hope for the man who seeks exemption from baptism when circumstances prevent him from obeying.

Despite the fact that this Old Testament account is not really compatible with the situation we face with respect to baptism, Hicks and Taylor have suggested that there are those who appear to have been transformed into Christ's image even though they have never received immersion in water for remission of sins. This transformation, they believe, gives us reason to hope these men and women are, indeed, children of God.

The proposal that certain un-immersed men and women appear to have been transformed from their previous life into a life that imitates Christ is certainly true. There are those among us who proclaim Jesus as Lord who have never been baptized; yet their way of life does seem to reflect that of Christ. They appear to be devoted to God and are giving toward other people, even to the point of sacrifice. Exactly how can we reconcile this with the teaching of Scripture?

The first thing we must recognize when considering this question is the fact that baptism is not defined in Scripture as the moment of one's transformation into a Christ-like being. Instead, it is presented as the moment of rebirth, forgiveness of sins, and receiving of the Holy Spirit as an integral part of our lives. Transformation into the image of Christ is a separate matter that cannot be confined to, or defined by, the moment of baptism, or even limited to those who have been immersed. Just as there are those who remain un-immersed who do undergo transformation, there are also those who are immersed who do not.

God does not zap us into a Christ-like existence at the moment of immersion in water. Baptism is simply the time appointed by God when we are offered the opportunity to start over as His children, having been adopted by Him (Galatians 4: 5) and united with Christ (Romans 6: 4). It is our opportunity to pursue, with a clean conscience from sin (1 Peter 3: 21), the transformation that God desires to see in us. Our transformation increases as we seek God through His Word. It is there that we discover the character of Christ that we are meant to imitate. Through reading the Bible and earnestly seeking God we are, over time, transformed. Although the Romans were already immersed believers (Romans 6: 1-4), Paul still urged them to be (or continue to be) transformed by the renewing of their minds rather than conforming to the ways of the world (Romans 12: 2).

It is certainly possible, and perhaps even inevitable, that we as men will become more and more Christ-like as we spend time in God's Word. Those who commit any significant amount of time to studying the Bible cannot help but be impacted by these inspired writings. That is a truth that overshadows obedience in baptism. Scripture is powerful (Hebrews 4: 12) and has that kind of effect on men regardless of their baptismal status. God's Word has the capability, in itself, to shape a person's character. Therefore, a man can be noticeably transformed without being baptized. Indeed, by the time someone chooses to receive Christ in baptism, his/her transformation may be well underway as a result of the discipleship (Matthew 28: 19) that has led to this very decision.

The greatest difficulty we face in establishing the redemption of *'transformed unimmersed believers'* is that God's Word recognizes no time other than baptism when a man's sins are forgiven and he becomes a new creature in Christ. The apostles offer no instruction about a time other than baptism when a man would receive the Holy Spirit or experience adoption as a child of God. In his letters, Paul consistently recognizes the members of the body as those who had submitted to Christ in Christian baptism. While a man may experience a marked transformation of character as a result of constant immersion in the Word, salvation for the un-immersed believer simply has no scriptural support despite any visible transformation that may have occurred.

What shall we say about the person who has been raised to believe that baptism has no salvation value and embraces that teaching with honest intentions? After all, it is a most difficult step for any man to reconsider theological views he has learned since childhood. It is like that person who, for many years, views a painting through a tinted lens. The shade of the lens affects his perspective. Observing the same image absent that lens, he may very well insist that it is a forgery.

The answer to this question is not an easy one. It is the hope of everyone who believes in Jesus as the Son of God that all men would be saved. However, Scripture does not offer greatly encouraging words for those who are disobedient when it comes to baptism, regardless of the circumstances. As Jesus completed the Sermon on the Mount, He addressed the matter of certain disciples who failed to obey God's commands (Matthew 7: 21-27). Jesus did not say that they were condemned because of insincerity, but disobedience. John stated that those who accept doctrine from men that does not harmonize with Jesus' teaching actually share in their *'evil deeds'* (2 John 9). We cannot judge the salvation or condemnation of anyone. Even so, it is true that Scripture offers no promise of salvation to the un-immersed; a reality that was stated eloquently by F. D. Srygley more than one hundred years ago.

As I understand the N.T., the 'pious unimmersed' ought to be immersed. And in case they are not immersed, I know of no promise in the N.T. that they will be saved. But as to whether God will make allowance for honest mistakes, and save those who think they are obeying him when in reality they are doing something he has not commanded in lieu of what he has commanded, is a question for God to settle, and I decline to take any part in it.[2]

The greatest challenge, however, concerns those who present themselves as teachers of God's doctrine, but fail to teach it appropriately. For these men, God seems to allow no excuses (Galatians 1: 6-9). Once a man lifts himself to the position of teacher in the eyes of men, he places upon himself a greater responsibility than that of other men, at least in the eyes of God. For this reason it is best for that man to be confident that his doctrine harmonizes completely with the fullness of Scripture.

No man will see heaven without an honest desire to please and honor God (2 Timothy 2: 22; 1 John 3: 19-20). Yet the Bible also places considerable emphasis upon doctrinal purity (Romans 6: 17; Ephesians 4: 14; 1 Timothy 1: 3; Titus 1: 9). Neither a sincere heart nor devoted obedience to the commands of God may be dismissed as we seek a relationship with Him and salvation through the blood of Christ. That being the case, perhaps we should regard purity of doctrine, including the doctrine of baptism, with the respect it is given in God's Word.

NOTES FOR CHAPTER 18

1. Hicks, John Mark, and Taylor, Greg, Down in the River to Pray, p. 180, Leafwood Publishers, 2004.

2. F. D. Srygley, 'From the Papers,' Gospel Advocate 32, March 26, 1890, p. 193.

Chapter XIX
The Apostles: Baptized in Jesus' Name?

Other than Ananias' baptism of Paul, we are not told within the pages of Scripture that the apostles were ever immersed *in Jesus' name*. This is, however, the baptism that was *taught* by the apostles. What can we determine from this curious scriptural silence? One of two possibilities exists. The first is that, indeed, the apostles did receive the baptism they taught. The second possibility views their foundational role in the establishment of the church (Ephesians 2: 20) as an indication that they may not have been required by God to submit to baptism in Jesus' name.

The baptism of the apostles *in Jesus' name* is a challenging topic simply because it is not discussed specifically in Scripture. The fact that it is not mentioned suggests that witnessing the apostles' baptism is not a critical matter in our relationship with God. Nonetheless, we will spend some time on the matter taking into consideration all available information.

Baptized by John

We can easily determine that the apostles received the baptism of John the Baptist. As John's disciples questioned him concerning the baptism that was being performed by Jesus' disciples, it was not a question about their *authority*, but seems to reflect jealousy on the part of John's disciples (John 3: 25). Additionally, the apostles would not have been among those who opposed the will of God by refusing to participate in John's baptism (Luke 7: 30).

Biblical support for the apostles' baptism by John the Baptist can be found in the first chapter of the book of Acts. When Peter called together the disciples in Jerusalem in order to replace Judas, one requirement was that the candidate must have been with them *beginning with John's baptism* (Acts 1: 21-22). Many look to this statement by Peter and assume that he is referring to the event of Jesus' baptism by John. However, the gospel writers do not place these men with Jesus at the time of His baptism.

When Jesus went to John to be baptized by him it was His first public appearance as the Messiah (Matthew 3: 13-17). After He had been baptized, Jesus went to the desert where He fasted and was tempted by Satan (Matthew 4: 1-11). It was not until after His time in the desert that Jesus went to Galilee where He chose the men who would later become His apostles. Therefore, when Peter spoke of selecting a replacement for Judas, declaring that the man should have been with them *'beginning from the baptism of John'* (Acts 1: 22), he could not have been referring to Jesus' baptism by John. These men were not present with Jesus at that time. Consequently, the only possibility is that Peter had in mind either the period of time during which John baptized or the candidate's immersion in water as performed by John. Since we can be confident that these men were not among those who refused baptism (Luke 7: 30), it is most reasonable to conclude that Peter is talking about a candidate who had received baptism at the hands of John.

Baptized in the Name of Jesus

We can conclude that the apostles were baptized by John the Baptist, but did they ever receive baptism *in Jesus' name*? In addressing this question, the first point we must consider is whether the apostles *needed* to experience baptism in Jesus' name. We look, then, to Paul's encounter with the Ephesians who had received the baptism of John (Acts 19: 1-7). Realizing that these men had not met the Holy Spirit in baptism, Paul baptized them *in Jesus' name*. The logical conclusion from this episode is that the baptism of John was insufficient within the covenant of grace, and that those who had previously submitted to John's baptism had not received the Holy Spirit.

Additional insight is offered in the verses just prior to Paul's re-baptism of these men in Ephesus. At an earlier time, while Aquila and Priscilla were in Ephesus, a Jewish man by the name of Apollos made his way there fervently teaching what he knew about the Lord. However, where baptism was concerned we find that *'he knew only the baptism of John'* (Acts 18: 25). As Aquila and Priscilla taught him more fully the things of God, we are never told that Apollos was actually baptized in Jesus' name. This seems to suggest a possible clash between the actions and understanding of Paul and that of Aquila and Priscilla regarding baptism.

A variety of arguments have been offered to address this apparent inconsistency. Some have suggested that the men of Ephesus with whom Paul met may have received John's baptism sometime *after* the Day of Pentecost. John was executed prior to Pentecost, but the pre-Pentecost baptism John practiced could have been administered by one of his disciples after his death and after

Pentecost – disciples like Apollos. If this was the case, it might mean that those who received the baptism of John before Pentecost may not need to be baptized in Jesus' name. Accordingly, if Apollos had received his baptism prior to Pentecost, this rationale would explain why we have no record of his re-baptism in Ephesus.

One problem with this logic becomes evident when we remember Paul's reason for re-baptizing the men at Ephesus. When they were originally baptized they had not received the Holy Spirit (Acts 19: 3-4). The promise of the Spirit is found only in baptism performed *in Jesus' name* (Acts 2: 38). Additionally, Paul did not ask the men of Ephesus *when* they had been baptized. He was only curious as to the nature of their baptism. Also, on the Day of Pentecost when Peter commanded his listeners to be baptized, there were surely those in the crowd who had received John's baptism (e.g., the one hundred twenty disciples). Yet Peter commanded baptism for every willing individual within the sound of his voice (Acts 2: 38). He did not differentiate between those who had received John's baptism and those who had not. Those who had been baptized by John were apparently baptized in Jesus' name at that time.

Since Apollos had received the baptism of John, his condition corresponded with those in the crowd on the Day of Pentecost who had received John's baptism. We can also liken his situation to that of the men at Ephesus in that, through the baptism of John, he would not have received the Spirit. Additionally, although we are not told specifically that Apollos was baptized in Jesus' name while at Ephesus, neither are we told that he failed to receive Christian baptism at that time. In fact, we have reason to believe this is exactly what happened.

From Luke's observation that Apollos knew *only* John's baptism, we can assume that there exists a baptism of greater significance – baptism in Jesus' name. Yet, according to Luke it is Apollos' perspective on baptism that was inadequate. He indicates that this was the chief issue Aquila and Priscilla would need to address with Apollos. When they *'took him aside and explained to him the way of God more accurately'* (Acts 18: 26), it is not difficult to picture Apollos receiving Christian baptism at that time, especially since he would later baptize others in the name of Jesus (1 Corinthians 1: 12). Since his situation mirrored both the disciples in Jerusalem and Ephesus, this is the most sensible conclusion.

Furthermore, we can infer from Luke's terminology and the context of the passage that Apollos *knew (επισταμαι)* the baptism of John in the same fashion that the Colossians *knew* the grace of God. Their knowing God's grace was reference to their receiving and experiencing it. Similarly, Apollos knew John's baptism in that he had received and experienced it (Colossians 1: 6). This was his shortcoming with respect to baptism. The word *επισταμαι* (*epistamai*) represents not just his knowledge of, but also his familiarity with, John's baptism. He *understood and had experienced* only John's baptism. This was the baptism upon which his conversion and teaching were based. Luke's remark that he *knew* John's baptism indicates that both Apollos' perception of baptism and his baptismal experience were deemed by Aquila and Priscilla to be incomplete in the new covenant.

Reading the account of Apollos, we are told that he was *'fervent in spirit'* (Acts 18: 25). Some men have suggested that this means Apollos received the Spirit at some time prior to Ephesus. However, the word *spirit* is not a reference to the Holy Spirit in this case, but points to Apollos' *spirit of enthusiasm*. This is why translators do not treat the word *spirit*, in this instance, as a proper name or title. However, when Paul taught the Ephesians, and as Peter addressed the crowd on the Day of Pentecost, the word points directly to the Holy Spirit in relation to Christian baptism.

What does all of this have to do with the baptism of the apostles? Since the narrative in these passages points to the inadequacy of John's baptism in the new covenant, and in the absence of any Scripture specifically exempting the apostles from baptism in Jesus' name, we have every reason to believe that this same principle would equally apply to them. While this is the most reasonable determination, based solely on what we know about John's baptism, there is actually additional evidence in the New Testament that speaks to the baptism of the twelve.

It is true that the apostles, on the Day of Pentecost, did not need to be baptized in Jesus' name in order to receive the Holy Spirit. They received the Spirit while *'they were all with one accord in one place'* (Acts 2: 1). However, at the house of Cornelius, when Peter saw that Gentiles had received the Holy Spirit in a manner similar to what he and the others had experienced on the Day of Pentecost, he immediately commanded that they be baptized in water (Acts 10: 45-47). Peter did not view the outpouring of the Spirit as license to dismiss the waters of baptism. Additionally, we are taught in Scripture that forgiveness of sins is provided at the time of baptism (Acts 2: 38). Since the apostles were not sinless, they were undoubtedly obedient in seeking forgiveness in the manner commanded by God, which is baptism (Acts 2: 38). While they had surely received forgiveness at the time of John's baptism, this was a new day and a new covenant.

It is doubtful that the apostles would have taught baptism to others as a command of God while resisting that command for themselves. We also find that, in the early stages of the church, many men sought desperately to discredit the work of the apostles. The very fact that no one ever questioned, within the pages of Scripture, why the apostles had not received the baptism they taught gives us reason to believe that they were baptized. Had such a question been raised, no doubt Paul would have addressed it in one of his epistles. Arguably, then, Scripture presumes, by its very silence on the subject, that the apostles were indeed baptized according to God's will.

Some may ask, *'If scriptural silence concerning the apostles' baptism leads us to believe they were, indeed, baptized, why would this not hold true for infants as well?'* That is a fair question that is easily answered. The primary answer is the baptism of the apostles does not conflict with apostolic instruction concerning the relationship between belief and baptism. This relationship is fundamental in New Testament instruction about baptism.

Furthermore, we find no concrete example of infant baptism in Scripture. However, we know that the apostle Paul was baptized in Jesus' name (Acts 22: 16). While he was bestowed with the same powers and fulfilled the same role as the other apostles who had received the outpouring on the Day of Pentecost, God saw fit that he should be baptized in water. Given the fact that we are provided a biblical example of a baptized apostle, there is no reason to question the baptism of the rest. In fact, the testimony of a baptized apostle should settle any argument to the contrary. Apostles were baptized. It seems, then, that the Bible is not completely silent on the subject.

Apparently the topic of the baptism of the apostles did arise during the life of Tertullian, a church leader who lived in the late second century. His response to those who accused the apostles of failing to receive the baptism of Christ was very direct.

> When, however, the prescript is laid down that "without baptism, salvation is attainable by none" (chiefly on the ground of that declaration of the Lord, who says, "Unless one be born of water, he hath not life"), there arise immediately scrupulous, nay rather audacious, doubts on the part of some, "how, in accordance with that prescript, salvation is attainable by the apostles, whom-Paul excepted-we do not find baptized in the Lord? Nay, since Paul is the only one of them who has put on *the garment of* Christ's baptism, either the peril of all the others who lack the water of Christ is prejudged, that the prescript may be maintained, or else the prescript is rescinded if salvation has been ordained even for the unbaptized." I have heard-the Lord is my witness-doubts of that kind: that none may imagine me so abandoned as to ex-cogitate, unprovoked, in the licence of my pen, ideas which would inspire others with scruple.

> And now, as far as I shall be able, I will reply to them who affirm "that the apostles were unbaptized." For if they had undergone the human baptism of John, and were longing for that of the Lord, *then* since the Lord Himself had defined baptism to be *one*; (saying to Peter, who was desirous of being thoroughly bathed, "He who hath once bathed hath no necessity *to wash* a second time; "which, of course, He would not have said at all to one *not* baptized;) even here we have a conspicuous proof against those who, in order to destroy the sacrament of water, deprive the apostles even of John's baptism. Can it seem credible that "the way of the Lord," that is, the baptism of John, had not then been "prepared" in those persons who were being destined to *open* the way of the Lord throughout the whole world? The Lord Himself, though no "repentance" was due from *Him*, was baptized: was baptism not necessary for *sinners*? As for the fact, then, that "others were not baptized"-they, however, were not companions of Christ, but enemies of the faith, doctors of the law and Pharisees. From which fact is gathered an additional suggestion, that, since the *opposers* of the Lord *refused* to be baptized, they who *followed* the Lord *were* baptized, and were not like-minded with their own rivals: especially when, if there were any one to whom they clave, the Lord had exalted John above him (by the testimony) saying," Among them who are born of women *there is* none greater than John the Baptist."

> Others make the suggestion (forced enough), clearly "that the apostles then served the turn of baptism when in their little ship, were sprinkled and covered with the waves: that Peter himself also was immersed enough when he walked on the sea." It is, however, as I think, one thing to be sprinkled or intercepted by the violence of the sea; another thing to be baptized in obedience to the discipline of religion. But that little ship did present a figure of the Church, in that she is disquieted "in the

sea," that is, in the world, "by the waves," that is, by persecutions and temptations; the Lord, through patience, sleeping as it were, until, roused in their last extremities by the prayers of the saints, He checks the world, and restores tranquillity to His own.

Now, whether they were baptized in any manner whatever, or whether they continued unbathed to the end-so that even that saying of the Lord touching the "one bath" does, under the person of Peter, merely regard *us*-still, to determine concerning the salvation of the apostles is audacious enough, because on *them* the prerogative even of first choice, and thereafter of undivided intimacy, might be able to confer the compendious grace of baptism, seeing they (I think) followed Him who was wont to promise salvation to every believer. "Thy faith," He would say, "hath saved thee;" and, "Thy sins shall be remitted thee," on thy believing, of course, albeit thou be not *yet* baptized. If that was wanting to the apostles, I know not in the faith of what things it was, that, roused by one word of the Lord, *one* left the toll-booth behind for ever; *another* deserted father and ship, and the craft by which he gained his living; *a third*, who disdained his father's obsequies, fulfilled, before he heard it, that highest precept of the Lord, "He who prefers father or mother to me, is not worthy of me." Tertullian, <u>On Baptism, Chapter X2. - Of the Necessity of Baptism to Salvation.</u>[1]

Tertullian claimed that if, for some reason, the apostles who received the initial outpouring of the Spirit on the Day of Pentecost did not receive water baptism, what we must recognize is their unequaled status in the church age. These were the very men through whom the Holy Spirit would make known His presence. Theirs was an unparalleled role at a unique time in history – a role that would/could never be equaled or repeated. Nonetheless, concluding that these men did not receive water baptism is a stretch given their leading role in the early church.

Baptism of the Apostles – A Most Reasonable Conclusion

Finally, it is reasonable to believe that the apostles were baptized *in Jesus' name* simply because this is the most sensible conclusion. The apostles walked before the people as examples of what God expected from His disciples (2 Thessalonians 3: 9). Since the apostles taught baptism we have no reason to question whether or not they experienced it. That is certainly the case with repentance. Who would even think of questioning whether or not the apostles actually repented of their sins? Repentance, like baptism, is a fundamental teaching of the apostles throughout the New Testament. However, other than the time Peter wept over his denial of Christ (Matthew 26: 75), the apostles' repentance for their sins is not detailed in Scripture. Nevertheless, we can, and do, assume that the apostles repented. In fact, they almost certainly repented on a daily basis.

While we are not told exactly *when* the apostles received baptism in Jesus' name, it is most reasonable to believe that it occurred on the Day of Pentecost since others who were baptized that day were *'added to them'* (Acts 2: 41). Prior to others becoming part of Christ's body, the foundation of the apostles must have been laid (Ephesians 2: 20).

Men actually gain nothing by questioning whether or not the apostles were baptized. The only imaginable reason for doubt is the opportunity to somehow discredit the redemptive value of baptism. However, the baptism of the apostles is irrelevant; it has no bearing on our salvation. For those of us who live in the church age, the call is uncomplicated. It does not rely on the baptismal status of the apostles. We are simply asked to respond to the instructions provided in the Bible regarding baptism and the normal pattern of salvation as it is presented in Scripture.

NOTES FOR CHAPTER 19

1. Anti-Nicene Fathers, Volume III, Chapter XII - Of the Necessity of Baptism to Salvation.

Tertullian suggests that it is unimportant to our salvation whether or not the apostles received baptism in water in the name of Jesus. This is because they received the Spirit as a matter of this divine manifestation of the Spirit similar to the manner by which the Spirit was received by Cornelius and the other Gentiles. If, indeed, the apostles were not baptized (other than John's baptism) divine intervention/revelation is the only reason.

Chapter XX
At the Feet of the Apostles

The Apostolic Fathers

Imagine how educational and inspirational it would have been to sit at the feet of the apostles and listen as they taught those in the first century about Jesus. The apostles were not just men who carried out an assignment for God. These men were specially selected to carry on the work that would help establish the very kingdom of God here on earth. Each one had spent considerable time with Jesus and understood things that go far beyond the grasp of other human beings.

Some men actually did have the opportunity to study under the direct leadership and guidance of the apostles. These men, many of whom became known as the *apostolic fathers*, were charged with the task of carrying forward the teachings of Jesus as the apostles, one by one, lost their lives. Living and working alongside the apostles offered these men the opportunity to not only read the words they had written, but have intimate conversations regarding the meaning of the written word. Reading their various works affords us the opportunity to take a look at the views of these men who received direct or indirect instruction from the apostles. This should provide a better perspective as to the apostles' intended meaning in their writings on baptism.

It is always risky to cite writings outside of Scripture in an effort to reinforce the teachings of the apostles. Often the works of other men reflect personal prejudices and doctrinal inconsistencies. It is true that those who followed after the apostles occasionally drifted from scriptural instruction. Therefore, the following excerpts are not intended to portray these men as authoritative on doctrinal issues. The Bible is, and must remain, our sole source of doctrine. Nonetheless, a review of the works of these men provides insight into the consistent and unified view of the role of baptism in the early church, despite any doctrinal differences that may arise in other areas.

In the early stages of the church The Epistle of Barnabas was believed to have been written by Barnabas, Paul's companion. More recently, however, some scholars have claimed that the letter may have been penned by either Barnabas of Alexandria or another apostolic student of the same name. Nevertheless, many of the early church fathers, attributing the work to Barnabas of Cyprus with strong conviction, considered the letter equivalent with Scripture, believing it might easily have been added to the Bible. In it we discover these words concerning the ceremony of baptism:

> Now let us see if the Lord has been at any pains to give us a foreshadowing of the waters of Baptism and of the cross. Regarding the former, we have the evidence of Scripture that Israel would refuse to accept the washing which confers the remission of sins and would set up a substitution of their own instead [Jer 22:13; Isa 16:1-2; 33:16-18; Psalm 1:3-6]. Observe there how he describes both the water and the cross in the same figure. His meaning is, "Blessed are those who go down into the water with their hopes set on the cross." Here he is saying that after we have stepped down into the water, burdened with sin and defilement, we come up out of it bearing fruit, with reverence in our hearts and the hope of Jesus in our souls. This He saith, because we go down into the water laden with sins and filth, and rise up from it bearing fruit in the heart, resting our fear and hope on Jesus in the spirit.[1]

*　　*　　*　　*　　*

One of the earliest and certainly better known students of the apostles was a man named Ignatius. We do not know exactly when he was born and when he died, although there is evidence that he died somewhere around AD 110 between the ages of 75 and 85. Known as Ignatius of Antioch, he was a student of the apostle John and may have done some studying under Paul. During his final journey to Rome, which ended in his martyrdom, he wrote several letters to churches and individuals. In The Epistle of Ignatius to the Ephesians we read the following passage:

> For our God, Jesus Christ, was, according to the appointment of God, conceived in the womb by Mary, of the seed of David, but by the Holy Ghost. He was born and baptized, that by His passion He might purify the water.[2]

In The Epistle of Ignatius to the Trallians we find:

> Wherefore also, ye appear to me to live not after the manner of men, but according to Jesus Christ, who died for us, in order that, by believing in His death, ye may by baptism be made partakers of His resurrection.[3]

On that same journey he wrote to his dear friend, Polycarp, these encouraging words:

> Let your baptism endure as your arms; your faith as your helmet; your love as your spear; your patience as a complete panoply. Let your works be the charge assigned to you, that ye may receive a worthy recompense. Be long-suffering, therefore, with one another, in meekness, as God is towards you. May I have joy of you for ever! [4]

In each of these letters Ignatius wrote concerning baptism. And what was the baptism to which he referred? From his letter to the Ephesians we learn that it was baptism in water. Coincidently, in his letter to the Trallians, he states plainly that this baptism is the very means by which we are, *'...made partakers of His resurrection.'* This is quite similar to Paul's explanation to the Romans and Colossians about the role of baptism in the church age (Romans 6: 1-22; Colossians 2: 11-12).

*   *   *   *   *

Polycarp, known as Polycarp of Smyrna, who was just mentioned in association with Ignatius, was another student of the apostle John. Born in AD 69, he was raised in the church and it is believed he was baptized around the age of 10 or 11. Although Polycarp was considerably younger than Ignatius, their difference in age could not prevent the two men from becoming very close friends.

Little is available in the way of written documents from Polycarp. Much of his teaching, however, is revealed in the writings of his best known student – a man named Irenaeus. The only confirmed writing directly from Polycarp is a letter he penned to the church at Philippi. He does not directly address the issue of baptism, presumably because he was writing to those who had already been baptized. In his letter, however, it is interesting to note this excerpt:

> The letters of Ignatius which were sent to us by him, and others as many as we had by us, we send unto you, according as ye gave charge; the which are subjoined to this letter; from which ye will be able to gain great advantage. For they comprise faith and endurance and every kind of edification, which pertaineth unto our Lord. Moreover concerning Ignatius himself and those that were with him, if ye have any sure tidings, certify us. [5]

Polycarp sent the letter written to him by Ignatius so that they *'will be able to gain great advantage.'* He wrote that these letters contained *'every kind of edification.'* He appears to find no fault with anything in the letter from Ignatius, including his reference to baptism.

The Ante-Nicene Fathers

The Ante-Nicene Fathers were a group of early Christian leaders who led the church in the post-apostolic period until the First Council of Nicea in A.D. 325. These men did not have the advantage of sitting at the feet of the apostles, but some of the earlier Ante-Nicene Fathers were students of men who were students of the apostles.

Irenaeus, born around AD 130, studied under the guiding hand of Polycarp. When confronted with those who, in his time, tried to deny the salvation value of water baptism, he wrote the following:

> And we come to refute them, we shall know in its fitting-place, that this class of men have been instigated by Satan to a denial of that baptism which is regeneration to God, and thus to a renunciation of the whole faith...For the baptism instituted by the visible Jesus was for the remission of sins.[6]

He also wrote:

> As we are lepers in sin, we are made clean from our old transgressions by means of the sacred water and the invocation of the Lord. We are thus spiritually regenerated as newborn infants, even as the Lord declared: "Except a man be born again through water and the Spirit, he shall not enter the kingdom of heaven."[7]

The writings of Irenaeus were based on the teachings of Polycarp, who had studied under the Apostle John. The Apostle John is the author of the gospel of John where we find the account of Nicodemus, which is referenced in the last quote. It is reasonable to conclude, then, that Polycarp, who did study under the Apostle John, understood Jesus' phrase *'born of water'* to be a direct reference to water baptism. Irenaeus also emphatically states that, *'...a denial of that baptism...'* is equivalent to, *'...a renunciation of the whole faith...'* He also wrote:

> Moreover, those things which were created from the waters were blessed by God, so that this might also be a sign that men would at a

future time receive repentance and remission of sins through water and the bath of regeneration -- all who proceed to the truth and are born again and receive a blessing from God.[8]

* * * * *

Justin Martyr was born very near the time of the death of the apostle John. He was not raised in a Christian home but, when he was a young man he converted to Christianity. While it is true that he could not have studied directly under the apostles, he was most certainly influenced by those who had heard the apostles. His First Apology was addressed to Emperor Marcus Aurelius.

I will also relate the manner in which we dedicated ourselves to God when we had been made new through Christ; lest, if we omit this, we seem to be unfair in the explanation we are making. As many as are persuaded and believe that what we teach and say is true, and undertake to be able to live accordingly, are instructed to pray and to entreat God with fasting, for the remission of their sins that are past, we praying and fasting with them. Then they are brought by us where there is water, and are regenerated in the same manner in which we were ourselves regenerated. For, in the name of God, the Father and Lord of the universe, and of our Saviour Jesus Christ, and of the Holy Spirit, they then receive the washing with water. For Christ also said, "Except ye be born again, ye shall not enter into the kingdom of heaven." Now, that it is impossible for those who have once been born to enter into their mothers' wombs, is manifest to all. And how those who have sinned and repent shall escape their sins, is declared by Esaias the prophet, as I wrote above; he thus speaks: "Wash you, make you clean; put away the evil of your doings from your souls; learn to do well; judge the fatherless, and plead for the widow: and come and let us reason together, saith the Lord. And though your sins be as scarlet, I will make them white like wool; and though they be as crimson, I will make them white as snow. But if ye refuse and rebel, the sword shall devour you: for the mouth of the Lord hath spoken it."[9]

'For at that time they obtain for themselves the washing in water in the name of God the Master of all and Father, and of our Savior Jesus Christ, and of the Holy Spirit. For Christ also said, "Unless you are regenerated, you cannot enter the kingdom of heaven."'[10]

Once again we find a reference to Jesus' conversation with Nicodemus and the true meaning of the phrase *'born of water.'* In his <u>Dialogue with Trypho</u>, we read the following:

"By reason, therefore, of this laver of repentance and knowledge of God, which has been ordained on account of the transgression of God's people, as Isaiah cries, we have believed, and testify that that very baptism which he announced is alone able to purify those who have repented; and this is the water of life. But the cisterns which you have dug for yourselves are broken and profitless to you. For what is the use of that baptism which cleanses the flesh and body alone? Baptize the soul from wrath and from covetousness, from envy, and from hatred; and, lo! the body is pure."[11]

Justin Martyr was a true believer in the efficacy of baptism by water. He understood that, if water only cleanses the flesh and body and is not accompanied by a truly repentant heart, it is of no use spiritually. His remark parallels Peter's statement regarding the salvation value of baptism as he declared, *'not the removal of the filth of the flesh, but the answer of a good conscience toward God'* (1 Peter 3: 21). Certainly it was a fundamental belief by Justin Martyr that water baptism was a requirement based on the teachings of the apostles.

*   *   *   *   *

Tertullian was a Christian leader in the second half of the second century and into the early third century. He wrote letters on special topics, including baptism. Consider the following writing regarding Paul, the Apostle:

But they roll back *an objection* from *that* apostle himself, in that he said, "For Christ sent me not to baptize", as if by this argument baptism were done away! For *if so*, why did he baptize Gaius, and Crispus, and the house of Stephanas? However, even if Christ had not sent him to baptize, yet He had given *other* apostles the precept to baptize. But these words were written to the Corinthians in regard of the circumstances of that particular time; seeing that schisms and dissensions were agitated among them, while one attributes *everything* to Paul, another to Apollos. For which reason the "peace-making" apostle, for fear he should seem to claim all *gifts* for himself, says that he had been sent "not to baptize, but to preach." For preaching is the prior thing, baptizing the posterior. Therefore the preaching came *first*: but I think baptizing withal was *lawful* to Him to whom preaching was.[12]

For those who argue against immersion as the *one baptism* addressed by Paul, consider the following excerpts from the works of Tertullian. They are very revealing with respect to Paul's statement.

> Thus, too, in *our* case, the unction runs carnally, (*i.e.* on the body,) but profits spiritually; in the same way as the *act* of baptism itself too is carnal, in that we are plunged in water, *but* the *effect* spiritual, in that we are freed from sins.[13]

> There is to us one, and but one, baptism; as well according to the Lord's gospel as according to the apostle's letters, inasmuch as *he says*, "One God, and one baptism, and one church in the heavens." We enter, then, the font *once: once* are sins washed away, because they ought never to be repeated. But the Jewish Israel bathes daily, because he is daily being defiled: and, for fear that *defilement* should be practiced among *us* also, therefore was the definition touching the one bathing made. Happy water, which *once* washes away; which does not mock sinners (with vain hopes); which does not, by being infected with the repetition of impurities, again defile them whom it has washed![14]

*   *   *   *   *

Clement of Alexandria, an early Greek theologian, was a contemporary of Tertullian. While his date of birth is unknown it is believed he died around AD 215. He, too, wrote regarding the purification that could be found in baptism alone and saw in Jesus' words to Nicodemus a call to rebirth involving baptism.

> 'It is the washing through which we are cleansed of our sins…We who have repented of our sins, renounced our faults, and are purified by baptism.'[15]

> But you will perhaps say, "What does the baptism of water contribute toward the worship of God?" In the first place, because that which has pleased God is fulfilled. In the second place, because when you are regenerated and born again of water and of God, the frailty of your former birth, which you have through men, is cut off, and so …you shall be able to attain salvation; but otherwise it is impossible. For thus has the true Prophet [Jesus] testified to us with an oath: "Verily, I say to you, that unless a man is born again of water….he shall not enter into the kingdom of heaven."[16]

*   *   *   *   *

The intent here is not to portray these writings as anything other than what they are: letters of the early leaders in the decades of the church following the death of the apostles. However, they do provide important confirmation that the apostles continued teaching immersion as the baptism of Scripture as long as they lived. Additionally, they affirm the changes that take place at the time of baptism as taught in the epistles. While these early Christian leaders did not agree in *all* things, and occasionally even strayed dramatically from some apostolic principles, especially near the end of the second century, there does seem to be unanimity on one topic. That agreement involves immersion in water as the biblical means to receive forgiveness of sins and enter the kingdom of God.

These writings also seem to offer implied confirmation that infant baptism would be fruitless. Justin Martyr wrote, *'that very baptism which he announced is alone able to purify those who have repented...'* He also noted that baptism was for, *'As many as are persuaded and believe that what we teach and say is true....'* Again he wrote that those who would be baptized *'are instructed to pray and to entreat God with fasting.'* Infants are incapable of repentance. Infants are incapable of belief. Infants are incapable of fasting and prayer.

As a side note, it is of interest that many of the men quoted here were eventually martyred for their beliefs. Marcus Aurelius beheaded Justin Martyr in AD 165 for his refusal to worship pagan gods. Ignatius was condemned and devoured by wild beasts in Rome somewhere around AD 110. In AD 155 Polycarp was burned at the stake in Smyrna at age 86. Irenaeus, in AD 202, was martyred under the rule of Emperor Lucius Septimus Severus.

The quotes offered in this chapter are but a small token of the literature available from the early church fathers concerning the efficacy of baptism. More would have been presented if it were possible that it would have any additional impact. The apostles taught and practiced water baptism (immersion) until the end of their physical lives. We have good witnesses who have been able to confirm this. For those who assert that water baptism was discarded during the ministry of Paul, it seems that these Christian teachers/historians disagree.

NOTES FOR CHAPTER 20

1. Barnabas, THE EPISTLE OF BARNABAS (c. A.D. 70), (11:1-10) – While some ascribe this letter to Barnabas of Alexandria, an early church father, most scholars agree that it is the work of Paul's companion.

2. Ignatius, The Epistle of Ignatius to the Ephesians, Chapter XV2I, THE GLORY OF THE CROSS.

3. Ignatius, The Epistle of Ignatius to the Trallians, Chapter 2, BE SUBJECT TO THE BISHOP, ETC.

4. Ignatius, THE DUTIES OF THE CHRISTIAN FLOCK, Chapter VI.

5. Polycarp, The Epistle of Polycarp 13: 2.

6.Irenaeus, CHAP. XXI.--THE VIEWS OF REDEMPTION ENTERTAINED BY THESE HERETICS.

7. Irenaeus, Cited by J. Pelikan, The Emergence of the Catholic Tradition (100-600), p. 164.

8. Irenaeus, ST. THEOPHILUS OF ANTIOCH (c. A.D. 181), (To Autolycus 2:16).

9. Justin Martyr, Chapter LXI.-Christian Baptism.

10. Justin Martyr, Apology I, 61.

11. Justin, Martyr, Dialogue with Trypho, Chapter XIV -- RIGHTEOUSNESS IS NOT PLACED IN JEWISH RITES, BUT IN THE CONVERSION OF THE HEART GIVEN IN BAPTISM BY CHRIST.

12. Tertullian, On Baptism, Chapter XIV-Of Paul's Assertion, that He Had Not Been Sent to Baptize.

13. Tertullian, Chapter V2.-Of the Unction.

14. Tertullian, Chapter XV.-Unity of Baptism. Remarks on Heretical And Jewish Baptism.

15. Clement, Clement Of Alexandria Instructor I. vi. 32:1.

16. Clement, *RECOGNITIONS OF CLEMENT* (c. A.D. 221), **(Recognitions 6:9).**

Conclusion

Many will read this book out of curiosity, seeing it as an opportunity to examine a different point of view. Most will already have developed their own doctrine with respect to the role of baptism within God's plan of salvation, and this book will not sway them. Given the prevailing view of baptism in the modern world, a vast number will undoubtedly consider this book offensive while others will vigorously condemn the teaching presented here.

It is true that the point of view expressed in this book is uncompromising when it comes to the teaching of baptism. That persistence is founded upon the words of Scripture. Paul, in his letter to the Galatians, identified baptism as the time that we cover ourselves with Jesus (Galatians 3: 27). He taught the Romans that we begin our new life as we rise from the baptismal waters (Romans 6: 4). Peter taught that baptism is necessary for forgiveness of sins (Acts 2: 38) and called it *'an antitype which now saves us... '* (1 Peter 3: 21). Jesus told the apostles, prior to His ascension, that it is the individual who believes and is baptized who will be saved (Mark 16: 16). He explained to Nicodemus, *'unless one is born of water and the Spirit, he cannot enter the kingdom of God'* (John 3: 5). We find that Jesus' words, too, are unbending. Therefore, if we believe that one who is not *born of water* cannot be saved, how can anything less be taught?

Challenging nearly five centuries of beliefs about baptism may appear on the surface to be a hopeless undertaking since apparently so few wish to hear it. Perhaps, however, there are those who will be influenced and make the decision to be baptized for the forgiveness of sins, just as the Bible teaches. At the very least, it is my hope that men will become curious enough to seriously reconsider, with an open and honest heart, biblical instruction related to baptism. It is for this reason and for my own conscience that this book has been written.

What is remarkable is the fact that so very few ever question the teaching of men that denies the role of baptism as it is presented in Scripture. Most men simply accept the claim that clear biblical instruction about baptism does not mean what it says. Rarely does anyone ask how Spirit-inspired teaching about baptism could be faulty.

The establishment of baptism as an essential command of God is easily determined from an honest study of God's Word. Baptism is recognized as a vital ingredient of the saving faith of which the apostles wrote. It is upon our shoulders, then, to dismiss the doctrine of men concerning baptism, as difficult as that may be, and found our beliefs on God's Word alone. It is the responsibility of each man to examine Scripture to learn God's will. If the apostles taught that we could be saved by baptism with the Holy Spirit alone, this book would not exist. Nor would it have been written if the apostles had taught that we *only* needed to believe or to repent or to confess to be saved. But, alas, that is not the lesson of Scripture.

Does God have the authority to save someone who has never received immersion in water? God's authority is not, and never has been, in question. He has the authority to do what He wills. Consequently, God has the power to save anyone He chooses in any manner He chooses. With that in mind, we must equally accept that He has the authority to establish baptism as essential for those who would receive forgiveness of sins and eternal life. Indeed, that is exactly what He has done.

While God has the authority to select how men will be saved, He has not granted us that same latitude. So the real issue when it comes to baptism is not God's authority, but the authority of mankind. We have not been given license to choose how we will be saved or to neglect God's commands. At no time have we been given authority to dismiss immersion as the method of baptism or to introduce the Sinner's Prayer as a means to salvation. In the end, we have no reason to believe that we will be measured by any scale, or any plan of salvation, established by men. When judgment comes, the only scale that really matters is God's and the only commands that matter are those proclaimed in Scripture.

It is not the aim of this book to identify, from a personal perspective, those who will or will not be saved. No man has that prerogative. However, it is fully meant to portray what God has to say, through Scripture, about who will receive eternal life. The intent is not to judge, but to teach. We as men can do no more, but we can certainly do no less. That is the mission with which we have been charged. Scripture depicts baptism as vital for the man or woman who earnestly seeks salvation. God's Word is so straightforward on this issue that it is actually difficult to understand how modern views of the role of baptism have become so popular. The numerous passages that identify baptism as a matter of justification (Acts 2: 38; 1 Corinthians 6: 11), rebirth/renewal (John 3: 5; Romans 6: 1-4; Titus 3: 5), and ultimately salvation (Mark 16: 16; 1 Peter 3: 21) are so uncomplicated that it seems like it would take considerable resolve to come to any other conclusion. If we are to remain faithful to the message of the gospel, it is critical that we recognize the role for baptism that God has revealed in His Word.

It is my plea that you consider the value placed upon immersion as it has been presented to us in Scripture. Is it Jesus' teaching? Certainly it is. Is a doctrine that resists baptism or diminishes its value a doctrine that is contrary to the teaching of Christ? I believe it is. What do you believe?

Bibliography

Ante-Nicene Fathers, On Baptism [Online], http://www.ccel.org/fathers2/ANF-03/anf03-49.htm.

Araujo, Luzia and Valerie Grundy, Larouse Portuguese English Pocket Dictionary, Larousse/VUEF, 2003.

Atkerson, Steven, 2003, Baptism's Practice [Online] http://www.ntrf.org/regen.html, (Accessed 01 June 2004).

Barclay, William, 1976, The Daily Study Bible Series, The Acts of the Apostles, The Westminster Press, Philadelphia, PA.

Beasley-Murray, G. R., 1994, Baptism in the New Testament, William B. Eerdsman Publishing Company, Grand Rapids, MI.

Brants, T. W., 1977, The Gospel Plan of Salvation, Gospel Advocate, reprint, Nashville, TN.

Brown, Robert K. & Comfort, Philip W., 1990, The New GREEK ENGLISH Interlinear New Testament, Tyndale House Publishers, Wheaton, IL.

Campbell, Alexander, 1839, The Christian System, Forrester & Campbell, Pittsburgh, PA.

Campbell, Alexander, 1851, Christian Baptism With Its Antecedents And Consequents, Alexander Campbell.

Chalmers, Marianne and Martine Pierquin, 2000, Pocket Oxford Hachette French Dictionary Second Edition, p. 337, Oxford University Press.

Conant, Thomas Jefferson, 2002, The Meaning and Use of Baptizein, The Wakeman Trust, London.

Copeland, Mark A., 2002, Baptism in the Preaching of the Apostles [Online] http://www.bible.ca/eo/ba/ba_01.htm, (Accessed 24 Feb 2005).

Copeland, Mark A., 2002, "Baptism in the Teaching of Paul" [Online] http://www.bible.ca/eo/ba/ba_02.htm, Mark A. Copeland, (Accessed 24 Feb 2005).

Copeland, Mark A., 2002, Baptism in the Teaching of Peter [Online] http://www.bible.ca/eo/ba/ba_03.htm, (Accessed 24 Feb 2005).

Cottrell, Jack, 1989, <u>Baptism A Biblical Study</u>, College Press Publishing Company, Joplin, MO.

Cox, Jack, 2000, <u>What the Bible Says About Baptism</u>, Star Bible Publications, Inc., Ft Worth, TX.

Dixon, Danny, 1901, <u>Essential Christian Baptism</u>, Star Bible Publications, Ft. Worth, TX.

Elliot, Jim, "Rightly Interpreting the Bible", [Online] http://www.ovrlnd.com/Apologetics/interpreting.html, (Accessed February 19, 2006).

Fletcher, David W., ed., 1992, <u>Baptism and the Remission of Sins</u>, College Press, Joplin, MO.

Goodrick, Edward W. & Kohlenberger, John R. 2I, 1990, <u>The NIV Exhaustive Concordance</u>, Zondervan Publishing House, Grand Rapids, MI.

Hall, Steve and Vickie, Principles for Understanding the Bible, [Online] http://www.aboundingjoy.com/hermeneutics.htm, (Accessed February 19, 2006).

Harrison, Everett F., ed., 1960, <u>Baker's Dictionary of Theology</u>, Baker Book House, Grand Rapids, MI.

Henry, Matthew, 2001, <u>Matthew Henry's Commentary on the Whole Bible</u>, Hendrickson Publishers, Inc., United States.

Hicks, John Mark and Greg Taylor, 2004, <u>Down in the River to Pray</u>, Leafwood Publishers, Siloam Springs, AR.

Johnson, B. W., 1891, The People's New Testament, [Online] http://www.ccel.org/j/johnson_bw/pnt/PNT00A.HTM, 11 Feb. 2005.

Kieszonkowy, Stownik, 2004, Larouse Polish English Pocket Dictionary, p. 116, Larousse/SEJER.

Luther, Martin, 1978, Luther's Large Catechism, Saint Louis, MO: Concordia.

Miller, David, 2005, "Is Mark 16: 9-20 Inspired?" Apologetics Press. Org,
[Online] http://www.apologeticspress.com/articles/2780, (Accessed December 6, 2007).

Padfield, David, "Baptism for the Remission of Sins", [Online] http://www.padfield.com/1995/sins.html, (Accessed August 15, 2007.

Practical Christianity Foundation, 2004, The General Epistles: A Practical Faith, Green Key Books, Holiday, FL.

Reese, Gareth, 2002, New Testament History Acts, Scripture Exposition Books, Moberly, MO.

Reese, Gareth, 1992, The New Testament Epistles – Hebrews, Scripture Exposition Books, Moberly, MO.

Simpson, D. P., 1987, Cassell's Latin English Dictionary, p. 111, Hungry Minds, Inc., © Macmillan Publishing, New York, NY.

Smith, Mont W., 1981, What the Bible Says About Covenant, College Press, Joplin, MO.

Southall, Timothy A. & Kimberly B., 1998, 1999, "A Biblical Look at Salvation", [Online]
http://www.bright.net/~1wayonly/biblical.html, 18 Feb 2005.

Srygley, F. D., Gospel Advocate 32, March 26, 1890.

Staten, Steven Francis, "The Sinner's Prayer", [Online] http://www.bible.ca/g-sinners-prayer.htm, (Accessed June 20, 2006).

Staten, Steven Francis, "Where Did We Get The Sinner's Prayer? Is it Biblical?", [Online] http://s8int.com/sinnersprayer.html, (Accessed June 20, 2006).

Strong, James, 1990, The New Strong's Exhaustive Concordance of the Bible, Thomas Nelson Publishers, Nashville, TN.

Thayer, Joseph Henry, D.D., Thayer's Greek-English Lexicon of the New Testament , Baker Book House, 1977.

Thompson, Della, The Oxford Russian Dictionary, p. 43, The Berkley Publishing Group, Oxford University Press, 1997.

Tertullian, On Baptism, Chapter X2I. - Another Objection: Abraham Pleased God Without Being Baptized. Answer Thereto. Old Things Must Give Place to New, and Baptism is Now a Law.

Webster's Everyday Spanish - English Dictionary, p. 129, Federal Street Press, 2002.

Welty, William, Acts 2:38 — "Baptism for Forgiveness?", [Online] http://isv.org/musings/musing15.htm, (Accessed June 24, 2006).

Zwingli, Huldreigh, "Of Baptism," in Zwingli and Bullinger, "Library of Christian Classics," Vol. 24, ed. And tr. G. W. Bromiley (Philadelphia Westminster Press), 1953.

GUARDIAN
PUBLISHING, LLC